medieval russia's epics, chronicles, and tales

St. George in the garb of a medieval Russian knight.
A sixteenth-century icon.

medieval Russia's epics, chronicles, and tales

EDITED, TRANSLATED, AND WITH
AN INTRODUCTION BY

Serge A. Zenkovsky

NEW YORK
E. P. DUTTON & CO., INC.
1963

FIRST EDITION

No part of this book may be reproduced in any form whatsoever without permission in writing from the publishers, except by a reviewer who wishes to quote brief passages in connection with a review written for inclusion in a magazine or newspaper or broadcasts.

Published simultaneously in Canada by
Clarke, Irwin & Company Limited,
Toronto and Vancouver.

ACKNOWLEDGMENTS

Grateful acknowledgment is made to the following for permission to quote from copyright material:

Selections from *The Russian Primary Chronicle* as translated by Samuel H. Cross in *Harvard Studies and Notes in Philology and Literature*, Volume XII, 1930, reprinted by permission of the Harvard University Press. Copyright, 1930, 1958, by The President and Fellows of Harvard College.

Selection from *The Correspondence between Prince A. M. Kurbsky and Tsar Ivan IV of Russia* translated by J. L. I. Fennell, 1955, reprinted by permission of the Cambridge University Press, London and New York.

LIBRARY OF CONGRESS CATALOG CARD NUMBER: 63-8606

PREFACE

IN PREPARING this volume for publication, I felt that at the present level of American and British scholarship in the field of Russian studies the time has come to offer readers and students a comprehensive anthology of Russia's medieval literature in translation. The works of modern Russian writers of the nineteenth century, especially those of the age of the great Russian novel as represented by Dostoevsky and Tolstoy, have long since become an inalienable part of American and British curricula of literary studies and of collections in public and school libraries. Also rather well known are the contemporary writings of Russia's Soviet period. Very different is the situation regarding the literature of previous centuries, especially that of the Russian Middle Ages, which lasted until the beginning of the eighteenth century. Indeed, there are available in English translation such masterpieces of medieval Russian letters as the *Primary Chronicle*, the *Lay of Igor's Campaign*, some adaptations and translations of the *Life*, or autobiography, of Avvakum, and of some other works written from the eleventh through the seventeenth centuries. Most of these translations, however, are either out of print or not readily available, having appeared in rare or expensive editions. Moreover, the tremendous remaining part of Russian medieval writings has never been translated either into English or into any other Western language.

The present anthology is therefore a pioneering effort to present to Western readers the finest works, a few in excerpt, of Russian literature from its very beginning, in the early eleventh century, through the seventeenth century, when Peter the Great forced Russia to rejoin the European family of nations and discard its medieval culture.

Russian medieval literature is very extensive. According to incomplete statistics, for example, there are over seven thousand versions of lives of saints written during Russia's Middle Ages, and many thousands of chronicles and tales. Therefore, the task of selecting for translation the most outstanding of these was not easy. I attempted to solve this problem by offering here as many recognized masterpieces of that period as possible, together with some lesser known works that also contribute to an understanding of the mentality, culture, and literary manners of Old Russia. My guiding principle was to offer entire works whenever possible, or at least complete narrative passages from such longer writings as the chronicles, in order to give the reader an opportunity to grasp the style and spirit of the Russians of that age. In a few cases—as, for instance, the long historical and polemical writings of the sixteenth and early seventeenth centuries—I decided, owing to the limitations of this volume, to include the most characteristic and interesting passages, in order to convey a more complete picture of the evolution of Russian letters.

When possible, already existing translations have been used; but the major part of the works published in this book appear for the first time in English. The translation of medieval Russian letters presents a number of technical difficulties. Their syntax, structure, and style are very different from the methods and devices of contemporary writers. Therefore, the translation of many passages required some adaptation to the mode of expression of modern English for them to be comprehensible to readers. For the sake of those who are not well acquainted with Russian medieval history, geography, and terminology, the words "prince," "city," or "river" have been added to avoid possible confusion. Since the Russian medieval calendar was 5,508 years behind the Western one, the corresponding Western dates have been supplied where necessary.

A customarily difficult problem is that of the transliteration of Russian names. For the titles of original Russian sources the system of the Library of Congress has been used, except for the diacritical signs. In the transliteration of Russian names and terminology, the Library of Congress system underwent some minor modification: for instance, the initial Russian soft vowels rendered by *ia* or *iu* have been changed to the more readable *ya* or *yu* (that is, "Yaroslav," not "Iaroslav"); the final *ii* and *yi* have been replaced by *y* (that is, "Kurbsky" instead of "Kurbskii"); and the final *iia* has been rendered by *ia* ("Dobrynia" in place of "Dobryniia"). Most of the proper names are given in their Russian form. Those of the clergy, such as "Theodosius" or "Sergius," are usually given in their original Greek or Latin version, and those of foreign rulers and writers in their original form, while common Christian names, such as "Alexander," "Nicholas," "Andrew," or "Helen," are given in the usual English manner.

Of the works previously translated into English and incorporated in the present collection, many have been revised against the original Russian texts and their transliteration of Russian names altered for the sake of consistency. It is my pleasant duty to acknowledge my gratitude to the following publishing houses, persons, and institutions for their permission to reproduce here the material listed:

1. to Harvard University Press, Cambridge, Massachusetts, for permission to reprint passages from *The Russian Primary Chronicle*, translated by Samuel H. Cross;

2. to G. P. Putnam's Sons, New York, and London, for permission to use portions of Leo Wiener's *Anthology of Russian Literature*;

3. to the Editorial Board of the *Slavonic and East European Review*, London, for permission to reprint *Adam's Address to Lazarus in Hell*, translated anonymously and published in Volume X (1932), pp. 145–152;

4. to Mr. Nicholas Zernov and The Society for the Promotion of Christian Knowledge, London, for permission to reprint *The Acts and Miracles of Our Dear and Holy Father, Sergius*, by Epiphanius the Wise, from *St. Sergius, Builder of Russia*, translated by Nicholas Zernov;

5. to Cambridge University Press, London and New York, for permission to reprint J. L. I. Fennell's translation of Prince Andrew Kurbsky's "First Epistle to Ivan IV," from *The Correspondence between Prince A. Kurbsky and Tzar Ivan IV of Russia*;

6. to Miss U. M. Lane and The Hogarth Press, Ltd., London, for permission to use *The Life of Archpriest Avvakum by Himself*, translated by Jane Harrison and Hope Mirrless.

In the preparation of this volume I was assisted by students in my graduate seminar on ancient Russian literature at the University of Colorado. The Reverend George Benigsen helped in translating *The Life of Yuliania Lazarevskyaya*, while Mr. Dan B. Chopyk translated Bishop Serapion's *Sermon on Merciless Heathens*. The remaining translations were made by myself in cooperation with my graduate student and assistant, Mr. Richard White. It is evident, however, that I am the only person responsible for all possible errors or shortcomings in selecting, translating, and commenting on the works in this book.

I am grateful to the Graduate School of the University of Colorado for financial help toward the completion of this volume when I was Professor of Slavic Languages and Literatures at that University.

Only I can fully appreciate the contribution made by my wife and colleague, Betty Jean, whose interest and editorial skill were so helpful in the planning and completion of *Medieval Russia's Epics, Chronicles, and Tales*.

SERGE A. ZENKOVSKY

CONTENTS

Contents

PART II: THE PERIOD OF FEUDAL DIVISIONS
(1240–1478)

Ideological Writings

PART III: THE MUSCOVITE PERIOD (1478–1700)

Military Tales

Epistolary Polemics

Historical Works from the Time of Troubles

Biographical Works

Secular Tales

Poetry

ILLUSTRATIONS

СЛЫШАТИ ДЕЛА
ШИТЬ

Ѩ ЦА МАРТА · СТРА
СТЫХ ҂МКЪ М
ЕВА · ОТ МАТ · ГЛА · С

РЕЧЕ ГЬ ПРИТЪ
УЖНИЖ ПОДО
БЬНО ЕСТЬ ЦРЬ
СТВИИ НБСЬНОЕ
ЧЛКОУ ДОМОВИ
ТОУ ИЖЕ ИЗИДЕ
КОУПЬНО ЗАОУТРА

A page from the Gospel of Ostromir written in 1056.
It is the oldest Russian book in existence.

INTRODUCTION

The Literature of Medieval Russia

THE term "Middle Ages" has a somewhat different connotation and time span for Russia than for Western Europe. In the West the Middle Ages began in the fifth century, when the Western Roman Empire fell under the blows of Germanic barbarians. They ended at the close of the fifteenth century or the beginning of the sixteenth, when Columbus discovered the New World, Luther broke the spiritual unity of the West, and secularized thought put an end to the "Age of Faith." The Russian Middle Ages began much later, only in the ninth century, and her Age of Faith came to an end in the early eighteenth century, when Russia adopted the secularized culture of Western Europe.

During the years that witnessed the fall of Rome, the Slavic tribes inhabiting the territory of present Russia were still in the age of prehistory. Only scattered data about the apparently Slavic "Antes" point to the inception of a loosely organized statehood in that area. Four additional centuries were needed for the appearance of a more solid national structure among the Eastern Slavs and for their emergence on the stage of history. The first indications of a firmly founded government among the Eastern Slavs, in the cities of Novgorod and Kiev, can be observed only in the ninth century when, in 862, according to legend, a certain Rurik became the prince of Novgorod. Since that time the word "Rus," or Russians, rapidly won a place in the pages of historical annals. In the tenth century the Kievan prince and conqueror Sviatoslav built a vast empire spreading from the Volga to the Dnieper and Danube rivers, and from Kiev to Novgorod. Despite these military and political successes, however, the culture of this early Russian state remained at a modest level. Only after the Christianization of Russia in 988 or 989 by Sviatoslav's son, Vladimir, did literacy and literature appear among these Slavs, and only from that time can historians observe the first blossoming of early Russian culture.

I. THE KIEVAN PERIOD ·(1030–1240)

1. CHURCH SLAVONIC

CHRISTIANITY came to Russia from Byzantium, or, as it was often called, the Eastern Roman Empire, at that time a powerful and highly developed nation culturally. Its flourishing capital, Constantinople, was still the most important political and cultural center of Europe and commanded a vast empire comprising the Balkan Peninsula, the Aegean Archipelago, all of Asia Minor, and parts of Italy. Its literary and state language was Greek; and Byzantium, as the preserver of both Christian thought and Greco-Roman arts and letters, was the main luminary of knowledge for still "dark" Western Europe. Despite Russia's conversion to Byzantine Christianity, however, Greek never won a position in Russia similar to that of Latin in the West, where for centuries Latin remained the exclusive liturgic and educational medium for medieval Catholic Europe. Indeed, from the very beginning of evangelization in Russia, the mass was read in Russian churches in Slavic, not in Greek. This does not mean that the Byzantine Greeks were not nationalists. To be sure, they always placed their language, the tongue of Homer, Plato, and the Gospel, above all others. Still, the wealth of the native cultures of non-Greek provinces of Byzantium compelled them at an early stage to permit the churches of the Middle East to use languages other than Greek. Later, when in 863 the Moravian prince Rostislav asked Constantinople to send missionaries for the Christianization of his realm—which occupied the present territories of Slovakia and Hungary—the Byzantine Church did not hesitate to permit the use of the Slavic tongue in the new churches.

The tasks of creating an alphabet for the Slavs and forming out of the primitive Slavic vernacular a suitable language for the mass and Gospel was entrusted to two brothers, Cyril and Methodius, Greek monks from the city of Saloniki. Linguists of genius, Cyril and Methodius created a Slavic alphabet (commonly called "Cyrillic") on the basis of the Greek one. They translated the ecclesiastic literature into one of the dialects of the Slavs of Macedonia, using Byzantine Greek stylistics and syntax. This new, somewhat artificial literary language—now called "Church Slavonic"—was perfectly Slavic in its vocabulary and grammar but rather Byzantine in its stylistic aspect.

Transplanted to Russia as a liturgic and literary language, Church Slavonic, which was very close to Old Russian, proceeded to absorb specific features of this Eastern Slavic language. Thus there developed a very interesting Russian literary language composed of Church Slavonic, with its original South Slavic linguistic features, interspersed with purely Russian characteristics. Surviving some periods of Russification, this adopted language remained the official literary language of Russia until the end of the seventeenth century, and the literary monuments written in it often have an elevated, solemn, even esoteric, coloration. As there were in medieval Russia no definite standards for the literary language, an erudite or sophisticated writer or cleric would couch his literary prose exclusively in Church Slavonic—which strongly reflected the refined and adorned stylistics of Byzantine letters—while in the same given period private correspondence, state documents, and even some simpler literary works were written in an almost pure and stylistically more naïve Old Russian vernacular. The possibilities for interweaving these two very close yet contrasting linguistic strata were innumerable and, since strict linguistic rules for the written language were established only in the eighteenth century, many Old Russian texts have a particular charm owing to a mingling of the vernacular with Church Slavonic. Unfortunately, this aspect of Old Russian literary monuments can not be reproduced at all in translation.

2. The Advantages and Limitations of Church Slavonic

The entire subsequent development of medieval Russian culture and literature was thus determined by the introduction and example of the Byzantine literary legacy in Church Slavonic translations. Initially, such adoption of a new culture in a linguistically comprehensible version offered a very considerable advantage for the Russians, who, contrary to the experience of the Catholic Germans or Poles, had not to learn a difficult foreign language, that is, Latin or Greek, in order to absorb the new religion and civilization. Byzantium's ecclesiastic and some of its secular literature, with all its stylistic patterns and genre models, became readily available to the Eastern Slavs in translation, and Russian letters were given a rapid start. Their beginning appears even spectacular when compared with the literary destinies of the Western Slavs—the Czechs and the Poles—who, having been Christianized by Rome, were obliged to adopt Latin in their mass and in their writing. Poland's first literary work in its native language did not appear until some three hundred years after its conversion to Christianity, and even five hundred years after evangelization the Poles continued to write in Latin more often than in Polish. A very similar delayed development can be observed among the Czechs. The first original Russian writings, however—some sermons by the Novgorodian and Kievan preachers, Bishop Luka Zhidiata and Metropolitan Hilarion—appeared as early as forty or fifty years after Russia's conversion. The *Primary Chronicle*, a significant work of liter-

ary, historical, and ideological interest came into being just a
little over a century after the appearance in Kiev of Christian
priests and Church Slavonic manuscripts, while the *Lay of Igor's
Campaign*, Russia's greatest monument in the heroic epic tradition, had already been written within two centuries after her
Christianization.

The spread of Byzantine culture to Russia in its Church
Slavonic versions, however, also had negative aspects. Because
Russian priests officiated in Church Slavonic, they were not
obliged to study Greek, and the knowledge of this language and
of antique, classical, culture for centuries remained extremely
limited in Russia. While Western Europe did not forget Virgil
and classical Latin even during the darkest years of its cultural
dormance—the fifth to eighth centuries—during the Russian
Middle Ages knowledge of the Greek language and acquaintance
with Byzantine literature in the original was restricted to but a
few representatives of the upper cultural strata. Numerous translations from Greek into Church Slavonic were made in Russia
but most of these were of theological or historical works. Neither
the wealth of pre-Christian Greek literature nor the entirety of
Byzantine secular writings became known to medieval Russians.
The Russian clergy was apparently afraid to translate and propa-
gate the works of pagan writers, while the Greeks themselves
were not especially interested in spreading education and their
cultural heritage among the Slavs. It can be surmised that
Byzantium was content to keep Russia as a cultural colony not
expected to attain the level of civilization of its cultural "mother
country." In any case, the Greeks sent to Russia neither teachers
for the purpose of forming a sophisticated cultural elite nor the
works of ancient Greece. Moreover, they preferred to appoint
Greeks to the head of the Russian Church than to prepare Russians for such positions, and did very little to raise the intellectual standard of the native Russian clergy. Thus, the humanistic,
scientific, and philosophic traditions of Byzantium put down no
substantial roots in Russia, and Byzantium's influence remained
limited primarily to the religious, political, and artistic spheres,
while the bulk of classical Greek, as well as Latin, thought and
letters remained almost unknown to Russians until the late
seventeenth century.

3. KIEVAN RUSSIA

As has been pointed out, the cultural history of Russia begins
largely with its Christianization at the end of the tenth century.
While an early Russian state had existed at least since the mid-

ninth century, and some scattered information concerning the national-state organization of the Russian, or Eastern, Slavs can be traced from the seventh century after Christ, or even the fifth (the state of the Antes), disappointingly little is known about the life of the pagan Russians and their culture. Judging from the quick flowering of their letters, art, and architecture after Christianization in 988–989, it can be presumed that the earliest contacts of the Eastern Slavs with Greece, Byzantium, the Caucasus, and peoples of the Eurasian steppes led to the formation in Eastern Europe of a very definite cultural type even before Christianity and letters came there. The trade routes from Scandinavia to Byzantium, from Central Asia and the Far East to Western Europe, passed through the territory of this early Russian state and certainly contributed to its cultural growth. The city of Kiev was at the crossroads of these two important trade routes, and its rise as the capital of a Russian state was largely due to the prosperity brought it by merchants who traveled to or through the city. After the Russians' conversion to Christianity at the instance of the Kievan Prince Vladimir (ruled 978–1015), Byzantine culture in its Slavicized forms won the dominant position among the Russians for the next seven centuries, and the years from A.D. 1000 to 1700 can be called the medieval or "Byzantinized" period of Russia.

Kiev itself became one of the wealthiest and most animated cities of medieval Europe, richer and more brilliant than Paris or London of the time. It was adorned with innumerable churches, and by the time of the reign of Vladimir's son, Yaroslav (ruled in Kiev 1019–1054) there were already numerous schools, hospitals, and libraries. In the eleventh and twelfth centuries Russia was an integral part of Europe, and Kievan princes maintained close dynastic ties with the ruling houses of Western countries. Their children married the sovereigns or princesses of England, Germany, France, Sweden, Hungary, and Byzantium. A daughter of Prince Yaroslav, Anna, married King Phillip of France and was the only literate member of the French royal family, for whom she signed state documents herself. Prince Vladimir Monomakh (who ruled in Kiev from 1112 to 1125), the grandson of Yaroslav, married Princess Gita, daughter of the last Anglo-Saxon king, Harold, whose family had been obliged to abandon England after the Norman Conquest and to live as emigrés in Kiev, where there were many foreigners. Western chronicles often mention the wealth and beauty of this early Russian capital. The German chronicler, Tittmar of Magdeburg, remarks that, during a fire, over four hundred churches burned

in Kiev. The city's main cathedral, St. Sophia (Holy Wisdom),
was lavishly decorated with delicate frescoes and mosaics. Its
marble pillars were brought from the Crimea, and even now,
despite centuries of mutilation and restoration, the cathedral's
proportions and dimensions produce a strong impression.

The Kievan era, however, was short-lived: from the late tenth
century to the early thirteenth. Yaroslav's children and grandchildren sundered the unity of Kievan Russia by indulging in
fratricidal feuds and Vladimir Monomakh was the last Kievan
sovereign obeyed by all the Russian princes. After his death the
Kievan state disintegrated into a number of large and small
principalities that competed and fought with one another. In
the face of increasingly frequent raids into the South Russian
territories by Turkic nomads—Pechenegs and, later, Kumans
(Polovetsians)—the Slavic population began to migrate from the
southern area of Kiev to the forests in the north, or westward
to the plains of Galicia and the Carpathian Piedmont. The prosperous merchant city of Novgorod in the northwest, Galich—
the capital of Galicia—in the extreme southwest, and the cities
of Suzdal and Vladimir—precursors of Moscow—in the northeast outgrew Kiev in prominence. With the conquest of the
Holy Land and Constantinople by the Crusaders, new trade
routes opened up from West to East and Kiev's importance as a
trading center rapidly diminished. The Mongol (Tatar) invasion
that took place in 1237–1240 under the leadership of the heirs
of Genghis Khan dealt the final blow to the dying Kievan state.
Kiev itself was sacked and burned, not to recover for centuries;
most other Russian cities were also devastated, and some two-
thirds of the Russian population perished. Thus weakened, most
of western and southern Russia then fell to the Lithuanians and
Poles, while the rest of Russia remained a vassal state of the
Mongol (Tatar) Empire for the following two centuries.

4. The Byzantine Literary Heritage of Kievan Russia

When Russia was Christianized by Prince Vladimir, some
Christian literature and several secular Byzantine works had already been translated from the Greek into Church Slavonic
by Cyril and Methodius or by Bulgarians, who formed a powerful Slavic state in the Balkans in the ninth and tenth centuries.
Bulgaria's proximity to Byzantium stimulated the knowledge of
Greek among the Bulgarians and an active translation of Greek
works into Church Slavonic, as well as the transmission of
Byzantine literary patterns from the Greeks to the Slavs. These

South Slavic translations from Greek became the first writings available to the Russians. Later, a considerable number of Byzantine writings were translated in Russia itself. Among the former, of capital importance were, of course, the Gospel and parts of the Old Testament, particularly the Psalms, which in Church Slavonic were readily understandable to all Russians who attended the Church service. Many of the liturgic texts had been composed by Byzantine theologians who were at the same time talented religious poets, such as St. John Damascene. Their aesthetic perfection, so clearly reflected in the ornate beauty of the Russian Church service itself, greatly influenced the subsequent spiritual and artistic development of the Russian people, while the stylistic and compositional influence of patristic writings on all genres of ancient Russian literature remained very great.

Among the translated literature, of prime importance also were writings of the early Christian Fathers and the "lives," or *vitae* (*zhitie*), of early Christian and Byzantine saints. Of the former, the most popular in Russia were the writings of St. John Chrysostom, which were continually translated and recopied throughout the whole seven centuries of the Russian Middle Ages. The spirit of this great Antiochian preacher of Christian social teachings influenced Russian religiosity almost as much as the Gospel itself; in any case, much more than the Old Testament—which, with the exception of the Psalms, was not often read by Russians. A collection of St. John Chrysostom's sermons, *Marguerite* (*The Pearl*), was printed in the 1630's long before the publication of the first full text of the Bible.

Saints' lives, often enhanced by fictional elements, were compiled in special collections in which the *vitae* were arranged in the order of the calendar; they remained for centuries the most edifying reading for Russians. Even as late as the nineteenth century, Greek, Syrian, Egyptian, and Russian *vitae* found an echo in the works of Tolstoy, Dostoevsky, Leskov, Turgenev, and other Russian authors, while for early Russian writers, especially the compilers of the *vitae* of native Russian saints, translated Byzantine hagiography constituted the main source for stylistic and spiritual inspiration.

Of similar attraction for the Russian reader were the Apocrypha—writings on subjects of the Old and New Testaments not recognized by the Church as authentic or canonic, translated from Greek into Church Slavonic either in Bulgaria or in Russia. Among them the apocrypha on King Solomon—whose wisdom eclipsed for Russian minds that of Aristotle and Plate—as well as the apocryphal tale *Descent of the Virgin Into Hell*, particularly absorbed the Russian reader. The latter was apparently considerably reworked in Russia and, in its content, was something of an Eastern counterpart to Dante's *Divine Comedy*. Russians liked especially its spirit of compassion for sinners, shown by the Holy Virgin's intercession on behalf of the souls condemned to perpetual torment. The Jobian theme of man's discontent with his fate was treated, in the form of a dialogue, in the apocryphal tale *Adam's Address to Lazarus in Hell*. This theme was taken up some six centuries later in an autobiographical *vita* by Monk Epiphany, a follower of the famous martyred Archpriest Avvakum.

A few works from Byzantine scholarly literature became known in Kievan and, later, in Muscovite Russia, such as the historical chronicles of John Malalas and George Hamartolas and the *History of the Judaic War* by Joseph Flavius. The style and manner of these writers were followed by the early Russian chroniclers.

Secular tales received by Russia from Byzantium included the legends of *Barlaam* and *Josaphat* and *Digenis Arkritas*, as well as the *Alexandria*. The first, of Indian origin, gives an account of the life of Buddha, who is presented as Prince Josaphat, a fictitious Christian hero and saint. It was reworked in Byzantium and Russia many times, and in the sixteenth century a Russian hymnologist, Markel Bezborody, composed a poetic church service in honor of this prince. The legend of *Digenis Akritas* originated within the confines of Byzantium and Persia and related the heroic deeds of Christian knights fighting the infidels. Although this Byzantine forerunner of the Spanish epic of El Cid was almost the only knightly tale known to Kievan Russia, its entire romantic element was expurgated from it by the austere Church authorities.

None of the great works of pre-Christian Greek poets, playwrights, and philosophers apparently found their way to Old Russian readers. It is true that Homer was known to them, at least by name, and some passages from his works were translated, but it can not be definitely stated that larger portions of his writings were ever in the hands of the literate Kievan. Almost the same can be said of the writings of Plato and Aristotle. While occasional quotations and passages from the works of these philosophers can be found in some ancient collections, as, for instance, *The Bee*, none of their works was ever entirely translated into Church Slavonic.

5. Earliest Russian Sermons and Thought

In the cultural life of every newly converted land, the clergy always occupies a position of pre-eminence. Therefore there is nothing astonishing in the fact that the first Russian writers and learned men were predominantly representatives of the Church. In Novgorod, soon after his elevation to the bishopric there in 1036, Luka Zhidiata wrote his *Instruction*, which is usually considered the oldest dated work in Russian literature. This is a didactic, rather dry homily consisting of admonitions and reminders concerning Church ritual. It is written in very simple language and can hardly be considered an inspiring piece of rhetoric.

Of completely different intellectual and literary value are the sermons of Metropolitan Hilarion, the first Russian—not Greek—head of the Russian Church, elevated to this position in 1051 by Yaroslav the Wise. Hilarion was a well-trained theologian and skillful writer who apparently knew Greek and was well versed in Byzantine religious literature. His main work, the *Sermon on Law and Grace*, is especially pointed and convincing, and despite its elaborate allegorical language the thought is clear and readily understandable. It begins with a treatment of the problem of the spiritual superiority of the New Testament over the Old: of the teachings of Christ over the law of Moses. Hilarion then switches very astutely from this topic to the thesis of the equality of newly converted Russia with older Byzantium. He considers that Russia has gained an honorable position in the Christian world because the religion of grace, ". . . the fount of the Gospel . . . overflowed upon our land . . . and, together with all Christians, we glorify the Holy Trinity." Hilarion presents the destiny of Russia in the general framework of world history and interprets it in the light of the divine plan for the general salvation of mankind. Strangely enough, this earliest Russian metropolitan is rather a philosopher of history than a preacher of purely religious, moralistic truths, and the appearance of a thinker of such depth of historical vision in the first decades of Russian Christian history is one of the most amazing phenomena of the early development of Russian culture.

While Hilarion is primarily anthropocentric, more concerned in his writings with the fate of man on earth or of the nation than with purely theological problems, Cyril of Turov, a preacher of the mid-twelfth century, is entirely theocentric. A member of a rich noble family, Cyril preferred the life of a monk to a military or court career. He subsequently became

bishop, but he always remained a man of contemplation, meditating on the mystical relation between God and man. Of his
numerous works, his sermons won the particular admiration of
his contemporaries and of later generations. Their main concern
is the problem of salvation, which he treats with great erudition
and oratorical skill. Perhaps he often exaggerates in the use of
complex allegories and metaphors, but it is precisely this perfect command of ornate Byzantine stylistics that lends his
writing great charm and elegance. For long centuries his sermons remained the best example of elevated rhetoric in Russian
literature, and Cyril can be called, without exaggerating, the
greatest preacher of medieval Russia.

A rather humanistic trend in the Russian sermon was represented by the works of Metropolitan Clement, a native of
Smolensk who was elected to the metropolitan see in Kiev in
1147. His contemporaries accused him of quoting more often
from Plato, Aristotle, and Homer than from the Bible or the
Church Fathers. The only fragment of his works which has been
preserved is an impressive example of early Russian scholarship
in the best Byzantine tradition. Clement's knowledge of Byzantine Greek learning seems to be very extensive, and there is
reason to believe that he completed his education not in Russia
but in some Greek monastery or school.

Very close in his cultural background and spirit to these
prelates of the Russian Church was Prince Vladimir Monomakh
(died 1125), grandson of Yaroslav the Wise. Monomakh had a
fluent command of five foreign· languages, was well read, and
left some significant writings. Among them, his *Instruction*, addressed to his children, stands out for its penetrating moral and
spiritual portrayal of the author himself. The work of a wise
layman, a stern though benevolent, indefatigable, and farsighted
ruler, the *Instruction* was written for the practical purpose of
advising his children. In his admonitions Vladimir shows himself to have a profound understanding of Christian teaching,
and illustrates his advice with examples from his own life. According to Monomakh, humility, contemplation, and the exami-
nation of one's own mind and life are the main instruments in
the hard task of the self-perfection of a ruler. He follows the
general patterns of the instructions of Byzantine and even
Anglo-Saxon rulers (it may be recalled that his wife was an
Anglo-Saxon princess). His ideas concerning a prince's obligations to his people and to himself are, however, original, yet
appropriate to the general framework of the developing Russian
spirituality: a ruler should never forget the teaching of Christ,

for humility is one of the outstanding qualities of a Christian man and prince.

Among the erudite men of Kievan Russia was also a certain Daniel, styled "the Exile," who was the author of a *Supplication* written circa 1200 and addressed to the prince of Suzdal, Yaroslav. More adroitly than any other stylist of the dawn of Russian writing, Daniel plays gracefully with quotations from the Bible and Greek writers, Russian folk sayings, and his own pointed witticisms. Apparently intended as a petition for patronage, Daniel's *Supplication* displays his superior command of literary Church Slavonic and contemporary learning.

6. CHRONICLES

The chronicle (*letopis*) forms the most important and sizable part of Russian literature of the Kievan Era. These chronicles—or, more precisely, annals, since they consist usually of annual entries organized chronologically—contain very heterogeneous material. Along with concise entries giving in one or several lines information on a ruler or an event in a city, there can be found various historical and diplomatic documents, treaties, and admonitions, as well as longer stories about the deeds, adventures, and campaigns of a prince or the prose recordings of heroic legends. The Russian chronicles were not the product of a single author but a complex and continuously maintained work that was copied, completed, and often re-edited by successive writers. The earliest Russian annals are the *Primary Chronicle*, or *The Tale of Bygone Years*—the most interesting and best written of them. There can be discerned various distinct layers in the *Primary Chronicle*, which was begun about 1040 and continued through 1118 by at least six different annalists, among whom the most remarkable were its first writer-editor, Monk Nikon, who worked on it in the 1060's, and Monk Nestor, one of its last editors and compilers, who practically completed the writing of this work. It is very difficult to determine now which of its various writers gave the chronicle its general tenor and main ideological line, but in any case this "collective" work, the compositional elements of which are so heterogeneous, still produces a very unified and sustained impression. The annalist, or annalists, consistently stress the necessity of preserving the unity of the Kievan state, appeal repeatedly to the princes to give up their fratricidal feuds and live in brotherly love because they are members of the same dynasty, "brothers who have the same father and the same mother," who are supposed to preserve, not destroy, the fruits "of the heavy labor" of their forefathers.

In the Prolegomenon to the *Primary Chronicle* the annalist studies the formation of different peoples and races, all of whom were the offspring of Noah, and succeeds in finding among them the Slavs, the descendants of Japhet, thus establishing an honorable biblical background for his own nation. Describing the legendary visit to Russia by the Apostle Andrew, the annalist does not fail to claim that this Disciple of Christ predicted the forthcoming blossoming of Christianity in Russia. Very cleverly interweaving the actual fabric of historical material with legendary accounts and reminiscences, the annalist succeeds in creating a religious and political tradition for his newly emerged country, and points out that Russia has won a respectable status among the other nations of the Christian world.

A considerable amount of historical information covering the centuries preceding the rise of Russia was evidently taken from Byzantine chronicles, but it is reworked stylistically and ideologically. The very structure of the Russian annals—their chronological yearly entries—is different from that of Byzantine historical works, which are usually organized into chapters covering the reigns of the emperors.

Stories and tales integrated into the historical entries convey considerable freshness and charm to the *Primary Chronicle*. Many of these accounts, as, for instance, of the death of Prince Oleg or the revenge of Princess Olga, have a clearly legendary background and were probably taken from the epic tradition. Others have the character of actual eyewitness accounts, as, notably, the dramatic story of the blinding of Vasilko, written by Priest Vassily, or the narratives about the life of the monks of the Kievan Crypt Monastery.

The *Primary Chronicle* was the earliest and most literary, but not the only, historical work of the Kievan period. Most leading cities, as well as certain branches of the Rurik dynasty, which then ruled Russia, maintained their own annals from the twelfth century. Among these, the *Galician-Volynian Chronicle* and the *Kievan Chronicle* (a continuation of the *Primary Chronicle*) are the more skillfully written, and contain many passages that were the work of gifted writers. Most of the chronicles were written by members of the clergy, mainly monks; only the *Galician-Volynian* and perhaps the twelfth-century *Kievan* chronicles, which emphasize details of army and court life, were composed probably by a member of the princes' retinue. The northern chronicles, on the other hand, especially those of the city of Novgorod, are much drier and more concise, and are characterized by their business-like, even abrupt, style.

The heroes of the chronicles are predominantly princes. Sometimes the chronicler mentions commanders, knights, or priests, but such characters are certainly secondary. The annalists of the Kievan Era gave simple yet impressive sculptural— even monumental, in the words of D. Likhachev—portrayals of their hero-princes, who are divided clearly into positive characters and villains. The portrayals are frequently stereotyped: a good prince is usually described as "a good man of war," "handsome of face," "mild of habits," or "detesting wrong and loving right." The main positive attributes are defense of the Russian land, protection of the Church, and generosity toward his subjects. Few feminine figures appear in the chronicles, indeed, in general, in all of early Russian literature. Those that do are either faithful wives or affectionate mothers, but never a participant in a romantic love intrigue. Contrary to the Western tradition, Russia's austere Middle Ages do not know any amorous or erotic themes such as can be found in the *chansons* of the troubadours, not to speak of such manuals on the art of love as *de Arte honesti amandi* (1170) or *La Clef d'Amour* (1250), which were completely unthinkable in Kievan and early Muscovite letters. No traces even of innocent romantic courtship can be found in Russian chronicles or tales until the seventeenth century. The only exception, the Tale of *Peter and Fevronia of Murom*, written in the fifteenth century, stands out strikingly in pre-seventeenth century Russian literature for its unusual love theme, but even here the motif is one of the affection and devotion between a husband and wife.

7. KIEVAN VITAE AND PATERICS

Narrative writing with extensive biographical, occasionally fictional or legendary, content can be found in Kievan literature in the *vitae* (*zhitie*, saints' lives or hagiography) and paterics (monk's lives). While these two genres, especially the *vitae*, adhered to strict compositional patterns, they were nevertheless often embellished with interesting details mirroring medieval psychology and the author's own imagination.

The tragic fate of the Princes Boris and Gleb, sons of Vladimir, Christianizer of Russia, who were killed in 1016 in a fratricidal feud by order of their elder brother, was described in *vita* form as well as in two other narratives. Written by Nestor, one of the authors of the *Primary Chronicle*, the *vita* version of the brothers' martyrdom is most detailed and realistic, and it places the fratricide within the framework of Russian religious history. In Nestor's eyes Boris and Gleb were martyrs for peace in Russia, preferring death to participation in internecine strife. Their pathos is heightened by the touching laments Nestor puts in their mouths in anticipation of their murder. The anonymous author of the *Legend* (*Skazanie*) about Boris and Gleb emphasizes less their desire to preserve peace in Russia than their voluntary acceptance of death after the example of Christ. Meditating just before his murder, Boris recalls, "The Lord resists the proud and gives his grace to the humble." In these lines, written toward the end of the eleventh century, appears for the first time one of the leading characteristics of Russian Christianity—humility and the acceptance of fate in imitation of the deeds of Christ. This idea can be traced through subsequent Russian literature even into the early twentieth century.

Another masterpiece of early Russian hagiography is the *Life of St. Theodosius*, co-founder of the Kievan Crypt Monastery. This work, also written by Nestor, is probably his best. He furnishes not only abundant material on the life of Abbot Theodosius, which makes the *vita* a vivid and realistic narrative, but also tries to convey the religious philosophy of this great Russian saint: simplicity in life, humility of attitude before God and people, and Theodosius' gentle, loving care toward the monks and his spiritual children.

The early *vitae* and stories of the paterics have many structural features in common, and usually consist of a number of episodes loosely woven into one continuous narrative. While both were intended as edifying religious literature for the Christian education of their readers, their final purposes are, however, different. The *vita* is the official biography of a saint, explaining his role in the development of Orthodox saintliness and the religious mind, and giving the reason for his canonization. It is always solemn, often begins and ends with a prayer or hymn, and, much more than the pateric narrative, stresses the spiritual aspect of its hero's life. The *vitae* were traditionally constructed according to a stereotyped pattern, with the ideal of sainthood outweighing an accurate presentation of the details of the saint's actual life, since the aim of the hagiographer was not to present the life story itself but rather the saintly example, for the edification of believers. The stories of the paterics, on the other hand, were simply instructive tales about the lives of monks, many of whom were never canonized. The pateric described the life and deeds of the monks of a given monastery, and consequently the name of the monastery was usually included in the title.

These two genres are not always clearly distinguishable, and some biographies of noncanonized monks are very similar to the hagiographic *vitae*. Toward the end of the Russian Middle Ages the *vita* lost its strict hagiographic purpose and developed into a new genre of secular biography. The narratives of the pateric, likewise, gradually assumed the form of a not strictly religious short story. Both the *vitae* and paterics were the most popular reading of medieval Russia, and innumerable versions of the lives of Russian saints were written and rewritten from the eleventh through the seventeenth centuries. Together with Byzantine paterics and hagiography, they formed the major part of the libraries of Russian monasteries and of private collections, since they were the medieval equivalent of modern short stories and novels and intermingled descriptions of everyday life, edification, and ebullient oriental phantasy.

8. THE EPOS

The greatest literary work of Kievan Russia is the *Lay of Igor's Campaign* (*Slovo o polku Igoreve*), which describes an unsuccessful raid by Russian princes against the nomadic Turkic tribe of Kumans, who, in the twelfth and thirteenth centuries, inhabited the plains north of the Black Sea. This raid, which took place in 1185 under the leadership of Igor, Prince of Novgorod-Seversk, became the subject of the only epic and purely poetic work of Kievan Russia, written probably within a year or two after Igor's return from Kuman captivity.

Against the rather uniform and undiversified background of the chronicles and religious literature of the Kievan period, the *Lay of Igor's Campaign* stands out as an exceptional specimen of strictly secular poetic letters. Its lyric pathos, rich imagery and symbolism, noble national spirit and pagan references contrast strikingly with the rest of the preserved wealth of early Russian literature. Literary historians usually classify the *Lay* as a typical example of epic poetry, but its loose structure, lyric and rhetorical digressions, and the author's addresses to his audience rather suggest its classification as a work of mixed genre in which the epic content is strongly diluted by lyric digressions and allusive admonitions.

The origins of the Russian epic tradition still remain in darkness despite decades of intensive research. Since the end of the eighteenth century a tremendous wealth of Russian epic songs, the *byliny*, have been discovered and collected. Much of this epic folklore deals with the time of Kievan Russia and the court of Prince Vladimir, "the bright sun," Christianizer of Russia, and his valorous knights—Ilia Muromets, Aliosha Popovich, Dobrynia

Nikitich, and many others—who formed around Vladimir a Russian counterpart of King Arthur's Round Table. Scholars, however, can not agree in their estimates of the actual age of the *byliny*. Indeed, Dobrynia was the real uncle of Vladimir, and is well known from the chronicles. The name of Ilia, "the Russian knight" or "cousin of Vladimir," can be found in Scandinavian and Lombardian epics penned as early as the eleventh and twelfth centuries. Moreover, while the oldest Russian work containing a reference to the *byliny* epics and their heroes dates only from the sixteenth century, the narrative parts of the *Primary Chronicle* itself, as well as such later works as, for instance, the *Tale of the Destruction of Riazan*, show very definite traces of the epic tradition. Hence, it is possible to assume that the Russian epic tradition goes back as far as the time of Kievan Russia, although their exact form and poetic devices can hardly be determined at the present stage of scholarship. It may only be surmised that at the time when the *Lay of Igor's Campaign* was written, the Russian poetic and epic tradition already had rather deep roots, especially since the *Lay* refers to the songs of a former bard, Boyan, who previously glorified the valor of Russian princes.

The subject and treatment of the *Lay* may be compared to some extent with the French *Chanson de Roland*. Both have for their topics a Christian army's fight for the honor of its country and its defeat by pagan warriors. Both treat nature as an almost animate participant in the military and national drama. Also, both use extensively fixed epithets in characterizing their heroes. A decade ago Roman Jakobson pointed out the *Lay*'s similarity to its contemporary Western counterpart in the use of pagan, pre-Christian motifs. He also showed the similarity of the poetic devices of the *Lay* to those studied and described by the Byzantine scholar Choiroboskos, whose treatise on poetic tropes and figures had been known in Russia since 1073. In view of these parallels with West European and Byzantine writings, it is possible to state that the *Lay* did not evolve exclusively from the Russian epic tradition but might also have been influenced by the general poetic environment of Western Europe and the Balkans, with which Russia was so closely connected at that time. In any event, the *Lay of Igor's Campaign* will probably continue to be an enigma for many more generations of scholars because it remains a unique specimen of unusually high quality in Kievan poetics.

The narrative part of the *Lay* is not very developed. Instead of reporting in detail the successive stages and episodes of the campaign, the author really only alludes to events and persons supposedly familiar to his audience or readers. Instead of communicating the minutiae of the battle, he impresses on his audience his own sorrow over the Russians' defeat and his desire to see Russia once again powerfully united in order to prevent further national calamity. The work strongly mirrors Russia's and the author's sorrow over the princes' feuds, their perpetual warring, and the political decline of Russian power.

The narrative structure given the *Lay* by its author, whose intent was apparently not so much to narrate as to warn his contemporaries of the perilous consequences of princely feuding, differs from that of most Western or later Russian epic works, whose usual purpose is to recall past deeds and glory. This might be explained by the fact that the *Lay* was composed almost immediately after Igor's stunning defeat, while the episodes of the campaign were still vividly preserved in the reader's memory.

The *Lay of Igor's Campaign* did not considerably influence Russian literature in the next decades and centuries. It was too different from the generally functional, didactic, and religious tenor of the other writings of the newly Christianized Russians. Its reference to the pagan Slavic gods, moreover, probably seemed to the clergy too hazardous to warrant any wide circulation, while the topic of defeat could not have been particularly popular among the princes, especially since in the very near future the relatively minor misfortunes of Igor's campaign were vastly overshadowed by a catastrophe of immensely greater magnitude. Therefore, it is not too surprising that the *Lay* was preserved only in a single manuscript and that only one other medieval Russian poetic work definitely reflects a strong stylistic and structural influence of the *Lay of Igor's Campaign*. This is *Zadonshchina*, written two hundred years later, on the occasion of the first major Russian victory, in 1380, over the nomads, Russia's historical enemy.

II. THE PERIOD OF THE TATAR YOKE AND FEUDAL DIVISION (1240–1478)

9. THE MONGOL INVASION

THE foreboding of the author of the *Lay of Igor's Campaign* and his apprehensions for Russia's future were soon justified by historical events. In 1223 the vanguards of Genghis Khan's

Mongol army, after a successful Caucasian campaign, unexpectedly crossed the Don River and inflicted a crushing defeat on regiments of the South Russian princes at the Kalka River. At this time the Mongols did not proceed to the conquest of Eastern Europe but crossed the Volga and disappeared into the Central Asian plains. In 1237, however, exactly half a century after the writing of the *Lay*, the Mongol hordes reappeared on the Volga, and in the following three years subjugated and devastated all of Russia.

It might be expected that the Mongol, or Tatar, Yoke ("Tatar" was the name of one of the Mongolian tribes of the Horde but became applied by the Russians to all of these Asian nomads) left a widespread influence on Russian culture and letters. Apart from the fact that Russian civilization was set back two centuries, however, this was not the case. Russian spiritual, artistic, and literary development remained entirely immune to the culture of these illiterate horsemen, while only a few political and military patterns of the Mongol Empire modified the previous Russian organizational forms. The Asian nomads—cattlemen and shepherds—did not settle in the Russian territories, but preferred the nearly uninhabited plains and grazing lands of the eastern and southern confines of present Russia to the forests and marshes of its central and northern parts, where most of the Slavic population lived. The tremendous differences in language, religon, and way of life between the sedentary Christian Slavs and the pagan (only subsequently Moslem) Asian nomads prevented the Russians from indulging in any widespread commerce with their conquerors, and there were few intermarriages between Russians and Tatars in the Middle Ages.

The century following the invasion was one of marked cultural decline but hardly of any perceptible changes in the basic features of Russian civilization. Monasteries and palaces had been burned, and the cultural elite decimated or abducted into slavery, but the surviving representatives of the Russian clergy and aristocracy tried to preserve the remnants of Russian civilization and literature although they were hardly able to develop them. The cultural decline was further intensified by the conquest of Western Russia by Poles and Lithuanians and the splitting up of Russian territories under the Mongols into innumerable small principalities that competed and fought among themselves. Only northern Russia, the republic of wealthy Novgorod, preserved the integrity of its immense territory, and the city itself became the center for burgeoning new forms in the arts, especially of architecture and painting.

10. MILITARY TALES

While no stylistic changes are perceptible in Russian writings of the first century after the Mongol conquest, their topics clearly evidence whether they were written before or after the collapse of Kievan Russia. One of the most popular subjects for thirteenth-century works was, of course, the Tatar invasion and therefore the military tale—already well known in Kievan literature, as seen from the *Lay of Igor's Campaign* and the chronicles—now became much more widespread. Of the new ones, two, the *Orison on the Downfall of Russia* and the *Tale of the Destruction of Riazan*, give an exceptionally artistic treatment of the invasion and the feelings of the survivors.

Still enigmatic in its origin, the *Orison on the Downfall of Russia* seems to be only an introduction to some now lost longer work. It speaks of the previous grandeur and glory of the realm founded by Vladimir and Yaroslav and is highly pathetic, but, unfortunately, the preserved fragments end exactly with the words that begin a description of the catastrophe.

Tales of the capture of various cities are poignant and numerous. Riazan, a city in the extreme southeast of Kievan territory, was the first to fall to the Tatar armies, and the description of its destruction is the most dramatic account of this type. The *Tale of the Destruction of Riazan* is a complex work in which four separate episodes and various genres are interwoven. The episode dealing with Evpaty Kolovrat, a *bogatyr* (knight) who challenged the Mongol army, has strong motifs of the oral epos, and is no less impressive than Western tales of heroic knightly deeds. Folklore elements can also be found in the laments of the princes. The narrative is considerably more vivid and dynamic than that of the *Lay of Igor's Campaign* or of earlier military tales. While some of the symbols and tropes have a close connection with those of the *Lay*, however, the *Tale* is far behind the *Lay* in its poetic and stylistic excellence. The dominant idea of the *Tale* is the juxtaposition of the Christian Russian army to the Tatar "infidels," and more than any other work of early Russian literature the *Tale* conveys the concept of Russia as the bulwark of Christian civilization against the hordes of pagan Central Asian nomads. Other military tales of the time deal with the conquest of Kiev and of other Russian cities that fell to the Tatars, as well as the first battle, in 1223, between Russians and Mongols on the Kalka River.

During these difficult years the Tatars were not the only conquerors of Russian lands. Poles and Lithuanians succeeded in occupying extensive regions in the west, from the Nemen to the Dniester rivers and from the Carpathian Mountains to Kiev and Smolensk. German knights of the Livonian Order took over present Latvia and Estonia and pushed against the ancient city of Pskov. Swedes appeared on the Neva River, attacking the confines of the territory of Novgorod. The defense of this northern border is the subject of many episodes of the *Life of Prince Alexander Nevsky* (called "Nevsky" for his defeat of the Swedes on the Neva River). In the manuscripts his *vita* usually follows the *Orison on the Downfall of Russia*, and some scholars even believe that the *Orison* was intended as an introduction to the life of this courageous prince who was so largely responsible for Russia's gradual rehabilitation after the Tatar conquest. Alexander, who died in 1263, was canonized primarily for his devotion to the cause of the Russian land and Church rather than for exceptional spirituality. Therefore, his *vita* is more a work of secular biography incorporating military tales than a piece of hagiography. The author widely used biblical portrayals and stylistics in Alexander's *Life*, and treated many events in the manner of the Byzantine chronicles and military stories. Alexander is compared to Roman emperors and biblical patriarchs. The *Life* ends with a touching miracle: when, during Alexander's burial, the metropolitan wanted to put in Alexander's hand a parchment remitting his sins, in accordance with Church ritual, the dead hero extended his hand to take it.

The defense of Pskov against the Lithuanians forms the background of the *Tale of Prince Dovmont*, written in the thirteenth century, while the miraculous deliverance of the city of Smolensk from the Tatars is related in the *Heroic Deeds of Mercurius of Smolensk*, written in the fourteenth, or even fifteenth, century. In no other Russian military tale does the miraculous element play such importance as in this story, which is treated in the hagiographic manner: beheaded by the Tatars, Mercurius returns to the city he had saved, holding his severed head in his hands.

The great battle in 1380 at the Don River, where the Russians inflicted their first decisive defeat upon the Tatars toward the end of the Tatar Yoke, supplied rich material for several literary works. *Zadonshchina* (*The Deeds Beyond the Don*), the best known of these, written by Sofony of Riazan, is to a large extent an inversion of the *Lay of Igor's Campaign*. Indeed, Sofony appropriated many of the compositional patterns and poetic devices of the *Lay*, and in places *Zadonshchina* adheres almost literally to the figures of speech and symbolism of the *Lay of*

Igor's Campaign. Like the author of the *Lay*, Sofony had recourse to poetic generalization rather than to a minute description of the details of battle, and let the lyric laments of Russian women express the sorrow of the Russian land at the losses suffered by the Russian army. Still, the narrative of *Zadonshchina* is somewhat more detailed, realistic, and sustained in plot than the great twelfth-century Russian lay. Its spirit is entirely Christian, and it lacks the pagan tendencies of the former. While not so adept poetically, Sofony was no less skillful in expressing his ideas than was the anonymous bard of Kiev. Both gave voice to Russia's hopes, sorrows, and expectations: the *Lay* deplored the princes' disunity; *Zadonshchina* praised their successful united effort to cast off the foreign yoke.

Two other works that treat the same Russian victory, less poetic but more informative than *Zadonshchina*, are the *Tale of the Battle on the Don* in the Simon and Ermolinsky chronicles and the *Legend* (*Skazanie*) of the *Rout of Mamai* (khan of the Tatar Horde). In the latter are some beautiful, highly poetic descriptions of the Russian army and of the night preceding the battle.

With *Zadonshchina* the era of the Kievan tradition in Russian literature came to a close. During the cultural revival that ensued in Russia in the late fourteenth and fifteenth centuries, new problems, topics, and literary methods came to the fore.

11. THE VITA OF ORNAMENTAL FORMALISM

At the end of the fourteenth century Russian letters came under the influence of a new spiritual and literary movement that had arisen among the monks of Byzantium and of the Slavic Balkan states. The participants in this movement, who called themselves "Hesychasts" (from *Hesychia*—quietude, silence, indirectly, contemplation), taught self-perfection and domination of the passions. According to their views, a believer could achieve direct vision of the Divine Light, a visual contemplation of the Creator. This teaching, which to a large extent was conditioned by renunciation of the passions and the pleasures of this world and led its followers away from the realities of this life, resulted in the field of literature in the development of a highly artificial and rhetorical style. At first primarily influencing hagiography, in the fifteenth and sixteenth centuries this style spread to other types of writing. For a Hesychast writer, not the recorded biography but the ideal truth of the saints' lives was important. Their *vitae* depict not the everyday deeds of the heroes but rather the supreme truth and eternal significance of the saints' actions. Like the modern impressionist or even contemporary abstract painter, the writer conveyed a portrayal of the saint as he visualized it and not as it necessarily was.

In their search for a medium worthy of describing spiritual perfection, the Byzantine and Balkan-Slavic Hesychasts developed a highly ornate language. Its elements were bookish words, compounds (*composita*) consisting of two or three words, complex syntactical structure with a multitude of subordinate clauses, numerous epithets, repetition of the same sound at the beginning of each rhythmic unit of the sentence, and archaic grammatical forms. These devices conveyed to the *vita* an especially elevated and solemn tone.

Callistos (Patriarch of Constantinople from 1350 to 1363) was the first writer to apply widely this formal, sophisticated, and ornate style which, from Byzantium, spread to Serbia and Bulgaria and, at the beginning of the fifteenth century, to Russia. The Balkan-Slavic writers of this period considerably reformed their literary language by reviving outlived ancient grammatical forms of Church Slavonic. When the Hesychast literary vogue came to Russia, it also became instrumental there in restoring to the literary language the archaic Church Slavonic grammar and phonetics. This "neo-Byzantine" literary influence in Russia, whose duration is referred to as the second Balkan, or South Slavic, period in Russian literature, dislodged from Russian letters purely East Slavic vernacular forms, renewing the archaic Church Slavonic. The outstanding Russian representative of this new ornamental formalism, which Russians termed "weaving of words," was Epiphanius, called "the Wise" for his writings (died in 1422). His masterpieces were the well-known *Lives* of St. Sergius and St. Stephen, evangelizer of Perm, a Finnic region west of the Urals. Despite his rich stylistics, Epiphanius successfully conveys a realistic portrayal of the saints, adorned with prayers, eulogies, and laments, and his writings remained for some two centuries the most imitated specimens of the formal, ornamental style in Russia. In the mid-fifteenth century his work was continued by Pachomius the Serb, an emigré from the Balkans who reworked some of Epiphanius' *vitae* and composed numerous new ones.

Ornamental formalism reigned in Russian literature until the seventeenth century. Not all the literary works of these two centuries were written in this style, but it became almost compulsory in hagiography, sermons, and historical writings. The result was the transformation of the *vita* into a uniform enumeration of the saint's virtues, and lengthy eulogies that frequently completely overshadowed the actual story of his life. In the mid-sixteenth century Metropolitan Macarius, tutor and adviser of the young Ivan IV, undertook a compilation (*Chetyi Minei*) of the finest in Russian spiritual literature, and at that time all the earlier *vitae* were reworked according to the exigencies of ornamental formalism.

Side by side with the erudite writers of rhetorical *vitae* and chronicles, however, there were other literary works of the late fourteenth and fifteenth centuries whose authors used a simple, almost vernacular, language without any particular embellishment. A good example of such unsophistication and even naïve narration are the early versions of the *vita* of St. Michael of Klopsko (its later versions were reworked by the Muscovite writers of ornamental style) in which the hagiographer concentrates rather on interesting episodes of the saint's life than on epithets and eulogies.

Also in the same unadorned, yet expressive, language is the *vita*-tale of Prince Peter of Murom and his wife, Fevronia. This is the only medieval Russian literary work with some romantic content, and it supplies many everyday details from the life of these saint-spouses. Fevronia, a peasant girl by origin, is placed against the background of rural life. The composition of this narrative is complex, containing legendary folklore motifs interwoven with the narrative. This charming story, which ends with a description of the hero's and heroine's death and posthumous miracles, may be considered a Russian counterpart of the Western legend of Tristan and Isolde.

12. Chronicles of the Fourteenth and Fifteenth Centuries

The writing of annals was almost completely interrupted by the Mongol invasion. Kiev and Vladimir, Russia's northern capital, were so thoroughly sacked by the invaders that cultural life there was entirely suspended. Therefore the main chronicles of the thirteenth and fourteenth centuries are those of Novgorod, Tver, and Rostov; in the fourteenth century, when Moscow arose as a new political rival, chronicle writing also commenced there. The transfer of the Russian metropolitan see to Moscow in 1325 made out of this previously insignificant princedom an important religious and cultural center. The Muscovite chronicles of the late fourteenth and early fifteenth centuries—the *Simon* and *Trinity* (*Troitsky*) chronicles—include the ancient *Primary Chronicle*, and use widely the annals of such other cities as Novgorod, Smolensk, Riazan, Tver, and others. They cultivate insistently the idea of Russian reunification under the aegis of the Muscovite prince. The fact that they are only compilations necessarily deprives them of inner unity and of the stylistic uniformity that characterizes the *Primary*, *Kievan*, and *Galician-Volynian* chronicles, and they often grow into tremendous codices, since they were supposed to contain ever-growing new material beside the wealth of early historical information. While the chronicler's task became increasingly difficult in these centuries, he continued to work according to the originally elaborated methods: yearly entries and the inclusion of heterogeneous material. Among the codices of the era the most important are the *Laurentian*, written in 1337 for Great Prince Dmitry of Suzdal and Nizhny-Novgorod; the *Hypatian*, compiled in the early fifteenth century; and the *Radzivil*, or *Königsberg*, completed in the late fifteenth century and given by Prince J. Radzivil to the Königsberg library. All of these contain the entire text of the *Primary Chronicle* and rich later material.

Since the late fifteenth century there developed in Russia a new type of historical work, the so-called chronograph, in which the material was organized into article-chapters in place of the customary yearly entries and in which surveys of world events were usually included along with events in Russian history. They were written in the new ornamental style with heavy panegyrics to the rulers and Church leaders, a style which spread to the chronicles themselves, whose compilation continued into the late seventeenth century.

13. POLITICAL LEGENDS AND TALES

From the mid-fourteenth to the mid-fifteenth century two principalities, Tver and Moscow, competed for supremacy and attempted to unify around themselves the central regions of Russia on the upper Volga and Oka rivers. The victor was Moscow, which subjugated Tver and won leadership over all central Russia. The subsequent unification of all of Great Russia was completed in 1478, when Ivan III (1462–1505), the founder of Muscovite power, forced Novgorod also to accept the suzerainty of Moscow.

Eager to justify their claims to the political leadership of Russia, the Muscovite dynasty and its ideologists elaborated, according to the medieval tradition, a number of political legends, most of which had their origin in Byzantine and Western historical myths. Among them, the *Legend of the Babylonian Kingdom* and the *Legend of the Princes of Vladimir* propagated the idea that only a powerful ruler could guarantee the security of the nation. The latter legend aimed, moreover, at providing the Muscovite princes with a respectable genealogy: according to this legend, the Muscovite dynasty descended not only from half-mythical Rurik but had its origins much deeper in history— its founder was said to be Prus, a wholly imaginary brother of the Roman Emperor Augustus.

The narrow purpose of the Muscovite political legends—to establish the prestige of the Muscovite dynasty and gain support for its political claims—to a large extent limited their circulation and popularity. More widely read was the Novgorodian *Tale of the White Cowl*. Novgorod, Moscow's main adversary, also sought historical tradition in defending its independence and republican institutions against encroachment by the Muscovite princes. The central idea of this tale is Russia's selection by God as the defender of Orthodoxy: the final kingdom of the Holy Spirit, which will replace both the Old Testamentary kingdom of law and the New Testamentary kingdom of grace, would become manifest in the Russian land. Novgorod and its archbishop are singled out in this legend as the heirs to one of the most sacred symbols of pure Christianity, the White Cowl, the possession of which endowed this old republican city with spiritual superiority and placed it on a level with Moscow in the sphere of Church tradition. The *Tale of the White Cowl* became particularly popular in the seventeenth century and had a profound influence on the subsequent development of Russian ideology. In connection with this legend there arose in the early sixteenth century the theory of Moscow, the Third Rome. This concept, however, differed considerably from that of the *Tale of the White Cowl*, which taught that the entire people of Russia, not only Moscow and its ruler, bore historical responsibility for the guardianship of true Orthodoxy.

III. THE MUSCOVITE PERIOD
A. MUSCOVITE RUSSIA'S FIRST CENTURY (1478–1598)

In 1478 Ivan III, by annexing the tremendous territory of the Republic of Novgorod, completed the main stage of the unification of Russia, which for centuries had remained divided into small feudal principalities. Two years later the Russians shook off forever the Tatar Yoke, and the Golden Horde disintegrated. Some seventy years later, in 1547, Ivan IV was crowned the first Tsar of Russia by the wise and erudite Metropolitan Macarius. Feudal Russia, with its endless fratricidal feuds and

princely warring, was replaced by one powerful, unified autocratic state. This process of unification and the rise of autocracy
required considerable military effort to preserve the new unity
and defend the young tsardom, as well as the further elaboration
of a new political philosophy justifying this newborn power. It
is therefore understandable that throughout the late fifteenth
and sixteenth centuries, during the reigns of Ivan III (1462–
1505). Vassily III (1505–1533) and Ivan IV (1533–1584),
Russian literature was dominated by two basic genres: the military tale and political polemics.

14. The New Military Tale

In the late fifteenth century there appeared a new type of
military tale—narratives about the siege and defense of fortresses
or cities. One of the first of these was the *Tale of the Taking of
Constantinople*, which fell to the Turks in 1453. It was written
by a certain Nestor Iskander, a professional Russian soldier who
had been captured by the Turks, forced to accept Islam, and
to join the Ottoman army. He was a writer of considerable
talent, and described colorfully as an eyewitness the siege and
storming of the city. While he is highly rhetorical, he nonetheless conveys a realistic picture of the battles. His original narrative was apparently reworked by some Muscovite writer who
added an ideological introduction and conclusion: after the conquest of the Balkans and the fall of the capital of Orthodoxy,
Russia was to take over the role of protector of Orthodoxy and
become responsible for its fate.

The siege of the Tatar capital, Kazan, which was taken in
1552 by Russian troops under Ivan IV, supplied the topic for
two very different narratives on the subject. One, the *Kazan
History*, was written in the 1560's by an anonymous Russian
who, similarly to Nestor Iskander, became prisoner of the Tatars
and spent two decades in Moslem captivity. He observed the
military operations from within the city, on the Tatar side, and
after the Russians' victory joined Ivan's army. His work, besides depicting the siege, covers an extensive period of time,
studies Russo-Tatar relations, the life of Russians in Tatar captivity, and the preparations for war. His literary devices are
patterned considerably after Iskander's tale. Although he depicts the heavy fighting and storming of Kazan in long and
ornate sentences, he provides very lively descriptions. Particularly impressive is his account of the tsar's return to Moscow
and the capital's jubilation. Another treatment of the same
siege was given by Prince Andrew Kurbsky, one of Ivan's com-

manders, in his *History of Tsar and Grand Prince Ivan Vassilie-vich*. Kurbsky is much more matter of fact, and uses the rich stylistics of his era with great taste and economy.

The *Story of Stephen Bathory's Campaign Against Pskov* exceeds all previous military tales in the extended employment of intricate, ornamented stylistics, allegory, metaphors, and epithets. The author belonged to a particularly sophisticated current in Russia letters, and had perfect command of all the subtleties of ornamental formalism. The use of compound words, figures of speech, and elaborate sentences makes this tale one of the best specimens of the heavy, embellished style of early Muscovite literature.

15. POLEMIC LITERATURE

Beginning in the early fifteenth century, polemics on theological and political problems form a prominent part of Russian letters of the early Muscovite era. The first polemic arose over the heresy of the Strigolniks, a movement for Church reform that denied the necessity of some sacraments and of an ordained clergy and that grew very strong in Pskov and Novgorod around 1400. A century later appeared the rationalistic Judaizers, who to some extent followed the teachings of the Strigolniks but also denied veneration of icons and the dogma of the Trinity, thus preceding by half a century the emergence of the West European Unitarianism of Servetus and Socinius. This movement spread to Moscow, and Ivan III himself was strongly suspected of being a secret sponsor of the sect. In any case, the main opponent of the Judaizers, Abbot Joseph of Volok, who finally won the struggle and succeeded in destroying the movement, clearly hinted at the "pernicious" role in Church affairs played by Ivan III, the founder of Russian political unity. The lively polemics for and against the heresy of the Judaizers lasted several decades and produced a number of important works.

The struggle against the Judaizers was not yet over when a new conflict arose between the supporters and opponents of monastic estates. Joseph of Volok once again came out forcefully in favor of the estates of the monasteries, which he called "the wealth of the poor" and which in his eyes were fundamental for maintaining and educating the clergy as well as for the Church's social work. In Joseph's opinion the Church was responsible for the souls and well-being of believers and was supposed to take the necessary action for preserving their spiritual condition. His adversaries were the contemplative hermit-elders from the hermitages of northern Russia beyond the Volga, who taught that the Church's wealth leads to corruption of the clergy and diverts the attention of the monks from their spiritual tasks. They opposed Church intervention in the inner life of believers, and considered that only a Christian's personal action may lead to his salvation. Their leader, Nil Sorsky, a pupil of the Greek Hesychasts, insisted that the way to God can be found only through suppression of the passions, self-perfection, and a believer's individual effort to understand and follow the divine commandments. His teaching in some respects also had certain points in common with later Western Protestantism, since he was against adornment of the Church and excessive ritualism, supporting a purely spiritual, nonsocial role for the clergy. The polemics between the followers of Joseph, called the "Josephites," and the Trans-Volga elders was largely a discussion of the necessity for discipline and the enforcement of Church law against spiritual freedom and an individual approach to God.

In the 1550's there arose in Moscow and northern Russia still another religious movement, this time under the very definite influence of the Western Reformation. Like the previous nonconformist sects, its leader disputed the value of the sacraments and the Church hierarchy. This new threat to Orthodoxy, however, was rapidly liquidated and did not leave many traces in Russian spirituality. The controversies around these various teachings led to the growth of a prolific polemic literature which, while neither fictional nor even particularly artistically written, is nonetheless an important witness to an intense spiritual and intellectual life in the first century of the Muscovite Era.

Purely political polemics are best seen in the *Story of Sultan Mehmed*, by Ivan Peresvetov, and in the correspondence between Ivan IV ("the Terrible") and Prince Andrew Kurbsky. In his story, written about 1550, Peresvetov describes conditions in Russia under the guise of those in the Ottoman Empire, and argues against the excessive power of the boyar aristocracy. He was a firm supporter of autocracy, in which he saw the best instrument for consolidating national power: "When the Tsar is gentle and weak, his Tsardom declines and his glory diminishes. When the Tsar is dread and wise, his Tsardom grows and his name is glorified on the earth," writes Peresvetov. It can be considered that the autocratic rule of Ivan IV was to a certain extent the result of Peresvetov's writings, in which the latter suggested breaking the power of the feudal lords.

Prince Andrew Kurbsky represented a completely different viewpoint. He defended the political role of princes, boyars,

and aristocracy in general, which he regarded as the bearer of
national stability, conservatism, and wisdom. According to
Kurbsky, autocratic rule necessarily leads to excesses, and a
proud ruler becomes instrumental in the decline of his nation.
A well-trained dialectician and writer, Kurbsky cleverly and
convincingly presents his views in his correspondence with Ivan
IV. He appeals to the tsar to cease persecuting the aristocracy
and to pardon the victims of his wrath. Ivan was hardly less
erudite than the prince, but he did not command his passions
and pen as well, and exploded in vituperative replies to Kurbsky,
his former friend and commander in chief of the Russian armies.
Ivan is sarcastic and biting, and does not shun using the most
offensive language in speaking of his enemies. The tsar's strong-
est argument is the boyars' misrule, which he describes in
recollecting his childhood. While Kurbsky is always concise and
to the point, Ivan is verbose, accumulating one argument after
another to prove his views. Very different in their respective
styles, Prince Kurbsky and Tsar Ivan are certainly the most
outstanding of Russian sixteenth-century polemists, and their
letters are the best example of the Muscovite epistolary art.

16. Encyclopedic Works

The greatest literary undertaking of the reign of the dread
Tsar Ivan IV were the encyclopedic compilations of various
types of Russian writings initiated and conducted under the
supervision of Macarius, Metropolitan of Moscow from 1543
to 1564. The most important of these works were the *Reading
Meneae* (*Chetyi Minei*), a collection of *vitae* and other spiritually edifying readings arranged for each calendar day. Altogether, there are in these *Meneae* some thirteen thousand folio
pages, the equivalent of thirty or forty modern volumes; most
of the existing *vitae* were rewritten for this new compilation in
the official style of ornamental formalism.

The other encyclopedic work, written in the same ponderous
formal manner, was the *Book of Grades* (*Stepennaia kniga*), an
extensive rewriting of the chronicles and chronographs in which
special attention was paid to the biographies of Russian rulers.
The main literary interest presented by this historical
work consists in the small stories and anecdotes incorporated in them
(often taken from oral folklore) which herald the nascence of
the fictional short story. Both of these works abound in neo-
logical compounds, epithets, and long rhetorical constructions.

The third important encyclopedic work of this time was the
Nikon Illustrated Codex of Chronicles, a monumental historical

encyclopedia covering not only Russian but also world history as far as it was known to sixteenth-century Muscovites. It consists of twelve enormous volumes richly illustrated with over ten thousand miniatures.

The completion of these catenae apparently exhausted the energies of Russian writers of the late Byzantine tradition and the talent of the ornamental formalists. After codifying and rewriting nearly all of previous Russian literature in these series, it was difficult and almost purposeless to invent any new sophistications in the adorned and heavy style. Thus, the *Reading Meneae, Book of Grades,* and *Illustrated Codex* became the final monuments of the period of exclusive Byzantine domination over Russian literature. While ornamental stylistics lasted into the seventeenth century, undergoing a final blossoming in 1615–1630, new currents and literary genres began to appear.

This last century of the undisputed domination of Byzantine stylistics over Russian writing was simultaneously the last century of the Rurik dynasty, which, according to legend, had ruled in Russia since 862. After the death of Ivan IV, his son, the last offspring of this dynasty—Tsar Theodore—reigned for some fifteen years, but with his death in 1598, the Rurik dynasty was extinguished. During the following fifteen years (1598–1613), called the "Time of Troubles" (*Smuta*), Russians witnessed four legitimate tsars from three new dynasties, two tsar-impostors, grave social disturbances, the breakdown of central government and foreign intervention, all of which brought the nation to the verge of another complete catastrophe. Only in 1613 was a new tsar, Michael (ruled 1613–1645), elected. Tsar Michael was the first of the Romanov dynasty, which reigned for the next 304 years, disappearing only with the revolution of 1917. His task was to rehabilitate the state, put an end to Polish and Swedish intervention, and bring social order to the nation. These tasks were fairly soon accomplished and order restored, but Russian culture and letters survived this historical trial very considerably changed.

B. THE WANE OF MEDIEVAL RUSSIA (1598–1700)

Erosion of the traditional Byzantine patterns in ancient Russian literature becomes perceptible from the second part of the sixteenth century. In historical works authors tend to prefer narration of the mythical legend in the manner of the Polish chroniclers to the down-to-earth style of early Russian annalists. Prose becomes more and more frequently interspersed with fragments of rhymed couplets. Job, Russia's first patriarch (from

1589 to 1605), included even in his *vita* of Tsarevich Dmitry long versified passages. One of the best, but now almost completely forgotten, medieval Russian hymnologists, Abbot Markel Bezborody, soon after his retirement in 1557, wrote a memorial church service to the saints Barlaam and Josaphat in the unusual form of a dramatic poem with vivid dialogues. Many hagiographers, especially those who did not belong to the official school of ornamental formalism but who wrote in a simple, unadorned manner, began to include the autobiographical reminiscences of their heroes, thus conveying a more realistic tenor to their *vitae*. Even the writers of these *vitae* began to lift the veil of anonymity, providing the reader with more information about themselves. Along with the steady growth of autobiographical elements in both the *vita* and in historical narratives, the Western picaresque tale and knightly novel became translated into Russian for the first time. Finally, fictional characters and a satirical portrayal of Russian life make their appearance, as in the short tale of *Shemiaka's Judgment,* written probably around the end of the sixteenth century.

This inauguration of new ways in Russian letters and the passing of the old literary tradition were accelerated by the events of the Time of Troubles, when large numbers of foreigners—Poles, Lithuanians, Swedes, and German and French mercenaries—came to Russia in the ranks of invading armies. At the same time many representatives of Russian society became closely acquainted with Western modes of life during their captivity in Poland, Lithuania, and Sweden. The reunion of "Little Russia"[1] with Muscovy in 1653 intensified Western, especially Polish, cultural influences. Moreover, the alienation from the hierarchy and the state of the conservative, Old Believer wing of the Church[2] considerably weakened the influence of traditionalists with the government and the cultural elite, and facilitated the further secularization and modernization of the Russian state, its culture, and letters.

To be sure, many Russian writers still continued until the middle of the seventeenth century to use the previously established literary manners, methods, and devices, but the more important and interesting part of literary production comes now from writers seeking new ways of expression. From the beginning of this century the *vita* was gradually replaced by secular biography, autobiography, and first-person confession. Ever-

---

[1] The southern part of Russia, with Kiev, now called "the Ukraine."
[2] For more detailed information on this movement, see the introduction to *The Life of Archpriest Avvakum by Himself* in this volume.

growing attention is given to the psychology of the heroes, and purely fictional characters come into being. The occasional rhymed couplets and versified fragments grow into larger poetic works, and lyric and epic songs open a new era in the expression of feelings and emotions.

17. HISTORICAL WORKS OF THE TIME OF TROUBLES

During the decades immediately following the Time of Troubles, historical works describing the calamities of social disturbance and foreign intervention played a dominant role in Russian letters. Both old and new literary methods characterize this transitional period. While some seventeenth-century writers achieved a high perfection in the employment of ornate stylistics, behind their rhetorical facade can frequently be found detailed portrayals of the character and psychology of their contemporaries as well as analyses of the reasons for the great cataclysm. The best stylist of the time was the *dyak* (high official) Ivan Timofeev, author of the well-known *Vremennik* (*Book of the Times*). His sentences are often built of rhythmic units with occasional rhyme, and are extremely rich in epithets, compound words, and a symbolic interpretation of names: for instance, artillery becomes "artifacts for the destruction of walls"; boats—"transporters over the water"; Theodore—"the gift of God"; John—"the Grace." The abundance of stylistic devices and allegories makes a reading of this clever analytical work— his study of the time of Ivan IV is particularly penetrating— extremely difficult. Timofeev's ideology is strictly conservative, the Time of Troubles being, in his mind, the result of the disappearance of the ancient dynasty and the rise of new social groups. Still, his conservatism does not preclude a severe judgment of the boyars, the upper class of this semifeudal society, whom Timofeev accuses of political irresponsibility and lack of civic virtue.

Other authors of historical works on the Time of Troubles— Palitsyn, Khvorostinin, Katyrev-Rostovsky, Shakhovskoy—use predominantly the same literary devices but, being more modest in displaying their stylistic ability, their works are more accessible to contemporary readers and translators. The most distinguished of these works is the *Povest'* (*Story*) written by Prince I. Katyrev-Rostovsky around 1626. Despite frequent rhetorical digressions, effusions of sympathy and indignation, he provides a well-organized, clear, and rather simply written account of events of the Time of Troubles. His versified fragments are skillfully rhymed, and refresh the prose recital of events. He

should be remembered as the first seventeenth-century writer
to present physical and psychological depictions of his heroes, as
well as descriptions of landscape. Palitsyn's *Skazanie* (*Narrative*),
the main part of which deals with the siege of the Holy
Trinity and St. Sergius Monastery near Moscow, is remarkable
for its powerful and severe philippic against the ruling classes
of Russia, which, in his eyes, neglected their Christian and
patriotic duties and, instead of caring for the nation and Church,
indulged in the accumulation of personal power and wealth. The
works devoted to the Time of Troubles are so numerous that it
is hardly possible even to enumerate them here, but at least
one other such work should be mentioned, the *Tale on the
Death of Prince Skopin-Shuysky*. It is notable for the touching
laments uttered by the prince's relatives after his poisoning.
The author made in these laments extended use of folklore
motifs, cleverly weaving them into the fabric of his tale.

18. LATE MUSCOVITE VITAE AND AUTOBIOGRAPHY

The drastic changes in the traditional genres are particularly
visible in the seventeenth-century *vita*. One of the earliest of
this century was written by K. Osoryin, who, soon after the
death of his mother in 1604, Yuliania Lazarevskaia, wrote the
story of her life. The matter-of-fact, simple, and realistic narrative
style of this *vita* opened a new era in Russian hagiography.
Yuliania, who later was canonized, is presented against
a background of the everyday life of rural Russia. In place of
the habitual eulogies and stereotyped enumeration of the saint's
virtues, Osoryin supplies details of family relations, of his
mother's daily household occupations, her generosity toward the
poor and the sick, and her help to the peasants during the
famine that struck Russia under Boris Godunov. Of course, there
are in this *vita* some descriptions of miracles performed by
St. Yuliania, but for the first time the heroine of a hagiographic
work is neither a nun distinguished by her holy life nor a pious
princess, but the simple and devout wife of a small nobleman.
The story's language is simple and unadorned, very fitting for a
description of the life of this charitable and unobtrusive woman.

Close to the realistic descriptions found in the *vita* of
Yuliania Lazarevskaia are the *vitae* of St. Dionysius, Abbot of
the Holy Trinity and St. Sergius Monastery, of Ivan Neronov, of
Boyarina Morozova—the two latter being important leaders of
the Old Believers—and of Theodore Rtischev, boyar and close
friend of Tsar Alexis (1645–1676). Although they preserve some
features of traditional hagiography, most of these works are

secular biographies of people of exemplary religious life, particularly the last, the story of a boyar noted for his welfare
work and his role in promoting enlightenment in Russia. These
vitae are almost completely devoid of rhetorical stylistics, and
frequently employ elements of the vernacular language.

In the 1670's leaders of the schismatic Old Believers wrote
the first true Russian autobiographies. *The Life of Archpriest
Avvakum by Himself* belongs among the most significant works
of medieval Russian literature, and modern Russian literary
historians are unanimous in considering Avvakum one of the
greatest masters of the Russian tongue. Concise, expressive,
biting, and sarcastic, Avvakum broke radically with the old
formalist tradition and the centuries-long use of Church Slavonic
as the written language of Russian letters. D. Mirsky feels that
Avvakum was the only Russian writer to use satisfactorily a pure
Great Russian vernacular (the spoken language of Muscovy,
present central and northern Russia) for a literary purpose:
"Avvakum molded it into a new form for his own purpose, re-
vamped it, widened its use and gave to this language new,
purely literary, importance. His style is active, original, literary,
creative." Avvakum reduced the length of the sentence, renounced the use of subordinate clauses, participles and gerunds,
multiple epithets and compounds. He saturated his short,
dynamic phrases—usually some eight to twelve words in length
—with nouns and verbs. This leader of the Old Believers was
not only a consummate stylist and expressionist but also a
master of psychological delineations, and from his pen issued
concise, pointed characterizations of his contemporaries. When
appropriate, however, Avvakum knew how to use rhetorical
stylistics in descriptions of his co-believers, as, for instance, in
that of Boyarina Morozova. While his *Life* was the best of his
numerous works, in most of Avvakum's writings can be found
his vivid, colorful, colloquial language and his unusual gift for
observation.

Another outstanding autobiography, or, rather, confession,
came from the pen of Avvakum's spiritual father, Monk
Epiphanius, who recorded his martyrdom and spiritual experi-
ences during the persecutions inflicted upon the Old Believers
by the Church and government. While Avvakum's *Life* treats
his sermons, tribulations, and struggle for the old faith,
Epiphanius' *Confession* presents the powerful, moving story of
the writer's inner life, his doubts and visions, mystical experi-
ences, and spiritual recoveries. This "Jobian" monologue is the
first instance in Russian literature of the "exposure of the soul,"

which later became so famous in the works of Dostoevsky and Tolstoy.

The emergence of secular biography, autobiography, and the literary confession signaled the end of the medieval literary patterns. With the secularization of life, literature turned away from purely religious-historical biography. New ways of life, together with freer cultural and spiritual criticism, demanded a new type of letters, greater realism, and a more penetrating portrayal of character and human psychology. A fictional hero replaced the historical or hagiographical one, and the novella and satirical tale made their appearance.

19. THE BIRTH OF FICTION

The rise of fiction was the most spectacular literary event of the last century of Muscovite Russia. Many literary historians classify all the fictional works of this time under the term *povest'* (tale, long story, or novella), but among these numerous works with fictional heroes and plots can be distinguished two different genres. One, of the novella type, centers upon the deeds of the main character. In the other, the satirical tale, the social aspect, and the criticism of conditions and mores, overshadow the narrative part and character delineation. Both of these types of *povest'* evidently arose under the influence of Western picaresque novels that were translated in the seventeenth century into Russian, as, for instance, *Peter of the Golden Keys, Brunswick, Prince Bova, Basil the Golden-Haired, Eruslan Lazarevich* (of Oriental origin), or the *History of Apollonius of Tyre*. The seventeenth-century Russian novella, however, has a simpler structure than Western picaresque novels. It is much more concise, contains fewer characters and adventures, and the narrative is provided a purely Russian socio–historical setting. The most interesting aspects of this new genre are its unexpectedly wide range of topics, its moral appraisals, linguistic facets, and manners of treatment.

The *Tale of Savva Grudtsyn*, which to some extent resembles the story of Dr. Faust's temptations, is probably the oldest Russian novella, the earliest version dating from the middle of the seventeenth century. Written in heavy Church Slavonic and interwoven with hagiographic motifs, the tale depicts Savva's amorous adventures, and its realistic, even naturalistic, depictions of the worlds of the merchant and soldier are strikingly novel. Savva's adventures are placed against an actual historical background, and even the name of this fictitious hero belongs to a well-known merchant family. The same theme—the down-

fall and moral recovery of a youth—is the basis of another
charming novella, this one in verse form, *Misery-Luckless-Plight*,
which, for its choice use of the vernacular, the extensive inclusion of figures of folk speech, and its impeccable structure, can
be considered one of the finest works of late medieval literature.

Shifting still further away from the earlier literary manners
is the *Tale of Frol Skobeev, the Rogue*. Any moral element is
entirely absent from this work, and the author obviously enjoys
relating the successful adventures of another new hero—a rogue
from the lower nobility whose swindles finally open for him the
door to the society of the upper aristocracy. While Savva
Grudtsyn is the victim of his own passions and of sorcery, Frol
Skobeev is simply an adroit, cynical scamp who cares nothing
for true love and for whom the seduction of aristocratic Annushka is merely a means to social success. The tale's language
shows a new stage in the development of literary Russian: in
place of the heavy Church Slavonic of *Savva Grudtsyn*, the
author of *Frol Skobeev* uses the vernacular extensively and does
not shun vulgarity.

An intermediate stage among these three novellas is represented by the tale *Karp Sutulov*, the story of a merchant's virtuous wife who cleverly maintains her virtue during her husband's
absence on a business trip. A contrasting evolution of amorous
motifs can be found in a touching *Novel in Verse*, written probably toward the very end of the century, about a young girl
whose father forces her to break with her true love and marry
another man. This tale is rich in colorful details of everyday life
during this culturally and socially transitional period. The *Tale
of Solomonia, the Possessed*, on the other hand, is the most
striking Russian medieval horror novella because of its demonological scenes. In most of these novellas the plots and characters
are given a precise setting as to locale and time.

No less rich is seventeenth-century satire, often written in
rhymed verse. Its oldest specimen, *Shemiaka's Judgment*, mentioned above, is charming for its naïve and abrupt style. The
judicial system of medieval Russia suffered strongly from the
partiality and graft of the judges, and supplied abundant material for satire. Shemiaka is the classic type of venal judge, and
this story, which became extremely popular in seventeenth- and
eighteenth-century Russia, is known in innumerable prose and
verse versions. A similar theme appears in the various prose
and verse versions of the satire *Yorsh Yorshovich* (*Ruff, Son of
Ruff*): *Proceedings of a Suit Brought by the Bream Against the
Ruff in the Case of the Lake and Rivers of Rostov*. This theme

of the partiality or impartiality of judges goes far back into history, to Buddhist, Tibetan, and Indian legends, Arabic tales, or ballads on the judgments of Charlemagne. Similar tales were certainly popular in oral form in Russia for centuries, but only now, with the relaxation of state and Church control over literature and the breakdown of a purely spiritually oriented culture, did they become available in written form. Other satirical poems and prose narratives have as their heroes drunkards, corrupt clerics and monks (as, for instance, in the *Supplication of Kaliazin* and the *Novella of Priest Savva*); the virtuous man and the sinner (as in the *Legend of the Rooster and the Fox*, the rooster being the symbol of polygamic man); or the debauched aristocracy, a jealous husband, and inefficient administrators. The number of novellas and satires penned in the seventeenth century is extremely large, and they clearly reflect the secularization of Old Muscovy and the collapse of its traditional mode of life and mentality.

20. POETRY

In the nineteenth century the beginning of Russian poetry was usually ascribed to Simeon Polotsky (1629–1680), a West Russian scholar and poet of Polish training and culture who, after coming to Moscow in 1664, became the writer of odes to the court and tutor to Tsar Alexis' children. Later research has discarded Polotsky not only as the initiator of Russian poetry but even as the first poet of the syllabic school of versification. As early as 1608 a nobleman, Ivanets Frunikov, wrote an ironical versified epistle, full of puns and folk witticisms, the *Letter of a Nobleman to a Nobleman*. With this oldest dated Russian work in verse not only Russian rhymed poetry began, but also its satirical and ironic ramifications—which later, after the middle of the century, produced verse versions of such satirical tales as *Shemiaka's Judgment, Yorsh Yorshovich,* or *Foma and Erema*. All of them use the vernacular, folk witticisms, and the rhymed couplet of the *skomorokhs,* folk jesters and entertainers. As every product of folk poetics, which abound in rhymed puns, colloquial sayings and vulgarisms, such works, unfortunately, are hardly fitted for translation.

At the same time, also in the beginning of the seventeenth century, there appeared the so-called "presyllabic" versification, of a more formal type, which was characterized by a regular use of rhymed couplets in a line of undetermined length, vacillating usually between eight and sixteen syllables, but with no specific meter. Patriarch Job in his *vita* of Tsarevich Dmitry, mentioned above, used a wealth of such couplets for the first time in a hagiographic work. Numerous similarly versified fragments can be found in the historical writings of the Time of Troubles, especially those of I. Katyrev-Rostovsky and G. Shakhovskoy, as well as in *The New Story About the Glorious Muscovite Tsardom* (*Novaya povest*) written around 1610. One of these earliest poets was Prince Ivan A. Khvorostinin, who in 1624 wrote the first large, formal poetic work, *Epistle Against Blaspheming Heretics*, a monumental theological poem abounding in autobiographical digressions. Directed against the propagation in Russia of Western religious beliefs, Khvorostinin's *Epistle* numbers over three thousand versified lines. The vogue for versification (*stikhobesie*) spread rapidly to various genres of Muscovite letters, and Khvorostinin's example was followed by scores of Russian versifiers who complied their theological and political treatises in rhymed form. Even many of the Old Believers, usually the staunch enemies of all new spiritual and cultural currents, succumbed to the temptations of this new vogue and also wrote some of their protests in verse form.

An attractive aspect of seventeenth-century Russian poetry can be found in lyric verses in which writers gave expression to their feelings, hopes, and sorrows. The earliest of these were recorded, surprisingly enough, by an English traveler in Russia in 1619, a certain Richard James, in whose transcriptions have been preserved the oldest known specimens of Russian lyric verse. The above-mentioned *Novel in Verse*, a huge work organized in alphabetic form with each chapter beginning with a consecutive letter of the alphabet, is partially a novella, partially a love poem. To the same transitional type also belongs *Misery-Luckless-Plight*. Toward the end of the century some remarkable lyric songs were written or recorded by Peter Kvashnin, S. Pazukhin, and other poets of this new Muscovite school. Most of them show the strong influence of folklore and are in the meter of folk lyrics, although some use the rhymed endings that developed under Western poetic influence, and a rather novel and sophisticated vocabulary.

The final stage of seventeenth-century Russian poetry is represented by the appearance of "syllabic" versification, which had come into ascendance in Polish poetry and made its way to Russia. The prosodic foundations of syllabic verse were a fixed number of syllables in each line, exclusively feminine rhyme, and a *caesura*, or break, in the middle of each line. This method of versification, so perfectly suited to the Polish language because of its constant accent on the penultimate syllable, was hardly appropriate for Russian, with its unstable stress. Therefore syllabic verse lasted only a short time in Russia, and syllabic poetry completely disappeared from Russian letters in the second quarter of the eighteenth century leaving very few traces on Russia's further poetic development. It was important, however, for acquainting Russians with the formal techniques of prosody.

This syllabic versification came to Muscovy from western and southern Russia (the Ukraine), where scholars and poets during the century of Polish domination were strongly influenced by Polish culture. The earliest syllabic poems appeared in Russian as early as the 1650's, but the first significant Russian syllabic poet was S. Polotsky, mentioned above, who was also the first Russian poet whose poems were printed during his lifetime. An erudite scholar and accomplished technician of *ars poetica*, Polotsky was not a man of real poetic inspiration. His copious work falls into two categories: odes written in his capacity as court panegyrist, and didactic poems revealing to Muscovites either ancient mythology or some achievement of Western scholarship. Skillfully constructed and often formed in geometric shapes and figures, in accordance with the mode of the time, his verses are dry and uninspiring, and should be classified rather as the writings of a leader of the enlightenment than of a genuine poet.

From the point of view of the development of the Russian literary language, Polotsky's verses—written in an artificial admixture of the Muscovite and Kievan versions of Church Slavonic—were a step backward, away from the increasingly simple, vernacular language of the novellas, satires, and autobiographies. Polotsky's importance in Russian literature is primarily historical because his work, which belongs more to baroque than to medieval literature, in the periodization suggested by D. Chizhevsky, brought Russia entirely into the literary sphere of the West. In the baroque period of the late seventeenth century, which signaled the end of the centuries-long medieval tradition, a prominent literary role was played by Polotsky's Muscovite followers, K. Istomin, S. Medvedev, and K. Khonykov, and later in the eighteenth century by A. Kantemir. Their language is somewhat easier than that of Polotsky, and they reveal more genuine poetic inspiration than did their teacher, but they do not excel him in erudition and poetic techniques.

The emergence of poetry was one of the most obvious manifestations of the profound changes in Russian literature. Western modes of life and culture rapidly won a place in Russia, and

Muscovy, in the second half of the seventeenth century, was very different not only from what it had been in the sixteenth century, but even in the *first* half of the seventeenth. The reunion of southern, formerly Kievan, Russia with Muscovy in 1653, as well as the Russian-Polish War of 1653–1668, were both instrumental in effecting these changes, since thousands of Kievan and West Russian scholars, noblemen, and merchants moved to Moscow or to the northern and eastern cities of the empire, carrying new Polish and Western modes with them. The Russian court was quick to adopt them, and in 1673 the first theatrical troupe performed in the palace of the tsar. Fourteen years later, in 1687, the first institution of higher education, the Muscovite Slavo-Greco-Latin Academy, was founded, and when, at the beginning of the eighteenth century, Peter I introduced his reforms—many of which only continued further the trends that had been taking place in preceding years—he, in effect, merely legalized the transformation of medieval Muscovite Russia into a Westernized empire and European power.

Part I

the kievan period

(1030–1240)

Russia Toward 1200 A.D.

THE PRIMARY CHRONICLE

THE *Primary Chronicle*, or, as it was called by its authors, *The Tale of Bygone Years*, is structurally a very complicated work compiled by various writers in the course of some three-quarters of a century, from about 1040 to 1118. Except for the introduction, which forms a prolegomenon to Russian history, the *Chronicle* starts with the year 852 (6360, according to the old Byzantine and Russian calendars) and is organized strictly on a yearly basis. Even when the chronicler had no event to record for a given year he recorded the year, leaving a blank space after it. Some of the entries are extremely laconic and are written in an almost telegraphic style, for example: "In the year 868(6376) Basil [Emperor of Byzantium] began to rule. In the year 869(6377) the entire Bulgarian land was Christianized. In the year 870 (6378) . . ." (no entry).

Besides these telegraphic entries, however, the *Chronicle* contains many colorful accounts of the deeds of the Russian princes, of legal documents—such as treaties between Russia and Byzantium, and the *Testament*, or *Instruction*, of Vladimir Monomakh—and lengthier descriptions of the feuds, wars, and other events that took place in old Russia.

In the opinion of the renowned Russian philologist A. A. Shakhmatov, which opinion is generally accepted by most contemporary investigators of *The Tale of Bygone Years*, the first draft of this chronicle was composed between 1037 and 1039. From 1060 to 1073 the task of its continuance was assumed by Nikon, a monk of the Kievan Crypt Monastery. Nikon recorded many events to which he was an eyewitness, and also re-edited the earlier entries. From 1093 to 1095 this version of the *Chronicle* was reworked in the Kievan Crypt Monastery, and the resulting redaction is usually referred to as the "Beginning Version" by literary historians. Around 1113 another monk of the Kievan Crypt Monastery, Nestor, rewrote the "Beginning Version," and it was probably he, also, who added the introduction with its historical and philosophical considerations. It was at this time, apparently, that the work received its present name, *The Tale of Bygone Years*. Nestor's version of the *Chronicle* also underwent redaction between 1117 and 1118, and this became the final form of the *Primary Chronicle*. As such, it was used as the initial part of most other Russian annals through the fourteenth and fifteenth centuries, as in the *Laurentian Chronicle*, the

Hypatian Chronicle, and the *Troitsky* (Trinity) *Chronicle*, the most important early Russian annals.

The text of the Prolegomenon and various stories taken from the *Primary Chronicle* are presented here in the translation by Samuel H. Cross. Some changes of geographical and historical names have been made for the sake of consistency in nomenclature and spelling throughout this volume.

◆ ◆ ◆

1. Prolegomenon

THIS IS THE TALE OF BYGONE YEARS: FROM WHENCE CAME THE RUSSIAN LAND, WHO FIRST RULED IN KIEV, AND FROM WHICH SOURCE THE RUSSIAN LAND HAD ITS BEGINNING

Let us begin this tale in this way: after the flood the sons of Noah—Shem, Ham and Japheth—divided the earth among them. To the lot of Shem fell the Orient, and his share extended lengthwise as far as India and breadthwise (from east to south) as far as Rhinocolura, including Persia and Bactria, as well as Syria, Media (which lies beside the Euphrates River), Babylon, Cordyna, Assyria, Mesopotamia, Arabia the Ancient, Elymais, India, Arabia the Mighty, Coelesyria, Commagene, and all Phoenicia.

To the lot of Ham fell the southern region, comprising Egypt, Ethiopia facing toward India, the other Ethiopia out of which the red Ethiopian river flows to the eastward, the Thebaid, Libya as far as Cyrene, Marmaris, Syrtis, Numidia, Massyris, and Mauretania over against Cadiz. Among the regions of the Orient, Ham also received Cilicia, Pamphylia, Mysia, Lycaonia, Phrygia, Camalia, Lycia, Caria, Lydia, the rest of Moesia, Troas, Aeolia, Bithynia, and ancient Phrygia. He likewise acquired the islands of Sardinia, Crete, and Cyprus, and the river Gihon, called the Nile.

To the lot of Japheth fell the northern and the western sections, including Media, Albania, Armenia (both little and great), Cappadocia, Paphlagonia, Galatia, Colchis, Bospore, Maeotis, Dervis, Sarmatia, Tauria, Scythia, Thrace, Macedonia, Dalmatia, Molossia, Thessaly, Locris, Pellene (which is also called the Peloponnese), Arcadia, Epirus, Illyria, the Slavs, Lychnitis, Adriaca, and the Adriatic Sea. He received also the islands of Britain, Sicily, Euboea, Rhodes, Chios, Lesbos, Cythera, Zacynthus, Cephallenia, Ithaca, and Corcyra, as well as a portion of the land of Asia called Ionia, the river Tigris flowing between the Medes and Babylon, and the territory to the north extending as far as the Pontus and including the Danube, the Dniester, and the Caucasian Mountains, which are called Hungarian, and thence even to the Dnieper. He likewise acquired dominion over other rivers, among them the Desna, the Pripet, the Dvina, the Volkhov, and the Volga, which flows eastward into the portion of Shem.

In the share of Japheth lie Russia, Chud, and all the gentiles: Meria, Muroma, Ves, Mordova, Chud beyond the hills, Perm, Pechera, Yam, Ugra, Litva, Zimegola, Kors, Setgola, and Liub. The Liakhs, the Prussians, and Chud border on the Varangian Sea. The Varangians dwell on the shores of that same sea, and extend to the eastward as far as the portion of Shem. They likewise live to the west beside this sea as far as the land of the Angles and the Italians. For the following nations also are a part of the race of Japheth: the Varangians, the Swedes, the Normans, the Rus [Russians], the Angles, the Gauls, the Italians, the Romans, the Germans, the Carolingians, the Venetians, the Genoese, and so on. Their homes are situated in the northwest, and adjoin the Hamitic tribes.

Thus Shem, Ham, and Japheth divided the earth among them, and after casting lots, so that none might encroach upon his brother's share, they lived each in his appointed portion. There was but one language, and as men multiplied throughout the earth, they planned, in the days of Yoktan and Peleg, to build a tower as high as heaven itself. Thus they gathered together in the plain of Shinar to build the tower and the city of Babylon round about it. But they wrought upon the tower for forty years, and it was unfinished. Then the Lord God descended to look upon the city and the tower, and said, "This race is one, and their tongue is one." So the Lord confused the tongues, and after dividing the people into seventy-two races, he scattered them over the whole world. After the confusion of the tongues, God overthrew the tower with a great wind, and the ruin of it lies between Assur and Babylon. In height and in breadth it is 5,433 cubits, and the ruin was preserved for many years.

After the destruction of the tower and the division of the nations, the sons of Shem occupied the eastern regions, the sons of Ham those of the south, and the sons of Japheth the western and the northern lands. Among these seventy-two nations, the Slavic race is derived from the line of Japheth, since they are the Noricians, who are identical with the Slavs.

For many years the Slavs lived beside the Danube, where the Hungarian and Bulgarian lands now lie. From among these Slavs, parties scattered throughout the country and were known by appropriate names, according to the places where they settled. Thus some came and settled by the river Morava, and were named Moravians, while others were called Czechs. Among these same Slavs are included the White Croats, the Serbs, and the Khorutanians. For when the Vlakhs attacked the Danubian Slavs, settled among them, and did them violence, the latter came and made their homes by the Vistula, and were then called Liakhs.[1] Of these same Liakhs some were called Polianians, some Lutichians, some Mazovians, and still others Pomorians. Certain Slavs settled also on the Dnieper, and were likewise called Polianians. Still others were named Derevlians, because they lived in the forests. Some also lived between the Pripet and the Dvina, and were known as Dregovichians. Other tribes resided along the Dvina and were called Polotians on account of a small stream called the Polota, which flows into the Dvina. It was from this same stream that they were named Polotians. The Slavs also dwelt about Lake Ilmen, and were known there by their appropriate name. They built a city which they called Novgorod. Still others had their homes along the Desna, the Sem, and the Sula, and were called Severians. Thus the Slavic race was divided, and its language was known as Slavic.

When the Polianians lived by themselves among the hills, a trade route connected the Varangians with the Greeks. Starting from Greece, this route proceeds along the Dnieper, above which a portage leads to the Lovat. By following the Lovat, the great lake Ilmen is reached. The river Volkhov flows out of this lake and enters the great lake Nevo. The mouth of this lake opens into the Varangian Sea. Over this sea goes the route to Rome, and on from Rome overseas to Constantinople. The Pontus, into which flows the river Dnieper, may be reached from that point. The Dnieper itself rises in the upland forest, and flows southward. The Dvina has its source in this same forest, but flows northward and empties into the Varangian Sea. The Volga rises in this same forest, but flows to the east, and discharges through seventeen mouths into the Caspian Sea. It is possible by this route to the eastward to reach the Bulgars and the Caspians, and thus attain the region of Shem. Along the Dvina runs the route to the Varangians, whence one may reach Rome, and go on from there to the race of Ham. But the

---

[1] Original Slavic name for Poles.

Dnieper flows through various mouths into the Pontus. This sea, beside which taught St. Andrew, Peter's brother, is called the Russian Sea.

2. *The Apostle Andrew Comes to Russia*

IN THE tenth or eleventh century the belief was held, based on the writing of Eusebius, that the Apostle Andrew, during his trip to the Greek colonies on the Black Sea, had visited the territories that were later to become Russia. This legend became very popular with the Russians and laid the foundation for the later-developed theory of Russia as the guardian of the Orthodox Christian faith. According to the *Primary Chronicle,* Andrew crossed through Russia from the mouth of the Dnieper River, passed the hills on which Kiev was later founded, and went as far north as the ancient city of Novgorod.

◆ ◆ ◆

When Andrew was teaching in Sinope and came to Kherson (as has been recounted elsewhere), he observed that the mouth of the Dnieper was nearby. Conceiving a desire to go to Rome, he thus went to the mouth of the Dnieper. Thence he ascended the river, and by chance he halted beneath the hills upon the shore. Upon arising in the morning, he observed to the disciples who were with him: "See ye these hills? So shall the favor of God shine upon them that on this spot a great city shall arise, and God shall erect many churches therein." He drew near the hills, and having blessed them, he set up a cross. After offering his prayer to God, he descended from the hill on which Kiev was subsequently built, and continued his journey up the Dnieper.

He then reached the Slavs at the point where Novgorod is now situated. He saw these people existing according to their customs, and on observing how they bathed and drenched themselves, he wondered at them. He went thence among the Varangians and came to Rome, where he recounted what he had learned and observed. "Wondrous to relate," said he, "I saw the land of the Slavs, and while I was among them, I noticed their wooden bathhouses. They warm them to extreme heat, then undress, and after anointing themselves with tallow, they take young reeds and lash their bodies. They actually lash themselves so violently that they barely escape alive. Then they drench themselves with cold water, and thus are revived. They think nothing of doing this everyday, and actually inflict such voluntary torture upon themselves. They make of the act not a mere washing but a veritable torment." When his hearers learned this fact, they marveled. But Andrew, after his stay in Rome, returned to Sinope.

3.   *The Founding of the City of Kiev*

THE story of the founding of Kiev by three brothers, Kii, Shchek, and Khoriv, constitutes one of the oldest historical legends of Russia. An Armenian historian of the seventh century, Zenob Glak, knew of a similar legend concerning the founding of the city of Kuar (Kiev) in the land of Poluni (Polianians) by three brothers, Kuar, Mentery, and Kherean. It is possible that this legend arose from the actual merging of three settlements that archaeological evidence shows to have existed within the limits of present-day Kiev.

◆   ◆   ◆

The Polianians lived apart and governed their families, for thus far they were brethren, and each one lived with his gens on his own lands, ruling over his kinfolk. There were three brothers, Kii, Shchek, and Khoriv, and their sister was named Lybed. Kii lived upon the hill where the Borich trail now is, and Shchek dwelt upon the hill now named Shchekovitza, while on the third resided Khoriv, after whom this hill is named Khorevitza. They built a town and named it Kiev after their oldest brother. Around the town lay a wood and a great pine forest in which they used to catch wild beasts. These men were wise and prudent; they were called Polianians, and there are Polianians descended from them living in Kiev to this day.

Some ignorant persons have claimed that Kii was a ferryman, for near Kiev there was at that time a ferry from the other side of the river, in consequence of which people used to say, "To Kii's ferry." Now, if Kii had been a mere ferryman, he would never have gone to Constantinople. He was then the chief of his kin, and it is related what great honor he received from the emperor when he went to visit him. On his homeward journey, he arrived at the Danube. The place pleased him, and he built a small town, wishing to dwell there with his kinfolk. But those who lived nearby would not grant him this privilege. Yet even now the dwellers by the Danube call this town Kievetz. When Kii returned to Kiev, his native city, he ended his life there; and his brothers Shchek and Khoriv, as well as their sister Lybed, died there also.

4. *The Beginning of the Russian State and the Arrival of Rurik*

THE expansion of the Norsemen in the ninth and tenth centuries was not limited to northwestern Europe—Germany, France, and England. Long before the Vikings established themselves in France and, under William the Conqueror, in England, other Norse warriors from Norway, Sweden, and Denmark had penetrated to the Mediterranean Sea and built strong principalities in southern Italy and Greece. Some of these Norsemen entered the service of Byzantium in Constantinople. Simultaneously, another current of Norse expansion extended into eastern Europe. Skillfully utilizing the river systems of Russia, with the Dnieper playing the most important role, the Vikings—or, as the Russians called them, the Varangians—crossed through Russia and began to attack Byzantium, their bands being reinforced by Slavs.

According to both the *Primary Chronicle* and archaeological evidence, some of these Varangians settled in various places on Russian territory. It is difficult to determine now how important their role was in the subsequent organization of the Russian state, but the *Chronicle* records that Rurik, the leader of a group of Varangians, was invited to rule over Novgorod in 862, and legend has it that Rurik became the founder of both the Russian state and the dynasty that ruled Russia until 1598, when Fedor, the son of Ivan IV, died without an heir. The legend of Rurik's founding of the Russian state has been contested by many distinguished scholars and has divided most Russian historians into the Normanists, or "Norsemanists," who believe the legend to be true, and the anti-Normanists, who reject it and consider the Russian state to have been founded long before the arrival of Rurik.

✦ ✦ ✦

859 (6367) The Varangians from beyond the sea imposed tribute upon the Chuds, the Slavs, the Merians, the Ves, and the

Krivichians. But the Khazars imposed it upon the Polianians, the Severians, and the Viatichians, and collected a squirrel skin and a beaver skin from each hearth.

860–862 (6368–6370) The tributaries of the Varangians drove them back beyond the sea and, refusing them further tribute, set out to govern themselves. There was no law among them, but tribe rose against tribe. Discord thus ensued among them, and they began to war one against another. They said to themselves, "Let us seek a prince who may rule over us, and judge us according to the law." They accordingly went overseas to the Varangian Rus: these particular Varangians were known as Rus, just as some are called Swedes, and others Normans, Angles, and Goths, for they were thus named. The Chuds, the Slavs, and the Krivichians then said to the people of Rus, "Our whole land is great and rich, but there is no order in it. Come to rule and reign over us." They thus selected three brothers, with their kinfolk, who took with them all the Rus, and migrated. The oldest, Rurik, located himself in Novgorod; the second, Sineus, in Beloozero; and the third, Truvor, in Izborsk. On account of these Varangians, the district of Novgorod became known as Russian (Rus) land. The present inhabitants of Novgorod are descended from the Varangian race, but aforetime they were Slavs.

After two years, Sineus and his brother Truvor died, and Rurik assumed the sole authority. He assigned cities to his followers, Polotzk to one, Rostov to another, and to another Beloozero. In these cities there are thus Varangian colonists, but the first settlers were, in Novgorod, Slavs; in Polotzk, Krivichians; at Beloozero, Ves; in Rostov, Merians; and in Murom, Muromians. Rurik had dominion over all these districts.

With Rurik there were two men who did not belong to his kin, but were boyars. They obtained permission to go to Constantinople with their families. They thus sailed down the Dnieper, and in the course of their journey they saw a small city on a hill. Upon their inquiry as to whose town it was, they were informed that three brothers, Kii, Shchek, and Khoriv, had once built the city, but that since their deaths, their descendants were living there as tributaries of the Khazars. Oskold and Dir remained in this city, and after gathering together many Varangians, they established their domination over the country of the Polianians at the same time that Rurik was ruling at Novgorod.

863–866 (6371–6374) Oskold and Dir attacked the Greeks during the fourteenth year of the reign of the Emperor Michael.

When the emperor had set forth against the Saracens and had arrived at the Black River, the eparch sent him word that the Russians were approaching Constantinople, and the emperor turned back. Upon arriving inside the strait, the Russians made a great massacre of the Christians, and attacked Constantinople in two hundred boats. The emperor succeeded with difficulty in entering the city. The people prayed all night with the Patriarch Photius at the Church of the Holy Virgin in Blachernae. They also sang hymns and carried the sacred vestment of the Virgin to dip it in the sea. The weather was still, and the sea was calm, but a storm of wind came up, and when great waves straightway rose, confusing the boats of the godless Russians, it threw them upon the shore and broke them up, so that few escaped such destruction. The survivors then returned to their native land.

5. *Prince Oleg's Campaign*
Against Constantinople

ACCORDING to the *Primary Chronicle,* Rurik died in 879, leaving the conduct of state affairs to his relative, Oleg, in view of the infancy of Rurik's son, Igor. Oleg was the first nonlegendary ruler of Russia. In 882 he moved the capital from Novgorod to Kiev, and consolidated most of the Russian and Eastern Slavic tribes under his rule. A successful warrior and cautious ruler, Oleg became a popular figure in Russian historical tradition, and was called "the Seer" by his contemporaries. His campaigns against the Byzantine Empire, referred to by the writer of the *Chronicle* as the "Greek Empire," were particularly successful.

The tribes mentioned in the following text are primarily of Slavic origin. The Krivichians were a Slavic people who inhabited the entire northwestern Russian territory between the present cities of Moscow, Leningrad, and Minsk. The Chuds, Merians, and Ves were Finno-Ugric tribes of northern Russia.

✦ ✦ ✦

904–907 (6412–6415)   Leaving Igor in Kiev, Oleg attacked the Greeks. He took with him a multitude of Varangians, Slavs, Chuds, Krivichians, Merians, Polianians, Severians, Derevlians, Radimichians, Croats, Dulebians, and Tivercians, who are Torks. All these tribes are known as Great Scythia by the

Greeks. With this entire force, Oleg sallied forth by horse and by ship, and the number of his vessels was two thousand. He arrived before Constantinople, but the Greeks fortified the strait and closed up the city. Oleg disembarked upon the shore, and ordered his soldiery to beach the ships. They waged war around the city, and accomplished much slaughter of the Greeks. They also destroyed many palaces and burned the churches. Of the prisoners they captured, some they beheaded, some they tortured, some they shot, and still others they cast into the sea. The Russians inflicted many other woes upon the Greeks after the usual manner of soldiers. Oleg commanded his warriors to make wheels, which they attached to the ships, and when the wind was favorable they spread the sails and bore down upon the city from the open country. When the Greeks beheld this, they were afraid, and sending messengers to Oleg, they implored him not to destroy the city, and offered to submit to such tribute as he should desire. Thus Oleg halted his troops. The Greeks then brought out to him food and wine, but he would not accept it, for it was mixed with poison. Then the Greeks were terrified and exclaimed, "This is not Oleg, but St. Demetrius, whom God has sent upon us." So Oleg demanded that they pay tribute for his two thousand ships at the rate of twelve *grivnas* per man, with forty men reckoned to a ship.

The Greeks assented to these terms, and prayed for peace lest Oleg should conquer the land of Greece. Retiring thus a short distance from the city, Oleg concluded a peace with the Greek emperors Leo and Alexander, and sent into the city to them Karl, Farulf, Vermund, Hrollaf, and Steinvith, with instructions to receive the tribute. The Greeks promised to satisfy their requirements. Oleg demanded that they should give to the troops on the two thousand ships twelve *grivnas* per bench, and pay in addition the sums required for the various Russian cities: first Kiev, then Chernigov, Pereiaslavl, Polotzk, Rostov, Liubech, and the other towns. In these cities lived princes subject to Oleg.

The Russians proposed the following terms: "The Russians who come hither shall receive as much grain as they require. Whosoever come as merchants shall receive supplies for six months, including bread, wine, meat, fish, and fruit. Baths shall be prepared for them in any volume they require. When the Russians return homeward, they shall receive from your emperor food, anchors, cordage, and sails, and whatever else is needful for the journey." The Greeks accepted these stipulations, and the emperors and all the courtiers declared: "If Russians come hither without merchandise, they shall receive no provisions. Your prince shall personally lay injunction upon such Russians as journey hither that they shall do no violence in the towns and throughout our territory. Such Russians as arrive here shall dwell in the St. Mamas quarter. Our government will send officers to record their names, and they shall then receive their monthly allowance, first the natives of Kiev, then those from Chernigov, Pereiaslavl, and the other cities. They shall not enter the city save through one gate, unarmed and fifty at a time, escorted by soldiers of the emperor. They may purchase wares according to their requirements, and tax-free."

Thus the emperors Leo and Alexander made peace with Oleg, and after agreeing upon the tribute and mutually binding themselves by oath, they kissed the cross, and invited Oleg and his men to swear an oath likewise. According to the religion of the Russians, the latter swore by their weapons and by their god Perun, as well as by Volos, the god of cattle, and thus confirmed the treaty.

Oleg gave orders that silken sails should be made for the Russians and linen ones for the Slavs, and his demand was satisfied. The Russians hung their shields upon the gates as a sign of victory, and Oleg then departed from Constantinople. The Russians unfurled their silken sails and the Slavs their sails of linen, but the wind tore them. Then the Slavs said, "Let us keep our canvas ones; linen sails are not made for the Slavs." So Oleg came to Kiev, bearing palls, gold, fruit, and wine, along with every sort of adornment. The people called Oleg "the Seer," for they were but pagans, and therefore ignorant.

6. *The Death of Oleg*

THE life of Oleg, the Seer, furnished material for several popular legends, one of which treats his death as predicted by the magicians.

✦ ✦ ✦

912 (6620) Thus Oleg ruled in Kiev, and dwelt at peace with all nations.

Now autumn came, and Oleg bethought him of his horse that he had caused to be well fed, yet had never mounted. For on one occasion he had made inquiry of the wonder-working magicians as to the ultimate cause of his death. One magician replied, "O, Prince, it is from the steed which you love and on which you ride that you shall meet your death." Oleg then reflected, and determined never to mount this horse or even to look upon it again. So he gave command that the horse should be properly fed, but never led into his presence. He thus let several years pass until he had attacked the Greeks. After he returned to Kiev, four years elapsed, but in the fifth he thought of the horse through which the magicians had foretold that he should meet his death. He thus summoned his senior squire and inquired as to the whereabouts of the horse which he had ordered to be fed and well cared for. The squire answered that he was dead. Oleg laughed and mocked the magician, exclaiming, "Soothsayers tell untruths, and their words are naught but falsehood. This horse is dead, but I am still alive."

Then he commanded that a horse should be saddled. "Let me see his bones," said he. He rode to the place where the bare bones and the skull lay. Dismounting from his horse, he laughed, and remarked, "Am I to receive my death from this skull?" And he stamped upon the skull with his foot. But a serpent crawled forth from it and bit him in the foot, so that in consequence he sickened and died. All the people mourned for him in great grief. They bore him away and buried him upon the hill which is called Shchekovitza. His tomb stands there to this day, and it is called the Tomb of Oleg.

7. *Igor's Death and Olga's Revenge*

AFTER Oleg's death, Igor became the ruler of Russia. He was neither succcessful in his military enterprises nor popular with the people. A campaign undertaken by him against the Slavic tribe of Derevlians, who lived between Kiev and the present-day Polish border, resulted in his death. His clever widow, Olga, cruelly revenged the death of her husband. Folklore motifs are evident in this story of her revenge, which is one of the most colorful narratives of *The Tale of Bygone Years*.

✦ ✦ ✦

945 (6453)   In this year, Igor's retinue said to him. "The servants of Sveinald are adorned with weapons and fine raiment, but we are naked. Go forth with us, O Prince, after tribute, that

both you and we may profit thereby." Igor heeded their words, and he attacked Dereva in search of tribute. He demanded the previous tribute, and collected it by violence from the people with the assistance of his followers. After thus gathering the tribute, he returned to his city. On his homeward way, he said to his followers, after some reflection: "Go forward with the tribute. I shall turn back, and rejoin you later." He dismissed his retainers on their journey homeward, but being desirous of still greater booty, he returned on his tracks with a few of his vassals.

The Derevlians heard that he was again approaching, and consulted with Mal, their prince, saying: "If a wolf comes among the sheep, he will take away the whole flock one by one, unless he be killed. If we do not thus kill him now, he will destroy us all." They then sent forward to Igor inquiring why he had returned, since he had collected all the tribute. But Igor did not heed them, and the Derevlians came forth from the city of Izkorosten, and slew Igor and his company, for the number of the latter was few. So Igor was buried, and his tomb is near the city of Izkorosten in Dereva even to this day.

But Olga was in Kiev with her son, the boy Sviatoslav. His tutor was Asmund, and the troop commander was Sveinald, the father of Mstikha. The Derevlians then said: "See, we have killed the Prince of Russia. Let us take his wife Olga for our Prince Mal, and then we shall obtain possession of Sviatoslav, and work our will upon him." So they sent their best men, twenty in number, to Olga by boat, and they arrived below Borichev in their boat. At that time, the water flowed below the heights of Kiev, and the inhabitants did not live in the valley, but upon the heights. The city of Kiev was on the present site of the palace of Gordiat and Nicephorus, and the prince's palace was in the city where the palace of Vratislav and Chud now stands, while the ferry was outside the city. Without the city there stood another palace, where the palace of the Cantors is now situated, behind the Church of the Holy Virgin upon the heights. This was a palace with a stone hall.

Olga was informed that the Derevlians had arrived, and summoned them to her presence with a gracious welcome. When the Derevlians had thus announced their arrival, Olga replied with an inquiry as to the reason of their coming. The Derevlians then announced that their tribe had sent them to report that they had slain her husband, because he was like a wolf, crafty and ravening, but that their princes, who had thus preserved the land of Dereva, were good, and that Olga should come and marry their Prince Mal. For the name of the Prince of Dereva was Mal.

Olga made this reply: "Your proposal is pleasing to me; indeed, my husband cannot rise again from the dead. But I desire to honor you tomorrow in the presence of my people. Return now to your boat, and remain there with an aspect of arrogance. I shall send for you on the morrow, and you shall say, "We will not ride on horses nor go on foot; carry us in our boat.' And you shall be carried in your boat." Thus she dismissed them to their vessel.

Now Olga gave command that a large deep ditch should be dug in the castle with the hall, outside the city. Thus, on the morrow, Olga, as she sat in the hall, sent for the strangers, and her messengers approached them and said, "Olga summons you to great honor." But they replied, "We will not ride on horseback nor in wagons, nor go on foot; carry us in our boat." The people of Kiev then lamented: "Slavery is our lot. Our prince is killed, and our princess intends to marry their prince." So they carried the Derevlians in their boat. The latter sat on the cross-benches in great robes, puffed up with pride. They thus were borne into the court before Olga, and when the men had brought the Derevlians in, they dropped them into the trench along with the boat. Olga bent over and inquired whether they found the honor to their taste. They answered that it was worse than the death of Igor. She then commanded that they should be buried alive, and they were thus buried.

Olga then sent messages to the Derevlians to the effect that, if they really required her presence, they should send after her their distinguished men, so that she might go to their prince with due honor, for otherwise her people in Kiev would not let her go. When the Derevlians heard this message, they gathered together the best men who governed the land of Dereva, and sent them to her. When the Derevlians arrived, Olga commanded that a bath should be made ready, and invited them to appear before her after they had bathed. The bathhouse was then heated, and the Derevlians entered in to bathe. Olga's men closed up the bathhouse behind them, and she gave orders to set it on fire from the doors, so that the Derevlians were all burned to death.

Olga then sent to the Derevlians the following message: "I am now coming to you, so prepare great quantities of mead in the city where you killed my husband, that I may weep over his grave and hold a funeral feast for him." When they heard these words, they gathered great quantities of honey, and brewed mead. Taking a small escort, Olga made the journey with ease, and upon her arrival at Igor's tomb, she wept for her husband. She bade her followers pile up a great mound, and when they had piled it up, she also gave command that a funeral feast should be held. Thereupon the Derevlians sat down to drink, and Olga bade her followers wait upon them.

The Derevlians inquired of Olga where the retinue was which they had sent to meet her. She replied that they were following with her husband's bodyguard. When the Derevlians were drunk, she bade her followers fall upon them, and went about herself egging on her retinue to the Massacre of the Derevlians. So they cut down five thousand of them; but Olga returned to Kiev and prepared an army to attack the survivors.

946 (6454) Olga, together with her son Sviatoslav, gathered a large and valiant army, and proceeded to attack the land of the Derevlians. The latter came out to meet her troops, and when both forces were ready for combat, Sviatoslav cast his spear against the Derevlians. But the spear pierced the ears of the horse, and struck the horse's foot, for the prince was but a child. Then Sveinald and Asmund said, "The prince has already begun battle; press on, vassals, after the prince." Thus they conquered the Derevlians, with the result that the latter fled, and shut themselves up in their cities.

Olga hastened with her son to the city of Izkorosten, for it was there that her husband had been slain, and they laid siege to the city. The Derevlians barricaded themselves within the city, and fought valiantly from it, for they realized that they had killed the prince, and to what fate they would in consequence surrender.

Olga remained there a year without being able to take the city, and then she thought out this plan. She sent into the town the following message: "Why do you persist in holding out? All your cities have surrendered to me and submitted to tribute, so that the inhabitants now cultivate their fields and their lands in peace. But you had rather die of hunger, without submitting to tribute." The Derevlians replied that they would be glad to submit to tribute but that she was still bent on avenging her husband.

Olga then answered: "Since I have already avenged the misfortune of my husband twice on the occasions when your messengers came to Kiev, and a third time when I held a funeral feast for him, I do not desire further revenge, but am anxious to receive a small tribute. After I have made peace with you, I shall return home again."

The Derevlians then inquired what she desired of them, and expressed their readiness to pay honey and furs. Olga retorted that at the moment they had neither honey nor furs but that she had one small request to make. "Give me three pigeons," she said," and three sparrows from each house. I do not desire to impose a heavy tribute, like my husband, but I require only this small gift from you, for you are impoverished by the siege."

The Derevlians rejoiced, and collected from each house three pigeons and three sparrows, which they sent to Olga with their greetings. Olga then instructed them, in view of their submission, to return to their city, promising that on the morrow she would depart and return to her own capital. The Derevlians reentered their city with gladness, and when they reported to the inhabitants, the people of the town rejoiced.

Now Olga gave to each soldier in her army a pigeon or a sparrow, and ordered them to attach by a thread to each pigeon and sparrow a match bound with small pieces of cloth. When night fell, Olga bade her soldiers release the pigeons and the sparrows. So the birds flew to their nests, the pigeons to the cotes, and the sparrows under the eaves. Thus the dovecotes, the coops, the porches, and the haymows were set on fire. There was not a house that was not consumed, and it was impossible to extinguish the flames, because all the houses caught fire at once. The people fled from the city, and Olga ordered her soldiers to catch them. Thus she took the city and burned it, and captured the elders of the city. Some of the other captives she killed, while she gave others as slaves to her followers. The remnant she left to pay tribute.

She imposed upon them a heavy tribute, two parts of which went to Kiev, and the third to Olga in Vyshegorod; for Vyshegorod was Olga's city. She then passed through the land of Dereva, accompanied by her son and her retinue, establishing laws and tribute. Her residences and hunting preserves are there still. Then she returned with her son to Kiev, her city, where she remained one year.

8. Sviatoslav's Campaigns and His Death

PRINCE Sviatoslav, son of Igor and Olga, reigned from 956 to 971. He was a great warrior who built a mighty empire that comprised the Khazars, the Caucasian tribes of Yasians and

Kassogians, and all the Slavic tribes from Novgorod to Kiev, including the Viatichians. During his reign a horde of Pechenegs, an Asian tribe of Turkic origin, invaded the prairies of southern Russia and began raiding its agricultural lands.

In 968 the Byzantine emperor requested Sviatoslav's aid in subduing the Bulgarian kingdom in the Balkans. This led to a long war, first against the Bulgarians, and finally against Sviatoslav's original ally, Byzantium.

✦ ✦ ✦

956–964 (6464–6472)   When Prince Sviatoslav had grown up and matured, he began to collect a numerous and valiant army. Stepping light as a leopard, he undertook many campaigns. Upon his expeditions he carried with him neither wagons nor kettles, and boiled no meat, but cut off small strips of horse-flesh, game, or beef, and ate it after roasting it on the coals. Nor did he have a tent, but he spread out a garment under him, and set his saddle under his head; and all his retinue did likewise. He sent messengers to the other lands announcing his intention to attack them. He went to the Oka and the Volga, and on coming in contact with the Viatichians, he inquired of them to whom they paid tribute. They made answer that they paid a sliver piece per plowshare to the Khazars.

965 (6473)   Sviatoslav sallied forth against the Khazars. When they heard of his approach, they went out to meet him with their prince, the Kagan,[1] and the armies came to blows. When the battle thus took place, Sviatoslav defeated the Khazars and took their city of Belovezha. He also conquered the Yasians and the Kassogians.

966 (6474)   Sviatoslav conquered the Viatichians and made them his tributaries.

967 (6475)   Sviatoslav marched to the Danube to attack the Bulgarians. When they fought together, Sviatoslav overcame the Bulgarians, and captured eighty towns along the Danube. He took up his residence there, and ruled in Pereiaslavetz, receiving tribute from the Greeks.

968 (6476)   While Sviatoslav was at Pereiaslavetz, the Pechenegs invaded Russia for the first time. So Olga shut herself up in the city of Kiev with her grandsons, Yaropolk, Oleg, and Vladimir. The nomads besieged the city with a great force. They surrounded it with an innumerable multitude, so that it was impossible to escape or send messages from the city, and

[1] A Turkic word for emperor.

the inhabitants were weak from hunger and thirst. Those who had gathered on the other side of the Dnieper in their boats remained on that side, and not one of them could enter Kiev, while no one could cross over to them from the city itself.

The inhabitants of the city were afflicted, and lamented, "Is there no one that can reach the opposite shore and report to the other party that if we are not relieved on the morrow, we must perforce surrender to the Pechenegs?" Then one youth volunteered to make the attempt, and the people begged him to try it. So he went out of the city with a bridle in his hand, and ran among the Pechenegs shouting out a question whether anyone had seen a horse. For he knew their language, and they thought he was one of themselves. When he approached the river, he threw off his clothes, jumped into the Dnieper, and swam out. As soon as the Pechenegs perceived his action, they hurried in pursuit, shooting at him the while, but they did not succeed in doing him any harm. The party on the other shore caught sight of him, and rowed out in a boat to meet him. They then took him into their boat, and brought him to their company. He thus reported to them that if they could not relieve the city on the next day, the inhabitants would surrender to the Pechenegs.

Then their general, Pryetich by name, announced: "Tomorrow we shall approach by boat, and after rescuing the princess and the young princes, we shall fetch them over to this side. If we do not bring this to pass, Sviatoslav will put us to death." When it was morning, they embarked before dawn in their boats, and blew loudly on their trumpets. The people within the city raised a shout, so that the Pechenegs thought the prince himself had returned, and accordingly fled from the city in various directions. Thus Olga went forth with her grandsons and her followers to the boats. When the prince of the Pechenegs perceived their escape, he came alone to Pryetich the general, and inquired who had just arrived. Pryetich replied that it was a boat from the opposite bank. The prince of the Pechenegs inquired whether Pryetich was the prince himself. The general then replied that he was the prince's vassal and that he had come as a vanguard but that a countless force was on the way under the prince's command. He made this statement simply to frighten the Pecheneg. So the prince of the Pechenegs invited Pryetich to become his friend, to which request Pryetich assented. The two shook hands on it, and the prince of the Pechenegs gave Pryetich his spear, sabre, and arrows, while the latter gave him his own breastplate, shield, and sword. The Pechenegs raised the siege, and for a time the inhabitants could no longer water their horses at the Lybed on account of the retreating enemy.

But the people of Kiev sent to Sviatoslav, saying: "O Prince, you visit and observe foreign lands. But while you neglect your own country, the Pechenegs have all but taken us captive, along with your mother and your children as well. Unless you return to protect us, they will attack us again, if you have no pity on your native land, on your mother in her old age, and on our children." When Sviatoslav heard these words, he quickly bestrode his charger, and returned to Kiev with his retinue. He kissed his mother and his children, and regretted what they had suffered at the hands of the Pechenegs. He therefore collected an army, and drove the Pechenegs out into the steppes. Thus there was peace.

969 (6477) Sviatoslav announced to his mother and his boyars: "I do not care to remain in Kiev, but should prefer to live in Pereiaslavetz on the Danube, since that is the center of my realm, where all riches are concentrated: gold, silks, wine, and various fruits from Greece, silver and horses from Hungary and Bohemia, and from Russia furs, wax, honey, and slaves."

But Olga made reply, "You behold me in my weakness. Why do you desire to depart from me?" For she was already in precarious health. She thus remonstrated with him and begged him first to bury her and then to go wheresoever he would. Three days later Olga died. Her son wept for her with great mourning, as did likewise her grandsons and all the people. They thus carried her out, and buried her in her tomb. Olga had given command not to hold a funeral feast for her, for she had a priest who performed the last rites over the sainted princess.[1]

Olga was the precursor of the Christian land, even as the dayspring precedes the sun and as the dawn precedes the day. For she shone like the moon by night, and she was radiant among the infidels like a pearl in the mire, since the people were soiled, and not yet purified of their sin by holy baptism. But she herself was cleansed by this sacred purification. She put off the sinful garments of the old Adam, and was clad in the new Adam, which is Christ. Thus we say to her, "Rejoice in the Russians' knowledge of God," for we were the firstfruits of their reconciliation with him.

She was the first from Russia to enter the kingdom of God, and the sons of Russia thus praise her as their leader, for since her death she has interceded with God in their behalf. The

[1] By that time Olga had become a Christian.

souls of the righteous do not perish. As Solomon has said, "The
nations rejoice in the praise of the righteous, for his memory is
eternal, since it is acknowledged by God and men" (Proverbs,
xxix, 2; Wisdom, iii, 4). For all men glorify her, as they behold
her lying there in the body for many years. As the prophet has
said, "I will glorify them that glorify me" (I Samuel, ii, 30). Of
such persons David also said, "The righteous shall be had in
everlasting remembrance, he shall not be afraid of evil tidings.
His heart is fixed, trusting in Jehovah, his heart is fixed, and
will not be moved" (Psalms, cxii, 7–8). And Solomon said,
"The righteous live forever, and they have reward from God
and grace from the Most High. Therefore shall they receive
the kingdom of beauty, and the crown of goodness from the
hand of the Lord. With his right hand will he cover them, and
with his arm will he protect them" (Wisdom, v, 16–17). For
he protected the sainted Olga from the devil, our adversary and
our foe.

970 (6478)   Sviatoslav set up Yaropolk in Kiev and Oleg in
Dereva. At this time came the people of Novgorod asking for
themselves a prince. "If you will not come to us," said they,
"then we will choose a prince of our own." So Sviatoslav promised them that a prince should be designated, but Yaropolk and
Oleg both refused, so that Dobrynia suggested that the post
should be offered to Vladimir. For Vladimir was son of Malusha,
confidante of Olga and sister of Dobrynia. Their father was
Malk of Liubech, and Dobrynia was thus Vladimir's uncle. The
citizens of Novgorod thus requested Sviatoslav to designate
Vladimir, and he granted their request. The Novgorodians took
Vladimir to be their prince, and he went forth to Novgorod
with Dobrynia his uncle. But Sviatoslav departed thence to
Pereiaslavetz.

971 (6479)   Sviatoslav arrived before Pereiaslavetz, and the
Bulgarians fortified themselves in the city. They made one sally
against Sviatoslav; there was great carnage, and the Bulgarians
came off victors. But Sviatoslav cried to his soldiery: "We seem
to be conquered here already. Let us fight bravely, brothers
and companions!" Toward evening, Sviatoslav finally gained the
upper hand, and took the city by storm. He then sent messages
to the Greeks, announcing his intention to march against them
and capture their city, as he had taken Pereiaslavetz. The Greeks
replied that they were in no position to offer resistance, and
therefore begged him to accept tribute instead for himself and
his soldiery, requesting him to notify them how many Russians
there were, so that they might pay so much per head. The

Greeks made this proposition to deceive the Russians, for the Greeks are crafty even to the present day. Sviatoslav replied that his force numbered twenty thousand Russians. So the Greeks armed one hundred thousand men to attack Sviatoslav, and paid no tribute.

Sviatoslav advanced against the Greeks, who came out to meet the Russians. When the Russians perceived their approach, they were terrified at the multitude of the Greek soldiery, and Sviatoslav remarked: "Now we have no place whither we may flee. Whether we will or no, we must give battle. Let us not disgrace Russia, but rather sacrifice our lives, lest we be dishonored. For if we flee, we shall be disgraced. We must not take flight, but we will resist boldly, and I will march before you. If my head falls, then look to yourselves." Then his vassals replied, "Wherever your head falls, there we too will lay down our own!" So the Russians went into battle, and the carnage was great. Sviatoslav came out victor, but the Greeks fled. Then Sviatoslav advanced toward the capital, fighting as he went, and destroying towns that stand deserted even to the present time.

The emperor summoned his boyars to the palace, and inquired what they should do, for they could not withstand Sviatoslav's onslaught. The boyars advised that he should be tempted with gifts, to discover whether Sviatoslav liked gold and silks. So they sent to Sviatoslav gold and silks, carried by a clever envoy. To the latter they gave command to look well upon his eyes, his face, and his spirit. The envoy took the gifts, and went out to Sviatoslav. It was reported to the prince that Greeks had come bringing greetings, and he ordered that they should be introduced. They then came near and greeted him, laying before him the gold and the silks. Sviatoslav, without noticing the presents, bade his servants keep them. So the envoys returned before the emperor; and the emperor summoned his boyars. Then the envoys reported that when they had come before Sviatoslav and offered their gifts, he had taken no notice of them, but had ordered them to be retained. Then another courtier said, "Try him a second time; send him arms."

This suggestion was adopted, and they sent to Sviatoslav a sword and other accouterments which were duly brought before him. The prince accepted these gifts, which he praised and admired, and returned his greetings to the emperor. The envoys went back to the emperor and reported what had occurred. Then the boyars remarked: "This man must be fierce, since he pays no heed to riches, but accepts arms. Submit to tribute." The emperor accordingly requested Sviatoslav to approach no

nearer, but to accept tribute instead. For Sviatoslav had indeed
almost reached Constantinople. So the Greeks paid him tribute,
and he took also the share of those Russians who had been slain,
promising that their families should receive it. He accepted
many gifts besides, and returned to Pereiaslavetz with great
acclaim.

Upon observing the small number of his troops, Sviatoslav
reflected that if haply the Greeks attacked him by surprise, they
would kill his retinue and himself. For many warriors had perished on the expedition. So he resolved to return to Russia for
reinforcements. He then sent envoys to the emperor in Silistria
(for the emperor was then at that place) indicating his intention
to maintain peaceful and friendly relations. When the emperor
heard this message, he rejoiced, and sent to Sviatoslav gifts even
more valuable than the former ones. Sviatoslav accepted these
gifts, and on taking counsel with his retinue declared: "If we do
not make peace with the emperor, and he discovers how few of
us there are, the Greeks will come and besiege us in our city.
Russia is far away, and the Pechenegs are hostile to us. So who
will give us aid? Let us rather make peace with the emperor,
for the Greeks have offered tribute; let that suffice. But if the
emperor stops paying tribute, we shall once more collect troops
in Russia in still greater numbers, and march again on Constantinople." His speech pleased his followers, and they sent
their chief men to the emperor. The envoys arrived in Silistria,
and reported to the emperor. He summoned them before him
on the following day, and gave them permission to state their
errand. They then replied, "Thus says our prince, 'I desire to
maintain true amity with the Greek emperor henceforth and
forever.'" The emperor rejoiced, and commanded his scribe to
set down on parchment the words of Sviatoslav. One envoy recited all his words, and the scribe wrote them down. He spoke
as follows:

"In accordance with the previous treaty concluded by Sviatoslav, Prince of Russia, and by Sveinald, with Johannes sur-
named Tzimiskes, written down by Theophilus the secretary in
Silistria during the month of July, in the year 971 (6479), the
fourteenth of the indiction, I, Sviatoslav, Prince of Russia, even
as I previously swore, now confirm by oath upon this covenant
that I desire to preserve peace and perfect amity with each of
the great Greek emperors, and particularly with Basil and Constantine, and with their successors inspired of God, and with all
their subjects. In this resolve concur all Russians under my
sway, both boyars and commons, forever. I will therefore con-

template no attack upon your territory, nor will I collect an army or foreign mercenaries for this purpose, nor will I incite any other foe against your realm or against any territory pertaining thereto, and particularly against the district of Kherson, or the cities thereto adjacent, or against Bulgaria. But if any other foe plans to attack your realm, I will resist him and wage war upon him. And even as I have given oath to the Greek emperors in company with my boyars and all my subjects, so may we preserve this treaty inviolate. But if we fail in the observance of any of the aforesaid stipulations, either I, or my companions, or my subjects, may we be accursed of the God in whom we believe, namely, of Perun and Volos, the god of flocks, and may we become yellow as gold, and be slain with our own weapons. Regard as truth what we have now covenanted with you, even as it is inscribed upon this parchment and sealed with our seals."

After making peace with the Greeks, Sviatoslav journeyed by boat to the cataracts of the Dnieper, and the general, Sveinald, advised him to ride around the falls on horseback, for the Pechenegs were encamped in the vicinity. The prince did not heed him, but went on by boat. The people of Pereiaslavetz informed the Pechenegs that Sviatoslav was returning to Russia after seizing from the Greeks great riches and immense booty but that his troop was small. When the Pechenegs heard this news, they ambuscaded the cataracts, so that when Sviatoslav arrived it was impossible to pass them. So the prince decided to winter in Beloberg, but the Russians had no rations, so that there was a severe famine, and they paid as much as half a *grivna* for a horse's head. But Sviatoslav wintered there nevertheless.

When spring came, in 972 (6480), Sviatoslav approached the cataracts, where Kuria, Prince of the Pechenegs, attacked him; and Sviatoslav was killed. The nomads took his head, and made a cup out of his skull, overlaying it with gold, and they drank from it. But Sveinald returned to Yaropolk in Kiev. Now all the years of Sviatoslav's reign were twenty-eight.

9. *Vladimir Christianizes Russia*

Vladimir, son of Sviatoslav, reigned from 980 to 1015, and solved the important problem of Russia's cultural orientation. He was faced with the need to choose a religion for his state, and vacillated between several: Islam, which had been carried to Central Asia by Arab armies and to the Upper Volga[1] by Arab missionaries; Judaism, to which belonged the upper class of the Khazars on the Lower Volga; the Christianity of the West, professed by the Germans; or the Christianity of the East, professed by Byzantium. Preachers of each of these religions were present in Kiev, and each tried to convert Vladimir to his particular faith. Finally, the Christianity of the East prevailed. This is not surprising, since for centuries Russia had been in close contact with Byzantium and, even earlier, with the Hellenic world. As early as the sixth and seventh centuries B.C., the Greeks had founded prosperous colonies in 'the Crimea, such as the important city of Kherson, and others at many places on the northern coast of the Black Sea, all of which became the focal point for Greek and, later, Byzantine, influence in eastern Europe. Lively trade relations between Kiev and Constantinople had been maintained for centuries, despite intermittent interruptions by Russian military campaigns against Constantinople —or, as the Russians of that time called it, "Tsargrad," the City of the Caesars.

✦ ✦ ✦

987 (6495) Vladimir summoned together his vassals and the city elders, and said to them: "Behold, the Bulgarians came before me urging me to accept their religion. Then came the Germans and praised their own faith; and after them came the Jews. Finally the Greeks appeared, criticizing all other faiths but commending their own, and they spoke at length, telling the history of the whole world from its beginning. Their words were artful, and it was wondrous to listen and pleasant to hear them. They preach the existence of another world. 'Whoever adopts our religion and then dies shall arise and live forever. But whosoever embraces another faith, shall be consumed with fire in the next world.' What is your opinion on this subject, and what do you answer?" The vassals and the elders replied: "You know, O Prince, that no man condemns his own possessions, but praises them instead. If you desire to make certain, you have servants at your disposal. Send them to inquire about the ritual of each and how he worships God."

Their counsel pleased the prince and all the people, so that they chose good and wise men to the number of ten, and directed them to go first among the Bulgarians and inspect their

---

[1] To the realm of the Volga Bulgarians, a Turkic state not to be confused with the Slavic Bulgarians of the Balkans.

faith. The emissaries went their way, and when they arrived at their destination they beheld the disgraceful actions of the Bulgarians and their worship in the mosque; then they returned to their own country. Vladimir then instructed them to go likewise among the Germans, and examine their faith, and finally to visit the Greeks. They thus went into Germany, and after viewing the German ceremonial, they proceeded to Constantinople where they appeared before the emperor. He inquired on what mission they had come, and they reported to him all that had occurred. When the emperor heard their words, he rejoiced, and did them great honor on that very day.

On the morrow, the emperor sent a message to the patriarch to inform him that a Russian delegation had arrived to examine the Greek faith, and directed him to prepare the church and the clergy, and to array himself in his sacerdotal robes, so that the Russians might behold the glory of the God of the Greeks. When the patriarch received these commands, he bade the clergy assemble, and they performed the customary rites. They burned incense, and the choirs sang hymns. The emperor accompanied the Russians to the church, and placed them in a wide space, calling their attention to the beauty of the edifice, the chanting, and the offices of the archpriest and the ministry of the deacons, while he explained to them the worship of his God. The Russians were astonished, and in their wonder praised the Greek ceremonial. Then the Emperors Basil and Constantine invited the envoys to their presence, and said, "Go hence to your native country," and thus dismissed them with valuable presents and great honor.

Thus they returned to their own country, and the prince called together his vassals and the elders. Vladimir then announced the return of the envoys who had been sent out, and suggested that their report be heard. He thus commanded them to speak out before his vassals. The envoys reported: "When we journeyed among the Bulgarians, we beheld how they worship in their temple, called a mosque, while they stand ungirt. The Bulgarian bows, sits down, looks hither and thither like one possessed, and there is no happiness among them, but instead only sorrow and a dreadful stench. Their religion is not good. Then we went among the Germans, and saw them performing many ceremonies in their temples; but we beheld no glory there. Then we went on to Greece, and the Greeks led us to the edifices where they worship their God, and we knew not whether we were in heaven or on earth. For on earth there is no such splendor or such beauty, and we are at a loss how to describe it. We know only that God dwells there among men, and their service is fairer than the ceremonies of other nations. For we cannot forget that beauty. Every man, after tasting something sweet, is afterward unwilling to accept that which is bitter, and therefore we cannot dwell longer here." Then the vassals spoke and said, "If the Greek faith were evil, it would not have been adopted by your grandmother Olga, who was wiser than all other men." Vladimir then inquired where they should all accept baptism, and they replied that the decision rested with him.

After a year had passed, in 988 (6496), Vladimir marched with an armed force against Kherson,[2] a Greek city, and the people of Kherson barricaded themselves therein. Vladimir halted at the farther side of the city beside the bay, a bowshot from the town, and the inhabitants resisted energetically while Vladimir besieged the town. Eventually, however, they became exhausted, and Vladimir warned them that if they did not surrender, he would remain on the spot for three years. When they failed to heed this threat, Vladimir marshaled his troops and ordered the construction of an earthwork in the direction of the city. While this work was under construction, the inhabitants dug a tunnel under the city wall, stole the heaped-up earth, and carried it into the city, where they piled it up in the center of the town. But the soldiers kept on building, and Vladimir persisted. Then a man of Kherson, Anastasius by name, shot into the Russian camp an arrow on which he had written: "There are springs behind you to the east, from which water flows in pipes. Dig down and cut them off." When Vladimir received this information, he raised his eyes to heaven and vowed that if this hope was realized, he would be baptized. He gave orders straightway to dig down above the pipes, and the water supply was thus cut off. The inhabitants were accordingly overcome by thirst, and surrendered.

Vladimir and his retinue entered the city, and he sent messages to the Emperors Basil and Constantine, saying: "Behold, I have captured your glorious city. I have also heard that you have an unwedded sister. Unless you give her to me to wife, I shall deal with your own city as I have with Kherson." When the emperors heard this message, they were troubled, and replied: "It is not meet for Christians to give in marriage to pagans. If you are baptized, you shall have her to wife, inherit the kingdom of God, and be our companion in the faith. Unless

[2] The city of Kherson was located in the Crimea.

you do so, however, we cannot give you our sister in marriage."
When Vladimir learned their response, he directed the envoys
of the emperors to report to the latter that he was willing to
accept baptism, having already given some study to their religion, and that the Greek faith and ritual, as described by the
emissaries sent to examine it, had pleased him well. When the
emperors heard this report, they rejoiced, and persuaded their
sister Anna to consent to the match. They then requested
Vladimir to submit to baptism before they should send their
sister to him, but Vladimir desired that the princess should herself bring priests to baptize him. The emperors complied with
his request, and sent forth their sister, accompanied by some
dignitaries and priests. Anna, however, departed with reluc-
tance. "It is as if I were setting out into captivity," she lamented;
"better were it for me to die here." But her brothers protested:
"Through your agency God turns the Russian land to repentance, and you will relieve Greece from the danger of grievous
war. Do you not see how much evil the Russians have already
brought upon the Greeks? If you do not set out, they may bring
on us the same misfortunes." It was thus that they overcame
her hesitation only with great difficulty. The princess embarked
upon a ship, and after tearfully embracing her kinfolk, she set
forth across the sea and arrived at Kherson. The natives came
forth to greet her, and conducted her into the city, where they
settled her in the palace.

By divine agency, Vladimir was suffering at that moment
from a disease of the eyes, and could see nothing, being in
great distress. The princess declared to him that if he desired to
be relieved of this disease, he should be baptized with all speed,
otherwise it could not be cured. When Vladimir heard her message, he said, "If this proves true, then of a surety is the God of
the Christians great," and gave order that he should be baptized. The Bishop of Kherson, together with the princess's
priests, after announcing the tidings, baptized Vladimir, and as
the bishop laid his hand upon him, he straightway received his
sight. Upon experiencing this miraculous cure, Vladimir glorified God, saying, "I have now perceived the one true God."
When his followers beheld this miracle, many of them were also
baptized.

Vladimir was baptized in the Church of St. Basil, which
stands at Kherson upon a square in the center of the city, where
the Khersonians trade. The palace of Vladimir stands beside this
church to this day, and the palace of the princess is behind the
altar. After his baptism, Vladimir took the princess in marriage.

Those who do not know the truth say he was baptized in Kiev, while others assert this event took place in Vasiliev, while still others mention other places.

Hereupon Vladimir took the princess and Anastasius and the priests of Kherson, together with the relics of St. Clement and of Phoebus his disciple, and selected also sacred vessels and images for the service. In Kherson he thus founded a church on the mound which had been heaped up in the midst of the city with the earth removed from his embankment; this church is standing at the present day. Vladimir also found and appropriated two bronze statues and four bronze horses, which now stand behind the Church of the Holy Virgin, and which the ignorant think are made of marble. As a wedding present for the princess, he gave Kherson over to the Greeks again, and then departed for Kiev.

When the prince arrived at his capital, he directed that the idols should be overthrown and that some should be cut to pieces and others burned with fire. He thus ordered that Perun should be bound to a horse's tail and dragged along Borichev to the river. He appointed twelve men to beat the idol with sticks, not because he thought the wood was sensitive, but to affront the demon who had deceived man in this guise, that he might receive chastisement at the hands of men. Great art thou, O Lord, and marvelous are thy works! Yesterday he was honored of men, but today held in derision. While the idol was being dragged along the stream to the Dnieper, the unbelievers wept over it, for they had not yet received holy baptism. After they had thus dragged the idol along, they cast it into the Dnieper. But Vladimir had given this injunction: "If it halts anywhere, then push it out from the bank, until it goes over the falls. Then let it loose." His command was duly obeyed. When the men let the idol go, and it passed through the falls, the wind cast it out on the bank, which since that time has been called Perun's Shore, a name that it bears to this very day.

Thereafter Vladimir sent heralds throughout the whole city to proclaim that if any inhabitant, rich or poor, did not betake himself to the river, he would risk the prince's displeasure. When the people heard these words, they wept for joy, and exclaimed in their enthusiasm, "If this were not good, the prince and his boyars would not have accepted it." On the morrow the prince went forth to the Dnieper with the priests of the princess and those from Kherson, and a countless multitude assembled. They all went into the water: some stood up to their necks, others to their breasts, the younger near the bank, some of them holding children in their arms, while the adults waded farther out. The priests stood by and offered prayers. There was joy in heaven and upon earth to behold so many souls saved. But the devil groaned, lamenting: "Woe is me! how am I driven out hence! For I thought to have my dwelling place here, since the apostolic teachings do not abide in this land. Nor did this people know God, but I rejoiced in the service they rendered unto me. But now I am vanquished by the ignorant, not by apostles and martyrs, and my reign in these regions is at an end."

When the people were baptized, they returned each to his own abode. Vladimir, rejoicing that he and his subjects now knew God himself, looked up to heaven and said: "O God, who hast created heaven and earth, look down, I beseech thee, on this thy new people, and grant them, O Lord, to know thee as the true God, even as the other Christian nations have known thee. Confirm in them the true and unalterable faith, and aid me, O Lord, against the hostile adversary, so that, hoping in thee and in thy might, I may overcome his malice." Having spoken thus, he ordained that churches should be built and established where pagan idols had previously stood. He thus founded the Church of St. Basil on the hill where the idol of Perun and the other images had been set, and where the prince and the people had offered their sacrifices. He began to found churches and to assign priests throughout the cities, and to invite the people to accept baptism in all the cities and towns.

He took the children of the best families, and sent them to schools for instruction in book learning. The mothers of these children wept bitterly over them, for they were not yet strong in faith, but mourned as for the dead. When these children were assigned for study, there was thus fulfilled in the Russian land the prophecy which says, "In those days, the deaf shall hear words of Scripture, and the voice of the stammerers shall be made plain" (Isaiah, xxix, 18). For these persons had not ere this heard words of Scripture, and now heard them only by the act of God, for in his mercy the Lord took pity upon them, even as the Prophet said, "I will be gracious to whom I will be gracious" (Exodus, xxxiii, 19).

10. *Yaroslav the Wise*

FRATRICIDAL warring among the sons of Vladimir ended in 1016 with the victory of Prince Yaroslav, who established a firm rule over Russia for nearly forty years, from 1016 to 1054. This was the "golden age" of Kievan Russia, the age when material, intellectual, and artistic achievements were particularly brilliant. Prince Yaroslav, called "Yaroslav the Wise" by his contemporaries because of the peace and prosperity that marked his reign, maintained lively relations with Byzantium and Western Europe, and his children and grandchildren married the royalty of various western European nations. His daughter, Ann, became queen of France, and ruled that country in the name of her son after the death of her husband, Henry I, the Capet. It is of interest to note that Ann was the only literate member of the French royal family, and signed most of the state documents for her husband and son.

✦ ✦ ✦

1037 (6545) Yaroslav built the great citadel at Kiev, near which stand the Golden Gates. He founded there also the metropolitan Church of St. Sophia, the Church of the Annunciation by the Golden Gates, and also the Monastery of Sts. George and Irene. During his reign, the Christian faith was fruitful and multiplied, while the number of monks increased, and new monasteries came into being. Yaroslav loved religious establishments and was devoted to priests, especially to monks. He applied himself to books, and read them continually day and night. He assembled many scribes, and translated from Greek into Slavic. He wrote and collected many books through which true believers are instructed and enjoy religious education. For as one man plows the land, and other sows, and still others reap and eat food in abundance, so did this prince. His father Vladimir plowed and harrowed the soil when he enlightened Russia through baptism, while this prince sowed the hearts of the faithful with the written word, and we in turn reap the harvest by receiving the teaching of books. For great is the profit from book learning.

Through the medium of books, we are shown and taught the way of repentance, for we gain wisdom and continence from the written word. Books are like rivers that water the whole earth; they are the springs of wisdom. For books have an immeasurable depth; by them we are consoled in sorrow. They are the bridle of self-restraint. For great is wisdom. As Solomon said in its praise: "I (Wisdom) have inculcated counsel; I have summoned reason and prudence. The fear of the Lord *is the beginning of wisdom*. Mine are counsel, wisdom, constancy, and strength. Through me kings rule, and the mighty decree justice.

Through me are princes magnified and the oppressors possess the earth. I love them that love me, and they who seek me shall find grace" (Proverbs, viii, 12, 13, 14–17). If you seek wisdom attentively in books, you will obtain great profit for your spirit. He who reads books often converses with God or with holy men. If one possesses the words of the prophets, the teachings of the evangelists and the apostles, and the lives of the holy fathers, his soul will derive great profit therefrom. Thus Yaroslav, as we have said, was a lover of books, and as he wrote many, he deposited them in the Church of St. Sophia which he himself had founded. He adorned it with gold and silver and churchly vessels, and in it the usual hymns are raised to God at the customary seasons. He founded other churches in the cities and districts, appointing priests and paying them out of his personal fortune. He bade them teach the people, since that is the duty which God has prescribed them, and to go often into the churches. Priests and Christian laymen thus increased in number. Yaroslav rejoiced to see the multitude of his churches and of his Christian subjects, but the devil was afflicted, since he was now conquered by this new Christian nation.

11. *The Blinding of Vasilko*

LIKE the Middle Ages in western Europe, the feudal period in Russia was characterized by cruel power struggles among the princes of the ruling house. The first victims of such a struggle were Boris and Gleb, whose story was recorded in the entry for the year 1015. No less tragic was the struggle between Princes Sviatopolk and David against their cousin, Prince Vasilko, who ruled Volynia and Galicia in western Russia. The struggle ended with the blinding of Vasilko by his cousins. This story was told to the chronicler by the priest Vasily, and is one of the most dramatic narratives in *The Tale of Bygone Years*.

◆ ◆ ◆

1097 (6605)   Satan now incited certain men to report to David son of Igor that Vladimir was conspiring with Vasilko against Sviatopolk and against himself. David gave credence to their false words, and endeavored to stir up Sviatopolk against Vasilko, saying: "Who killed your brother Yaropolk? Now he plots against me and against you, and has conspired with Vladimir. Take thought for your own head."

Sviatopolk was thus perturbed, and wondered whether these allegations were true or false. He was uncertain, and replied to David: "If you speak aright, may God be your witness. But if you speak from motives of jealousy only, God will punish you for it."

Sviatopolk was concerned for his brother and himself, and wondered whether the rumor were true. He finally believed David, who thus deceived Sviatopolk, and the two of them set out to plot against Vasilko. Now Vasilko and Vladimir were ignorant of this fact. David remarked, however, that if he and Sviatopolk did not seize Vasilko, neither of them could be sure of the domains they then held. And Sviatopolk believed him.

Vasilko arrived on November 4th, crossed over to Vydobychi, and went to make his reverence to St. Michael in the monastery, where he also supped. He pitched his camp on the Ruditsa. At evening, he returned to his camp. When it was morning, Sviatopolk urged him by messenger not to depart before his name day. Vasilko refused, urging that he could not wait that long, or there would be disorder in his domain. Then David begged him not to depart, but rather to obey his elder kinsman. Vasilko, however, was still reluctant to comply.

Then David remarked to Sviatopolk: "See, he sets no store by you, though he is in your power. If he departs to his domain, you shall see whether he does not seize your cities of Turov and Pinsk, and other towns which belong to you; then you will perhaps remember my words. Call the men of Kiev and take him prisoner; then deliver him over to me."

Sviatopolk followed his advice, and sent word to Vasilko, saying, "If you are unwilling to remain until my name day, at least come and embrace me now, and then we shall meet with David." Vasilko promised to go, and did not perceive the treachery which David was planning against him. Vasilko thus mounted his horse and rode off. One of his servants then met him and urged him not to go, because the princes were plotting to take him prisoner. But Vasilko heeded him not, as he thought to himself: How can they intend to take me prisoner? They joined me in the oath that if any one of us should attack another, the holy cross and all of us should be against him. Having thus reflected, he crossed himself, and said, "God's will be done."

He thus rode with a small escort to the prince's palace. Sviatopolk came out to meet him, and they went into the hall. David entered, and all sat down. Then Sviatopolk begged Vasilko to remain until the festival.

Vasilko replied, "I cannot remain, kinsman; I have already ordered my camp to move forward."

David sat silent as if struck dumb, till Sviatopolk invited Vasilko to breakfast with them, and Vasilko accepted. Then Sviatopolk said, "Remain seated here a moment while I go out and make certain dispositions." He thus went out, leaving David and Vasilko alone together. Vasilko tried to open a conversation with David, but there was no voice nor hearing in him, for he was afraid, and had treachery in his heart. After he had sat awhile, he inquired where his kinsman was. The answer was given that he was standing in the vestibule. David then rose and asked Vasilko to remain seated while he went in search of Sviatopolk. He thus stood up and went thence. When David had thus gone out, others seized upon Vasilko and fettered him with double fetters, setting guards over him by night. This treachery took place on November 5th.

In the morning, Sviatopolk assembled the boyars and the men of Kiev and informed them of what David had told him, to the effect that Vasilko had been responsible for his brother's death, was plotting with Vladimir against him, and intended to kill him and seize his cities. The boyars and the populace replied: "It behooves you, O Prince, to protect your own life. If David spoke aright, let Vasilko suffer the penalty. If David has spoken falsely, let him suffer the vengeance of God and answer before God."

When the priors heard of the circumstances, they interceded with Sviatopolk in Vasilko's behalf, but he protested that it was all David's affair. When David heard of all this, he urged that Vasilko should be blinded, on the ground that if Sviatopolk did nothing and released Vasilko, neither he himself nor Sviatopolk would be able to retain their thrones much longer. Sviatopolk was in favor of releasing him, but David kept close watch over him and would not consent.

During the night, they thus took Vasilko to Belgorod, which is a small town ten versts from Kiev. The transported him fettered in a cart, and after removing him from the vehicle, they led him into a small house. As he sat there, Vasilko saw a Tork[1] sharpening a knife, and then comprehending that they intended blinding him, he cried out to God with loud weeping and groaning. Then came the emissaries of Sviatopolk and David: Snovid, the son of Izech, the squire of Sviatopolk, and Dmitry, David's

---

[1] Torks were a Turkic tribe of southern Russia.

squire, and they laid a rug upon the floor. After they had spread it, they seized Vasilko and endeavored to overthrow him. He offered a violent resistance, so that they could not throw him. Then others came and cast him down. They bound him, and laid upon his chest a slab taken from the hearth. Though Snovid, the son of Izech, sat at one end and Dimitri at the other, they still could not hold him down. Then two other men came, and after taking a second slab from the hearth, they too sat upon him, and weighed upon him so heavily that his chest cracked. Then a Tork, Berendi by name, a shepherd of Sviatopolk, came up with his knife, and though intending to strike him in the eye, missed the eye entirely and cut his face. This scar Vasilko bears to this day. Afterward, however, he struck him in one eye, and took out the pupil, and then in the other eye, and also removed the pupil of the latter.

At that moment Vasilko lay as if dead. They raised him in the rug, laid him fainting in the wagon, and carried him off to Vladimir. While he was being thus transported, they happened to halt with him at a marketplace after they had crossed the bridge at the town of Zvizhen. They took off his bloody shirt, and gave it to a priest's wife to wash. After she had washed it, the woman put it on him while the others were eating, and she began to weep, for he was as if dead. He heard her weeping, and inquired where he was. They replied that the town was Zdvizhden. He then begged for water. They gave him some, and after he had drunk the water, full consciousness returned to him. He remembered what had occurred, and feeling his shirt, he lamented: "Why did you take it from me? I had rather have met my death and stood before God in this bloody shirt."

When they had eaten, they rode on swiftly in the cart with him, and over a rough road, for it was then the month of *Gruden*, called November. They arrived with him at Vladimir on the sixth day. David accompanied them, and behaved as if he had captured some prize. They quartered Vasilko in the Vakeev palace, and placed over him a guard of thirty men, as well as two servants of the prince named Ulan and Kolchko.

Blinded Prince Vasilko asks for water.
A miniature from the *Radzivil Chronicle* of the fourteenth century.

12. *Metropolitan Hilarion*
Sermon on Law and Grace

THE *Sermon on Law and Grace* is arranged in two distinct parts: "The Sermon on the Law of Moses Given to Him by God and on the Grace and Truth Brought to the Earth by Jesus Christ," and "The Eulogy to Our Kagan, Vladimir."

This famous sermon by Metropolitan Hilarion is one of the oldest Russian literary-philosophical works and is the earliest Russian sermon preserved. It was written several decades before the *Primary Chronicle* and the most ancient Russian *vitae*, probably between 1037 and 1050. Its author, Hilarion, became in 1051 the first Russian (non-Greek) head of the Russian Church and Metropolitan of the city of Kiev. He was one of the most erudite and brilliant Russian preachers and writers of the Kievan age. Despite his clearly Byzantine cultural background, he manifests the Russian national spirit.

Besides the *Sermon on Law and Grace*, there has also been preserved Hilarion's *Confession of Faith*, in which he emphasizes the Trinitarian foundation of Christian dogma and the dual nature of Jesus Christ. In this work he wrote, "He suffered for me as a man. . . . He revived as God, . . . and after three days he arose from the dead, as a victor, Christ, my King."

In his *Sermon on Law and Grace* Metropolitan Hilarion reveals himself to be an astute preacher. The central idea of the sermon is the juxtaposition of the faith of the Old Testament with that of the New Testament. For a biblical comparison, he uses the story of the two sons of Abraham: the first, Ishmael, who was not free, but the son of Hagar, Sarah's handmaid; the second, who was free, being the son of Abraham by his wife, Sarah. For Hilarion, Christianity is the faith of freedom and liberation, while the religion of the Old Testament was one of law, compulsion and strict obedience.

Hilarion's attitude toward the problem of salvation is very characteristic of early Eastern Christianity: salvation through "baptism and good deeds," through Christian mercy and charity. This is remote from Luther's and Calvin's teachings of salvation solely through faith and, concomitantly, moral behavior.

This sermon, despite its clear tendency to raise the prestige of the Russian nation and the Russian Church, was composed in a typical Byzantine style, and is saturated with repeated parallels between Hagar and the Old Testament, and between Sarah and the New Testament. When Hilarion wrote that "Divine Grace announced to God" and that "the Father did as he was told by Divine Grace," he apparently referred to "Holy Sophia," that is, the Divine Omniscience of the three hypostases of the Trinity. The teaching of "Holy Wisdom," or "Holy Sophia," was widespread throughout Byzantium and Russia at that time, and is attested to by the fact that cathedrals in Kiev, Constantinople, and Novgorod were dedicated to "Holy Sophia."

Having adroitly presented his point, which is the supreme nature of the Christian faith, Hilarion turned to the destiny of the Russian people. In his eyes, when the Russians adopted Christianity they became the equal of all Christian peoples, including the Greeks. He regarded the Russian Church as having the same dignity, status, and rights as the Byzantine Church. It must be remembered that both Yaroslav and Hilarion attempted to liberate the Russian Church from Byzantine supervision and that Hilarion was the first native Russian to head the Russian Church and to defend its autonomy from Constantinople.

Hilarion ends his sermon with a highly rhetorical panegyric to Prince Vladimir, whom Russians consider a saint for having Christianized Russia. Optimistic, bright, even triumphant notes can easily be discerned in Hilarion's treatment of history. Russia had become enlightened by the Christian faith, and therefore its future would lie in Christ's hands.

The following translation is based upon the text of Metropolitan Hilarion's sermon published by A. B. Gorskii in *Pamiatniki dukhovnoi literatury vremeni velikogo kniazia Yaroslava I-ogo*, Moscow, 1844.

❖ ❖ ❖

THE SERMON OF THE LAW OF MOSES GIVEN TO HIM BY GOD, AND OF THE GRACE AND TRUTH BROUGHT TO EARTH BY JESUS CHRIST

Blessed be the God of Israel, the God of Christianity who visited his people and brought them salvation. He did not disdain his creation which was for ages possessed by pagan darkness and by worship of the devil, but he enlightened the Children of Abraham by giving them his Law tablets, and later he saved all nations, sending them his Son, his Gospel, and his baptism, and by giving them resurrection to eternal life.

Law was the precursor and the servant of Grace and Truth.
Grace and Truth were the servants of the future life and immortal life. Law led its people of the Old Testament toward the
blessing of baptism, and baptism led its sons to the life eternal.
Moses and the prophets announced the coming of Christ, but
Christ and the Apostles announced resurrection and the future
age.

And what could the Law achieve? And what could Grace
achieve? First was the Law and then Grace. Hagar and Sarah
are the pictures of Law and Grace: Hagar was a handmaid and
Sarah was free. First one is the handmaid and then one is free.
And he who reads (the Bible) must understand this. Abraham,
since his youth, had Sarah for his wife and she was free and not
a slave, and so God decided before all ages to send his Son into
the world that Grace might appear through him (but sent him
to man only later). But Sarah was restrained from bearing children, since she was unfruitful. But she was not actually unfruitful, but was chosen by divine Providence to bear in her old age.
The wisdom of God was not revealed to anyone, but concealed
from both angels and men. This wisdom was not shown, but was
concealed to be revealed at the end of the age.

It was Sarah who said unto Abraham:

"Behold now, the Lord has prevented me from bearing
children; go in to my maid; it may be that I shall obtain
children by her."

And so the divine Grace (of the Son) announced to God, the
Father:

"It is not yet my time for descending to the earth and to
save the world. Descend to Mount Sinai and give them the
Law."

And, just as Abraham did as Sarah told him and went into
Hagar, so God, the Father, did as he was told by the divine
Grace and descended to Mount Sinai.

And Hagar, the handmaid, bore from Abraham a servant (not
a truly free man), and Abraham gave him the name Ishmael.
And Moses brought from Mount Sinai the Law and not the
Grace, the shade and not the Truth.

When Abraham and Sarah were old, God appeared to Abraham by the oaks of Mamre, as he sat at the door of his tent in
the heat of the day. And he ran to meet him, and bowing lowly
to the earth, he hastened into the tent (to Sarah). And so,
when the end of the age was nearing, God appeared to the
humankind, descended to the earth, and blessed the womb of

the Virgin. And he was received by the Immaculate Virgin into the tent of the flesh. And the Virgin said to the angel:

"Behold I am the handmaid of the Lord; let it be to me according to your word."

Once the Lord gave Sarah to bear a child, and she begat Isaac, the free son of a free father. And, when once more our Lord visited the humankind, he appeared unknown and hidden from men and then was born Grace and Truth, but not the Law. And now it was the Son and not the servant.

And the child grew up and was weaned; and Abraham made a great feast on the day that Isaac was weaned. And when Christ was upon the earth Grace did not reveal Itself and Christ was hiding himself until he was thirty. And when he had grown and was weaned, then there, in the river Jordan, Grace was revealed by a man. And our Lord invited many and made a great feast and offered up the fatted calf of the age, His beloved Son, Jesus Christ, and God then called to this feast many of heaven and earth and they the angels and men into one (Church).

This blessed faith spreads now over the entire earth, and finally it reached the Russian nation. And, whereas the lake of the Law dried up, the fount of the Gospel became rich in water and overflowed upon our land and reached us. And now, together with all Christians, we glorify the Holy Trinity, while Judea remains silent.

THE EULOGY TO OUR KAGAN VLADIMIR

Rome, with voices panegyrical, praises Peter and Paul through whom they came to believe in Jesus Christ, the Son of God:

Asia, Ephesus, and Patmus praise John the Theologian;

India praises Thomas;

Egypt, Mark.

All lands, cities, and men honor and glorify their teacher who brought them the Orthodox Faith. Thus, let us, through our own strength, humbly praise our teacher and mentor, the great Kagan of our land Vladimir, the grandson of Igor of yore and son of glorious Sviatoslav, who ruled in their day with courage and valor, becoming famed in many lands for their victories and fortitude. And they did not reign in a poor and unknown land, but in Russia, which is known and celebrated by all to the ends of the earth.

A good attestation of your devotion, blessed one, is the Holy Church of the Blessed Virgin, the Mother of God, which you

build on the orthodox foundation and where your valorous body
now lays at rest and awaits the archangel's trumpet.

A good and certain attestation is your son, George [Yaroslav's
Christian name], whom God has made the heir to your throne,
> who does not destroy your laws, but confirms them,
> who does not diminish works of piety, but extends them,
> who does not undo, but strengthens,
> who finishes that which you have left unfinished
> even as Solomon finished the works begun by David;
> who has built a great and holy temple to God's omniscience
> that it may hallow your city;
> who has embellished with all manner of things beautiful,
> with gold and silver and precious stones
> and with sacred vessels;
> so that the church is a wonder to all surrounding lands
> and so that the like cannot be found in all the northern
>   land,
> nor in the east nor the west;
> who has given your famous city of Kiev the crown of glory,
> who has turned your city and its people
> to all-glorious Mother of God,
> who is always ready to succor Christians
> and for whom he has built a church with doors of gold
> in the name of the first holy day of the Lord of the
>   Annunciation,
> that the veneration, which the archangel will offer to the
>   Virgin,
> may also be upon this city.
> To her he speaks, saying:
>> "Rejoice, Blessed One, the Lord is with you!"
> And to the city he speaks, saying:
>> "Rejoice, faithful city, the Lord is with you!"

Arise from your grave, venerated prince,
Arise and shake off your sleep.
You are not dead,
but only sleep to the day of resurrection.
Arise! You are not dead,
for it is not right that you should die,
for you have believed in Christ,
the Sustainer of the whole world.
Shake off your deep sleep
and lift up your eyes
that you might see what honor the Lord has granted you,

and you still live upon this earth,
unforgotten through your sons.
Arise! upon your son, your beloved son,
whom God has brought forth from your loins.
See him embellishing the throne of your land.
Rejoice and be of good cheer!
Look upon the pious wife of your son, Irina.
Look upon your grandchildren
and your great-grandchildren.
See how they live and how they are cared for by God.
See how they preserve devotion in your tradition,
how they partake of the Sacraments of the Holy Church,
how they glorify God,
and how they bow before his Holy Name.
See your city radiant with grandeur.
See your blossoming churches,
See Christianity flourishing.
See your city gleaming,
adorned with holy icons and
fragrant with thyme,
praising God and filling the air with sacred songs.
  And seeing all this, rejoice and be of good cheer, and praise
the Lord, the Creator of all which you have seen.

13. *Cyril of Turov*
Sermon on the First Sunday After Easter

AMONG Russian writers of the Kievan period, Cyril, Bishop of
Turov, was probably the most accomplished master of Orthodox
theology and the Byzantine style of writing. He had an excellent
command of Greek and his literary achievements surpass those
of any other Russian man of letters of that era. He wrote
numerous epistles, prayers, and sermons, all of which are distinguished by their elegant and elaborate style. They show
clearly the author's gift for composition and his extensive knowledge of the Bible and early Church history. In his works he
quotes the patriarchs and prophets of the Old Testament with
unusual adroitness for that time. Though full of symbolism and
allegory, his writings are nonetheless lucid and fully comprehensible, and they gained the admiration of endless generations
of Russians. Even as late as the seventeenth century, many of
Cyril's stylistic patterns were still popular with writers of the

conservative literary tradition. Of all his works, Cyril's triumphant description of spring as the symbol of the resurrection is the most popular.

Very little is known of the author's life except that he lived in the middle of the twelfth century and was Bishop of Turov. His best-known works are eight sermons delivered on the occasion of the eight Sundays beginning with Palm Sunday. The *Sermon on the First Sunday after Easter,* perhaps his most famous single composition, is offered here in a translation by Leo Wiener.

◆   ◆   ◆

The Church needs a great teacher and a wise orator to celebrate the holiday properly, but we are poor in words and dim in mind, not having the fire of the Holy Ghost—the enjoyment of words useful to the soul; yet for the love of my brethren who are with me, we shall say something about the renewal of the Lord's resurrection. In the past week of the Easter there were joy in heaven and terror in the nethermost regions, a renewal of life and liberation of the world, a destruction of hell and victory over death, a resurrection of the dead, and annihilation of the enticing power of the devil; a salvation of the human race by the resurrection of Christ; an impoverishment of the Old Testament and enslavement of the Sabbath; an enrichment of the Church of Christ, and enthronement of the Sunday.

Last week there was a change of all things, for the earth was opened up by heaven, having been purified from its satanic impurities, and the angels with their wives humbly served at the resurrection. All creation was renewed, for no longer are the air, the sun, the fire, the springs, the trees, thought to be gods; no longer does hell receive its due of infants sacrificed by their fathers, nor death its honors, for idolatry has come to an end, and the satanic power has been vanquished by the mystery of the cross. The Old Testament has become impoverished by the rejection of the blood of calves and sacrifices of goats, for Christ has given himself to the Lord as a sacrifice for all. And with this, Sunday ceased to be a holiday, but the Sunday was sanctified on account of the resurrection, and Sunday is now supreme, for Christ arose from the dead on that day. . . .

Today the heavens have been cleared from the dark clouds that enshrouded them as with a heavy veil, and they proclaim the glory of God with a clear atmosphere. . . .

Today the sun rises and beams on high, and rejoicing warms the earth, for there has arisen for us from the grave the real

sun, Christ, and he saves all who believe in him. Today the
moon descends from its high place and gives honor to the
greater lights. The Old Testament, as had been prophesied, has
stopped with its Sabbath, and with its prophets gives honor to
the Testament of Christ with its Sunday. Today the winter of
sin has stopped in repentance, and the ice of unbelief is melted
by wisdom. Today spring appears spruce, and enlivens all
earthly existence; the stormy winds blow gently and generate
fruits, and the earth, giving nurture to the seed, brings forth
green grass. For spring is the beautiful faith in Christ which,
through baptism, produces a regeneration of man, and the
stormy winds are the evil, sinful thoughts that, being changed
to virtue through repentance, generate soul-saving fruits; but
the earth of our being, having received the Word of God like a
seed, and, passing through an ecstatic labor, through the fear of
him, brings forth a spirit of salvation.

Today the newborn lambs and calves frisk and leap about
joyfully and returning to their mothers gambol about, so that the
shepherds, playing on their reeds, praise Christ in joy. The
lambs, I say, are the gentle people from among the pagans, and
the calves—the idolaters of the unbelieving countries who, having accepted the Law through Christ's incarnation and the
teachings of the Apostles and miracles, and having returned to
the holy Church, suck the milk of its teachings; and the teachers
of Christ's flock, praying for all, praise Christ, the Lord, who
had collected all the wolves and sheep into one herd.

Today the trees send forth buds and the fragrant flowers
bloom, and behold, the gardens already emit a sweet odor, and
the workers laboring in hope acclaim Christ the giver of fruits.
We were before like the trees of the forest that bear no fruit,
but today the faith of Christ has been grafted on our unbelief,
and those who already held to the roots of Jesse have burgeoned
with the flowers of virtue and expect through Christ a regeneration in heaven, and the saints who labor for the Church expect
a reward from Christ. Today the plowman of the Word leads
the oxen of the Word to the spiritual yoke, sinks the plow of
baptism into the furrows of thought and deepening them to
furrows of repentance plants in them the spiritual seed and
rejoices in the hope of future returns. Today everything old has
taken an end, and all is new for the sake of the resurrection.
Today the apostolic rivers are full, and the pagan fish let out
their broods, and the fishermen, having examined the depth of
the divine incarnation, drag in full nets into the Church. . . .
Today the industrious bees of the monastic order show their

wisdom and set all to wonder, for living in the wilderness and providing for themselves, they astonish both angels and men, just as the bee flies upon the flowers and forms combs of honey in order to furnish sweetness to man and what is needed in the Church. . . .

Today there is a feast of regeneration for the people who are made new by the resurrection of Christ, and all new things are brought to God: from heathens, faith; from good Christians, offerings; from the clergy, holy sacrifices; from the civil authorities, God-pleasing charity; from the noble, care for the Church; from the righteous, humility; from the sinners, true repentance; from the unhallowed, a turning to God; from the hating, spiritual love.

THE LIVES OF SAINTS AND MONKS

14. Nestor: The Martyrdom of Boris and Gleb

AFTER the death of Vladimir, a fratricidal struggle broke out among his sons. The eldest, Sviatopolk, seized power and began plotting the elimination of his brothers, Boris, Gleb and Yaroslav. The murder of Boris and Gleb is described in a touching manner by the chronicler: the two refused to take up arms against their elder brother in order to prevent further bloodshed. They decided to accept their fate passively, following the example of Christ. This was the earliest imitation in the Middle Ages of Christ as a humble martyr dying for the sins of man. In both Western and Byzantine Christianity at that time, Christ's image was that of a pantocrat: an awe-inspiring, omnipotent ruler of the universe, to be dreaded. The humble aspect of Christ was stressed neither in Byzantine nor in Western Christianity until the time of St. Francis, some two hundred years after the martyrdom of Boris and Gleb.

The text presented here is the Samuel H. Cross translation.

✦ ✦ ✦

Sviatopolk settled in Kiev after his father's death, and after calling together all the inhabitants of Kiev, he began to distribute largess among them. They accepted it, but their hearts were not with him, because their brethren were with Boris. When Boris returned with the army, after meeting the Pechenegs, he received the news that his father was dead. He mourned deeply for him, for he was beloved of his father before all the rest.

When he came to the Alta, he halted. His father's retainers then urged him to take his place in Kiev on his father's throne, since he had at his disposal the latter's retainers and troops. But Boris protested: "Be it not for me to raise my hand against my elder brother. Now that my father has passed away, let him take the place of my father in my heart." When the soldiery heard these words, they departed from him, and Boris remained with his servants.

But Sviatopolk was filled with lawlessness. Adopting the device of Cain, he sent messages to Boris that he desired to live at peace with him, and would increase the territory he had received from his father. But he plotted against him how he might kill him. So Sviatopolk came by night to Vyshegorod. After secretly summoning to his presence Putsha and the boyars of the town, he inquired of them whether they were whole-heartedly devoted to him. Putsha and the men of Vyshegorod replied, "We are ready to lay down our lives for you." He then commanded them to say nothing to any man, but to go and kill his brother Boris. They straightway promised to execute his order. Of such men Solomon has well said: "They make haste to shed blood unjustly. For they promise blood, and gather evil. Their path runneth to evil, for they possess their souls in dishonor" (Proverbs, i. 16–19).

These emissaries came to the Alta, and when they approached, they heard the sainted Boris singing vespers. For it was already known to him that they intended to take his life. Then he arose and began to chant, saying: "O Lord, how are they increased who come against me! Many are they that rise up against me" (Psalms, iii, 1). And also, "Thy arrows have pierced me, for I am ready for wounds and my pain is before me continually" (Psalms, xxxviii, 2, 17). And he also uttered this prayer: "Lord, hear my prayer, and enter not into judgment with thy servant, for no living man shall be just before thee. For the enemy hath crushed my soul" (Psalms, cxl, 1–3). After ending the six psalms, when he saw how men were sent out to kill him, he began to chant the Psalter, saying, "Strong bulls encompassed me, and the assemblage of the evil beset me. O Lord my God, I have hoped in thee; save me and deliver me from my pursuers" (Psalms, xxii, 12, 16, vii, 1). Then he began to sing the canon. After finishing vespers, he prayed, gazing upon the icon, the image of the Lord, with these words: "Lord Jesus Christ, who in this image hast appeared on earth for our salvation, and who, having voluntarily suffered thy hands to be nailed to the cross, didst endure thy passion for our sins, so help me now to endure my passion. For I accept it not from those who are my enemies, but from the hand of my own brother. Hold it not against him as a sin, O Lord!"

After offering this prayer, he lay down upon his couch. Then they fell upon him like wild beasts about the tent, and overcame him by piercing him with lances. They also overpowered his servant, who cast himself upon his body. For he was beloved of Boris. He was a servant of Hungarian race, George by name, to whom Boris was greatly attached. The prince had given him a large gold necklace which he wore while serving him. They also killed many other servants of Boris. But since they could not quickly take the necklace from George's neck, they cut off his head, and thus obtained it. For this reason his body was not recognized later among the corpses.

The desperadoes, after attacking Boris, wrapped him in a canvas, loaded him upon a wagon, and dragged him off, though he was still alive. When the impious Sviatopolk saw that he was still breathing, he sent two Varangians to finish him. When they came and saw that he was still alive, one of them drew his sword and plunged it into his heart. Thus died the blessed Boris, receiving from the hand of Christ our God the crown among the righteous. He shall be numbered with the prophets and the Apostles, as he joins with the choirs of martyrs, rests in the lap of Abraham, beholds joy ineffable, chants with the angels, and rejoices in company with the choirs of saints. After his body had been carried in secret to Vyshegorod, it was buried in the Church of St. Basil.

The impious Sviatopolk then reflected, "Behold, I have killed Boris; now how can I kill Gleb?" Adopting once more Cain's device, he craftily sent messages to Gleb to the effect that he should come quickly, because his father was very ill and desired his presence. Gleb quickly mounted his horse, and set out with a small company, for he was obedient to his father. When he came to the Volga, his horse stumbled in a ditch on the plain, and broke his leg. He arrived at Smolensk, and setting out thence at dawn, he embarked in a boat on the Smiadyn. At this time, Yaroslav received from Predslava the tidings of their father's death, and he sent word to Gleb that he should not set out, because his father was dead and his brother had been murdered by Sviatopolk. Upon receiving these tidings, Gleb burst into tears, and mourned for his father, but still more deeply for his brother. He wept and prayed with the lament, "Woe is me, O Lord! It were better for me to die with my brother than to live on in this world. O my brother, had I but seen thy angelic countenance, I should have died with thee. Why am I now left alone? Where are thy words that thou didst say to me, my brother? No longer do I hear thy sweet counsel. If thou hast received affliction from God, pray for me that I may endure the same passion. For it were better for me to dwell with thee than in this deceitful world."

While he was thus praying amid his tears, there suddenly arrived those sent by Sviatopolk for Gleb's destruction. These emissaries seized Gleb's boat, and drew their weapons. The servants of Gleb were terrified, and the impious messenger,

Goriaser, gave orders that they should slay Gleb with dispatch. Then Gleb's cook, Torchin by name, seized a knife, and stabbed Gleb. He was offered up as a sacrifice to God like an innocent lamb, a glorious offering amid the perfume of incense, and he received the crown of glory. Entering the heavenly mansions, he beheld his long-desired brother, and rejoiced with him in the joy ineffable which they had attained through their brotherly love.

"How good and fair it is for brethren to live together!" (Psalms, cxxxiii, 1). But the impious ones returned again, even as David said, "Let the sinners return to hell" (Psalms, ix, 17). When they returned to Sviatopolk, they reported that his command had been executed. On hearing these tidings, he was puffed up with pride, since he knew not the words of David, "Why art thou proud of thy evildoing, O mighty one? Thy tongue hath considered lawlessness all the day long" (Psalms, lii, 1).

After Gleb had been slain, his body was thrown upon the shore between two tree trunks, but afterward they took him and carried him away, to bury him beside his brother Boris in the Church of St. Basil. United thus in body and still more in soul, ye dwell with the Lord and King of all, in eternal joy, ineffable light, bestowing salutary gifts upon the land of Russia. Ye give healing to other strangers who draw near with faith, making the lame to walk, giving sight to the blind, to the sick health, to captives freedom, to prisoners liberty, to the sorrowful consolation, and to the oppressed relief. Ye are the protectors of the land of Russia, shining forever like beacons and praying to the Lord in behalf of your countrymen. Therefore must we worthily magnify these martyrs in Christ, praying fervently to them and saying: "Rejoice, martyrs in Christ from the land of Russia, who gave healing to them who draw near to you in faith and love. Rejoice, dwellers in heaven. In the body ye were angels, servants in the same thought, comrades in the same image, of one heart with the saints. To all that suffer ye give relief. Rejoice, Boris and Gleb, wise in God. Like streams ye spring from the founts of life-giving water which flow for the redemption of the righteous. Rejoice, ye who have trampled the serpent of evil beneath your feet. Ye have appeared amid bright rays, enlightening like beacons the whole land of Russia. Appearing in faith immutable, ye have ever driven away the darkness. Rejoice, ye who have won an unslumbering eye, ye blessed ones who have received in your hearts the zeal to fulfill God's only commandments. Rejoice, brethren united in the realms of golden light, in he heavenly abodes, in glory unfading, which ye through your merits have attained. Rejoice, ye who are brightly irradiate with the luminance of God, and travel throughout the world expelling devils and healing diseases. Like beacons supernal and zealous guardians, ye dwell with God, illumined forever with light divine, and in your courageous martyrdom ye enlighten the souls of the faithful. The light-bringing heavenly love has exalted you, wherefore ye have inherited all fair things in the heavenly life: glory, celestial sustenance, the light of wisdom, and beauteous joys. Rejoice, ye who refresh our hearts, driving out pain and sickness and curing evil passions. Ye glorious ones, with the sacred drops of your blood ye have dyed a robe of purple which ye wear in beauty, and reign forevermore with Christ, interceding with him for his new Christian nation and for your fellows, for our land is hallowed by your blood. By virtue of your relics deposited in the church, ye illumine it with the Holy Spirit, for there in heavenly bliss, as martyrs among the army of martyrs, ye intercede for our nation. Rejoice, bright daysprings, our Christ-loving martyrs and intercessors! Subject the pagans to our princes, beseeching our Lord God that they may live in concord and in health, freed from intestine war and the crafts of the devil. Help us therefore who sing and recite your sacred praise forever unto our life's end."

15. Nestor

The Narratives of the Kievan Crypt Monastery

THE Crypt Monastery, located on the hilly banks of the Dnieper River on the outskirts of the city of Kiev since its foundation in the eleventh century, became the main spiritual and cultural center of early Russia. Its founders, Sts. Antonius and Theodosius, were remarkable religious leaders whose lives and teachings inspired endless generations of the Russian people. Until the revolution of 1917, the Crypt Monastery remained the principal place for Russian devotional pilgrimages, and even now its churches and crypts attract numerous pilgrims.

Works describing life in the monastery are collected either in the *Primary Chronicle*, their author apparently being Nestor, a monk of this monastery, or in the *Kievan Crypt (Monastery) Paterikon* (the Greek word *paterikon* means a collection of lives of saints or stories about the life of monastery inhabitants). The *Kievan Crypt (Monastery) Paterikon* was written in the first quarter of the thirteenth century by Bishop Simon and Monk Polycarpe, both having been monks of this monastery. Later, more stories were added to the *Paterikon* by other writers. Despite the fact that Simon and Polycarpe lived some hundred and fifty years after Nestor, the style of their work differs very little from his. In both collections can be found historical accounts of life in the monastery, edifying tales about its inhabitants, some half-legendary stories with considerable mystic or fantastic elements, and finally demonological narratives describing the struggles of the monks with the devil.

The stories of the Kievan Crypt Monastery were entered by Nestor under the years 1051 and 1074. However, as often happens in the *Primary Chronicle,* these tales were not necessarily connected with the given year but describe life in the monastery over most of the second half of the eleventh century. Nestor himself belonged to the monastery, and witnessed many of the events described by him.

The text of this work is that of Samuel H. Cross as translated by him in the *Primary Chronicle.*

❖ ❖ ❖

THE FOUNDING OF THE CRYPT MONASTERY AND THE LIFE OF ST. ANTONIUS

1051 (6559)   Yaroslav, after assembling the bishops, appointed Hilarion Metropolitan of Russia in St. Sophia.

Let us now relate why the Monastery of the Crypts bears this name. Prince Yaroslav was fond of Berestovoe and the Church of the Holy Apostles there situated. He gathered a large company of priests, among whom was a presbyter named Hilarion, a virtuous man, learned and ascetic. Hilarion used often to walk from Berestovoe toward the Dnieper to a certain hill, where the old Crypt Monastery now is, and made his orisons there. He dug a little crypt two yards deep, and often went thither from Berestovoe to chant the hours and offer his prayer to God in secret. Then God inspired the prince to appoint him Metropolitan in St. Sophia; and the crypt remained as it was.

Not many days afterward, there was a certain man, a layman from the city of Liubech, in whose heart God inspired the desire to go on pilgrimage. He made his way to Mount Athos,[1] beheld the monasteries there, and upon examining them and

---

[1] Mount Athos, or the "Holy Mount," has long been the most important monastic center of Eastern Christianity. It is located in Greece in the vicinity of the city of Saloniki.

being charmed by the monastic life, he entered one of the local monasteries, and begged the prior to confer upon him the monastic habit. The latter complied with his request and made him a monk, calling him Antonius, and after he had admonished him and instructed him in his monastic obligations, he bade him return to Russia accompanied by the blessing of the Holy Mount, that many other monks might spring from his example. The prior blessed him and dismissed him, saying, "Go in peace." Antonius returned to Kiev, and reflected where he should live. He went about among the monasteries and liked none of them, since God did not so will, and subsequently wandered about among the hills and valleys seeking the place which God should show him. He finally came to the hill where Hilarion had dug the crypt, and liked this site, and rejoiced in it. He then lifted up his voice in prayer to God, saying amid his tears, "O Lord, strengthen me in this place, and may there rest upon it the blessing of the Holy Mount and of the prior who tonsured me." Thus he took up his abode there, praying to God, eating dry bread all the day long, drinking water in peace, and digging the crypt. He gave himself rest neither day nor night, but endured in his labors, in vigil, and in prayer. Afterward good men noticed his conduct, and supplied him according to his necessities. Thus he acquired distinction as the great Antonius, and those who drew near to him besought his blessing.

When the Great Prince Yaroslav died, Iziaslav his son inherited his domain and settled in Kiev, while Antonius was celebrated throughout Russia. Iziaslav observed his manner of life, and came with his retainers to request his blessing and prayers. The great Antonius was thus remarked and revered by everyone. Brothers joined him, and he welcomed and tonsured them. Brethren thus gathered about him to the number of twelve. They dug a great crypt and a church, and cells, which exist to this day in the crypt under the old monastery. When the brethren had thus assembled, Antonius said to them, "God has gathered you together, my brethren, and ye are under the blessing of the Holy Mount, through which the prior at the Holy Mount tonsured me, and I have tonsured you also. May there be upon you first the blessing of God and second that of the Holy Mount." And he added this injunction: "Live apart by yourselves, and I shall appoint you a prior; for I prefer to go alone to yonder hill, as I formerly was wont when I dwelt in solitude." So he appointed Barlaam as their prior, and betook himself to the hill, where he dug a grotto, which is under the new monastery, and in which he ended his life, enduring in virtue, and for the space of forty years never issuing forth from the crypt in which his bones lie to the present day.

The brethren thus abode with their prior, and as the number of monks in the crypt increased, they considered the establishment of a monastery outside the original crypt. Thus the prior and the brethren approached Antonius and said to him, "Father, the brethren have increased in numbers, and we can no longer find room in the crypt. If God and thy prayers so direct us, we might build a small church outside the crypt." Antonius then bade them so to do. They obeyed him, and built a little chapel over the crypt and dedicated it to the Assumption of the Holy Virgin.

God continued to augment the number of the brotherhood through the intercession of the Holy Virgin, and the brethren took counsel with the prior as to constructing a monastery. The friars again visited Antonius, and said, "Father, our brethren increase in numbers, and we are desirous of building a monastery." Antonius rejoiced, and replied, "Blessed be God for all things, and may the prayers of the Holy Virgin and of the fathers of the Holy Mount be with you." Having thus spoken, he sent one of the brotherhood to Prince Iziaslav with the message, "My Prince! Behold, God strengthens the brotherhood, but their abode is small; give us therefore the hill which is above the crypt." When Iziaslav heard these words, he rejoiced, and sent his servant, and gave to them the hill. The prior and the brethren founded there a great church, and fenced in the monastery with a palisade. They constructed many cells, completed the church, and adorned it with icons. Such was the origin of the Crypt Monastery, which was so named because the brethren first lived in the crypt. The Crypt Monastery thus issued from the benediction of the Holy Mount.

ST. THEODOSIUS, ABBOT OF THE CRYPT MONASTERY

Now, when the monastery was completed during the priorate of Barlaam, Iziaslav founded the Monastery of St. Demetrius, and appointed Barlaam prior therein, since he intended, by virtue of his material wealth, to make it superior to the ancient monastery. Many monasteries have indeed been founded by emperors and nobles and magnates, but they are not such as those founded by tears, fasting, prayer, and vigil. Antonius had neither silver nor gold, but accomplished his purpose through tears and fasting, as I have recounted.

When Barlaam had departed to St. Demetrius', the brethren held a council, and then once more visited the ancient Antonius with the request that he should designate them a new prior. He inquired whom they desired. They replied that they desired only the one designated by God and by his own selection. Then he inquired of them, "Who among you is more obedient, more modest, and more mild than Theodosius? Let him be your prior." The brethren rejoiced, and made their reverence before the old man. Being twenty in number, they thus appointed Theodosius to be their prior. When Theodosius took over in the monastery, he began to practice abstinence, fasting, and tearful prayer. He undertook to assemble many monks, and thus gathered together brethren to the number of one hundred.

He also interested himself in searching out the monastic rules. There was in Kiev at the time a monk from the Studion Monastery named Michael, who had come from Greece with the Metropolitan George, and Theodosius inquired of him concerning the practices of the Studion monks. He obtained their rule from him, copied it out, and established it in his own monastery to govern the singing of monastic hymns, the making of reverences, the reading of the lessons, behavior in church, the whole ritual, conduct at table, proper food for special days, and to regulate all else according to prescription. After obtaining all this information, Theodosius thus transmitted it to his monastery, and from the latter all others adopted the same institutions. Therefore the Crypt Monastery is honored as the oldest of all.

While Theodosius lived in the monastery, following a virtuous life and the monastic rule, and receiving everyone who presented himself, I, a poor and unworthy servant, came to him, and he accepted me in my seventeenth year. Hence I have set down and certified what year the monastery came into being, and why it is named the Crypt Monastery; but to Theodosius' life we shall recur later.

1074 (6582) In this year the Church of the Crypts was founded by the Prior Theodosius and the Bishop Michael, while George the Metropolitan was absent in Greece and Sviatoslav was reigning in Kiev.

Theodosius, the Prior of the Crypt Monastery, passed away. We shall therefore supply a brief account of his assumption. When the Lenten season approached, upon the eve of Quinquagesima Sunday, Theodosius was accustomed, after he had embraced the brethren according to his practice, to instruct them how to pass the Lenten period in prayer by night and by day, and how to guard against evil thoughts and the temptations of the devil. "For," said he, "demons incite in monks evil thoughts and desires, and inflame their fancy so that their prayers are impaired. One must combat such thoughts when they come by using the sign of the cross and by saying, 'Lord Jesus Christ our God, have mercy on us, Amen!' With this end in view, we must practice abstinence from many foods, for evil desires develop out of excessive eating and immoderate drinking, and by the growth of such thoughts sin is caused. By this means," said he, "oppose yourselves to the influence of the demons and their malice, guard against laziness and too much sleep, be zealous in churchly song, in the traditions of the fathers, and in the reading of the Scriptures. For it befits monks above all things to have upon their lips the Psalter of David, and thereby to expel the weaknesses caused by the devil. It befits all young persons to show toward their elders love, obedience, and attention, and it behooves all older persons to offer the younger brethren their love and admonition, and to be an example by their continence and vigil, their self-restraint and humility, to counsel and console the youthful, and to spend Lent in such pursuits."

"For," he added, "God has given us these forty days in which to purify our souls. This is a tithe given to God by the body. For the days of the year are three hundred and sixty-five, and giving to God each tenth day as a tithe makes a fast of forty days, during which the soul is cleansed and happily celebrates the resurrection of the Lord as it rejoices in God. For the Lenten season purifies the heart of man. In the beginning, fasting was first imposed upon Adam, so that he should not taste of one tree. Moses fasted forty days to prepare himself to receive the law upon Mount Sinai, and then he beheld the glory of God. During a fast, Samuel's mother bore him. Through their fasting, the Ninevites averted the wrath of God. By his fasting, Daniel prepared himself for great visions. After his fast, Elijah was taken up to heaven to receive celestial sustenance. Through their fasting, the Three Children quenched the violence of the fire. And our Lord, by fasting forty days, made known to us the Lenten season. By means of their fasting, the Apostles rooted out the teaching of the devil. By virtue of their fasts, our fathers appeared to the world as beacons that continue to shine after their decease. They exhibited great labors and continence; for example, the great Antonius, Euthymius, Savva, and the other fathers. Let us imitate them, my brethren."

After thus instructing the brotherhood, he kissed them, calling each by name, and then left the monastery, taking with him but a few loaves of bread. He entered a crypt, closed the door behind him, and covered himself with dust. He spoke to no one, unless some object was needful to him, and in any case he conversed only on Saturday and on Sunday through a small window. Upon other days, he remained in fasting and in prayer, maintaining strict abstinence. He returned to the monastery on the eve of Friday, St. Lazarus' day. For on this day ends the forty days' fast, which opens on the first Monday after the week of St. Theodore and concludes on Friday, the feast of St. Lazarus. Holy Week is then observed as a fast on account of our Lord's passion. Theodosius thus returned according to his custom, embraced the brethren, and with them celebrated Palm Sunday.

When Easter Day came, he celebrated it brilliantly as usual, and then fell ill. When he was taken ill, and had been sick for five days, he bade them carry him in the evening down into the courtyard. The brethren laid him upon a sled and set him before the church. He then desired that the whole brotherhood should be summoned, so the brethren struck upon the bell, and all assembled together. Theodosius then said to them, "My brethren, my fathers, and my children! I now depart from you, for God made known to me, while I was in the crypt during the Lenten season, that I must now quit this world. Whom do you desire for your prior, that I may confer my blessing upon him?"

They made answer, "You have been a father to us all. Whomsoever you yourself select shall be our father and our prior, and we shall obey him even as we obey you." Then our father Theodosius said, "Go apart from me and designate him whom you desire, except the two brothers Nicholas and Ignatius: but choose from the rest whomever you prefer, from the eldest down to the youngest."

They obeyed his behest, and upon withdrawing a short distance in the direction of the church, they took counsel together, and then sent two of the brethren back to Theodosius to beg him to designate the one chosen by God and his own holy prayer, and who should be agreeable to Theodosius himself. Theodosius then made answer, "If you desire to receive your prior from me, then I will appoint him not so much from my own choice as by divine disposition," and he designated the presbyter James. This nomination did not meet with the approval of the brotherhood, who objected that James had not taken orders in the monastery, since he had come thither from Letetz with his brother Paul. They demanded rather Stephen the Cantor, who was then a pupil of Theodosius, and therefore said, "He has grown up under your hand and has served with you; appoint him as our prior."

Then Theodosius said, "By the commandment of God, I designated James, but you prefer that the appointment should coincide with your own wishes." He gave way to their desire, however, and appointed Stephen to be their prior, and blessed him, saying: "My son! I give over to you this monastery. Guard it with care, and maintain what I have ordained in its observances. Change not the traditions and the institutions of the monastery, but follow in all things the law and our monastic rule."

The brethren then raised him up, carried him to his cell, and laid him upon his bed. At the beginning of the sixth day, while he was seriously ill, Prince Sviatoslav came to visit him with his son Gleb. While the prince was sitting beside him, Theodosius said: "I depart from this world and entrust this monastery to your guardianship in the event that some disorder arises in it. I confer the priorate upon Stephen; desert him not in his hour of need."

The prince embraced him, and after promising to care for the monastery, departed from him. When the seventh day was come, while Theodosius was steadily growing weaker, he summoned Stephen and the brotherhood, and spoke to them these words: "Upon my departure from this world, if I have found favor with God and he has accepted me, then this monastery, after my decease, will grow and prosper through his help. In that event, know that God has accepted me. But if, after my death, the monastery begins to lose in membership and income, be assured that I shall not have found favor in the sight of God."

When he had spoken thus, the brethren wept, saying, "Father, intercede with God for us, for we know that he will not scorn your labors." They thus sat out the night with him, and at the beginning of the eighth day, being the second Saturday after Easter, in the second hour of the day, he commended his soul into the hands of God, upon May 3rd, in the eleventh year of the indiction. The brethren thus mourned for him.

Theodosius had given command that he should be buried in the crypt where he had performed many good works. He had also directed that his body should be buried by night, and they followed his injunction in this respect. When evening was come, the brethren took up his body and laid it in the crypt, after conducting it thither in all honor with hymns and candles to the glory of our God Jesus Christ.

BROTHER ISAAC AND THE DEMONS

There was also another monk, named Isaac. While still in

the world, he was very rich, since in the secular life he was by birth a merchant of Toropetz. But he resolved to become a monk, and distributed his fortune to the needy and to the monasteries. He then approached the great Antonius in the crypt, and besought him to receive him into the order. Antonius accepted him, and put upon him the monastic habit, calling him Isaac, for his secular name was Chern. Isaac adopted an ascetic mode of life. He wrapped himself in a hair shirt, then caused a goat to be bought, flayed it, and put on the skin over his hair shirt, so that the fresh hide dried upon him. He shut himself up in a lonely gallery of the crypt in a narrow cell only four ells across, and there lamented and prayed to God. His sustenance was one wafer, and that only once a day, and he drank but moderately of water. The great Antonius carried it to him, and passed it in to him by a little window through which he inserted his arm. Thus Isaac received his food. He subsisted thus for seven years without seeing the light of day or even lying down upon his side, for he snatched what sleep he could in a sitting posture.

Once, when evening had fallen, he had knelt till midnight singing psalms, as was his wont, and when he was wearied, he sat down upon his stool. As he sat there, and had as usual extinguished his candle, a light suddenly blazed forth in the crypt as if it shone from the sun, and strong enough to take away man's vision. Two fair youths then approached him. Their faces were radiant like the sun, and they said to him: "Isaac, we are angels; Christ is drawing near to you. Fall down and worship him."

He did not understand their devilish artifice nor remember to cross himself, but knelt before the work of the demons as if to Christ himself. The demons then cried out and said, "Now, Isaac, you belong to us."

They led him back into his cell and set him down. They then seated themselves around him, and both the cell and the aisle of the crypt was filled with them. One of the devils, who called himself Christ, bade them take flutes and lyres and lutes and play, so that Isaac could dance before them. So they struck up with flutes, lutes, and lyres, and began to make sport of him. After they had tormented him, they left him half alive, and went away when they had beaten him.

The next day at dawn, when it was time to break bread, Antonius came to the window according to his custom and said, "May the Lord bless you, Father Isaac." But there was no answer. Then Antonius said, "He has already passed away," so he sent into the monastery in search of Theodosius and the brethren. After digging out the entrance where it had been walled up, they entered and lifted him up, thinking him dead, and carried him out in front of the crypt. They then perceived that he was still alive, and Theodosius the prior said, "This comes from the devil's artifice." They laid him upon a bier, and Antonius cared for him.

About this same time it happened that Iziaslav returned from Poland, and was angry with Antonius on account of Vseslav, so that Sviatoslav caused Antonius to escape by night to Chernigov. When Antonius arrived there, he was attracted by the Boldiny hills, and after digging another crypt, he settled there. At that spot in the Boldiny hills, there is a monastery dedicated to the Virgin even to this day. When Theodosius learned that Antonius had fled to Chernigov, he came with his brethren, took Isaac, and bore him to his own cell, where he cared for him. For Isaac was so weakened in body that he could not turn from one side to the other, nor rise up, nor sit down, but he lay always upon one side, and relieved himself as he lay, so that numerous worms were caused under his back by his excrement. Theodosius washed and dressed him with his own hands, and for two years cared for him thus. It is wondrous and strange that he lay thus for two years, tasting neither bread nor water nor any other food nor fruit, nor did he speak with his tongue, but lay deaf and dumb for the whole two years.

Theodosius prayed to God in his behalf, and offered supplications over him by day and by night, until in the third year he spoke and heard, rose upon his feet like a babe, and began to walk. He would not go faithfully to church, but the brethren carried him thither by force; they also taught him to go to the refectory, but seated him apart from the rest of the brethren. They set bread before him, but he would not take it unless they placed it in his hand.

Theodosius then said, "Leave the bread before him, but do not put it in his hand, so that he can eat of his own volition."

For a week he ate nothing, but gradually he became aware of the bread, and tasted it. Thus he began to eat, and by this means Theodosius freed him from the craft of the devil.

Isaac then assumed severe abstinence. When Theodosius was dead and Stephen was prior in his stead, Isaac said: "Demon, you deceived me once when I sat in a lonely spot. I must not confine myself in the crypt, but must vanquish you while I frequent the monastery." He then clad himself in a hair shirt, and put on over this a sackcloth coat, and began to act strangely. He undertook to help the cooks in the preparation of food for the brotherhood. He went to matins earlier than the others, and stood firm and immovable. When winter came with its heavy frosts, he stood in shoes so worn that his feet froze to the pavement, but he would not move his feet till matins were over. After matins, he went to the kitchen, and made ready the fire, the water, and the wood before the other cooks came from the brotherhood.

There was one cook who was also named Isaac, who mocked at Isaac and said, "There sits a black crow; go and catch it." Isaac bowed to the ground before him, then went and caught the crow, and brought it back to him in the presence of all the cooks. They were frightened, and reported it to the prior and the brotherhood, who began to respect him. But not being desirous of human glory, he began to act strangely, and to play tricks, now on the prior, now on the brethren, and now on laymen, so that others dealt him blows. Then he began to wander through the country, acting like an idiot. He settled in the crypt where he had formerly lived, for Antonius was already dead. He gathered young men about him and laid upon them the monastic habit, so that he suffered blows from the Prior Nikon as well as from the parents of these youths. But he suffered these hardships, and willingly endured blows and nakedness and cold by day and by night.

One night he lit the stove in a cabin by the crypt. When the stove was heated, fire began to issue forth from the crevices, for it was old and cracked. Since he had nothing to put over the stove, he braced his bare feet against the flame till the stove burned out, and then left it. Many other stories were told about him, and I myself witnessed some such occurrences.

Thus he won his victory over the demons, holding their terrors and apparitions of as little account as flies. For he said to them: "You did indeed deceive me the first time in the crypt, since I did not perceive your craft and cunning. But now that I have on my side the Lord Jesus Christ and my God and the prayers of my father Theodosius, I hope to vanquish you." Many times the demons harassed him, and said, "You belong to us, for you have worshiped us and our leader." But he replied, "Your chief is Antichrist and you are demons," and signed his countenance with the cross. At this they disappeared. Sometimes, however, they came upon him again by night, and frightened him in his dreams, appearing like a great company with mattocks and spades, and saying, "We will undermine the crypt, and bury this man within it," while others exclaimed, "Fly, Isaac, they intend to bury you alive." But he made answer, "If you were men, you would have come by day; but you are darkness and come in darkness, and the darkness shall swallow you up." Then he made the sign of the cross against them, and they vanished.

On other occasions, they endeavored to terrify him in the form of a bear, sometimes as a wild beast and sometimes as a bull. Now snakes beset him, and now toads, mice, and every other reptile. But they could not harm him, and said to him, "Isaac, you have vanquished us!" He replied, "You conquered me in the image of Jesus Christ and his angels, of whose sight you are unworthy. But now you rightly appear in the guise of beasts and cattle or as the snakes and reptiles that you are, repulsive and evil to behold." Thereupon the demons left him, and he suffered no more evil at their hands. As he himself related, his struggle against them lasted for three years. Then he began to live still more strictly, and to practice abstinence, fasting, and vigil.

After thus living out his life, he finally came to his end. He fell sick in his crypt, and was carried in his illness to the monastery, where he died in the Lord upon the eighth day. The Prior John and the brethren clothed his body and buried him.

Such were the monks of the monastery of Theodosius, who shine forth like radiant beacons since their decease, and intercede with God in behalf of the brethren here below, as well as for the lay brotherhood and for those who contribute to the monastery in which to this day the brotherhood abides together in virtuous life amid hymns, prayers, and obedience, to the glory of Almighty God, and protected by the intercession of Theodosius, to whom be glory, Amen.

16. *Bishop Simon and Monk Polycarpe*
The Kievan Crypt Paterikon

THE narratives of this *Paterikon* come from the pen of Simon, Bishop of Vladimir and Suzdal, who apparently began his ecclesiastical career in the Crypt Monastery; and from the pen of Polycarpe, a monk of the same monastery. Simon, who became bishop in 1214 and died in 1226, wrote his narratives as an appendix to his epistle to Polycarpe. In this epistle Simon endeavors to reconcile Polycarpe, who was dissatisfied with his life in the monastery, with his brethren and abbot, and to convince him that the monastery was the spiritual center of the land.

Apparently Polycarpe wanted to become a bishop and his relations with the other monks were rather strained. That portion of the *Paterikon* written by Polycarpe was done some years later, when he had become reconciled with the monastery. It is addressed to Abbot Akindin, and has about the same structure as the first part—that is, an epistle with eleven tales about the lives of the monks, but is in a style less personal than the work of Simon. It was written for wide circulation both within and without the monastery, whereas the work of Simon was meant to be read only by Polycarpe.

In the thirteenth century both works were made into one, and to them was added the story of "The Brethren of the Crypt Monastery" (Damian, Jeremy, and Matthew) and "Isaac and the Demons" from the *Primary Chronicle* by Nestor. Later, more narratives were added to this *Paterikon,* and it became one of the most popular collections of this genre in Russia.

Bishop Simon wrote the first four stories of this collection, while the last one, "Marko the Gravedigger Who Was Obeyed by the Dead," is the work of Polycarpe. The translations here presented are based on the text published by D. Abramovich, *Kievo-Pecherskii paterik,* Kiev, 1931.

◆ ◆ ◆

Bishop Simon

PRINCE SVIATOSHA OF CHERNIGOV

This blessed and faithful Prince Sviatosha, called Nicholas after he became a monk, was the son of Prince David and the grandson of Prince Sviatoslav. This prince came to the conclusion that all things in this vain life are illusive and that everything on the earth comes to its end and passes away, but that the blessings of the future life are eternal and everlasting and that the Kingdom of Heaven, which God has prepared for those who love him, is unending. And he relinquished his princedom together with all his honor, glory and power, seeing no worth in all these things. And he came to the Crypt Monastery and became a monk. This happened in 1106 (6614) on the 17th day of February. All the monks who were living in the monastery at that time are witnesses to his virtuous life and his fulfillment of the vows of obedience.

For three years he remained in the kitchen working with his brethren. With his own hands he chopped wood for the preparation of meals, carrying it on his shoulders, often from the river

Dnieper. And his brothers, Iziaslav and Vladimir, were hardly able to keep him from such heavy labor. However, he asked and begged that they permit him to work at least one more year in the kitchen with his brethren. Thereafter, he was placed in charge of the monastery gates, for in every type of work he was skillful and diligent. He remained in there, at the gates, for three years, never leaving except to attend church services. From there he was told to go and serve in the refectory. Finally, according to the will of the abbot and all the brethren, he was permitted to have his own cell, which he himself built. This cell is called Sviatosha's cell to this very day, and the vegetable garden, which he planted with his own hands, is also called after his name still. People say of him that no one has ever seen him idle. He was always occupied with some kind of work, and thus he earned his keep. On his lips permanently was a prayer to Jesus: "Jesus Christ, have mercy upon us." He never ate anything more than the monastery meals. He had considerable wealth, but he gave everything away to pilgrims and the poor and for the building of churches. Up to now there are many books given by him to your monastery. When he was still ruling, this blessed Sviatosha had a very skilled physician, Peter, who was from Syria. This Peter came with him to the monastery, but, seeing that the prince voluntarily accepted poverty and worked in the kitchen and at the gate, he left him and, settling in Kiev, became a doctor for many citizens of this city. This physician used to come often to Prince Sviatosha at the monastery and, seeing his bitter sufferings and endless fasting, tried to convince him to change his way of living, saying: "Prince, you should care for your health and not ruin your body with endless labor and abstinence. You will become so ill, that you will not be able to carry the burden which, for God's sake, you have voluntarily accepted. God does not desire unbearable fasting and labor, but only a humble and contrite heart. You are not accustomed to hardships such as you, working like a slave, must now endure. Your pious brothers, Iziaslav and Vladimir, feel that your poverty is a reproach to them. How could you turn away from such glory and honor to such wretchedness and how can you exhaust your body with such food? I wonder about your stomach; once sweet meals were too heavy for it, and now it accepts and endures simple herbs and dry bread. Beware, for sometime all your maladies will attack you at once, and you, deprived of resistance, will succumb, and I will not be able to help you. You will leave your inconsolable brothers to mourn after you. Also, your boyars, who once served you, hoped to become powerful and glorious with your help. Now they are deprived of your love, and they complain about you. They have built large houses for themselves, but they remain in them in great grief. You yourself have not even a place to lay your head, remaining in this backyard. They consider that you have become insane. Who among the princes has done anything of this nature? Did your blessed father, David, or your grandfather, Sviatoslav, do so? Or who among the boyars has acted in this way? Or who even intended to do anything similar, excepting Barlaam, who was the abbot here? And if you don't follow my advice, you will meet an untimely death."

So he used to talk with Prince Sviatosha, now Monk Nicholas, sitting with him in the kitchen or at the gate. And he was instructed to do so by Prince Sviatosha's brothers. But Prince Sviatosha answered him, saying: "Brother Peter, I have thought for a long time and I have decided not to spare my flesh so as to prevent it from arousing in me a new struggle. It is better to keep it submissive under the burden of heavy labor, for it is said: 'Strength is achieved through weakness,' and, 'These present temporary passions are nothing worse in comparison with the glory which will be revealed in us.' I thank God for he has liberated me from the slavedom of this world and made me the servant of his servants, these blessed monks. And my brothers had better look after themselves, for each man must bear his cross alone. They should be satisfied with having my patrimony—all of what I had: my wife and children, the house and power, brethren and friends, serfs and estates, I gave up for Christ's sake so as to inherit eternal life. I became poor for the sake of God, so that I might gain God's favor.

"And even yourself, when you treat people, don't you prescribe refraining from excessive eating? To die for Christ would be a real acquisition of fortune for me. And sitting here in the backyard next to the refuse heap is the winning of a real kingdom. It may be that no prince has done as I do now. Then I will be the first example for them. Perhaps one of them will want to imitate my example and follow in my footsteps. As far as my life is concerned, it should not be of concern to you, nor to those who have asked you to come to me."

When the blessed prince was sick, his physician, Peter, usually prepared some medicine for the illness, such as severe heartburn or other pains that had occurred to the prince. But before the physician could reach the prince, the prince was already cured. And he never permitted himself to be treated by a physician. And so it happened many times. Once, when the

physician himself became ill, Prince Sviatosha sent him a messenger to say: "Don't take your medicine and you will be cured.
And if you don't obey me, you will suffer bitterly."

But the latter, relying on his medical skills, drank the medicine, hoping to be cured of his illness; but instead of being
cured, he almost died. And only the prayer of the blessed prince
helped and cured him.

Another time the physician again became ill, and the blessed
prince sent his messenger once more to say, "If you don't
attempt to cure yourself, you will be completely recovered in
three days."

The Syrian obeyed him, and on the third day he recovered,
according to the words of the blessed prince. As soon as he had
recovered, the blessed one asked him to come to the monastery,
and there he enjoined the physician to become a monk, saying,
"In three months from now, we shall part." With these words
Prince Sviatosha predicted the death of the physician.

The Syrian misunderstood the prince's words, thinking that
not his own death but that of the prince was nearing. He fell
before the prince's feet and tearfully implored him, saying:

"Alas, woe is me, my lord and benefactor!
Who will help me, a foreigner?
Who will feed so many people who are hungry?
Who will be the intercessor of the offended?
Who will be merciful with the poor?
Have I not told you, my prince,
that you will be mourned by all your inconsolable brothers?
You cured me not only through the words and power of
    God,
but also with the help of your prayers.
Where will you depart to, my good pastor?
Tell me what fatal illness you have,
and I will cure you.
And, if I cannot,
then my head shall be given for your head,
and my soul for your soul.
Oh, my lord, don't leave me
without telling me how you learned of your death.
I would give my life for you.
If God has announced your passing away to you,
please pray to him that I might die in your place.
Where would I be able to mourn my loss,
if you leave me?

Should I do it here, at this refuse heap,
or at the gate where you live?
And what can you leave me if you die?
You yourself are almost naked, and when you die
you will be buried in your patched and tattered garments.
Help me through your prayers
as once Prophet Elijah gave Elisha his mantle
to get through paradise
under the shelter of the wonderful house of the Lord.
Even the beast knows where the sun will rise
before it goes to its lair.
And the bird knows how to find its abode
and the turtledove knows how to find the nest
where it raises its fledglings."

But the blessed one answered him: "It is better to place one's hopes in the Lord than to rely upon many; God knows how to feed his creatures and how to protect and save his poor. My brothers should not worry about me, but about themselves and their children. I never wanted any treatment by a physician during my life, because when the hour of death has come the physician cannot help." And the prince went with the physician down into the crypt and dug a grave for himself, and he asked the Syrian, "Which of us wants this grave the more?"

And the Syrian replied: "It should come to pass as each of us desires. But you should live, and I should be buried here."

And then the blessed prince told him, "Let it be as you do desire."

The Syrian physician became a monk, and passed three months weeping incessantly both day and night. The blessed one consoled him, saying, "Brother Peter, do you wish that I should take you with me?"

And the physician answered tearfully: "I want you to release me and let me die in your place. Please, pray for me."

And the blessed prince told the physician, "Prepare for death, my son, and in three days you will depart to the lord."

And after three days the physician took Holy Communion, lay down on his bed, adjusted his robes, stretched out his legs, and gave up his soul into the hands of the Lord, as it was predicted by Blessed Prince Sviatosha.

Prince Sviatosha lived after this for another thirty years, never leaving the monastery again. And when he died, almost the entire city of Kiev came to his burial. Learning of Blessed Sviatosha's death, his brother, Prince Iziaslav, sent a messenger

to the abbot, asking that he be given the crucifix of Prince
Sviatosha, his pillow, and the board upon which he had knelt.

The abbot gave them to the prince, saying, "It will renew
your faith."

The prince accepted them and carefully preserved them at
home. And he gave the abbot three pieces of gold so as not to
receive this blessing of the abbot for nothing.

Once, this prince became so ill that all his family lost hope
and, seeing that he was about to die, his wife, children, and
boyars went to his chambers and remained with him. He raised
up slightly and asked for some water from the well of the Crypt
Monastery, and then he became mute.

In the meantime a messenger went to the monastery for the
water. The abbot took Sviatosha's hair shirt,[1] put it first on the
grave of St. Theodosius, and then gave it to the prince's messenger, telling him to put this shirt on Prince Iziaslav. Before
the messenger had returned with the water and hair shirt, the
ill prince suddenly uttered the words, "Go beyond the gates of
the city and meet St. Theodosius and St. Nicholas."

And when the messenger returned with the water and the
hair shirt, the prince exclaimed, "Nicholas—Nicholas Sviatosha!"

And the prince was given the water, and the hair shirt was
placed on his body, and he recovered immediately. And everyone glorified God and his saints. And each time Iziaslav became
ill, he would put on this hair shirt, and he always recovered.
And in all battles he wore this hair shirt, and he remained unharmed. But once, a poor sinner, he dared not put on the hair
shirt, and he was slain in battle. And he was buried in this hair
shirt, as he had requested. And the brethren still remember
other great deeds of the saint. Until this day the monks of the
Crypt Monastery still hold Blessed Prince Sviatosha in their
memory.

Bishop Simon

VIKING SHIMON AND ST. THEODOSIUS

THE BUILDING OF THE CHURCH OF THE HOLY VIRGIN
OF THE CRYPT MONASTERY

And now I will come to other stories. Everyone should know
how, according to the will of God and the prayers and desires
of the Holy Virgin, the beautiful and great Church of the Crypt

[1] Hair shirt—a shirt made of horsehair, and worn as a penance.

Monastery, dedicated to the Holy Virgin, was founded and built. This is the church of the great abbey of all the Russian land, the monastery of St. Theodosius.

There was in the land of the Vikings[2] a certain prince whose name was Africanus, the brother of Yakun, who, when he and Prince Yaroslav were fighting against evil Prince Mstislav, lost his gold-embroidered mantle when he was fleeing from battle. This Prince Africanus had two sons, Friand and Shimon. After Prince Africanus' death, his brother, Yakun, drove his nephews from their patrimonies. And thus Shimon came to our faithful Prince Yaroslav. And Yaroslav received him with honor and sent him to his son, Vsevolod, appointing him to be the senior counselor to Vsevolod. And through this position Shimon gained great influence. The reason for Shimon's devotion to the Holy Crypt Monastery is explained in the following narrative.

During the reign of Prince Iziaslav in Kiev, the Kumans came to the Russian land, this being in 1068 (6576). And the sons of Yaroslav, Princes Iziaslav, Sviatoslav, and Vsevolod, decided to attack them. And Shimon went with Prince Vsevolod. When they came to the great and holy Father Antonius and asked him for his blessing and prayers, the abbot opened his lips, which had been sealed for a very long time, and clearly foretold of their forthcoming demise. Then Shimon the Viking fell at the abbot's feet and begged him to tell how he, Shimon, might escape this fate.

And the blessed abbot told him: "My son, many of you will fall in battle, pierced by swords. And when many of you attempt to escape from the enemy, you will be pursued and struck down by weapons or drowned in the river. But you, my son, will escape, and later you will be buried in the church that you will build."

And the Russian regiments engaged in battle on the river Leta, and because of God's wrath the Christians were defeated and routed. And many *voevodas*[3] and warriors fell in battle. Among those who had fallen in battle lay Shimon, who was wounded. He raised his eyes to the heavens and there saw a great church, the same that he had seen once at sea. And, remembering the words of the Savior, he said, "Lord! Deliver me from bitter death through the prayers of your most holy Mother and the reverend fathers Antonius and Theodosius."

And at that moment a certain power took him from the

---

[2] Apparently Shimon came to Russia from Sweden.
[3] Military commanders.

clutches of death. He became cured of his wounds and soon found that all his family was safe and in good health.

And then he returned to the great Antonius and told him of this wonderful miracle, saying: "My father, Africanus, once made a cross on which was the figure of Christ with pieces of gold that weighed fifty grivnas.[4] And on his head he placed a golden crown. When my uncle, Yakun, drove me from my patrimony, I took with me the girdle and the crown from this image of Jesus. And when I did so, I heard coming from the cross a voice that was directed to me, and it said:

" 'Man, never put this crown on your own head, but take it to the place that I have chosen. And there the Reverend Father Theodosius will erect a church in honor of my Mother. Place this crown in his hands and tell him to hang it over my altar.'

"And I fell to the ground, seized with awe, and I lay there motionless, as if dead, for a long time. Then I got up and went to a ship. When we were crossing the sea, there occurred a great storm, and we all feared for our lives. And I began to pray, 'Lord! Forgive me, for I am perishing because of the crown I took from your revered and holy image.'

"And I saw in the heavens a church, and I began to wonder what this vision meant. And then there came from above a voice that announced:

" 'This is the church that should be built by the Reverend Father Theodosius in the name of the Mother of God. And in this church you are to be buried.'

"And I saw the size and the height, and I measured it with the golden girdle and found it to be twenty feet wide and thirty feet high, and the walls and the roof were fifty feet. And we all glorified God and, becoming consoled, we experienced great joy at having escaped a bitter death. Until now, I did not realize where the church, shown me both at sea and at the river Leta where I was lying at death's door, was to be built. And then I heard from your revered tongue that I will be buried here in the church that will be erected."

And Shimon took out the golden girdle, and said, "Here are the measurements and the plan, and here is the crown that should be hung above the holy altar."

And Abbot Antonius glorified God, and told the Viking, "My child, from this day on you will never be called Shimon, but Simon."

---

[4] Old Russian unit of money.

And Antonius invited Blessed Father Theodosius to come to him, and he told him, "Here is Simon who wants to build such a church." And Antonius gave Theodosius the girdle, crown, and plans. And from that day Simon loved holy Theodosius very much, and he gave him his wealth and estate for the needs of the monastery.

Once Simon came to Blessed Theodosius, and after the usual talk he told the holy one, "Father, I ask you to give me a gift."

And Theodosius answered, "Oh, my child, what can you, a powerful man, ask from me, a humble one?"

And Simon answered, "The gift I ask of you is most important, and beyond my power to obtain."

And Theodosius replied: "My child, you know how poor we are and that often we don't even have enough bread for the daily meal. And I know not what else we may have."

But Simon said: "If you want to give me this gift, you can do so, thanks to the grace that you have received from God, who called you a 'Reverend Father.' When I had taken the crown from the head of Jesus, he told me:

"'Take it to the place that I have chosen. And there the Reverend Father Theodosius will erect a church in honor of my Mother.'

And so I now ask you to give me your word that your soul will bless me both during our lives and after our deaths."

And the saintly father answered: "What you ask me is beyond my power, but if the church is built, and if after my passing the rituals and traditions are preserved in this church, then know that I shall dare to ask God. But now I know not whether my prayers would be acceptable."

And Simon said: "God is my witness that I was told about you by the purest lips of his holy image. Therefore, I beg you, pray for me, for my son, George, and for his descendants, in the same way in which you pray for your monks."

The saint promised this to Simon the Viking, and then added: "I don't pray for my monks only, but for everyone who for my sake loves this holy monastery."

Then Simon bowed deeply to the earth, and spoke: "My father, I won't leave you until you have confirmed in writing what you have said."

Theodosius felt compelled to do so, since Simon loved him. And he wrote, "In the name of the Father, and of the Son, and of the Holy Ghost. . . ." And these words became the prayer which, from that time to this, is always placed in the hands of

the dead. And since that time it has become the custom to put
such letters in the coffins of the dead. No one did this before.
And the following was written in the prayer:

"Remember, me, O Lord, when thou comest into thy kingdom, and when thou judgest everyone according to his deeds,
then permit, O Lord, that thy servants Simon and George remain on the right side of thy glory, and hear thy blessed voice
saying, 'Come, O blessed of my Father, and inherit the kingdom
that has been prepared for you since time immemorial.'"

And Simon asked, "My father, please ask the Lord also to
absolve the sins of my father and my relatives."

And Theodosius raised his hands to the heavens and said,
"Be blessed by the God of Zion, and you, and everyone to the
last of your line, shall view the beauty of Jerusalem."

Simon received this holy blessing and this prayer as a price-
less gift. Once he was a Viking, and now, thanks to the grace
of God, he became an Orthodox Christian. He was instructed
by our holy father Theodosius, and, for the sake of the miracles
performed by holy Antonius and Theodosius, he gave up his
Western heresy and became a believer of the one true faith.
And this he did with all his household and all his priests, and
they numbered about three thousand. And Simon was the first
to be buried in the church of the Crypt Monastery. Since that
time Simon's son, George, also loved this holy place exceedingly.
Prince Vladimir Monomakh sent George, the son of Simon, to
the land of Suzdal, and entrusted to him his son, Yury. Many
years later this Prince Yury became the ruler of Kiev, and he
entrusted to George the land of Suzdal as if George were his
own father.

Bishop Simon

THE COMING OF THE GREEK ICONOGRAPHERS
FROM CONSTANTINOPLE TO ABBOT NIKON

Once, several Greek iconographers from Constantinople came
to Abbot Nikon of the Crypt Monastery and began to complain,
saying: "Bring before us the men who hired us. We wish to have
a trial. They hired us to embellish a small church, and we made
the agreement in front of witnesses, but this church is very
large. Take back your gold (which we received as payment),
and we'll return to Constantinople."

Abbot Nikon (not understanding of what they were speaking)

asked them, "Who were the people who made this agreement with you?"

And the Greeks described these people and gave their names as being Antonius and Theodosius.

But the abbot answered them, saying: "My children, we cannot bring them before you, for they departed this world ten years ago. But they still continue to pray incessantly for us; they steadily safeguard this church; they care for this monastery; and they protect all those who live in it."

Hearing these words, the Greeks were awestruck. However, they brought before the abbot numerous merchants, Greeks and Abkhasians,[1] who had traveled with them from Constantinople to Kiev. And the iconographers declared: "We made the agreement and accepted gold for payment from those who hired us in the presence of these merchants. But since you, Abbot, do not wish to bring to us those who commissioned us, or are unable to bring them here, then show us their images so that our witnesses can see them."

When the abbot brought them the icons of Sts. Antonius and Theodosius, the Greeks and Abkhasians, upon seeing them, bowed deeply and said: "Verily, they are their image! And we believe that even after death they still live and can protect, save, and succor those who turn to them for aid." And they decided to give the mosaic, which they had brought with them from Constantinople to sell, for the embellishment of the altar.

And the iconographers began to confess their sins: "When we arrived in our boats at the city of Kanev on the river Dnieper, we had the vision of a mountain on which was a large church. And we asked other travelers, 'What church is this?' and they answered, 'It is the church of the Crypt Monastery in which you are to paint the icons.'

"And, becoming angry,[2] we decided to go back, and started down the river. But that same night there occurred a severe storm on the river, and when we awoke the next morning we found that we were at the village of Tripole, farther up the river, and that a certain power was pulling us always up river. And only with great difficulty were we able to stop our boat. And we remained there the whole day, contemplating the meaning of this event, since in one night, and without any rowing,

---

[1] Abkhasians: a tribe in the western Caucasus.

[2] They were upset because having seen the size of the church they realized that their work would have to be much more extensive than they had expected.

we went up the river for a distance that usually requires three days of travel.

"The next night we again had the same vision of the church, and in the church was an icon of the Holy Virgin, and from this icon there came a voice announcing: 'Men! Why do you worry? Why do you not submit yourself to my will and that of my Son? If you do not obey, but try to escape, you, together with your boat, will be taken from this place and placed in the church. And know that you will never leave the monastery, but will there receive the tonsure, and will there end your days. But you will be granted mercy in the life eternal for the sake of the builders of the monastery, Abbots Antonius and Theodosius.'

"And the next day, when we awoke, we once more attempted to escape, and made a great effort to row downstream; but the boat moved continually upstream. And soon it landed at the shore under the monastery, and of its own accord."

After the Greeks had finished their narration, they and the monks glorified God, the miraculous holy icon of his most pure mother, and the holy fathers Antonius and Theodosius. And actually, having become monks, the iconographers and builders did end their days in the Crypt Monastery. And they were buried near the altar, and their robes still hang there and their books are preserved in the monastery for the commemoration of this miracle.

Bishop Simon

JOHN AND SERGIUS

There were two men from this great city (of Kiev) who were very close friends, and their names were John and Sergius. Once, both of them went into the Church of the Crypt Monastery, which was built by the will of God. And there they saw that from the icon of the Holy Virgin there emanated a bright light, even brighter than the rays of the sun. And so they decided to pledge themselves to become spiritual brothers.

Many years later John became very ill and was on his deathbed, leaving a son, Zacharias, who was only five years old. Before his death John called for the abbot of the Crypt Monastery, and gave him all his personal wealth for distribution to the poor. The part that belonged to his young son, which consisted of one thousand *grivnas* of silver, and one hundred *grivnas* of gold, he left in trust with his spiritual brother, Sergius. John also asked his spiritual brother to care for his son, Zacharias, telling Sergius, "Give this gold and silver to my son when he comes of age."

When Zacharias was fifteen years old, he wanted to obtain his gold and silver from Sergius. But Sergius, incited by the devil, decided to keep the money for himself, and in so doing to lose his soul. Therefore he told the youth: "Your father gave his entire estate to God, and you should ask God for your gold and silver. He owes it to you, and, being merciful, perhaps he will return it to you. But I don't owe your father even a single gold coin, for he, having lost his mind, gave away all his wealth and left you in poverty."

Hearing these words, the youth became sad and once more he begged Sergius for his money, but this time asking for only one-half of his money, letting Sergius keep the second half. But Sergius began to reproach the son and the son's father in strong words.

Zacharias then attempted to obtain from Sergius at least one-quarter or even one-tenth of his money; but seeing that he would not receive anything from Sergius, he spoke to him, saying, "Come and avow in the Church of the Crypt Monastery, before the miraculous icon of the Virgin, the same icon before which you pledged to be my father's spiritual brother, that you received no money from my father."

And Sergius promised to avow before the icon that he had received neither one thousand *grivnas* of silver nor one hundred *grivnas* of gold from John. But as Sergius approached the icon to avow, an invisible power prevented him from nearing it. And suddenly he began to shout: "Holy Angels and St. Theodosius! Enjoin this merciless angel not to slay me. Pray to the Holy Virgin to drive away the devils who attack me! Take your gold and silver! It is in a sealed vessel in my house!"

Everyone was seized with awe. And from that day it was forbidden to pronounce avowals on this icon. Men were sent to Sergius' house, and there they found the sealed vessel, and in it were two thousand *grivnas* of silver and two hundred *grivnas* of gold, for God had miraculously increased the fortune of the poor, knowing that Zacharias would give his fortune to the abbot of the Crypt Monastery. Zacharias remained at the monastery to the end of his days, and his fortune was used to erect the Church of St. John the Baptist. This church was dedicated to the memories of John and Zacharias, since their gold and silver had erected it.

Monk Polycarpe

MARKO THE GRAVEDIGGER WHO WAS OBEYED BY THE DEAD

We sinners imitate the ancient writings on the saints. But the ancient writers, with great difficulties, sought the saints in he wilderness, in the mountains, and in the abysses. Some of these authors have themselves seen these saints, while of other saints they have heard stories of their lives, works, miracles, and deeds, and have composed the *Paterikon*, which we read and in which we enjoy spiritual narrations. I, an unworthy one, have not yet been able to comprehend the truth of reason, and I have seen nothing of this kind. I tell only what I have heard. This narration was told to me by Bishop Simon, and I wrote it down for you, my reverend father. I have never been in holy places, nor have I seen Jerusalem nor Mount Sinai. Therefore I am unable to add anything to this narration for the purpose of embellishment, as is the habit of those who are clever with words. I do not want to praise anything but this Holy Crypt Monastery, the monks who live therein, and the lives and miracles of the latter. I shall rejoice when I remember them, for I, a sinner, hope that the saintly fathers will pray for me. And here I shall begin the narration concerning the gravedigger Marko.

St. Marko used to live in the crypt, and during his life there the body of our father, Theodosius, was taken from the crypt into the great holy church. This Marko dug graves in the crypt with his own hands, and carried the earth away on his shoulders. He worked hard all day and all night to do these pious deeds. Though he dug many graves for the burial of his brethren, he never accepted payment for doing so. If someone gave him money, he would take it and distribute it among the poor and crippled.

Once, according to his custom, he dug a grave and, laboring very much, became tired. However, the grave was not sufficiently wide. It so happened that this very day one of the brothers passed to God, and there was no grave available except this narrow one. The dead man was brought to the crypt, but because the grave was so very narrow he could not be placed in it. And the brethren began to grumble at Marko, for it was neither possible to adjust the dead man's robes nor to anoint him with holy oil. Marko, the monk of the cave, bowed to everyone with humility and said, "Forgive me, my fathers, but I could not finish the grave because of my poor health."

But the monks continued to reproach him still more. Then Marko addressed the dead man: "Brother, your grave is so narrow we cannot even anoint you with holy oil. Take the oil and anoint yourself."

The dead man raised up slightly, extended his hand, took the oil, and anointed his face and chest, making the sign of the cross. He then returned the vessel, adjusted his robes, lay down, and once more died. Awe and trembling seized everyone because of the miracle.

Some time later, after a long illness, another brother died. One of his friends cleansed the body with a sponge and went to the crypt to view the grave where his friend was supposed to lie. He asked Marko about the grave, and Marko answered, "Go to the dead brother and tell him, 'Wait until tomorrow, until I dig your grave, and then you can enter into rest.'"

But the brother, who had come to the crypt, said: "Brother Marko, I have already cleansed the dead man's body with a sponge. How can you now ask me to speak to him?"

Marko once again spoke to him: "You can see for yourself that the grave is not finished. I enjoin you to go and tell the dead man that sinful Marko tells him: 'Brother, live one more day, and then tomorrow you will pass to God in peace. When I have prepared a place for you, I will send for you.'"

The brother who had come to Blessed Marko obeyed. When he returned to the monastery, all the brothers were standing around the dead man and were singing the usual hymns. The monk stood before the dead brother, and said, "Brother Marko has told me to tell you that your grave is not ready and that you should wait until tomorrow."

Everyone was astounded by these words. But as soon as they were spoken by the monk who had returned from Marko, the dead brother's soul returned to his body. The whole day and night he remained with his eyes open, but talked with no one at all.

The next day his friends once more returned to the cave to find out if the place was ready. And Blessed Marko told them: "Go and tell the following to one who has become alive: 'Abandon this provisional life and pass into the life eternal. Here the place is ready for your body. Give your soul to God, and your body will be buried here with many holy brothers.'"

The brothers came and told all this to the dead one who had come alive. Immediately the latter, in the presence of all who had come to visit him, closed his eyes and passed away. And he was placed with honors in the new place in the cave. And everyone wondered about this miracle. How could it be that, with just one word from Blessed Marko, the dead would become alive, and then die once more after Marko ordered it?

Two other brethren in this great Crypt Monastery had since their youth been united by the great love in their hearts. They had the same thoughts and the same desires, which were directed to God. And they begged Blessed Marko to prepare them a common grave where they would be able to lie together when God should order them to do so. Many years later the elder brother, Theophile, left the monastery on business. In the meantime the younger brother became ill and died and was laid in the grave prepared for him. Theophile returned only some days after the burial. Having learned of the death of his brother, he became very sad and, taking some other monks, went to the cave to see in which place the deceased was laid.

Having noticed that his brother was buried in a place that was higher than the place reserved for himself, he was seized by wrath, and began to complain to Marko, saying: "Why did you put him there? I am the older, and therefore should be put in the higher place. But you have buried him in my place."

Marko, the monk of the cave, being a humble man, bowed to Theophile, and said, "Excuse me, my brother, I have sinned before you." Then he said to the deceased, "Brother, give your place to your elder brother and lie down in the lower place." And immediately after these words of Blessed Marko, the dead man got up in the presence of all the monks and lay down in the lower place. Everyone saw this terrible and awe-inspiring miracle.

Then brother Theophile, who had reproached Marko, fell to his knees and said: "Brother Marko, I have sinned by moving my brother from his place. Tell him to return to the original place."

But Blessed Marko told Theophile: "God ended the enmity between us. He did so because you complained and so that you might be prevented from lasting enmity and evil feelings toward me. Even this soulless body has demonstrated its love to you, respecting your seniority even after death. I should like you to make use of your seniority by not leaving this crypt, but by lying down in this place. But you are not ready for passing away. Therefore, go and care for your soul. In some days from now you will be brought to this place. The resurrection of the dead is the work of God, whereas I am only a miserable sinner.

Look on your dead brother, who was not able to bear the reproaches with which you covered me. And he left you a half of the place that was prepared for both of you. God can raise the dead, but I cannot say, 'Go down and lie in the lower place,' and then say, 'Go up and lie in the higher place.' If you want him to go back to his former place, order it, and perhaps he will go back to the place he left before."

Having heard these words, Theophile became saddened, and he thought that he would be unable to walk back to the monastery. When he returned to his cell, he began to cry disconsolately. He distributed everything he had, and kept only his mantle and robe. From that time forth, he was in permanent expectation of death, and no one could bring an end to his bitter crying and no one could convince him to eat well.

At the beginning of the day he would say to himself, "I don't know whether I shall live till evening." When evening was approaching, he would cry and say: "What should I do? Shall I be able to live till morning? Many people who arose this morning were not able to live until evening, but were obliged to lie down and were unable to get up again. And what of me? For I was told by Blessed Marko that my end was very near." And he spent each day mortifying his flesh with fasting, praying, and incessant weeping, expecting each day that his final hour was approaching. The expectation that his soul would soon be separated from his body exhausted him to such an extent that it became possible to count his ribs. Many people wished to console him, but this made him weep only the more. Finally, because of his incessant tears, he became blind. And so Theophile spent his days in great abstinence, thereby winning the grace of God by his exemplary life.

When Marko learned the hour of his own passing to God, he asked Theophile to come, and he told him: "Brother Theophile, forgive me for having caused you great sadness, lo! these many years. Now I leave this world. Pray for me. If I receive God's mercy, I shall not forget you. Let us pray that we may see each other with our fathers, Antonius and Theodosius, in the next life."

And Theodosius answered tearfully: "Father Marko, why do you leave me here? Why don't you return my sight to me?"

Marko told him: "Brother, don't grieve. Thanks to God you have lost your physical sight, but you have won the insight for understanding him with your spiritual eyes. My brother, I was responsible for your blindness, for I prophesied your death. But I did so for the sake of your soul, for I wanted to turn your pride into humility, and God rejects neither the contrite heart nor the humble man."

And Theophile answered him, saying: "I know, my father, that I should have fallen dead for my sins when you raised my dead brother. But, because of prayers, the Lord gave me new life, hoping for my repentance. Now I beg you, please, either take me with you to the Lord or return my sight to me."

Marko replied: "There is no need for you to see this transitory world. Pray to the Lord that you may see his glory in the next world. Your hour will come, even if you do not wish it to. Nevertheless, I shall give you a foretoken of your passing. Three days before your death, you will regain your sight. And, passing to God, you will there see endless light and unspoken glory." And Blessed Marko passed to God, being buried in the crypt in a grave he himself had dug.

This separation from Brother Marko added greatly to Theophile's suffering and increased his weeping. He shed whole torrents of tears, and the tears continually increased. He had a special vessel, and because his tears would always reappear when he began praying, he would put this vessel before himself so that his tears would fall into it. Some days this vessel would be full of tears, since every day Theophile expected the end of his life as Blessed Marko had predicted. When Theophile felt that his day of passing to God was drawing near, he began to pray zealously, saying: "Our Lord who loves man, my God, my most holy King, you do not want the death of a sinner; you anticipate their conversion to righteousness. You know our weaknesses, our gracious Comforter. You are health to the ill and salvation for the sinner. You are succor for the exhausted and an uplifting for the fallen. O Lord, I, an unworthy one, pray to you in this hour to show me your amazing grace and to reveal to me the unfathomable depths of your mercy. Deliver me from temptation. Do not permit the enemy to overcome me in my ordeal, but give me strength for the sake of the prayers of your saints and our great fathers, Antonius and Theodosius, and for the sake of the prayers of all saints who have served you since the beginning of time."

And in this moment a beautiful youth appeared before him, and said, "You pray well, but why are you so saddened by the vanity of your tears?" And the youth, taking a vessel much larger than that which Theophile had, and which was filled with the fragrance of myrrh, said: "Here are the tears that have poured forth from your contrite heart during your prayers to

God. All your tears that you dried neither with your hand nor with your robe nor with a cloth fell from your eyes to the earth. All of them, at the command of the Creator, I gathered and preserved in this vessel. Now I have been sent to you to announce tidings of joy. With joy will you go to the one who said, 'Blessed are they that mourn, for they shall be comforted.' Having spoken these words, the youth disappeared.

After this, Blessed Theophile asked the abbot to come to his cell, and he told him of the appearance of the angel and of the angel's words. He showed the abbot both vessels, one of which was filled with tears and the other with a fragrance that could not be compared to any other. And Blessed Theophile asked that the contents of both vessels be poured over his body after his death.

Three days later, Blessed Theophile passed to the Lord and was buried in the crypt near the grave of Marko the gravedigger. And when the contents of the angel's vessel were spread over his body, the entire crypt was filled with a wondrous sweet fragrance. And the monks also poured the contents of the vessel of tears over him, doing this so that he who had shed these tears might harvest the fruits of his labor.

APOCRYPHA

17. *The Descent of the Virgin into Hell*

AFTER the Christianization of Russia under Prince Vladimir, canonical books, such as the Bible, liturgic texts, and the works of the early Church Fathers, circulated through the Russian land. In addition to these, a considerable number of apocryphal or noncanonical writings came to Russia. Patterned after the Bible and written at the time of the New Testament, they were never recognized by the Church. Among such works, *The Descent of the Virgin Into Hell*, or, as it was called by Russians, *The Visitation to the Torments by the Mother of God*, is the most distinguished owing to its concept of divine mercy and the originality of its composition. "A visit to hell" was a subject common to both Eastern and Western Christianity, its most famous version being, of course, Dante's great poem *The Divine Comedy*.

The juxtaposition of eschatological concepts with the concept of divine mercy, as presented in this work, greatly influenced the Russian religious mind and was reflected in medieval Russian *vitae*, spiritual songs, and icons.

This translation is based on the text of a seventeenth-century manuscript that was revised and corrected by Professor N. K. Gudzy according to a twelfth-century manuscript, and it appeared in his *Khrestomatiia po drevnei russkoi literature*, Moscow, 1955, pages 92–98. Some portions of this translation follow that of Professor L. Wiener.

◆ ◆ ◆

The Holy Virgin wished to see the torments of the souls, and so she said to the archangel, Michael, "I ask that you tell me all things which are upon the earth." And the archangel answered, "I shall tell you all things which are upon the earth, Blessed One, as you would have it." And the Holy Virgin asked him, "How many torments does the Christian race suffer?" And the archangel said, "Innumerable are those torments." And then the Holy Virgin replied, "Show me what is in heaven and upon the earth."

Then the archangel ordered the angels to come from the south, and Hell was opened. And she saw those that were suffering in Hell, and there were a great number of them and there was much weeping. And the Blessed Virgin asked the archangel: "Who are these that they suffer so?"

And the archangel answered: "These are those who did not believe in the Father, the Son, and the Holy Ghost, but forgot God and believed in those things which God created for our sakes. They called the sun and the moon, beast and reptiles, earth and water God. And they made gods out of the devils Troyan, Khors, Veles, and Perun, and they worshiped these evil devils. And even now they are possessed by evil darkness, and therefore they suffer such torments."

And the Holy Virgin saw great darkness in another place. And she asked, "What is this darkness and who are those who dwell therein?" And the archangel answered, saying, "Many souls dwell in this place." And the Holy Virgin said, "Let the darkness be dispersed that I may see the torment." And the angels who watched over the torment answered, "We have been enjoined not to let them see light until the coming of your blessed Son, who is brighter than seven suns." And the Holy Virgin was saddened, and she raised her eyes to the angels and looked at the invisible throne of her father and said: "In the name of the Father, and the Son, and the Holy Ghost! Let this darkness be dispersed that I may see this torment."

And the darkness was dispersed and seven heavens appeared and there was a great multitude of men and women. And there were loud weeping and wailing in this place. And seeing them, the Holy Virgin said, weeping: "What have you done, wretched and unworthy people? What has brought you here?" But there was no voice nor any answer from them. And the watching angels spoke, "Wherefore do you not speak?" And one who was tormented replied, "Blessed One! For ages we have seen no light and we cannot look up." The Holy Virgin, looking on them, wept bitterly.

And a tormented one, seeing her, said: "How is it, Holy Virgin, that you have visited us? Your blessed Son came upon the earth and did not ask us, nor did Abraham the Patriarch, nor Moses the Prophet, nor John the Baptist, nor Paul the Apostle, the favorite of the Lord. But you, most Holy Virgin, are an intercessor and protector for the Christian people. You have prayed to God for us, but how did it come to pass that you have visited us, wretched as we be?"

Then the Holy Virgin inquired what was the sin of these tormented ones, and Michael answered: "These are they who did not believe in the Father, the Son, and the Holy Ghost, nor in you, Holy Virgin! They did not want to proclaim your name, nor that from you was born our Lord Jesus Christ who, having come in the flesh, has sanctified the earth through baptism. It is for this that they are tormented in this place."

Weeping, the Holy Virgin spoke to them. "Wherefore do you live in error? Do you not know that all creation honors my name?" And when the Holy Virgin finished speaking, darkness once more fell upon them.

And Michael said to her: "Whither, Blessed One, do you wish to go now: to the south or to the north?" And when the Virgin replied that she would go to the south, there appeared cherubim and seraphim and four hundred angels who took the Holy Virgin to the south. And there the Holy Virgin saw a river of fire. There was a multitude of men and women who stood in this fiery river. Some stood in the river to their waists, some to their shoulders, some to their necks, and some above their necks. Seeing this, the Holy Virgin exclaimed in a loud voice, "Who are they that stand in the fire up to their waists?" And the Archangel answered, "They are those that have been cursed by their fathers and mothers, and being so cursed, they are tormented here." And when the Holy Virgin inquired who were those who stood in the fire to their shoulders, Michael replied, "They are those who have cursed and indulged in lechery, and therefore are tormented in this place." And the Virgin asked, "Who are those that are in the fiery flame up to their necks?" And Michael answered, saying: "They are those who have eaten human flesh. For this they are tormented here." And the Holy Virgin then asked, "Those who are immersed in the fiery flame above their heads, who are they?" Michael the Archangel replied: "They are those, Lady, who, holding the cross, have sworn falsely. Such is the power of the cross that it is worshiped with awe by the angels and they tremble before it. And so, when a man swears by the cross and then lies, he is punished by such a torment."

And then the Holy Virgin saw a man who was hanging by his heels, and worms were devouring him. And she asked the archangel who he was and what were his sins. And the archangel answered, "They are those who took interest on their silver and gold, and therefore are tormented in this place."

And then she saw a woman who was hanging by one tooth, and various serpents came from her mouth and were devouring her. The Holy Virgin, seeing this, asked Michael: "Who is this woman? What is her sin?" And the archangel answered, "Lady, this one is she who used to say evil words and gossiped, which led to evil discourse among her neighbors, and therefore she is damned." And the Holy Virgin replied, "Blessed be the woman who does not give birth to such a sinner."

And then Michael said, "Holy Virgin, you have not yet seen the greatest torments." And the Holy Virgin replied: "Let us go and visit so that I may see all torments." And, when Michael inquired where she should like to go, the Holy Virgin asked to go to the north. And then seraphim and cherubim and four hundred angels took the Blessed One to the north where there was a great fiery cloud, and in this fiery cloud there were fiery places to lie down. In these places were a great many men and women. And the Holy Virgin, weeping, asked who these men and women were and what were their sins. And the archangel replied: "Lady, those are the ones who, during holy weeks, did not get up to attend the Easter Midnight Service, but lay in bed lazily as if dead. Therefore, they are tormented in this place." And the Holy Virgin asked, "And those who were not able to get up, are they also condemned as sinners?" And Michael answered, "Holy Lady, only those who cannot get up even when their house be in flame on all four sides do not sin when they do not go to church."

And the Holy Virgin saw a big iron tree with branches of iron on which there were iron barbs. On these barbs hung a great many men and women by their tongues. Seeing them, the Holy Virgin began to sob, and asked Michael who these people were and what was their sin. And the archangel replied, "These people are calumniators and gossipers who separate brother from brother and husband from wife."

And she saw women hanging by their fingernails, and fire came from their mouths and burned them. And serpents came out of the flames and tormented them. And they cried out, saying, "Be merciful unto us, for we are tormented beyond all other torments." And the Holy Virgin asked what were their sins. And Michael answered, "These are the widows of priests who did not revere the office of the priesthood, but married other men after the death of their priestly husbands."

And the Virgin saw other women who were lying in fire and were devoured by various serpents, and Michael said, "These are nuns from convents who sold their bodies for lechery, and therefore they are tormented."

And the archangel said to the Blessed Virgin, "Come hither, Holy Virgin, and I will show you the place where many sinners are tormented." And the Holy Virgin saw the river of flames. And the river appeared as if it were flowing blood and it covered the whole earth. In the middle of this river were a great many sinners. Seeing these, the Virgin wept, and asked, "What is their sin?" And the archangel Michael answered, "These are the whores and the adulterers, those who listen to gossip, the match-makers and calumniators, the drunkards, merciless princes, bishops, and archbishops, tsars who did not fulfill the will of God, the usurers, who collected interest, and the lawbreakers." Hearing this, the Blessed Virgin wept, and said, "Oh, these evil sinners, it would have been better if they had never been born!"

And Michael asked her: "Wherefore do you weep, Holy One? Have you never seen such great torments before?" And the Blessed Virgin answered, "Take me farther, that I may see all torments that are." And Michael asked, "Where do you wish to go, Blessed One, to the east or to the west, to the right into paradise or to the left where are the greatest torments?" And as soon as the Virgin replied that she wished to go to the left, there appeared seraphim and cherubim and four hundred angels and they took the Most Holy One to the east, to the left. And in the vicinity of the river there was a great darkness, and in the river there came many men and women, and it appeared as if the water were boiling. And great waves broke upon the sinners, and when the waves rose they drowned the sinners in a thousand feet of water, so that they were not even able to utter, "Righteous Judge, be merciful unto us!" And there was much gnashing of teeth in this place, since the sinners were devoured by the worms.

And seeing the Holy Virgin, the host of angels that watched over the sinners exclaimed in unison: "Holy, Holy, Holy! Holy God and you, Holy Virgin, we bless you and the Son of God born of you. For ages we have not seen light, but now, praise be to you, we have seen the light." And once more all of them exclaimed: "Rejoice, Blessed Virgin. Rejoice, Source of Light Eternal. Rejoice, Holy Archangel Michael and pray to our Lord for the entire world, for we have seen the sinners who are tormented, and we are very saddened."

The Holy Virgin, seeing the angels saddened and filled with sorrow because of the torments of the sinners, began to weep. And all exclaimed in unison, saying: "It is good that you have come to this darkness, for now you have seen their torments. Most Holy Lady and Archangel Michael, pray for them." And she heard the sobs and voices of the sinners who raised their laments, saying, "God have mercy upon us!" And the Virgin said, "God have mercy upon them." And as soon as she had said this, the tempest on the river of fiery waves ceased. And the sinners gained the hope in a tiny mustard seed. And the Holy Virgin, seeing this, wept and said, "What is this river and of what are its waves?" And Michael answered: "This river is a river of hot pitch, and its waves are of flame. And the Jews are tormented here because they tormented our Lord, Jesus Christ. And those who were baptized in the name of the Father, the Son, and Holy Ghost and still believed in demons and rejected God and baptism are also tormented in this place. And those who committed lechery with their mothers and daughters, and those who murdered with poisons or who killed with weapons, or who strangled their children are tormented in this place. Because of such deeds they are tormented. And the Holy Virgin said, "They deserve this for their sins." And when she had said these words the fiery waves once again enveloped the sinners, and darkness betook them. And Michael said to the Holy Virgin, "There is no thought of God for those who are lost in darkness." And the Most Holy One said: "O evil sinners, the flame of this fire shall never become extinguished."

And then the Holy Virgin spoke, saying: "I have only one request. Let me also enter, that I may suffer together with the Christians, for they have called themselves the children of my Son." And the archangel said, "Rest yourself in paradise!" And the Holy Virgin replied, "I beg you, move the host of the angels that we may pray for the sinners, and God may accept our prayer and have mercy upon them."

The archangel replied, saying: "Great is the name of our Lord God. Seven times in the day and seven times in the night do we bring praises and worship our Lady for the sake of the sinners. And we hope that our Lord will listen to our prayers." And the Holy Virgin answered, "I beg you, order that the angelic host carry me to the heavenly height and take me before the invisible Father."

And the archangel so ordered, and there appeared cherubim and seraphim, and they carried the Blessed One to the heavenly height, and put her down at the throne of the invisible Father. She raised her hands to her Blessed Son and said: "Have mercy, O Lord, upon the sinners, for I have seen them, and I could not endure. Let me be tormented together with the Christians." And there came a voice to her which said: "I see nails in my Son's hands. How can I have mercy upon them?" And she said: "I do pray for the infidel Jews, but for the Christians I ask thy mercy." And a voice again came to her, saying: "I see how they have had no mercy upon my brethren, so I can have no mercy upon them."

And the Holy Virgin again spoke, saying: "Have mercy, O Lord, upon the sinners, the creation of thine own hands, who proclaim thy name over the whole earth and even in their torments, and who in all places say, 'Most Holy Lady, Mother of God, intercede for us.' And when a child is born people say, 'Most Holy Virgin, help us.'"

Then the Lord spoke to her: "Hear, Holy Virgin! There is not a human being who does not praise thy name. I will not abandon them, neither in heaven nor upon the earth." Then the Holy Virgin asked: "Where is Moses the Prophet? Where are all the prophets? And you, Fathers, who have never committed a sin? Where is Paul, God's favorite? Where is Sunday, the pride of the Christian? And where is the power of the pure cross through which Adam and Eve were delivered from their curse?"

Then the Archangel Michael and all the angels cried, "Have mercy, O Lord, upon the sinners!" And Moses wept aloud and said, "Have mercy upon them, O Lord, for I have given them thy Law!" And John wept and cried out, "Have mercy, O Lord, for I have preached thy Gospel to them." And Paul wept and said: "Have mercy, O Lord, for I carried thine epistles to the churches." [Here a fragment is missing, but it is apparent from the text that follows that God did not concede to the prayers of the Holy Virgin and the saints.] And the saints, hearing the voice of the Lord, did not dare to answer.

The Most Holy Virgin, seeing that she could not intercede and that God would neither listen to their pleas nor take mercy on the sinners, said: "Where is the Archangel Gabriel who announced to me, 'Rejoice, because you have heard the Father before all ages and he will take away his reproach among men?' . . . [fragment missing]. And where are the servants of the throne and where is St. John the Theologian? Wherefore did they not appear with us to pray for these Christian sinners? Don't you see that I shed tears for the sinners? Come, all angels which are in the heavens. Come, all righteous people acquitted by God, since you are given the right to pray for sinners. And come you, Michael, for you are the first incorporeal one and are next to the throne. Let us all pray to the invisible Father for mercy, and let us not move away as long as he will not have mercy unto the sinners."

And Michael bowed to the ground before the throne, and with him bowed all those who are in heaven and all the incorporeal angels. Then the Lord, seeing the intercession of the saints, became merciful for his Son's sake, and said, "Come down, my beloved Son, and listen to the prayers of the saints and appear before the sinners."

And the Lord came down from the invisible throne, and all sinners who were in the darkness exclaimed in unison, "Have mercy upon us, King of All Ages! Have mercy upon us, Son of God!"

And the Lord then said: "Hear all! I have planted paradise, and have created man in my own image, and made him lord over paradise, and gave him life eternal. But they have disobeyed me and sinned in their selfishness and delivered themselves unto death. And since I did not want to see deeds done by hands which were forced by the devil, I came to earth and became incarnate through the Virgin. And I was raised to the cross to free them from slavery and the original curse. And I asked for water, but I was given gall mixed with vinegar. My hand created man and man put me into the grave. I descended to Hell and defeated the enemy and raised the selected ones. And I blessed the river Jordan to save you from original sin, but you did not care to repent for your sins. You became Christians only in words, and did not keep my commandments. For this you find yourselves in the fire everlasting, and I ought not to have mercy upon you! But today, by the mercy of my Father who sent me to you, and through the intercession of my Mother who has wept much for you, and through Michael, the archangel of the Gospel, and through the multitude of martyrs who have labored much in your behalf, I give you from Good Thursday to Holy Pentecost, day and night, for rest and for praising the Father, and the Son, and the Holy Ghost!"

And they all answered, "Glory be to thy mercy!" Glory to the Father, and to the Son, and to the Holy Ghost, now and forever. Amen.

18. *Adam's Address to Lazarus in Hell*

AMONG early Russian writings that cannot be dated with certitude a very prominent place is occupied by *Adam's Address to Lazarus in Hell*. Its style and content indicate that this work was written in the Kievan era and probably in the same century as the *Lay of Igor's Campaign*, with which it has many parallels. Its content is definitely apocryphal, but it is still difficult to

determine whether the original text is Byzantine or Russian.
The topic of this work is Adam's address to Lazarus in hell before he had been raised from the dead by Jesus. The address
consists of two rather different parts, the first being poetic and
original, while the second is composed of quotations from the
Gospel, and apparently has been corrupted by the scribes.

The final text has been established by M. Hruchevsky, who
divided the work into poetic lines. The translation offered here
was published anonymously in *The Slavonic Review*, Volume
X, 1931, pages 246–252. Several stylistic corrections have been
made by the present editor.

◆ ◆ ◆

Hear, heaven, attend, earth,
   how speaks the Lord.
"I bore sons and exalted them,
   and they have rejected me.
The ass recognizes his master's manger,
But my people have not recognized me.
And behold I will not give my glory to another
   but will send my Word on earth
   that I may save my people from the meshes of Satan."

"Brethren, let us today sing songs,
   let us cast aside grief, and be full of joy,"
spoke David, seated in infernal Hell,
   setting his eyed fingers on the live strings.
And he struck the lute and said:
"For now has come a joyful time,
   for now has come the day of salvation.
For I hear shepherds
   playing the reed in the cave,
And their voice passes the gates of Hell
   and enters my ears.
And I hear the trampling of feet of Persian horses,
   that carry the Magi with their gifts for him,
   from their kings to the King of Heaven,
   who has today been born on earth.
And him, brethren,
   we have been awaiting for many days,
   whose throne is heaven
   and whose feet rest on the earth.
The maiden mother
   wraps him in swaddling cloths

who wraps the heavens in clouds
and the earth in darkness.
And she speaks bending over him:
"O great and heavenly king,
how hast thou willed
to descend to us on the earth in poverty?
Hast thou desired this cave,
and this manger,
in which thou liest now?
And lo, how soon does the furious Herod
shake as he sharpens his sword against thee,
wishing to kill thee,
whose throne is heaven
and whose feet rest on the earth."
And Adam spoke,
to those that were with him in Hell:
"Come, ye prophets
and all ye just men,
let us send a message to the Lord,
into the living world,
to the Lord Christ
asking him with tears
whether he wishes
to release us
from these torments?"
And Isaiah and Jeremiah,
upbraiding Hell
and his impotent power,
said to David:
"But who can carry the message
from us to him?
Gates of brass,
posts of iron,
locks of stone,
solidly sealed."
Then David spake to them clearly:
"Isaiah, Jeremiah, Aaron,
Ezekiel, Solomon,
Adam, Abraham, Isaac,
Jacob, Samuel, Daniel,
and all the seventeen prophets
attend to my voice:
Tomorrow will go from us
Lazarus the four-dayed,

friend of Christ.
He from us
will carry the message."

And hearing this, Adam,
first-created of men,
began beating his face
with his hands.
Groaning heavily,
he exclaimed and said:
"Tell the Lord about me,
Lazarus, glorious friend of Christ:
Thus cries to thee
thy first-created Adam:
Was it for this, Lord, thou createdst me
to be on this earth
for but a short age
only to condemn me
to be tormented in Hell for many years?
Was it for this, O Lord, that thou madest the earth full?
For now thy beloved ones,
my grandchildren, lie in darkness
in the pit of Hell—tormented by pain
and finding their joy in their grief.
They wash their eyes with tears
and gladden their hearts with grief
and are downcast exceedingly.
For on this earth
but a short while did we know prosperity,
and now in this sorrow
many years are we in duress.

For a short while was I king
of all God's creatures,
and now for many days
am I slave to Hell
and captive to devils.

For a short while did I see thy light,
and now it is many a year
that I do not see thy bright sun
nor hear the stormy winds,
O Lord.

If I have sinned
worse than any man,

it is according to my deserts
thou hast assigned to me these torments,
I do not complain, O Lord.

But this is what fills me with pity—
I was created in thine image,
and now I am upbraided,
cruelly tormented by the devil,
who oppresses me, O Lord.

If I, Adam,
while I lived in nature,
broke thy divine commandment,
behold, O Lord,
Abraham, first patriarch,
and thy friend
who for thy sake was ready
to sacrifice his son,
his beloved Isaac,
but thou saidst:
Through thee, Abraham, all the generation on earth
    shall be blessed.
In what way has he sinned
that he should be tormented here in Hell
and sigh heavily?
Descend, O Lord, for the sake of Abraham,
or has Abraham, too, sinned unto thee, O Lord?

And behold thy servants
Isaac and Jacob his son
lying in thraldom in the infernal Hell.

And behold Noah, the just,
whom thou, O Lord,
deliveredst from fierce deluge,
and canst thou not deliver him from Hell?
Or maybe he too has sinned
like myself?

And behold thy great prophet Moses,
who led the Jews through the Red Sea,
and spoke with thee on the Mountain of Sinai
and in the burning bush face to face,
in what way, O Lord, has he sinned
that he too should lie with us in the darkness of Hell?
Or maybe, Moses, too, O Lord, has sinned unto thee?

And David, O Lord,
whom thyself exaltedst on earth
and gave him to reign over many men,
and he did make the psalter and lute,
in what way has he sinned, Lord?
But he too is tormented together with us in this Hell,
and sighs, as he groans frequently,
or maybe he too has sinned
in the same way as myself?

And here, O Lord, is thy prophet Isaiah,
who from his mother's womb was lifted to heaven
and then returned into his mother's womb,
like as thou too, O Lord, didst descend into the womb
   of a maiden,
and he too, O Lord, is with us in Hell,
or maybe Isaiah, too, has sinned, O Lord?

And here is thy great prophet Daniel,
son of Ezekiel the prophet,
who carried about a wooden rack in a frame,
who prefigured thy divine passion,
who smote the golden body in Babylon
and was cast into the lions' den,
and he, Lord, is with us in Hell
or maybe Isaiah, too, has sinned, O Lord?

And here, Lord, is Solomon son of David
who erected for thee a house in Jerusalem
and cast two eagles of gold
like unto cherubim and seraphim,
and spake: If God is on earth,
the Holy Ghost will descend on the two eagles.
And the two eagles flew round the church
and ascended to heaven.

And here is John, great among prophets,
The Lord's Precursor, the Baptist,
who was born from the annunciation of Gabriel,
who from youth grew up in the wilderness,
eating wild honey.
In what way has he sinned, O Lord?
On earth he was dishonored by Herod,
and now together with us he is tormented in Hell.

And here thy prophets complain,
Elijah and Enoch who pleased thee
more than all just men on earth.
No longer, O Lord, do we see
Thy resplendent sun
nor thy gratifying light,
but instead are possessed by sorrow
and downcast with grief.
Or maybe the prophets too have sinned unto thee?

Is it for the sake of our sins that thou wilt not release
    us?
or art thou biding thy time?
If thou willst descend thyself,
thou alone knowest it,
But we are yearning men
and thou art longsuffering and without malice.
Come to us soon,
release us from Hell and bind the devil,
that the mutinous Jews may know thee,
and we all may worship thee."

And hearing this the Lord went to Bethany, to Mary the
sister of Lazarus and of Martha; and Mary and Martha, as soon
as they heard that he was coming, hastened forth and falling at
his feet and wiping his feet with their hair said, "Lord, if thou
hadst been here, our brother Lazarus had not died." And the
Lord said to Martha and Mary, "Your brother shall rise again."
And Hell spake to the devil:
        "I hear.
        My soul is sad at having to release Lazarus,
        and I am sore pressed to cast forth Adam."
And the Lord said to Mary and Martha: Where have ye laid
him? And they came to the grave, and the Lord told them to
take away the stone from the entrance of the grave. And Mary
and Martha said: Lord, by this time he stinketh, for he hath
been dead four days. And the Lord said: If ye would believe,
ye should see the glory of God. And he lifted up his eyes and
said, Lazarus, come forth. And Lazarus rose at once, bound with
grave clothes, and the Lord said, Loose him.
    And when Lazarus had risen from Hell, he spake to the Lord:
"Lord, thy prophets in Hell cry unto thee, Adam the first-
created and Abraham the patriarch with Isaac his son and Jacob

his grandson. David cries unto thee on behalf of Solomon his son, 'Lead us out of Hell.' "

And the Lord spake to Lazarus: "Had it not been for David my beloved servant, I would have destroyed Solomon in Hell." And the Lord descended to Hell in person, and a multitude of heavenly warriors with him, Semiel, and Raguel, and Ismael, and Nanael, Tartarus, Gabriel, Michael, and all the angels advanced with the cross against Hell, saying, "Lift the gates of eternity and let the gates of sorrow be taken, that the King of Glory may enter."

And the angels and the prophets spake: "The Lord is strong and terrible in battle, for he is the King of Glory. Let them be taken."

And the great king David spake: "When I was alive . . .[1] that the gates of brass be overthrown and the posts of iron be broken.

And then will the Lord overthrow the gates of brass and break the posts of iron."

And the Lord spake to Adam: "This hand created thee from the beginning of time, and the same will lead thee out of corruption."

And then Jesus arose and said to his apostles: "Go Forth, preach to all lands, baptising in the name of the Father, the Son, and the Holy Ghost, teaching to obey them . . ." And the Lord himself ascended to heaven and was seated on the right hand of the Father, and all over the earth is his glory, of Christ Jesus our Lord.

[1] An apparent lacuna.

MILITARY TALES

19. The Lay of Igor's Campaign

WRITTEN on the occasion of Prince Igor's unfortunate campaign against the Kumans in 1185, the *Lay of Igor's Campaign* (*Slovo o polku Igoreve*) is unanimously acclaimed as the highest achievement in Russian literature of the Kievan era.

Igor was himself a well-known historical personality, a prince of Novgorod-Seversk (not to be confused with Novgorod "the great," the metropolis of northern Russia). Novgorod-Seversk, now a small city on the border between the Russian and Ukrainian S.S.R.'s, was at that time one of the Russian strongholds against the Kumans, nomads of Turkic origin who inhabited the prairie of southern Russia. Prince Igor (1151–1202), one of the leaders of Russian political and military activities of that region, began his campaign in 1185 to drive out these nomadic invaders, who, every year, would raid Russian territories, burn the cities and take the inhabitants as slaves. Relying only on his own military forces and those of his relatives, Igor moved into the prairie with no support from the other Russian rulers. This campaign ended in defeat and in Igor's capture by the Kumans, although he later escaped from them.

Though much is known about Igor, practically nothing is known about the author of the *Lay of Igor's Campaign*. One can only presume that he belonged to Igor's court, was a warrior, and, as is evident from his *Lay*, was very familiar with the life and environment of the prairie. Even less can be said of the literary antecedents of the work and of the epic tradition previous to it. It is true that the writer of the *Lay* often mentions Boyan, a bard who apparently lived in the eleventh century, but no details are known either of his life or of his poetic works.

The *Lay* is a poetic masterpiece and a highly sophisticated literary work. The word "poetic" should not be understood here in its narrower sense, since the *Lay* is neither rhymed nor organized in verses, nor does it follow any metrical pattern. The rhythm and the length of the sentences to some extent replace verse organization. Beside rhythm, the poetic elements of the *Lay* comprise an extremely rich imagery constructed primarily on parallels with nature, symbolism, poetic address, and lyric lamentation. Among other devices, the author of the *Lay* employs the repetition of characteristic images, stylized descriptions of military action, assonance and alliteration. Unfortunately, the latter are impossible to reproduce in translation. The structure of the *Lay* is by no means that of a narrative poem; and rather than being an epic tale, per se, it is much more a lament over the feudal discord in medieval Russia, a stern admonition to the princes responsible for the fratricidal feuds. The writer's forebodings of impending disaster in the Russian land proved to be true, for only fifty years after Igor's defeat and the writing of the *Lay*, Russia was subjugated by the Mongol-Tatars and lost her independence for two hundred years.

Three distinct structural planes can be discerned in the *Lay*. The first concerns the destiny of Prince Igor, his campaign, defeat, and escape from the Kumans. This plane, the narrative core of the work, is somewhat clouded by invocations to the late bard, Boyan, reminiscences of past glory, and the allusive atmosphere of foreboding. The second plane consists of portents and lamentations over the outcome of the campaign and Russia's fate, such as the dream of Prince Sviatoslav of Kiev and the lament of Yaroslavna, the wife of Igor. The final plane consists of the author's admonitions to the princes to unite, and his censure of their feuding.

Unfortunately, the *Lay* was preserved in only one copy, discovered at the end of the eighteenth century and first printed in 1800. This single copy, which was subsequently destroyed in a fire in Moscow during the Napoleonic invasion in 1812, was itself defective, and so the first edition of the *Lay* was an unsatisfactory one reflecting the low standard of scholarship and interpretation of ancient manuscripts of that time. Many portions were apparently misread or misinterpreted, and in some places inadequately deciphered. Despite the efforts of generations of scholars and voluminous research, several passages in the *Lay* still remain incomprehensible, and have lent themselves to contradictory interpretations. In the present translation such passages have been placed in brackets.

The text that was used for the present translation of the *Lay of Igor's Campaign* is that revised by S. D. Likhachev and published in the series *Literaturnye pamiatniki*, Moscow-Leningrad, 1950. However, the present translator has made wide use of the text and interpretations of Professor Roman Jakobson of Harvard University, who offers numerous and extremely ingenious explanations of certain unclear passages, while others have been interpreted in the light of such research as that on nature symbolism by N. V. Charlemagne.

The *Lay's* complex symbolism, structure, imagery, and philosophy require a more detailed commentary than any other medieval Russian work. Notes on the symbolism of the *Lay* and on Russian literary tradition appear at the bottom of each page, as well as comments pertaining to historical and geographical names specific to the work. Finally, references of a more general type can be found in the Introduction and in the Glossary.

The typographical arrangement and the chapter and stanza form given here are in agreement with authoritative publications of the *Lay* and also reflect this editor's feeling that they contribute to readability. For the sake of better understanding, some explanatory words have been added in parentheses and proper names have been preceded by the words "prince," "river," or "city."

◆　◆　◆

I. Invocation

Might it not behoove us, brethren
to commence in ancient strains
the stern lay of Igor's campaign,
　Igor, son of Sviatoslav?
Then let this begin
according to the events of our time,
and not according to the cunning of Boyan.[1]
For he, Boyan the Seer,
when composing a song to someone,
soared in his thoughts over the tree (of wisdom[2]),
ran as a gray wolf over the land,
flew below the clouds as a blue-gray eagle.

When he recalled the feuds of former times
he would let loose ten falcons upon a flock of swans.
　And the first swan overtaken
　was the first to sing a song
　to old Yaroslav,[3]

[1] Apparently a bard who lived in the eleventh century and who composed songs in honor of the Russian princes.
[2] Apparently this refers to the tree of wisdom or thought, a common symbol of Eastern mythology.
[3] Prince of Kiev from 1019 through 1054. He is considered the greatest ruler of Russia during the Kievan era.

to brave Mstislav,[4]
who slew Rededia[5] before the Kasog regiments,
and to handsome Roman,[6] son of Sviatoslav.

Boyan, however, did not let loose ten falcons
upon the flock of swans.
But rather he lay his wise fingers
    upon the living strings
    and they sounded lauds to the princes.
Let us begin this narration, brethren,
from the old times of Vladimir[7] to this present time of Igor,
    who strengthened his mind with courage,
    who quickened his heart with valor
    and, thus imbued with martial spirit,
    led his valiant regiments
    against the Kuman land
    in defense of the Russian land.

II. Prince Igor Prepares His Campaign

Igor looked up at the bright sun,
and saw that all his warriors
became enveloped in darkness.[8]
And Igor spoke to his army:
    "Brethren and warriors!
    It is better to be killed in battle,
    than to become a captive.
    Let us mount our swift steeds, brethren!
    Let us view the blue river Don."

And the prince's mind was seized by ambition.
And the desire to drink from the great river Don
concealed the evil omens from him.
And he spoke:
    "I want to break a lance at the Kuman frontier.
    I want, oh, my Russians,

[4] Mstislav the Brave, the brother of Yaroslav the Wise and Prince of Tmutorakan, a principality located on the Caucasian shore between the Black and Azov seas.

[5] A prince of the Kasogs, now called the Cherkess, who was slain by Mstislav.

[6] Roman the Handsome, a prince of Tmutorakan who was killed by the Kumans in 1079.

[7] Apparently Vladimir the Saint, the Christianizer of Russia.

[8] The author probably meant that the sun was eclipsed. An eclipse of the sun occurred on May 1, 1185.

    either to drink with you Don (water) from my helmet,
    or to leave my head there."
Oh, Boyan, the nightingale of yore!
If you were to sing the glory of the (Russian) campaign,
like a nightingale would you soar over the tree (of wisdom),
soaring in your mind up under the clouds
and singing the glory of both these ages.[9]
You would race along the trail of Trojan,[10]
over the prairies and the mountains.
And the god Veles' grandson
would sing Igor's song (thusly),
    "It is not a storm that has driven
    the falcons over the wide prairies.
    It is a flock of jackdaws
    racing toward the great river Don."

Or you, Boyan the Seer, grandson of god Veles, would sing:
    "Steeds neigh beyond the river Sula.
    Glory resounds in the city of Kiev.
    Trumpets blare in the city of Novgorod.
    Banners fly over the city of Putivl."[11]
Igor awaits his dear brother, Vsevolod.
This fierce auroch, Vsevolod,[12] (comes to him and) speaks:
    "My only brother, Igor,
    you are my only bright light.
    We are both the sons of Sviatoslav.
    Brother, order the saddling of your swift steeds,
    as my (swift steeds) are ready.
    They were already saddled at the city of Kursk.
    And my men of Kursk are famed as warriors.
    They were swaddled under trumpets.
    They were brought up under helmets.
    They were fed at lance point.
    The roads are known to them.
    The ravines are familiar to them.
    Their bows are taut,

[9] The glorious age of Vladimir and this age of Igor. (See "Invocation.")
[10] Trojan: the meaning of this word is not clear. It may refer to Trajan, Emperor of Rome (98–117), who campaigned in southern Russia, to a Slavic and Balkan deity, or the city of Troy.
[11] Novgorod-Seversk and Putivl: important cities in Igor's principality.
[12] Fierce auroch Vsevolod: Igor's brother, who died in 1196, was prince of Trubchevsk and Kursk.

their quivers are open,
their sabers have been sharpened.
They race into the prairie like gray wolves,
seeking honor for themselves
and glory for their prince."

III. The Omens

Then Prince Igor set his foot in the golden stirrup
and rode into the open prairie.
The sun barred his way with darkness[13]
and night, moaning with tempest, awoke the birds.
The whistling of the beasts arose.
And the Div[14] arose and from the treetops it cried,
enjoying unknown lands to listen:
    the land of the Volga,
    the land on the Azov Sea,
    the land at the river Sula,[15]
    the city of Surozh,
    the city of Kherson,[16]
    and you, the idol of the city of Tmutorakan.[17]

The Kumans hastened by untrodden ways
to the great river Don.
Their carts squeak at midnight,
one may say, as dispersed swans.
Igor leads his warriors to the river Don.
The birds in the forests of oak portend his misfortune.
The wolves conjure the tempest in the ravines.
The screeching eagles call the beasts to the feast of bones.
Foxes bark at crimson shields.

O Russian land! You are already far beyond the hills.

IV. The First Day of Battle: The Russians Are Victorious

Evening was fading late into the night.
Finally the glow of dawn faded.
Mist enveloped the prairie.

---

[13] Again the author wishes to say that the sun was eclipsed.
[14] A deity in the form of a bird that represented foreboding for the Russians.
[15] A tributary of the river Dnieper.
[16] Surozh and Kherson: Greek cities in the Crimea.
[17] Idol of Tmutorakan: probably a colossal idol that was held in veneration by the Kumans.

The song of the nightingale had died out.
The daws have begun to caw.
Russian warriors barred the wide prairie
with their crimson shields.
They seek honor for themselves
and glory for their prince.

Early in the morning of Friday
the Russians trampled the infidel Kuman armies,
and, spreading like arrows over the prairie,
they galloped away with beautiful Kuman maidens.
And with them they took:
   golds and brocades,
   and costly velvets.
With cloaks and coats and fur mantles
and with all kinds of Kuman garments
they began to bridge their way over the swamps and marshes.
The crimson banner,
the white gonfalon,
the scarlet panache, and
the silver lance
were taken to brave Igor,
son of Sviatoslav.

Brave Oleg's[18] clan slumbers in the prairie.
They have flown away.
They were born to be offended
   neither by the falcon,
   nor by the gyrfalcon,
   nor by you, the black ravens,
   the infidel Kumans.
Khan Gza flees like a gray wolf.
Khan Konchak[19] shows him the way to the great river Don.

V. The Second Day of Battle: The Victory of the Kumans

Very early on the second morn
a bloody dawn announced the day.
Black clouds arise from the sea
and want to envelop the four suns.[20]
Blue lightning shows through the clouds.

[18] Oleg was the grandfather of Igor and prince of the principal city
of Igor's domain, Chernigov.
[19] Gza and Konchak: Kuman khans.
[20] "Four suns" refers to the four princes who lead the Russian
armies: Igor, Vsevolod, Oleg, and Sviatoslav.

There is to be a mighty thundering.
The rain of arrows will come from the great river Don.
Here, on the river Kaiala,[21]
here, on the great river Don,
lances will be broken
and swords will be dulled on Kuman helmets.
O Russian land! You are already far beyond the hills.

Here the winds, grandsons of god Stribog,
blow the arrows from the sea
against the regiments of brave Igor.
The earth groans.
The rivers become turbid.
Dust covers the prairie.
The pennants announce:
  "The Kumans have come from the river Don
    and from the sea.
    They encircle the Russian regiments from all sides."
The devil's children bar the prairie with their battle cries.
The brave Russians bar it with their crimson shields.

Fierce auroch Vsevolod!
Your defense is firm,
Your arrows rain down upon Kuman warriors.
Your Frankish swords[22] clang on Kuman helmets.
Where you, fierce auroch, gallop gleaming in your golden
    helmet,
there will lie the heads of infidel Kumans.
There Avar helmets[23] are cloven at your hands,
fierce auroch Vsevolod.
What wound can matter, brethren,
to one who has forgotten honors and fortune,
and his father's golden throne in the city of Chernigov,
and the habits and ways of his dearly beloved
and beautiful wife,
the daughter of Prince Gleb?[24]

[21] The river at which Igor was defeated. Its location remains unknown but apparently it was a tributary of the Donets, itself a tributary of the river Don.
[22] Frankish swords or lances: weapons made of steel imported from Western Europe.
[23] Apparently helmets made in the Avar style. The Avars were nomads who in the seventh and eighth centuries lived in southern Russia and Hungary.
[24] The daughter of Prince Gleb, the ruler of Pereyaslavl-Seversk.

VI. CENSURE OF THE PRINCES' FEUDS

There were the eras of Trojan.
There passed the years of Yaroslav.
And there were the campaigns of Oleg,
Oleg, son of Sviatoslav.[25]
That Oleg fostered feuds with his sword
and sowed the Russian lands with arrows.
In the city of Tmutorakan
he used to put his foot in the golden stirrup
and its clinking could be heard by great Yaroslav,
who lived long ago.
And Prince Vladimir, son of Vsevolod,
would stop his ears in the city of Chernigov.[26]

And the dubious glory of Prince Boris,[27]
son of Vyacheslav,
brought him to his final Judgment,
and he remained in eternal sleep
on a burial shroud of green grass
for offending brave and young Prince Oleg.

On the river Kaiala Sviatopolk ordered
that his father be taken between two ambling Hungarian
    horses
to be buried in the Cathedral of St. Sophia in Kiev.[28]

Then, in the era of Oleg, son of misfortune,
the feuding spread and grew.
The fortune of god Dazhbog's[29] grandson was destroyed.
Human lives became shortened through the princes' discord.
In those days the plowman spoke but rarely,

[25] Prince Oleg was responsible for the fratricidal warring among the Russian princes. Oleg Sviatoslavovich, previously mentioned as Igor's grandfather, was an antagonist of Vladimir Monomakh, whose feudal wars shattered the unity of Russia. He died in 1115.

[26] So that he might not hear the clinking of Oleg's stirrup.

[27] Boris, son of Vyacheslav, was the first Russian prince to fight other Russian princes in alliance with the Kumans. Boris was killed in this campaign, while his brother, Oleg, escaped to the Kumans.

[28] Sviatopolk's father was killed in battle in 1078 and was taken to Kiev for burial. Slain warriors were carried in a carpet between two horses.

[29] Dazhbog: an ancient Russian deity; Dazhbog's grandson refers to the Russians. Veles and Stribog were also pre-Christian deities.

and the ravens often cawed, dividing corpses among them-
     selves.
And the daws talked in their own tongue,
before flying to feed on corpses.

VII. THE RUSSIAN DEFEAT

And so it used to be.
There were battles and campaigns,
but there had never been such battle as this.
From early morning to night,
from evening to dawn
there flew tempered arrows,
swords rained down upon helmets,
Frankish lances resound,
and all this in the unknown prairie,
in the Kuman land.
The black earth under the hooves
was strewn with bones,
was covered with blood.
Grief overwhelmed the Russian land.

What noise do I hear?
What clinking comes to my ears
so early in the morning, before the dawn?
It is Prince Igor who has led away his troops.
He is saddened by the fate of his brother, Vsevolod.
They fought for one day.
They fought for another day.
At noon on the third day Igor's banners fell.
Here, on the shores of the swift river Kaiala,
the brothers parted.
The wine of this bloody banquet was drunk to the last drop.
The Russians gave their guests to drink from the same cup.
They died for the Russian land.
     The grass withered from sorrow,
     and the saddened trees drooped earthward.

VIII. THE AUTHOR'S LAMENTS

And now, brethren, unhappy times have arrived.
The prairie overwhelmed the Russian forces.
Grief reigned over the forces of god Dazhbog's grandsons.
Grief, like a maiden, entered the land of Trojan.
She splashed her swan wings at the river Don,
by the blue sea,

The Kumans attack Prince Igor's army. The Russian horses fall from exhaustion. A miniature from the *Radzivil Chronicle* of the fourteenth century.

and splashing, she put an end to the times of good fortune.
The princes' fight against the infidel came to an end.
And brother said to brother:
    "This is mine,
        and that also is mine."
And the princes began to argue about trifles,
calling them important matters,
and began to create discord among themselves.
The infidels from all lands began to invade
the Russian land and to win victory.

Oh, too far toward the sea has the falcon flown, slaying birds!
And Igor's valiant regiments cannot be resurrected!
He is mourned by Grief and Sorrow,
and they spread across the Russian land.
[Shaking the embers in the flaming horn],[30]
the Russian women begin to lament, saying:
    "No more, our dear husbands,
        can you be envisioned in our thoughts,
        nor can you reappear in our dreams,
        nor can you be seen with our eyes,
        and never again shall we jingle gold and silver."
And, brethren, the city of Kiev began to groan from grief,
and the city of Chernigov also, from their misfortune.
Anguish spread over the Russian land.
Deep sadness flew through the Russian land.
And the princes created discord among themselves.
The infidels, victoriously invading the Russian land,
levied a tribute of one vair from each household.

All this happened because Igor and Vsevolod,
two valiant sons of Sviatoslav,
once more revived evil forces
which were curbed by their cousin, (another) Prince
    Sviatoslav.[31]
This stern prince of Kiev
held (everyone) in fear and awe,
for, as a tempest, his powerful regiments

---

[30] A part of the mourning ritual (?)
[31] Sviatoslav III, the great prince of Kiev (1177–1194) and theoretical ruler of all Russia. He was the cousin and godfather of Igor and Vsevolod. In 1183 he defeated Khan Kobiak on the shores of the Azov Sea and took him as a prisoner to Kiev.

and his Frankish swords defeated and attacked the Kuman
  lands.
They trampled under Kuman hills and ravines,
made turbid Kuman rivers and lakes,
dried out Kuman streams and marshes.
Like a tornado, he seized Khan Kobiak
from amongst his great iron regiments
on the shore of the sea bay.
And Kobiak fell in the city of Kiev,
in the hall of Prince Sviatoslav.

Now the Germans and the Venetians,
the Greeks and the Moravians
sing the glory of Prince Sviatoslav
and reproach Prince Igor,
who has lost his fortune on the bottom of the river Kaiala
and filled the Kuman rivers with Russian gold.
And here Prince Igor exchanged his golden saddle of a prince
for the saddle of a slave.
And the cities became saddened
and joy vanished.

IX. THE DREAM OF PRINCE SVIATOSLAV OF KIEV

Sviatoslav had a troubled dream
in Kiev, on the hills:
  "Early this night I was clothed in a black shroud
    upon a bed of yew.
  They ladled out for me
    a blue wine mixed with sorrow.
  From the empty quivers of the infidel strangers
    there poured large pearls into my lap.[32]
  They comforted me.
  And the beams of my gold-roofed palace
    were already without girding.[33]
  During the entire night, since evening,
    the gray-blue ravens were croaking.
  [And at the foothills of the city of Plesensk[34]

---

[32] Pearls were the symbols of forthcoming tears for the Russians.
[33] It was the custom among Russians to remove the girding of
orches before removing the dead from a house.
[34] Plesensk was a fortified city in the Galician mountains. Probably
  e allusion here is to the funeral of the Galician warriors, country-
  en, or Igor's wife, who was the daughter of the prince of Galicia.

appeared a sledge,[35]
and this sledge was racing to the blue sea."]
And the boyars told the prince:
"O Prince, sorrow has seized your mind.
There were two falcons who flew
From their father's golden throne,
either to conquer the city of Tmutorakan
or to drink the water of the river Don with their helmets.
But their wings were clipped by the sabers of the infidels,
and they themselves were put in irons.
It became dark on the third day.
The two suns[36] were eclipsed.
[Two purple columns[37] faded into the sea
Two young moons—Oleg and Sviatoslav—became en-
     veloped in darkness,[38]
On the river Kaiala darkness overcame the light,[39]
and the Kumans, like a brood of panthers,
spread across the Russian land.
And great violence came from the nomads.]
Already shame has eclipsed glory.
Already violence has defeated freedom.
Already the Div has descended to earth.
And now beautiful Gothic maidens[40]
have begun their song on the shore of the blue sea.
They jingle Russian gold.
They sing of the foreboding time.
They glorify the revenge of Sharokan.[41]
And we, the army, are without joy."

And then great Sviatoslav let fall his golden words
mixed with tears, saying:
"Oh, my young cousins, Igor and Vsevolod,
too early did you begin to disturb
the Kuman lands with your swords, seeking glory,
but you won it without honor,

[35] In ancient Russia sledges were used for funerals.
[36] Igor and Vsevolod.
[37] Apparently symbols of the two armies of Igor and Vsevolod.
[38] Young Prince Sviatoslav, Igor's nephew, and Igor's son, Prince Oleg.
[39] Darkness symbolizes the infidel Kumans, and light, the Russian army.
[40] In the twelfth century the Goths still maintained settlements in the Crimea, where they penetrated in the third century.
[41] Sharokan: a Kuman khan defeated several times by the Russians.

for you spilled the blood of the infidels
without winning glory for yourselves.
Your valiant hearts are forged of Frankish steel
and are tempered in valiance.
What have you done to my silver-gray hairs?
No longer do I behold my powerful
and wealthy,
and well-girded brother,
Yaroslav of Chernigov,[42]
nor his lords.
With his Moguts and Tatrans,
with his Shelbirs and Topchaks,
with his Revugas and Olbers.[43]
They used to defeat the regiments (of the infidels),
and without shields,
only with their knives and ancestors' war cries.
But you said:
'Let us be valiant.
    Let us assume the glory of the past.
    Let us divide amongs ourselves
    the glory of tomorrow.'
What is there to wonder, brethren,
when an old man feels like a young one?
When a falcon molts, he chases birds high and away
and does not permit harm to come to his nest.
But there is great misfortune,
and the Russian princes are no help to me."

X. THE BARD APPEALS TO THE RUSSIAN PRINCES

THE APPEAL TO VLADIMIR, SON OF GLEB[44]

Gloomy times have arrived.
The Russians cry out at the city of Rim
under the Kuman swords.
Prince Vladimir is covered with wounds.
Grief and sorrow to you Vladimir,
son of Gleb.

---

[42] Prince of Chernigov and borther of Sviatoslav, Prince of Kiev.
[43] Moguts, Tatrans, Shelbirs, Topchaks, Revugas, and Olbers: apparently Turkic tribes, but their identification is not certain. They settled in the land of Chernigov; in the principality of Yaroslav.
[44] Vladimir, son of Gleb: In 1185 the Kuman Khans Gza and Konchak invaded the Russian land, destroying the city of Rim on the river Sula. During this invasion Vladimir Glebovich was mortally wounded.

THE APPEAL TO VSEVOLOD, PRINCE OF SUZDAL[45]

Great Prince Vsevolod!
Do you not intend to come from far away
to watch over your paternal golden throne?
For you, with the oars (of your fleet),
can scatter the river Volga into droplets.
With the helmets (of your army)
you can pour out the river Don.
If you were here, then (Kuman) slave girls
would go for a *nogata*,
and (Kuman) male slaves for only a *rezana*.
And you can shoot over the dry land
with the fiery arrows,
with the courageous sons of Gleb.

THE APPEAL TO PRINCES RURIK AND DAVID[46]

O valiant Rurik and David!
Was it not your warriors who swam through blood
under the gilded helmets?
Was it not your army that roared like aurochs,
wounded by tempered swords in the unknown prairie?
Lords, set your feet in the golden stirrups
to avenge the outrage of the present day,
of the Russian land,
of Igor's wounds,
wounds of the daring son of Sviatoslav.

THE APPEAL TO PRINCE YAROSLAV OF GALICH[47]

O Yaroslav of Galich,
the prince of eight senses!
You sit high on your throne wrought of gold.
Your iron regiments defend the Hungarian mountains.
You bar the way to the (Hungarian) king.

[45] Vsevolod was called "the great nest" because of his numerous and powerful family. He was prince of Suzdal, a powerful principality in the vicinity of present-day Moscow, the latter being at that time only a small village in the Suzdalian principality.

[46] Rurik and David: Princes of Belgorod and Smolensk who died in 1215 and 1198. They were known for their courage during the fratricidal wars.

[47] Yaroslav of Galich, Prince of Galicia (1152–1187). Igor's father-in-law, he was called *Osmomysl* (eight-sensed) apparently because of his qualities for ruling. His land bordered on the Kingdom of Hungary, and he practically controlled the river Danube.

You close the gates of the river Danube.
You hurl stones over the clouds.
Your law reigns up to the river Danube.
Your thunder resounds above the lands,
You keep the gates of Kiev open,
From your father's golden throne you shoot at the sultans
beyond the (Russian) lands.
Lord, shoot at Konchak, the infidel slave,
for the revenge of the Russian land,
for the wounds of Igor,
the wounds of the valiant son of Sviatoslav.

THE APPEAL TO PRINCES ROMAN OF VOLYNIA AND MSTISLAV OF GRODNO[48]

And you, daring Roman and Mstislav,
your courageous thoughts direct your minds to action.
In your bravery you soar to valiant deeds,
like a falcon over the winds,
which desires, in its daring, to surpass the bird.
Your iron men are under Latin helmets[49]
and they make the earth tremble,
and (they make) many nations (tremble):
   the Nomads,
   the Lithuanians,
   the Deremelas,
   the Yatvags,[50]
   the Kumans.
(All of them) have dropped their lances
and have bowed their heads under your Frankish swords.

But Prince Igor, the sunlight has already dimmed for you.
And, by misfortune, the tree lost its foliage.
The enemies have already divided amongst themselves
the cities of the rivers Ross and Sula.[51]
The valiant regiments of Igor will not be resurrected.
The river Don appeals to you, Prince,
and summons the princes to victory.
O valiant princes, grandsons of Oleg,
you are ready for the battle.

[48] Roman (died 1205) and Mstislav (died 1226): Princes of Volynia, a region east of Galicia.
[49] Refers to the helmets of Latin or Western origin.
[50] Deremelas and Yatvags: Lithuanian tribes who lived at the northwestern Russian border.
[51] Tributaries of the Dnieper.

THE APPEAL TO MSTISLAV'S SONS

Ingvar and Vsevolod and you three sons of Mstislav![52]
You are six-winged falcons[53] of no mean nest.
You have not won your patrimonies by deeds of victory.
To what avail are your golden helmets,
    your Polish lances and shields?
Bar the gates of the prairie with your sharp arrows
        for the Russian lands,
        for the wounds of Igor,
        the wounds of the daring son of Sviatoslav.

EVOCATION OF PRINCE IZIASLAV'S[54] DEATH IN THE BATTLE OF
GORODETS (1162)

No more do the silver streams of the River Sula
protect the city of Pereyaslavl.
And the river Dvina, which flows to Polotsk,
that city of stern men,
became turbid under the cries of the infidels.

Only Iziaslav, son of Vasilko,
rained his sharp arrows upon Lithuanian helmets
and tarnished the glory of his grandfather Vseslav.
And, having been worsted by the Lithuanian swords,
he fell upon the bloody grass
[(as if it were) the marriage bed,]
under the crimson shields.

And Boyan said:
    "Prince, the wings of birds cover your warriors
        and the beasts already have begun to lick their blood."

Neither his brother, Briachislav,
nor the other brother, Vsevolod, was there (in battle).
And (you, Iziaslav) remained alone.
And you let drop from your valiant body,
through the golden necklace of a prince,
the pearl of your soul,
and voices became saddened,

[52] Princes of Volynia.
[53] Some of the Russian falcons have wings that have three distinct
sections, and are therefore called "six-winged falcons."
[54] Prince Iziaslav was killed at Gorodets in a war between the Russians and Lithuanians.

and joy ceased to be,
And the trumpets mournfully resound at the city of Gorodets.

THE APPEAL TO PRINCE YAROSLAV OF CHERNIGOV AND VSESLAV'S[55] HEIRS

O sons of Yaroslav and the grandsons of Vseslav,
lower your banners!
Put your dented swords into their sheaths!
You do not deserve the glory of your ancestors,
since, through your feuding,
you brought the infidels into the Russian land,
into the domain of Vseslav.
Your warring brought Kuman violence (into Russia).

THE EVOCATION OF PRINCE VSESLAV THE SORCERER

During the seventh age of Trojan
Vseslav cast lots for the maiden he desired, and,
cunningly leaning on the lance,
he leaped to the city of Kiev and
touched the golden throne of Kiev
with the staff of his lance.
Like a fierce beast he leaped from Belgorod at midnight,
under the cover of blue mist.
[He managed to cast thrice a lucky lot:]
    he opened the gate of the city of Novgorod,
    he tarnished the glory of Prince Yaroslav, and
    he leaped like a wolf from Nemiga [to Dudutki].

On the river Nemiga they built haystacks of heads.
They are threshed with steel flails
and lives are left behind on the threshing floor.
Souls abandon their bodies.
The bloody shores of the river Nemiga
    were sown with misfortune,
    were strewn with the bones of Russia's sons.

Prince Vseslav used to judge the people.
And, as prince, he ruled over the cities.
But, in the night, he prowled like a werewolf.

[55] Vseslav (d. 1101): Prince of Polotsk who in 1067 attacked and burned Novgorod, but was defeated at the river Nemiga. In 1068 he became Prince of Kiev for seven months. The "maiden" he cast lots for was the city of Kiev. He was considered a sorcerer.

He was able to go from Kiev to Tmutorakan
before the cock could crow.
And, prowling as a werewolf, he crossed
the way of great god Hors.[56]
At the Church of St. Sophia of Polotsk
the bells tolled the matins for him,
and he could hear them in Kiev.
His magician's soul lived in a valiant body,
but he still often suffered miseries.
Of him Boyan the Seer said wisely in his refrains:
    "Neither a crafty man,
        nor a clever man,
        nor a clever bird,
        can escape divine judgment."

O Russian land, you must mourn,
remembering your early age, your early princes.
And Vladimir of yore
could not be retained by the hills of Kiev.[57]
But now his banners have become the banners of Rurik,
and some of them have become the banners of David.
Thus, they are blown (by the wind) in different directions.

XI. Igor's Wife, Euphrosinia, Daughter of Prince Yaroslav
        of Galich, Laments of the Walls of Putivl

At the river Danube lances sing their song,
but it is the voice of Yaroslavna which is heard.
Since morning, she sings like an unknown seagull:[58]
    "Like a seagull I will fly along the river Danube.
        I will dip my beaver-trimmed sleeve into the river Kaiala.
        I will cleanse the bloody wounds of my prince,
        on his mighty body."

Since morning Euphrosinia has lamented on the walls
of the city of Putivl, saying:
    "O wind, why do you, my lord wind,
        blow so fiercely?
        Why do you bring on your light wings
        Kuman arrows against the warriors of my beloved?

---

[56] God of the sun in ancient Russia.
[57] Because he unceasingly campaigned against his enemies.
[58] The seagull was considered to be the bird of mourning.

Isn't it enough for you to blow under the clouds,
to loll the ships on the blue sea?
Why, my lord, did you scatter my joy
over the feathergrass of the prairie?"

Since morning Euphrosinia has lamented on the walls
of the city of Putivl, saying:
"O river Dnieper, son of Slovuta,
it is you who have broken through
the stone mountains[59] of the Kuman land.
You lolled the boats of Sviatoslav
(when he went to meet Khan Kobiak's army.
O my lord wind, loll my beloved
and (bring) him to me that I might not
send him my tears to the sea so early in the morning,
at dawn."

Since morning Euphrosinia has lamented on the walls
of the city of Putivl, saying:
"O my bright and thrice bright sun!
For everyone you are warm and beautiful.
Why did you spread, my lord, your burning rays
upon the warriors of my beloved?
In the waterless prairie you parched their bows
and closed their quivers with misfortune."

XII. PRINCE IGOR FLEES FROM KUMAN CAPTIVITY

The seas splashed at midnight
and the tornado rushes through the mist.
God shows the way to Igor,
the way from the Kuman land,
to the Russian land,
to his father's golden throne.

The glow of the sunset had faded.
Igor sleeps.
Igor keeps his vigil.
Igor's thoughts cross the prairie,
from the great river Don
to the small river Donets.

59 Stone mountains: apparently a reference to the cataracts in the
er Dnieper, and the surrounding rocky shores.

Beyond the river, Ovlur whistles,[60]
having caught a horse.
He warns the prince.
Prince Igor will not remain a prisoner.
The earth rumbled,
the grass rustled,
and the Kuman tents began to stir.
Prince Igor raced to reeds like an ermine,
like a white duck (he races) on the water.
He leaps to his swift steed.
He (later) springs from it, like a gray wolf.
He rushed toward the curve of the river Donets.
He flew under the clouds like a falcon
which kills geese and swans
    for lunch,
    for dinner,
    and for supper.

If Prince Igor flies like a falcon,
then Ovlur races like a wolf,
shaking off the chilling dew.
And both of them exhausted their swift steeds.

XIII. IGOR SPEAKS WITH THE RIVER DONETS

The river Donets speaks:
    "Oh, Prince Igor,
      there will be no small glory for you,
      but dislike for Konchak,
      and joy for the Russian land."

And Igor spoke:
    "Oh, my river Donets!
      There will be no small glory for you,
      for you have lolled the prince on your waves,
      for you have spread for him green grass
      on your silver shores,
      for you have enveloped him in your warm mists
      in the shadow of green trees,
      for your drakes watched over him on the water,
      and your seagulls on the streams,
      and your black ducks in the winds."

[60] Ovlur was Igor's faithful servant.

But different words came to him from the river Stugna.
Its stream is weak.
It has swallowed up other brooks and rivulets,
[and, therefore, has grown wide at its delta.
It hid young Prince Rostislav.[61]
It concealed him on its bottom near its dark bank.]
And Rostislav's mother mourned the young prince.
Flowers withered from sorrow,
and the saddened trees dropped earthward.

XIV. THE KUMAN KHANS PURSUE IGOR

It is not the magpies which have begun croaking,
it is Khans Gza and Konchak
who search for Igor's path.
At that time the crows did not caw.
The daws became silent and
the jackdaws did not chatter.
Only the snakes were crawling,
and the woodpeckers show the way to the river with their
    sounds.
The nightingale announces the dawn with its gay song.

And Khan Gza told Khan Konchak:
    "If the falcon fly to his nest,
    we will shoot at the falconet[62]
    with our gilded arrows."

And Khan Konchak replied to Khan Gza:
    "If the falcon flies to his nest,
    we will enmesh the falconet
    with the charms of a beautiful maiden."

And Khan Gza said to Khan Konchak:
    "If we enmesh him with the charms of
    a beautiful maiden,
    we will have neither the falconet
    nor the beautiful maiden,
    and (their) birds will start fighting us
    in the Kuman prairie."

[61] Prince Rostislav was drowned at the age of twenty-two in 1093,
during a fording of the river Stugna, a tributary of the Dnieper.
[62] The term "falconet" refers to Igor's son, Vladimir, who remained
a prisoner of the Kumans.

XV. Apodosis

And Boyan, [the bard of olden times,
said of the time of Sviatoslav,
  of Yaroslav,
  and of Kagan Oleg:]
    "It is difficult for a head
     to be without shoulders.
     But it is also a misfortune
     for the body to be without the head."
And so it is difficult for the Russian land
to be without Prince Igor.
The sun gleams in the sky.
Prince Igor is in the Russian land.
Maidens sing on the Danube.
Their voices reach across the sea to Kiev.
Igor rides along the Borichev[63]
to the Church of the Holy Virgin of Pirogoshch.
The lands are jubilant.
The cities rejoice.
Once the glory of the princes of yore was sung,
now glory will be sung for the young.
Glory to Igor, son of Sviatoslav,
to fierce auroch Vsevolod,
and to Vladimir, son of Igor.
Hail to the princes and the armies
who fight for Christendom against the infidel hosts.
Glory to the princes and to the army. Amen.

20. Prince Roman, Khan Otrok, and the Wormwood

THE *Galician and Volynian Chronicle,* from which this tale is
taken, gives a rather detailed account of the fate of southern
Russia in the thirteenth century. The authors of the first part
demonstrate an unmistakable talent for narration and some

---

[63] Borichev: a location of the Dnieper shore in the vicinity of Kiev
where a church was built in honor of the Holy Virgin of Pirogoshch.
This name comes from the name of an icon in a tower (*pyrios* is
Greek for "tower") in Constantinople.

poetic inclination. The present excerpt gives a short but poetic account of the circumstances under which Khan Otrok returned to his native land.

The text upon which this translation is based is to be found in N. K. Gudzy's *Khrestomatiia po drevnei russkoi literature,* Moscow, 1955.

❖ ❖ ❖

Great Prince Roman, the unforgettable ruler of all Russia, died. He was the one who conquered all the heathen nations and with wisdom fulfilled all the divine commandments. He would strike against the infidels (Kumans) like a lion. He could be as full of wrath with them as is a lynx. He annihilated them like a crocodile. Many were the times he crossed their lands like an eagle. He was as courageous as an aurochs. He continued the deeds of his grandfather, Prince Vladimir Monomakh, who destroyed the infidel sons of Ishmael, who are usually called Kumans. He drove Khan Otrok from the steppes to beyond the Iron Gates (of the Caucasian Mountains) into Abkhasia.[1] Only the horde of Khan Syrchan remained on the river Don, and he had only fish for food. It was that time when Prince Vladimir Monomakh drank water from the river Don with his golden helmet. He conquered the entire Kuman land and drove away these accursed sons of Hagar.[2]

After the death of Prince Vladimir Monomakh, Khan Syrchan sent his bard, Oria, to his brother, Khan Otrok, who was still in the land of Abkhasia. And Syrchan told Oria to tell his brother: "Vladimir is dead. Come back, brother; return to your native land." And he added to Oria: "Tell these words I have spoken to my brother and sing him our Kuman songs. But, if he does not want to return, let him smell the fragrance of our prairie grass that is called wormwood."

When Khan Otrok wanted neither to return nor to listen to the songs of his brother's bard, the bard presented him a bouquet of wormwood from the prairie.

And when Khan Otrok inhaled the fragrance of the prairie wormwood, he began to weep, and said: "It is still better to die in one's native land then to win glory in a foreign one." And thus Khan Otrok decided to return to his native land.

[1] A small nation on the eastern shores of the Black Sea.
[2] Following the Byzantine tradition, the Russians considered all nomads to be the descendants of Ishmael, the son of Hagar.

21. *Tales from the Novgorodian Chronicle*

IN southern and central Russia the princes eventually established their undisputed rule over the Russian cities and principalities, and the ancient people's assembly, the *Veche,* which had played an important role in Russia before the eleventh and twelfth centuries, gradually declined in importance. But in the cities of Novgorod and Pskov, in northwestern Russia, the power of the princes was curbed and the *Veche* became the principal ruling institution. The princes, who served as commanders of the army, the *posadniks,* who headed the civil administration, other administrators, and the bishops were all elected by the *Veche,* and often removed by it if its members became dissatisfied with them. Like such European merchant cities as Venice, Genoa, Hamburg and Lubeck, both Pskov and Novgorod had a powerful merchant class. Novgorod became a member of the Hanseatic League and maintained lively trade relations with Germany and other nations of northern Europe.

The style of the *Novgorodian Chronicle* strongly reflects the commercial atmosphere that prevailed in these two cities. The entries tell little about political events, but furnish details concerning matters of commerce, such as the state of the harvest, the prices of merchandise, trade activities, and climatic conditions that might have a bearing on the economic situation. Most of the longer stories in these northern annals are of southern origin, and were taken from the Kievan or central Russian chronicles.

The translation of the *Novgorodian Chronicle* presented here is based on *Novgorodskaia pervaia letopis,* Second Version, published by the Academy of Science of the U.S.S.R., Moscow and Leningrad, 1950.

◆ ◆ ◆

LIFE IN THE CITY OF NOVGOROD

1128 (6636)   Kiriak, the Abbot of St. George, died. In the same year John, son of Vsevolod, grandson of Mstislav, died on the 16th of April. In the same year Zavid Dmitrevich was made *posadnik* in Novgorod. This was a cruel year: an *osminka* of rye cost a *grivna;* the people ate lime leaves, birchbark; they ground wood pulp and mixed it with husks and straw; and some ate buttercups, moss, and horseflesh. And the corpses of those who had fallen from starvation were in the streets, the marketplace, the road, and everywhere. And they hired men to carry the dead out of town, for the serfs could not go out. Sorrow and misery befell all. Fathers and mothers would give their children as gifts to merchants or put them to death. And many people went to other lands. Thus a blight was brought upon our land for our sins. And this year the water of the river Volkhov was very high, and it carried away many houses. And Prince Boris Vsevolodovich of Polotsk died, and Zavid Dmitrevich, *posadnik* of Novgorod, died.

1143 (6651) All this autumn was rainy; from Our Lady's Day of Nativity until the winter solstice it was warm and wet. The water was very high in the river Volkhov, and it carried away hay and wood. The lake froze, and there was great coldness in the night. And the wind broke up the ice and carried it into the river Volkhov, where it broke the bridge and carried away four of the bridge piles. In the same year Sviatopolk married in Novgorod. He brought his bride from Moravia between Christmas and Epiphany. And in the same year the Korelians campaigned against the Yamians, but were forced to retreat.

1156 (6664) The Novgorodians expelled Sudila, the *posadnik* of the city, and he died five days later. And they gave the position of *posadnik* to Yakun Miroslavovich. In the same spring, on April 29th, Archbishop Nifont passed away. Before he died he went to Kiev to oppose the metropolitan bishop, but many people say that he went to Constantinople after having plundered the Cathedral (St. Sophia in Kiev). They say many things about him, but it is their sin for doing so. We should remember that he was the one who embellished the Cathedral (St. Sophia of Novgorod), who decorated the porches, who made the icon case, and who adorned the church on the outside. He also built the Church of the Holy Savior in Pskov and the Church of St. Clement in Ladoga. I believe that God, because of our sins, did not desire that we should have his grave for our consolation and so he sent him to Kiev, where he died. And he was buried in the Crypt Monastery.

In the same year the whole populace of the city gathered and decided to elect as bishop a holy man, Arkady, who was chosen by God. And all the people went to the Monastery of the Holy Mother of God and took him, Prince Mstislav, the entire clergy of the Cathedral of St. Sophia, and all the priests, abbots, and monks of the city and brought them to the court of St. Sophia. And they entrusted the bishopric to Arkady until the Metropolitan of Russia should arrive and consecrate him.

And in the same year the merchants from over the seas erected the Church of Good Friday on the market square.

1157 (6665)   There was malice among the people, and they rose against Prince Mstislav Yurievich and began to drive him from Novgorod, but the merchants took up arms for him. And brother quarreled with brother. The bridge over the river Volkhov was seized. Guards took their stand on either side of the town gates, and it nearly came to the shedding of blood between them. And then Sviatoslav Rostislavich and David Rostislavich arrived. That very night Mstislav fled from Novgorod. And in three days Rostislav himself arrived. And the brothers came together, and no harm came of it.

In the spring Prince George died at Kiev, and the people of Kiev set Iziaslav Davidovich on the throne. In the same year Andrew, Abbot of the Church of the Holy Mother of God, died. And Alexis was appointed in his place. And in the fall the weather was fearsome with thunder and lightning, and on November 7th, at five in the night, there was hail of the size of apples.

NOVGOROD AT WAR WITH SUZDAL

THE chronicle entries for the years 1169 and 1170 which follow below, give a clear picture of the struggle between the princes of Novgorod and those of central Russia. First the princes of Suzdal and later those of Moscow tried to unify all Russia and to bring the prosperous merchant city of Novgorod under their sway. The struggle described in these two entries is against the armies of Suzdal, led by the autocratic Prince Andrey, and their allies, led by Prince Roman and Prince Mstislav. At this time the troops of Novgorod were commanded by young Prince Roman. These entries are written in short, telegraphic style. For a better understanding of the text some explanatory notes have been added in parentheses.

◆ ◆ ◆

1169 (6667)   Danislav Lazutinich went with his troops beyond the Volok[1] to collect tribute, but (Great Prince Andrew) sent his army against them. And it came to a battle. There were only four hundred men of Novgorod against seven thousand soldiers from Suzdal, but God helped the Novgorodians, and the Suzdalians suffered thirteen hundred casualties, while Novgorod lost only fifteen men. Novgorod retreated, but then

---

[1] Volok (Portage) was the name of the region which formed the watershed between the West Dvina and Dnieper.

returned and collected tribute (beyond the Volok), and received tribute also from the peasants of Suzdal. And all returned home in good health.

In this same year in the winter the army of Suzdal, under the command of the son of Prince Andrew, Prince Mstislav, and Prince Roman, and with troops from Smolensk, Toropetz, and Murom; the armies of Riazan led by two princes, the Prince of Polotsk with his armies, and men from the entire Russian land all approached the city of Novgorod. But the people of Novgorod were firmly behind their leader, Prince Roman, and their *posadnik*, Yakun. And so they built fortifications about the city. On Sunday (the emissaries of the princes of Suzdal) came to Novgorod to negotiate, and these negotiations lasted for three days. On the fourth day, Wednesday, February 25th, the Day of St. Tarasy, Patriarch of Constantinople, the Suzdalians attacked the city and fought the entire day. Only toward evening did Prince Roman, who was still very young, and the troops of Novgorod manage to defeat the army of Suzdal with the help of the holy cross, the Holy Virgin, and the prayers of the Right Reverend Bishop Elias. Many Suzdalians were massacred, many were taken prisoner, while the remainder escaped only with great difficulty. And the price of Suzdalians prisoners fell to two *nogatas*.

1170 (6678) There were high prices in Novgorod. A barrel of rye cost four *grivnas*, bread cost two *nogatas*, and honey ten *kunas* a pood. After deliberations, the Novgorodians decided to renounce Prince Roman. And they sent their emissaries to Great Prince Andrew Bogoliubsky (of Suzdal), suing for peace. They asked Prince Andrew to give them another prince who would preserve their liberties. In the same year on the 4th day of October, St. Erofey's Day, Prince Rurik Rostislavich (the prince sent to Novgorod by Prince Andrew) arrived in Novgorod. This same year the God-loving archbishop, Elias, and his brother, Gabriel, founded a monastery and erected the Church of the Annunciation of the Holy Mother of God. And this year Prince Mstislav Iziaslavich, the grandson of Vladimir, died. In the same year Prince Gleb Giorgivich died at Kiev, and (the Kievans) put in Vladimir Mstislavovich.

THE ELECTION OF ARCHBISHOP MANTURY, AND NOVGOROD WARS AGAINST THE UGRIANS

The entry for the year 1193 gives an interesting account of the election and consecration of a new archbishop. The second part of the entry is concerned with the description of a Novgorodian campaign against the people of Ugra (kinsmen of the present-day Hungarians) who occupied the area both east and west of the northern Urals. The Novgorodians began building their colonial empire in what is now northern Russia. By the fifteenth century, when this empire was nearing its end, it extended into Siberia and covered an area the size of present-day France, Germany, and Italy combined.

✦ ✦ ✦

1193 (6701) The archbishop of Novgorod, Gabriel, passed away on May 24th, the Day of Our Holy Father St. Simon. And he was solemnly buried in the porch of the Cathedral of St. Sophia next to his brother whose name was George after he took the holy vows. And then the people of Novgorod, the abbots, the Chapter of St. Sophia, and the clergy began their deliberations as to who should be the new archbishop. Some wanted to elect Mitrofan, while others wanted to elect Mantury, and still others wanted Grichina in this office. There was a great feud among them, and they decided to cast lots after High Mass in the Cathedral of St. Sophia. And they prepared the lots, and after the service they sent for a blind man and he was given to them by God. And with the help of divine Grace the blind man cast, and Mantury was chosen. And they sent for Mantury and they brought him to the Court of the Archbishop.

And they announced his election to the Metropolitan of Kiev, and he sent for Mantury with great honors. And Mantury went to Kiev with the patricians of Novgorod. And he was received there with love by Prince Sviatoslav and the metropolitan. He was consecrated on the 10th day of December, the day celebrated for the deaths of the holy martyrs Mina, Hermogen, and Eugraph. And Mantury returned to Novgorod on January 16th, the Day of the Falling Off of the Fetters of the Holy Apostle Peter.

In the same year the Novgorodian troops under Voevoda Yadreik reached the land of Ugra and took a town. And they went to another town and besieged it. And they remained there five weeks, and the people of Ugra sent the Novgorodian forces a deceitful message saying the following: "We are collecting silver and sables and other valuables for you, so that you should neither destroy us nor your own tribute." And in the meantime the Ugrians began collecting their forces, and when their army had been gathered, the city sent a message to Voevoda Yadreik saying the following, "Come to the city bringing with you twelve men."

And Voevoda Yadreik went to the city, taking with him the priest John Legena and other leading men, and they were cut to pieces by the Ugrians on the eve of St. Barbara's Day. And then they took thirty of the best Novgorodian warriors prisoner and cut them to pieces. And later fifty more Novgorodian warriors were cut down by the Ugrians.

And then Savka (apparently a Novgorodian) came to the Ugrian prince and said: "Prince, if you don't kill Jacob Prokshenich (presumably the second-in-command of the Novgorodian forces), but let him live to reach Novgorod, he will bring more warriors and will devastate your land." And the Ugrian prince called Jacob Prokshenich before him and ordered that he be killed, but Jacob said to Savka: "Brother, God and Holy Sophia will judge you if you have in mind the spilling of your brothers' blood. And you will appear before us and God, and you will be responsible for our blood." And after he said this he was killed, for Savka had secret connections with the Ugrian prince.

And then the army of Novgorod was starving because they had remained for six weeks, being induced to do so by Ugrian deceit. And on the Holy Day of St. Nicholas they broke camp and were all cut to pieces by the Ugrian army. And there were sorrow and misery among those who remained alive, and there were only eighty of them. During the whole winter there was no word in the city of Novgorod as to whether the men of the army of Voevoda Yadreik were dead or alive. And in Novgorod the prince, the archbishop, and the entire people of the city grieved.

In the same year a son, Rostislav, was born to Yaroslav in Novgorod. And they built a wooden church called Zhivoglozha to the Holy Apostles, and another church to St. Joan the Merciful at the Gates of Resurrection.

THE BATTLE ON THE RIVER KALKA

IN 1224 the Mongols, united under Ghenghis Khan, invaded southern Russia for the first time. They came there more or less accidentally, returning to central Asia after conquests in Persia and the Caucasus. (The Mongols became known to Russians by the name Tatar. The Tatars were actually a Mongolian tribe from which were taken the shock troops for the advancing Mongolian army.) After having defeated the Russian princes and their allies, the Kumans—who joined with the Russians the better to resist the invasion—the Mongols disappeared into the central Asian steppes and deserts. They returned twelve years later, and this time they held the Russian land for nearly two and a half centuries. The report of this first decisive battle on the river Kalka is apparently of southern origin, and was incorporated into the *Novgorodian Chronicle* under the year 1224.

✦ ✦ ✦

1224 (6732)   In the same year, for our sins, there came unknown tribes. No one knew who they were nor what was their origin, faith, or tongue, and some people called them Tatars, while others called them Taurmen, and still others called them Pechenegs. Some say that these are the same people of whom Methodius of Patras spoke and that they came from the Yetrian Desert, which is between North and East. Methodius said that at the end of time there will appear those whom Gideon drove away, and they will conquer the whole land from the Tigris and Euphrates rivers to the Pontic Sea, with the exception of Ethiopia. Only God knows who these people are or from whence they came. The wise man, who understands the Books, knows who they are, but we do not. Here we record them in memory of the misfortunes of the Russian princes that came about at their (the Tatars') hands. We have heard that they have conquered many lands and have killed many Yasians, Abkhasians, Kossogians,[1] and godless Kumans. And many Kumans were driven away and many others were killed, owing to the wrath of God and his Immaculate Mother. Much evil has befallen the Russian land at the hands of these Kumans, and therefore most merciful God desired that these godless Kumans, son of Ishmael, should die in order to revenge the Christian blood that was upon them, these lawless ones.

These Taurmen (Mongols) came across the whole Kuman land and came close to the Russian border. And the remnants of these godless Kumans under the leadership of Khotian and other princes came to the so-called Kuman Wall, where many were killed together with princes David Koviakovich and George. This Khotian was the father-in-law of Mstislav Mstislavich, the Russian Prince of Galich. And he (Khotian) arrived in Galich with greetings for his son-in-law, Mstislav Mstislavich, and all the other Russian princes. He brought them numerous presents: horses, camels, buffaloes, and girls. And he presented

---

[1] Yasians, Kossogians, and Abkhazians were Caucasian tribes.

these gifts to them, and said the following: "Today the Tatars took away our land and tomorrow they will come and take away yours." And Khotian begged his son-in-law (for help). And Mstislav Mstislavich began to beg his brothers, the Russian princes, saying, "Brethren, if we do not help them, they will turn to the Tatars, and so later they (the Kumans) will be more powerful."

And hence, having deliberated for some time, they decided to start a campaign, responding to the appeals of the Kuman princes. And the warriors began to gather in their respective regions, and began a march against the Tatars after the whole Russian land was united. Soon the Russian army came to a place called Zarub on the Dnieper.

The Tatars, learning that the Russian princes had begun to march against them, sent their envoys to them, saying: "We hear that you, having followed the advice of the Kumans, do march against us. But we have neither occupied your lands nor your cities and villages, and we are not campaigning against you. We came because God let us conquer the godless Kumans who are our slaves and cattle herders. You should make peace with us. If the Kumans came to you, fight them and take all their belongings. We tell you this because we understand that they have done much harm to you and that is why we fight them."

The Russian princes paid no heed to these speeches, but killed the envoys and marched against the Tatars. They set up camp on the Dnieper in the vicinity of Oleshie. And the Tatars once again sent envoys, and they said the following: "You have listened to the Kumans and have killed our envoys. Come, then, though we have not occupied your lands, and it will be an injustice against God and everyone." And the Russians permitted the envoys to go away.

And Prince Mstislav Mstislavich forded the Dnieper and charged the Tatar outpost and took it with a thousand warriors. The rest of the Tatars of this outpost escaped to the Kuman Hills under the command of Gwemia Beg. Since the Tatars found no assistance, they hid their leader, Gwemia Beg, underground so that he would not be killed. But they were attacked at that place by the Kumans, and Gwemia Beg was killed with the approval of Mstislav Mstislavich.

As soon as the other Russian princes learned of this action, they all crossed the Dnieper, and after nine days they came to the river Kalka. They sent the Kuman vanguard, under the command of Yarun, ahead, while the Russian princes and their armies set up camp. Yarun began fighting with the Tatars, but his Kuman warriors failed, and retreated in such haste that they galloped over the Russian camp and trampled it underfoot. And there was not time for the Russian forces to form ranks. And so it came to complete confusion, and a terrible slaughter resulted.

Mstislav, Prince of Kiev, having witnessed this misfortune, decided not to retreat, but took his position over the river Kalka. It was a rocky, rugged place on which he built a stockade and fought off the Tatars for three days. In this fortification with Prince Mstislav there remained his brothers-in-law, Andrew and Alexander of Dubrovich. The Tatar troops that besieged the fortification were led by Chigyz Khan and Teshu Khan. With the Tatars there were also a number of Brodniki (Cossacks) under the command of Ploskyn. This accursed commander pledged by the holy cross that Prince Mstislav and his two brothers-in-law would not be killed, but released for ransom. But this accursed Ploskyn lied, and he bound the princes hand and feet and turned them over to the Tatars. The princes were taken by the Tatars and crushed beneath platforms placed over their bodies on the top of which the Tatars celebrated their victory banquet. And the fortified camp of Mstislav was taken, and all his warriors were slain.

The other princes were pursued to the Dnieper, and six of them were killed there: Sviatoslav of Yanev, Iziaslav, son of Ingvar, Sviatoslav of Shumsk, Mstislav of Chernigov and his son, and George of Nesvizh. But Prince Mstislav Mstislavich, Prince of Galich, escaped by crossing the Dnieper, and he cut loose the boats from the shore to ensure his escape. Only one Russian warrior in ten lived through this battle; in returning to their homelands, many of these were killed by the Kumans for their horses and clothes.

In such a way did God bring confusion upon us, and an endless number of people perished. This evil event came to pass on the Day of Jeremiah the Prophet, the 31st day of May. As for the Tatars, they turned back from the Dnieper, and we know neither from whence they came nor whither they have now gone. Only God knows that, because he brought them upon us for our sins.

Part II

the period of feudal divisions

(1240–1478)

Russia Toward 1480 A.D.

22. *Orison on the Downfall of Russia*

THE *Orison on the Downfall of Russia* belongs to a well-known, but still obscure Russian thirteenth-century literary fragment. It is usually found in miscellanies that contain the *Tale of the Life and Heroic Deeds of the Great Prince Alexander Nevsky*, and always precedes it. However, its style differs strikingly from the tale of Alexander Nevsky. It is very probable that it is the beginning of a longer orison or lamentation bewailing the conquest of Russia by the Mongols. It ends abruptly with the indication that a catastrophe befell Russia. Its style is both rhetorical and pathetic, and reflects a strong nationalistic spirit embittered by the catastrophe. One can presume that a longer description of the Mongol invasion originally followed this introductory part.

Although this orison was not written in verse, it can easily be divided into short rhythmic units, many of which rhyme, as for instance, lines three to eleven. The rhyme and diction of this work have many features in common with those of the *Lay of Igor's Campaign*. Since the author mentions the ruler at the time of the orison's writing as being Yaroslav (Great Prince of Vladimir, 1238–1246), it can be concluded that this work was composed no earlier than 1237, the year the Tatars invaded Russia, and no later than 1246, the year of Yaroslav's death.

This translation is based on the Russian text of Kh. Loparev to be found in *Pamiatniki drevnei pismenosti i iskusstva*, Volume LXXXIV, St. Petersburg, 1892.

✦ ✦ ✦

O Russian land, brightest of the bright,
most beautifully adorned,
thou art marvelous to us, with thy many beauties.
Marvelous are thy numerous lakes,
thy rivers and venerated springs,
steep mountains, high hills,
oak forests, beautiful fields,
many beasts and countless birds,

great cities, wonderful villages, and monastery gardens,
honorable boyars and countless lords,
Christian churches and stern princes.
Thou, Russian land, art rich in wealth
and the Orthodox Christian faith.
Thou spreadest from Hungary to Poland and Bohemia,
from Bohemia to the land of the Yatvags,
from the land of the Yatvags to the Lithuanians and
          Germans,
from the land of the Germans to Karelia,
from Karelia to Ustiug
where live the pagan Toymians,
and beyond the breathing sea,
and from the sea to the Bulgars,
from the Bulgars to the Burtasians,
from the Burtasians to the Cheremiss, and
from the Cheremiss to the Mordvians.
All these vast areas and the people that live on them
were subjugated by God to the Christian people (of Russia)
and to Great Prince Vsevolod
and to his father, Yury, Prince of Kiev,
and to his grandfather, Vladimir Monomakh,
with whose name the Kumans frightened
their children in their cradles,
and in whose reign the Lithuanians
did not dare show themselves from their swamps,
and in whose reign the Hungarians fortified
the stone walls of their cities with their iron gates
so that great Vladimir might not pass through.
And at that time the Germans did rejoice
in being so far (from the Russians) beyond the sea.
And the Burtasians, Cheremiss, Votiaks, and Mordvians
worked hard to pay tribute to Vladimir the Great.
And even the Emperor of Byzantium, Manuel,
fearing lest Vladimir the Great take Constantinople,
was sending rich presents to him.

And so it used to be.
But now a great misfortune has befallen the Russian land,
the land that was once ruled by the great Yaroslav and
          Vladimir,
and is now ruled by Prince Yaroslav
and his brother, Yury, Prince of Vladimir. . . .

23. *Tale of the Destruction of Riazan*

THE *Tale of the Destruction of Riazan* is one of the most interesting and best written accounts of the invasion of Russia by the Mongols under the leadership of Batu. Though the writer of this tale called Batu "tsar," meaning emperor, Batu was actually only a commander of the Mongolian armies that operated in Europe. The Mongolian emperor resided either in Mongolia or in northern China.

This story is contained in many manuscripts of the sixteenth and seventeenth centuries. Apparently it once formed a part of a miscellany that was composed and revised many times by the clergy of the Church of St. Nicholas of Zaraisk, which, according to legend, is located on the very spot where Princess Eupraxy killed herself. The composition of this account, which in our translation is divided into distinct parts, shows its heterogeneous origins. The first contains typical chronicle entries slightly embellished by the usual phraseology of old Russian military tales. The story of the knight, Eupaty Kolovrat, is one of the oldest examples of the Russian heroic type and has several stylistic features to be found also in Russian *bylinas*, or heroic epic songs. Many features of this knightly tale resemble those of the deeds of medieval knights in western Europe. The joust between Eupaty and the Tatar knight, Hostovrul, and Batu's respect for the body of Eupaty Kolovrat and the survivors of his army, would fit perfectly well into the knightly tradition of western Europe. Other details seem to be patterned after the *Lay of Igor's Campaign*, such as the appeal by Great Prince Yury Ingvarevich to the princes of Riazan. In the last part, with its description of the mourning over and burial of the princes who fell on the field of battle, and in the remarkable lamentation of Prince Ingvar Ingvarevich, folkloric and biblical styles are skillfully blended.

It is evident that this is a fictionalized account of the destruction of Riazan and that it was actually written many years after the events occurred. The author apparently used for his source material a short account of the events and a list giving the names of the princes of Riazan but not the dates of their deaths. Therefore, the writer oversimplified the family relationships among the Riazan princes and also mentioned several princes who had actually died either before the battle or some time after: *i.e.*, Prince Vsevolod and Prince Oleg the Handsome are mentioned as heroic defenders of the Riazan land. Actually, Prince Vsevolod died in 1208 and Prince Oleg in 1258. Still, most of the facts and details given in this tale do not correspond to information provided in other documents and chronicles.

This translation is based on the Russian text published by V. P. Adrianova—Peretts in *Voinskie povesti drevnei Rusi*, Moscow and Leningrad, 1949, pages 9–17, 18, and 19.

✦ ✦ ✦

I. Batu Invades Russia

Within twelve years after bringing the miraculous icon of St. Nicholas from Kherson, the godless Emperor Batu invaded the Russian land with a great multitude of his Tatar warriors and set up camp on the river Voronezh in the vicinity of the principality of Riazan. And he sent his faithless envoys to the city of Riazan, to Great Prince Yury Ingvarevich, demanding tithes from everyone—from the princes and from all kinds of people. And they also demanded one-tenth of all the horses in the city. As soon as Great Prince Yury Ingvarevich learned of the invasion by godless Batu, he sent his people to the city of Vladimir, to the faithful and Great Prince George Vsevolodovich, asking that he either send succor against the godless emperor or come personally with his army. However, the great prince neither came personally nor sent help, since he had decided to fight Batu himself. And the Great Prince Yury Ingvarevich, having learned that he would receive no help from the Grand Prince of Vladimir, immediately sent to his kin for help, to Prince David Ingvarevich of Murom, to Prince Gleb Ingvarevich of Kolomna, to Prince Oleg the Handsome, and to Prince Vsevolod of Pronsk, and to other princes. And they started to deliberate as to how to satisfy the godless emperor with tribute. And the Great Prince Yury Ingvarevich decided to send his son, Fedor Yurevich, to Batu with many gifts and supplications that he not invade the land of Riazan.

Prince Fedor came to the Emperor Batu whose camp was on the river Voronezh. And he pleaded with the emperor. The godless, false, merciless emperor accepted the gifts and deceitfully promised not to launch a campaign against the principality of Riazan, but he bragged, and threatened to conquer all other Russian lands. And the emperor began to entertain the Riazan princes, and after this entertainment asked that they send their sisters and daughters to be his concubines. And one envious Riazan courtier told Batu that the wife of Prince Fedor belonged to the Byzantine Imperial Family and that she had a most beautiful body. Emperor Batu, who was false and merciless, became excited, and told Prince Fedor, "Prince, give me your wife so that I may enjoy her beauty."

But Prince Fedor laughed at Batu's suggestion, and said: "It is not our Christian custom to bring to you, the godless emperor, our wives so that your lust may be satisfied. If you conquer us, then you will be the ruler of our wives."

The godless Emperor Batu felt offended, and became angry. He ordered the immediate death of Prince Fedor, and commanded that his body be thrown in a field where it would be devoured by beasts and birds. And the retinue and the warriors of Prince Fedor were also put to death.

One of the servants of Prince Fedor, by name Aponitsa, managed to escape, and wept bitterly, seeing the body of his master. Having noticed that no one guarded the corpse, he took his beloved master's body and buried it secretly. Then he hurried to Princess Eupraxy and told her that Emperor Batu had killed her husband. At that moment the princess happened to be on the upper floor of the palace with her infant son, Prince Ivan. When she heard from Aponitsa that her husband had been slain, she was seized with grief, and threw herself from the window with the child in her arms. And so both were killed.

When Great Prince Yury Ingvarevich learned of his son's death and of the deaths of his son's retinue and warriors, he fell to mourning with Princess Agrippina. And for a long time there were lamentation and sorrow throughout the city. As soon as the great prince recovered from his bereavement, he began to gather an army and to groom his regiments. When Great Prince Yury Ingvarevich saw his kin, his boyars, and his voevodas fearlessly and bravely astride their horses, he raised his hands to the heavens and said with tears in his eyes: "Save us, God, from our enemies and those that march against us. And preserve us from the faithless and make their way dark and difficult."

And then he said to his men: "O my lords and brethren! Since we have received from God his blessing, we must also accept his punishment. It is better, through death, to win eternal glory than to be under the power of the heathen. And I, your brother, am ready to sacrifice my life for the holy divine Church, for the Christian faith, and for the country of our father, Great Prince Ingvar Sviatoslavovich."

And then he went to the Church of the Assumption of the Blessed Virgin, and prayed there. And he cried before the icon of the Blessed Virgin and prayed to the great worker of miracles, St. Nicholas, and to his holy kin, Sts. Boris and Gleb. And for the last time he kissed Great Princess Agrippina. And he received the blessings of the bishop and the priests.

II. Batu Defeats Prince Yury

And they marched against the infidel Batu, and meeting him on the border of the principality of Riazan, attacked and began to fight both fiercely and bravely. And it was a terrible and awesome battle, and many of Batu's regiments were defeated. And Emperor Batu, seeing how fiercely and bravely did the warriors of Riazan fight, became frightened. But who can resist the wrath of God? Batu's forces were innumerable and invincible. Each Riazan warrior had to fight with a thousand of the enemy. And every two Riazan warriors had to fight with ten thousand of the enemy. And Prince Yury Ingvarevich saw the slaying of his brother, David, and exclaimed in anguish: "O my kind brothers and dear warriors, the flower of Riazan's troops, be brave and resist mightily. Our dear brother, Prince David, was the first to drink the bitter cup to the dregs, and we shall do the same."

And the princes and the warriors changed horses and once again began to fight fiercely. And they cut through the many strong lines of the Tatar regiments, fighting bravely and fiercely. And all the Tatar regiments were struck with awe upon seeing the bravery and power of the Riazan armies. And they fought with such intensity that even the earth began to moan, and confusion reigned in the ranks of Batu's armies. The strong Tatar regiments were hardly able to overcome the Riazan offensive. In this battle were killed Great Prince Yury Ingvarevich, Prince David Ingvarevich of Murom, Prince Gleb Ingvarevich of Kolomna, Prince Vsevolod Ingvarevich of Pronsk, and many other brave Riazan princes, powerful voevodas, and warriors. Heroes and brave warriors, the flower of Riazan's army, all drank the same bitter cup to the dregs, and fell on the field of battle.*
And Prince Oleg was taken prisoner half alive. All of this happened according to the will of God and because of our sins.

And the Emperor Batu, seeing that numerous regiments of his army had been defeated, was seized by awe and grief. He began conquering the Riazan lands, ordering that everyone and everything be cut down and burned without mercy. And he lay

---

* None of the men of Riazan deserted the battlefield; all were slain.

low the cities of Pronsk, Belgorod, and Izheslavets, killing everyone in these cities without mercy. And Christian blood flowed like a great river. And all this because of our sins.

When Emperor Batu saw Prince Oleg Ingvarevich, the most handsome and bravest of the Riazan princes, dying from his grievous wounds, he wanted to heal his wounds and win him over to his faith. But Prince Oleg began to reprimand Batu, and called him godless and the enemy of all Christendom. And fire came from the evil heart of Batu, and he ordered that Prince Oleg be cut to pieces. And so he became the second Stephen the Martyr, having received the crown of suffering from the all-merciful God. And he drank his bitter cup to the dregs with all his brethren.

III. THE TAKING OF RIAZAN

The accursed Batu began the conquest of the land of Riazan, and soon approached the city of Riazan itself. They encircled the city and fought without surcease for five days. Batu changed his regiments frequently, replacing them with fresh troops, while the citizens of Riazan fought without relief. And many citizens were killed and others wounded. Still others were exhausted by their great efforts and their wounds. On the dawn of the sixth day the pagan warriors began to storm the city, some with firebrands, some with battering rams, and others with countless scaling ladders for ascending the walls of the city. And they took the city of Riazan on the 21st day of December. And the Tatars came to the Cathedral of the Assumption of the Blessed Virgin, and they cut to pieces the Great Princess Agrippina, her daughters-in-law, and other princesses. They burned to death the bishops and the priests and put the torch to the holy church. And the Tatars cut down many people, including women and children. Still others were drowned in the river. And they killed without exception all monks and priests. And they burned this holy city with all its beauty and wealth, and they captured the relatives of the Riazan princes, the princes of Kiev and Chernigov. And churches of God were destroyed, and much blood was spilled on the holy altars. And not one man remained alive in the city. All were dead. All had drunk the same bitter cup to the dregs. And there was not even anyone to mourn the dead. Neither father nor mother could mourn their dead children, nor the children their fathers or mothers. Nor could a brother mourn the death of his brother, nor relatives their relatives. All were dead. And this happened for our sins.

IV. EUPATY THE FEARLESS

Seeing this terrible letting of Christian blood, the heart of godless Batu became even more hardened, and he marched against the cities of Suzdal and Vladimir, intending to conquer all Russian lands, to uproot the Christian faith, and to destroy the churches of God. At that time a Riazan lord, Eupaty Kolovrat, who was in Chernigov at the time of the destruction of the city of Riazan, heard of Batu's invasion. He left Chernigov with a small force and hurried to Riazan. When he came to the land of Riazan he saw it devastated and the cities destroyed, the rulers killed, and the people dead. And he rushed to the city of Riazan and found it destroyed, the rulers killed, and the people slaughtered. Some of them were cut down, while others were burned, and still others were drowned. And Eupaty wept with great sorrow and his heart became angry. He gathered a small force of seventeen hundred men who had been preserved by God outside the city. And they hurriedly pursued the godless emperor. And with difficulty they caught up with him in the principality of Suzdal, and suddenly fell upon his camp. And there began a battle without mercy, and confusion reigned. And the Tatars lost their heads from fear as Eupaty fought so fiercely that his sword became dull, and, taking a sword from a fallen Tatar, he would cut them down with their own swords. The Tatars thought that the Russians had risen from the dead, and Eupaty was riding through the ranks of the Tatar regiments so bravely that Batu himself became frightened.

With great effort the Tatars managed to capture five men from Eupaty's regiments, and then only because they were exhausted from their wounds. They were brought before the Tatar emperor, and he asked them, "Why do you cause me such evil?"

The warriors answered: "We are of the Christian faith, knights of the Great Prince Yury of Riazan, and from the regiment of Eupaty Kolovrat. We were sent by Prince Ingvar Ingvarevich to you, the powerful emperor, to honor you, to chase you away with honors, and to render unto you all honors. Do not wonder, Emperor, that we have not had time to serve up the bitter cup to your entire army." And the emperor admired their witty answers. And he sent his brother-in-law, Hostovrul, against Eupaty, and with Hostovrul went strong regiments. Hostovrul bragged to the emperor, and promised to bring back Eupaty alive.

Eupaty was encircled by Tatar troops because they wished to take him alive. And Hostovrul rode out against Eupaty, but

Eupaty was a giant, and with one blow he cleft Hostovrul to the saddle. And once more he began to cut down the Tatar troops, and he killed many of Batu's best knights. Some were cut down, while others were cleft to their waist, and still others were cleft to their saddles. The Tatars became afraid, seeing what a giant Eupaty was. And then they brought up catapults and began showering rocks upon him. And they finally killed Eupaty Kolovrat, but only with great difficulty.

Eupaty's body was brought before Batu, and the emperor sent for his princes, lords, and commanders, and all marveled at the courage, power, and bravery of the Riazan warriors. And the lords, commanders, and princes told Batu: "We were in many battles with many emperors in many lands, but never have we seen such courageous heroes, and even our fathers never told us of such. They are winged people. They do not think about death, and they fight bravely and courageously on their horses, one against a thousand, and two against ten thousand warriors. None of them would abandon the battlefield alive."

And Batu looked at Eupaty's body, and said: "O Kolovrat Eupaty, you have honored us with your courage, and you, with your small army, have killed many knights of my powerful horde and have defeated many of my regiments. If such a knight would serve with me, I would keep him very close to my heart." And he gave up Eupaty's body to the remainder of the Riazan force that had been captured on the battlefield. And Batu gave orders that the prisoners should be released and that no harm should come to them.

V. Prince Ingvar Buries the Dead

Prince Ingvar Ingvarevich (the brother of Great Prince Yury Ingvarevich of Riazan) returned from Chernigov, having been there with his relative, Prince Michael, at the time of the destruction of Riazan. And so he was preserved by God from the enemy of all Christendom. Prince Ingvar Ingvarevich found his fatherland devastated, and learned that all his brothers had been killed by the impure, lawbreaking Batu. And he came to the city of Riazan and found the city destroyed, and his mother and sisters-in-law, his relatives, and many other people lying dead. And he found the churches burned and all valuables taken from the common treasury of Chernigov and Riazan. When Prince Ingvar saw this great and enduring destruction he shrieked aloud in his sorrow, sounding as a trumpet summoning the army or as an organ resounding. And after these rending shrieks and horrifying lamentations, Prince Ingvar fell to the ground as if dead. With great difficulty and the help of water and a fresh breeze did he recover. And finally his soul did revive in his body.

Who would not so lament such a catastrophe? Who would not bewail the deaths of so many Orthodox people? Who would not mourn the death of so many rulers? Who would not mourn such a dispersion?

And Prince Ingvar searched through the bodies, and found the body of his mother, Princess Agrippina, and those of his brothers' wives. And he called a priest from villages that were preserved by God, and he buried his mother and the wives of his deceased brothers with great lamentations in place of the psalms and chants. And he cried and lamented terribly. And he buried the bodies of the other dead and he cleaned the city. And he had the city blessed by a priest and he gathered the few survivors and comforted them. And he lamented for a long time, thinking of his mother, his brothers, his relatives, and all the people of Riazan who had met such untimely deaths.

And all this happened because of our sins. There used to be the city of Riazan in the land of Riazan, but its wealth disappeared and its glory ceased, and there is nothing to be seen in the city excepting smoke, ashes, and barren earth. All churches and the cathedral were burned. And not only this city, but many others were conquered. There is neither the ringing of the church bells nor church services. And instead of joy, there are only uninterrupted lamentations.

And Prince Ingvar went to the place where his brethren were killed by the impious emperor Batu. Great Prince Yury of Riazan, Prince David of Murom, Prince Vsevolod of Pronsk, Prince Gleb of Kolomna, many other princes, boyars, voevodas, and warriors —indeed, all the best souls of Riazan—were lying on the barren earth and frozen grass. And they were covered with snow and ice, and no one cared for them. Beasts devoured their bodies, and a multitude of birds tore them to pieces. And they were lying together, even as they had fallen together. They all drank the same bitter cup to the dregs.

And when Prince Ingvar Ingvarevich saw this great number of corpses lying on the earth, he shrieked bitterly, like a trumpet resounding. He fell to the ground, and tears flowed from his eyes in a stream. And Prince Ingvar spoke in great sadness:

"O my dear brethren and warriors!
O my treasured lives!
How could you close your eyes

and leave me alone in such misfortune?
How could you disappear from my sight,
treasures of my life?
O my beautiful flowers!
O my unripened vineyard!
Why won't you speak to me, your brother?
Never again will you make my life sweet.
Why won't you look at me?
Why won't you talk with me?
How could you, fruitful gardens,
born of the same father,
and from the same womb of Great Princess Agrippina,
and fed by the same breast, forget me?
To whom have you forsaken me, your brother?
You did fade too early, my dear eastern stars.
You set so early, my dear suns.
You lie on this deserted land watched over by no one!
No one renders you honor or glory.
Indeed, your days of glory have dimmed.
Where is your power?
You, who used to be rulers of many lands,
now lie on this barren earth,
and your faces darken from decay.
O my dear brothers!
O my dear warriors!
Never again shall we share joys.
O my bright lights,
Why were you extinguished?
I have not had enough joy with you!
If God hears your prayers,
pray that I, your brother, might join you!
After days of joy have come those of tears and sorrow.
After pleasures and happiness,
have come lamenting and mourning.
O, why did I not die before you
so that I would not have had to see your deaths?
This is my bitter fate!
Do you hear my unhappy words that fall so sadly?
O mother earth!
O forest of oak, lament with me!
And how shall I describe these days
in which perished
so many rulers and warriors,
so many brave and dashing heroes of Riazan?

> None returned,
> but all drank the same bitter cup to the dregs.
> My tongue does not obey me,
> my lips close,
> my sight darkens,
> my strength ebbs,
> for great is the sorrow of my soul."

And there was great sorrow and sadness, tears and sighs, fears and trembling, because of the evil ones that attacked our land. Great Prince Ingvar raised his hands to the heavens, and prayed tearfully:

> "O Lord, my God,
> I place my hope in thee.
> Save and preserve me from my persecutors.
> O my most holy Mother of Christ, my Savior,
> don't forsake me in my hour of grief.
> Boris and Gleb, our great martyrs and ancestors,
> be of help to me in battle, lowly sinner that I am.
> My brethren and warriors,
> help me with your prayers in my struggles against the
>   enemy,
> these children of Hagar,
> these grandchildren of Ishmael."

And then Prince Ingvar began to search among the bodies of the dead, and he took for burial the bodies of his brothers, Great Prince Yury, Prince Gleb of Kolomna, and of other princes related to him, as well as those of many other boyars and voevodas well known to him. And he transported the bodies to the city of Riazan, and buried them with honor. And the bodies of the others, which were lying on the devastated earth, he buried and had the last rites pronounced over them. Having buried all of them, Prince Ingvar then went to the city of Pronsk where he gathered the pieces of his slain brother, the peaceful and Christ-loving Prince Oleg. And he ordered the body returned to the city of Riazan, and he himself carried the venerable head of Prince Oleg to the city. And he kissed it with respect, and placed the body in the same coffin with the body of Great Prince Yury. In the vicinity of this grave were buried the remains of Princes David and Gleb in a single coffin. And then Prince Ingvar went to the river Voronezh where Prince Fedor Yurevich had been killed at the order of Batu. And

Prince Ingvar shed many tears over the body of Prince Fedor and he brought it to the city of Riazan, and in the vicinity of the icon of the great maker of miracles, St. Nicholas, he buried Prince Fedor together with his wife, faithful Princess Eupraxy, and his son, Prince Ivan. And he placed stone crosses over the graves. . . .

Then faithful Prince Ingvar, whose baptismal name was Cosmas, took the throne of his father, Ingvar Sviatoslavovich. And he restored the land of Riazan and he erected churches and monasteries. And he consoled the settlers and gathered his people together. And he was a great joy for the Christians who, with the help of God's strong hand, had escaped the godless infidel, Emperor Batu. And he put Prince Michael Vsevolodovich of Pronsk in his father's patrimony.

24. Sofony of Riazan: Zadonshchina

ON SEPTEMBER 8, 1380, Russian troops, under the command of the Great Prince of Moscow, Dmitry, defeated the Tatar armies, 300,000 strong, lead by Mamay, Khan of the Golden Horde. It was the first time, after one and a half centuries of Tatar domination over the Russian land, that the Russians defeated the Tatars. This battle did not bring an immediate end to the Tatar yoke, but it was a great victory for the Russians, both weakening the domination of the Tatars and fostering the unification of the Russian lands. Thus, it is not surprising that this important historical event is recorded in various literary works. Among them, the most interesting is the *Lay of Great Prince Dmitry Ivanovich and his Brother, Prince Vladimir Andreevich*, written by Sofony of Riazan. It is known in Russian as *Zadonshchina*, meaning "The Tale of Events Beyond the Don," because the battle took place not far from the Don River, on the Kulikovo prairie. *Zadonshchina* was the title used in one of several extant manuscripts by Sofony of Riazan.

The purpose of this poetic lay was not to give a detailed historical account of the background and development of this battle, one of the most memorable in Russian history. The author omitted a considerable number of events that were of importance to the final outcome of the conflict, while many others were consolidated for the sake of poetic unity. Instead, the author wished to give an epic account of the Russians' efforts, and to stress the importance of this, the first decisive victory over the Tatars.

For the basic patterns of this lay, Sofony of Riazan turned to the greatest poetic work of Kievan Russia, the *Lay of Igor's Campaign*. In many respects he imitated this work, using its symbolic parallelisms, metaphors, alliterative patterns, and poetic imagery. Some sentences are taken word for word from the text of the earlier *Lay* (*Slovo*). Still, Sofony of Riazan created a lay that is very different from that about Igor, not only in its historical perspectives and political conceptions but also in its structure and in the development of narrative line.

Like the author of the tale of Igor, Sofony of Riazan, in writing this work, had in mind not only a poetic account of the battle but also an appeal to Russian unity and Russian national feelings. But, whereas the *Lay of Igor's Campaign* is primarily a lyrical appeal, *Zadonshchina* has a very definite narrative scheme that gives a more realistic account of events. Unlike the *Lay*, the lyrical elements in this work are minimized, and the reminiscences of past feuds, so central to the *Lay*, are practically absent. *Zadonshchina*, like the *Lay*, was written not in verse but in rhythmic prose consisting of clearly distinguishable units.

The present translation is based on the text edited by V. P. Adrianova-Peretts, which is itself based on various medieval manuscripts of the work. This text was published in *Voinskie povesti drevnei Rusi*, in the series *Literaturnye Pamiatniki*, Moscow and Leningrad, 1949, pages 33–41. The division into chapters and stanzas, as well as the typographic arrangement, was made by the translator to facilitate reading.

✦ ✦ ✦

Proemium

Great Prince Dmitry Ivanovich, with his brother,[1] Prince Vladimir Andreevich, and his voevodas, attended a banquet at the house of Mikula Vasilievich. (And Prince Dmitry Ivanovich spoke, saying:)

"Do you know, dear brothers, that Emperor Mamai
 invaded the Russian land at the swift river Don
 and is advancing into the midnight land?
Let us go, brothers, into that midnight land,
 the lot of Japheth, the son of Noah,

---

[1] Prince Vladimir was actually his cousin, but among close relatives it was customary to call each other "brother."

from whom has come most glorious Russia.
Let us ascend the mountains of Kiev
and view the glorious river Dnieper.
Let us view the entire Russian land
and beyond the east, the lot of Shem,
the son of Noah, from whom were born
the pagan nomads, the Moslem Tatars."

I. EXHORTATION

They have defeated the race of Japheth on the river Kalka.[2]
And since that time the Russian land has been sad.
And, from the battle on the Kalka to the defeat of Mamai,
the Russian land has been covered with grief and sorrow,
shedding tears and lamenting the loss of her children.
Princes, boyars, and all courageous men!
Let us leave our homes, our wealth, our women and children,
    our cattle,
that we may receive glory and honor in this world.
Let us lay down our lives for the Russian land and the Christian
    faith.
First, the sorrow of the Russian land did I describe,
as it has been done before in the books.
Then, I have described my sorrows and my glorifications
of the Great Prince Dmitry Ivanovich
and his brother, Vladimir Andreevich.
Let us come together, brothers, friends, and sons
of the Russian land.
Let us knit word after word.
Let us encourage the land of Russia
and cast sorrow on the eastern country, the lot of Shem.
Let us sing of the defeat of Mamai, the infidel.
Let us sing glory to the Great Prince Dmitry Ivanovich
and to his brother, Prince Vladimir Andreevich.

Let us say the following words:
"It behooves us, brothers, to begin with new words
    the telling of the glorious tale of the army of Prince Dmitry
        Ivanovich
    and his brother, Prince Vladimir Andreevich, great-
        grandsons
    of holy Prince Vladimir of Kiev."

[2] In most of the manuscripts the river is called Kaiala, but Sofony
apparently refers to the river Kalka, the site of the battle with the
Mongols in 1223.

Let us tell the tale in the tradition of yore.
Let us race in thought across the lands.
Let us remember the deeds of former years.
Let us glorify wise Boyan, the great bard of Kiev,
for he, wise Boyan, would put his nimble fingers
on the living strings and would sing the glory of
the princes of Russia, of Igor Rurikovich, the first Great
       Prince of Kiev,
of Great Prince Vladimir Sviatoslavovich and
of Great Prince Yaroslav Vladimirovich.
So let us glorify with our melodies and powerful lyrics
this Great Prince Dmitry Ivanovich
and his brother, Prince Vladimir Andreevich,
great-grandsons of those princes who devoted all their
bravery and efforts to the Russian land and the Christian
       faith.

II. THE RUSSIANS PREPARE FOR THE CAMPAIGN

Great Prince Dmitry Ivanovich and
his brother, Prince Vladimir Andreevich,
strengthened their minds with valor,
quickened their hearts with courage, and
imbued their thoughts with martial spirit.
And they gathered their regiments throughout the Russian
       land.
And they remembered the deeds of their great-grandfather,
Prince Vladimir of Kiev.

Skylark, joy of beautiful days!
Fly high into the beautiful blue sky.
Look on the powerful city of Moscow,
sing the glories of Great Prince Dmitry Ivanovich
and his brother, Prince Vladimir Andreevich.
The storm will bring the gyrfalcon
from the Russian lands into the Kuman prairie.
Steeds neigh in Moscow.
Glory rings out over all Russian lands.
Trumpets blare in Kolomna.
Drums resound in Serpukhov.
Banners are raised at the shore of the great river Don.
Bells resound in the great city of Novgorod,
but men of Novgorod remain in Holy Sophia, saying,
   "O brethren, we shall not have time to help
   Great Prince Dmitry Ivanovich."

It seems that eagles fly from the midnight land,
but they are not eagles.
They are Russian princes who fly together
to help Prince Dmitry Ivanovich and his brother,
Prince Vladimir Andreevich, telling them such words:
"Lord, Great Prince, the infidel Tatars have begun
       advancing into our lands.
They take from us our patrimony.
They camp on the river Mech,
between the rivers Don and Dnieper.
Our lord, we will go beyond the swift river Dnieper.
We will win glory for our land in the tradition of old.
We will gain memories for our youth.
We will put our brave warriors to the test
for the Russian land and the Christian faith."

And then Prince Dmitry Ivanovich said:
"Brethren and princes of the Russian land,
we are all descendants of Prince Vladimir of Kiev.
Since our birth we have never permitted ourselves to be
       offended,
neither by the falcon nor the gyrfalcon,
nor by the black raven nor by the infidel Mamai."

If only the nightingale could sing the glories
of the two brothers of the Lithuanian land,
Andrew and Dmitry, the sons of Olgerd,
and of Dmitry of Volynia,
for these courageous sons, gyrfalcons in time of battle,
our brave army captains,
were swaddled under trumpets,
were raised under helmets, and
were fed at lance point in the Lithuanian land.

And Andrew, son of Olgerd, spoke to his brother, Dmitry:
"We are two brothers, sons of Olgerd,
grandsons of Adiman, great-grandsons of Skolomend.
Let us gather together our dear brethren,
the nobles of brave Lithuania, bold and brave fellows.
Let us mount on swift steeds.
Let us view the swift river Don.
Let us drink the water of the Don from our helmets,
Let us test our Lithuanian swords on Tatar helmets,
and our German javelins on the armor of the Muslims."

And Dmitry, son of Olgerd, said to him:
  "Brother Andrew, let us not spare ourselves
    in defense of the Russian land and the Christian faith,
    and in defense of the honor of Prince Dmitry Ivanovich.
    Already, brother, thunder resounds and clamor raises in
                  the stone city of Moscow.
    But it is not thunder, brother.
    It is the clamor of the powerful army of Dmitry Ivanovich.
    The brave Russian warriors thunder in their gilded armor
    and with their crimson shields.
    Andrew, saddle your swift steed,
    for mine has been long saddled.
    Let us go, brother, into the open fields.
    Let us go, brother, and view our regiments."

III. The Coming of the Tatars

Already from the sea there have begun blowing strong winds
into the mouth of the rivers Don and Dnieper.
And they have wafted great clouds over the Russian land,
and these clouds made the sunsets as crimson as blood,
and blue lightning flashes through these clouds.
There will be great clamor on the river Nepriadva,
between the rivers Don and Dnieper.
Many men will fall on the field of Kulikovo,
and blood will be shed on the river Nepriadva.

The carts (of the nomads) have begun to creak
between the Don and the Dnieper.
The Tatars march into the Russian land.
Gray wolves follow after them
from the mouths of the Don and the Dnieper.
They howl on the river Mech and
they wish to advance into the Russian land.
But they are not wolves.
They are the infidel Tatars who wish
to march into the Russian land and conquer it.

The geese have begun to cackle on the river Mech.
Swans have begun to flutter their wings.
But it is not geese that cackle
nor swans that flutter their wings.
It is the infidel Mamai who has entered the Russian land,
and he brought his warriors there.
These winged birds have been brought by misfortune.

They fly high under the clouds.
Ravens croak and magpies speak in their own speech.
The eagles screech menacingly, wolves howl,
and foxes bark, waiting for bones.
O, Russian land, you are far away beyond the hills.

IV. THE RUSSIAN ARMY MARCHES TO BATTLE

Already the falcon and the gyrfalcon
and the goshawks of Belozersk[3] race from the stone city
    of Moscow,
fly high under the blue sky,
ring their golden bells,[4]
and prepare to swoop down upon numerous flocks
of geese and swans.
And so the brave knights of Russia prepare
to strike the great armies of the infidel, Mamai.

Great Prince Dmitry Ivanovich sets in the golden stirrup
and takes his sword in his right hand.
The sun shines brightly from the east,
showing him the road (to victory).
What rumbles? What roars so early before the dawn?
It is Prince Vladimir Andreevich
who prepares his regiments for battle
and leads them to the great river Don.
And he speaks to his brother:
  "Prince Dmitry, Great Prince, don't yield to these Tatars,
    for these infidels destroy our fields and
    invade our fatherland."
Prince Dmitry Ivanovich speaks to his brother:
  "My dear brother, Vladimir Andreevich,
    we are two brothers.
    Our voevodas are appointed and our armies are well known
        to us.
    We mount swift steeds and we wear gilt armor.
    We have Circassian helmets and Muscovite shields.
    We have German javelins and Frankish lances,
    and our swords are made of steel.
    The roads are known to us.
    The rivers are prepared for fording.
    The armies are eager to sacrifice their lives

---

[3] Allusion to the princes of Belozersk.
[4] Hunting falcons had small bells attached to their talons.

for the Christian faith.
Our banners flap in the wind,
and Russians seek honor and glory."

V. The Battle Begins

Already the falcons, the gyrfalcons, and
the goshawks from Belozersk swiftly cross the river Don.
And they strike against flocks of geese and swans.
They are Russian sons who strike against the great Tatar
      army,
And who, with their steel lances, clash against Tatar armors,
whose tempered swords sunder Tatar helmets,
on the field of Kulikovo,
at the small river, Nepriadva.

The earth became black from horse hooves.
The field became strewn with Tatar bones.
Much blood was spilled upon the field.
Strong regiments came together and clashed,
and they trampled the hills and the meadows.
The calm waters of rivers and lakes became stirred up.
The Div[5] called out in the Russian land,
calling all lands to listen.
And the glory of the Russian princes resounded,
from the roar of battle to the Iron Gates,
to Rome and to Kafa-on-the-Sea,
to Tyrnovo and to Constantinople.[6]
O great land of Russia.
you have defeated Mamai on the field of Kulikovo.

The storm clouds began to gather
and from them shone lightning,
and thunder roared mightily.
It was the clash of the sons of Russia
with the Tatar infidels, for they seek revenge for Tatar
      offenses.
The gilt armor of the Russian princes gleamed.
Their steel swords rained upon the Tatar helmets.
It is not aurochs that roar upon the field of Kulikovo.

---

[5] A god or bird of misfortune that was mentioned in the *Lay of
Igor's Campaign*.
[6] Iron Gates: a narrow canyon on the lower Danube; Kafa-on-the-
Sea: an Italian city in the Crimea; Tyrnovo: the capital of medieval
Bulgaria.

It is the wailing of Russian princes, boyars, and voevodas of
   Prince Dmitry,
and the princes of Belozersk who were defeated at the swift
river Don.
And there voevodas Fedor Semionovich, Timofey Valuevich,
Andrey Serkizovich, Mikhail Ivanovich,
and a great many warriors were cut to pieces by the Tatars.
And their bodies lie on the shore of the river Don.
And then a boyar of Briansk, Monk Peresvet,
was ordered to the place where he was fated to meet death.
And Monk Peresvet said to Prince Dmitry Ivanovich:
 "It is better that we fall in battle
  than become slaves of these infidels."
And Peresvet, galloping on his horse,
filled the air with his battle cry.
And his armor gleamed as he called
to his younger brother, Osliabia:
 "Well, brother, it is time for those who are old
  to feel young and for the young to win glory
  by trying the arms of brave warriors."
And the brother, Monk Osliabia, answered:
 "Brother Peresvet, I already see that there
  will be heavy wounds on your body and
  that your head will lie on the feathergrass.
  I can see that my son, Jacob, will also lie in the green grass
  on the field of Kulikovo and for the defense
  of the Christian faith and revenge of the offenses
  done to Great Prince Dmitry Ivanovich."

And at that time in the land of Riazan
at the river Don there was heard neither
the voice of the plowman nor of the shepherd.
Only the crows cawed and the cuckoos cuckooed,
circling above the corpses.
And it was awesome and bitter to look about,
for the grass was covered with blood
and the trees bowed down to the earth in their sorrow.

VI. The Lamentation of the Widows

The birds began to sing their songs of sorrow.
And the princesses and wives of the boyars and voevodas
began to lament the deaths of their husbands.
Maria Dmitrievna, the wife of Mikula,
cried early in the dawn on the fortress wall of Moscow:

"O river Don, my swift river,
 mountains crumble before you, and
 you flow to the land of the Kumans.
 Oh, that you might bring me from there my lord, Mikula!"
And Fedosia, the wife of Timofey Valuevich, also lamented:
 "Joy has abandoned the glorious city of Moscow.
 Never again will I see my dear lord, Timofey Valuevich."
And Maria, the wife of Andrey,
and Xenia, the wife of Michael, lamented since dawn:
 "For both of us the sun has set in the glorious city of
  Moscow.
 News of our relatives has come from the swift river Don
 and has brought great sorrow upon us.
 Russian knights have dismounted their swift steeds
 on the fateful field of Kulikovo."

And the Div cries under the Tatar sabers,
and there the wounded Russian knights weep.

And since dawn nightingales sing sadly
from the walls of the city of Kolomna.
But these sad songs are not sung by nightingales,
but by the wives of Kolomna who lamented:
 "O Moscow, Moscow, our swift river,
 why did you take our husbands from us to the Kuman
  land?"
And they addressed their great prince, saying:
 "Oh, our Lord, why wouldn't you close
 the river Dnieper with your oars?
 Why wouldn't you empty the swift river Don
 with the helmets of your warriors?
 Why wouldn't you build a dam
 on the river Mech from Tatar corpses?
 Why wouldn't you close the gates of the river Oka,
 that we might be preserved from the infidels,
 for our husbands have succumbed in battle."

VII. The Defeat of the Tatars

Prince Vladimir Andreevich, with the Prince of Volynia,
threw seventy thousand warriors from his right flank against
  the infidels.
And they rapidly struck down the infidel Tatars,
their golden helmets gleaming,
their tempered swords raining on Tatar helmets.

And Prince Dmitry praises his brother:
"Brother, Prince Vladimir, you are our shield of iron
   in this time of evil.
   Don't let your regiments cease fighting.
   Don't give in to these evil Tatars.
   Don't pardon these traitors,[7]
   for these infidels destroy our fields
   and have killed most of our valorous army.
   Oh, my brother, it is so sad to see
   so much Christian blood spilled!"
And then Prince Dmitry Ivanovich addressed his boyars:
"Fellow boyars, voevodas, and sons of boyars,
   This is not a banquet for drinking sweet Muscovite mead.
   This is not a court in which to win higher ranks.
   This is the place to win glory for your names.
   This is the place where an old man must act as a young
      man,
   and the young man must win glory."

And it seemed that a falcon flew to the swift river Don,
but it was not a falcon that flew beyond the swift Don.
Prince Dmitry galloped with his regiments beyond this river.
And Prince Dmitry said:
"Brother, Prince Vladimir,
   now is the time to drink of the cup.
   Let us attack the infidel army, brother,
   with our strong regiments."

And the princes advanced onto the field of battle.
Once more tempered swords rained upon Tatar helmets.
Now the infidels can protect their heads only with their arms.
The infidels begin to retreat swiftly from the princes.
Banners flap in the wind.
The infidels flee while Russian cries of victory cover the field.
Their gilt armor gleams.
The aurochs have taken the stronger position.

Indeed, the tide turned, and the Russian
regiments began to cut the Tatars to pieces.
And despair seized the infidels.
Princes fell from their mounts,

---

[7] Apparently some of the Russian leaders hesitated in attacking the Tatars.

and Tatar corpses began to cover the field.
And blood flowed in a stream.
The infidels began fleeing on all sides.
They fled by impassable routes to the sea,
and they gnashed their teeth
and they clawed their faces in despair, saying:
  "Alas, brothers, we shall never escape to our land.
  We shall never again see our children.
  We shall never again caress our wives,
  but we must kiss the damp earth.
  We shall never again campaign against Russia.
  We shall never again receive tribute from the Russian
      princes."

And the Tatar lands began to mourn,
and sorrow and sadness covered the land.
And they lost their courage for campaigning against the
      Russian land.
Their joy disappeared.
The sons of Russia pillaged the Tatars of
cloths and silks, weapons and horses,
oxen and camels, wines and sugars,
jewelry and velvets, and they carried
the wealth of the Tatars to their wives.
Tatar gold jingled in the hands of Russian women.
Joy and happiness spread over the Russian land.
Russian glory was exalted,
while shame was brought upon the Tatars.
And the Div was enthroned, and the fear
of Russian princes spread over the earth.

Oh, great princes of Russia,
fight the enemy with your valorous army.
Fight for the Russian land and the Christian faith,
fight against the infidel emperor, Mamai.

And the infidels threw down their weapons,
and they bowed their heads to the Russian sword.
Their trumpets stopped sounding, and their voices became
      saddened.

VIII. The Escape of Mamai

Like a gray wolf, the infidel emperor, Mamai,
ran away with his guards.

And he came to the city of Kafa-on-the-Sea.
And the Italians asked him:
"Infidel Mamai, how did you dare to attack the Russian
lands?
Once Tatar power spread over the Russian forests,
but the time of Emperor Batu has long passed.
Emperor Batu had four hundred thousand, and he
conquered the whole Russian land,
the whole earth, from the east to the west.
And God punished the Russian land for its sins.
But this time you, Emperor Mamai,
came to the Russian land with a large army,
with nine hordes and seventy princes,
and yet you run away to the sea, and with only eight
soldiers.
And there is no one to pass the winter with you in the
prairie.
Did the Russian princes treat you so badly
that there are no longer princes or commanders with you?
Did they really become drunk with your own blood
on the field of Kulikovo, on the feathergrass?
Go away from us, infidel Mamai!
Go from us, as you went from the Russian forest!"

IX. APODOSIS

We love the Russian land as a mother loves her dear child.
The mother caresses her child and praises it for good deeds,
but she also punishes it for bad deeds.
In the same way, our Lord God
was merciful unto the Russian princes
who fought between the Don and the Dnieper,
unto the Great Prince Dmitry Ivanovich,
unto his brother, Vladimir Andreevich.

And so Princes Dmitry Ivanovich and Vladimir Andreevich
remained victorious on the bone-strewn field of Kulikovo,
on the river Nepriadva.
And Prince Dmitry Ivanovich said:
"It is horrible, brethren, to see the earth
covered with the corpses of Christians,
even as the field is covered with haystacks.
And it is horrible to see that the river Don
has flowed blood-red for three days."

And then Prince Dmitry Ivanovich commanded:
  "Count how many voevodas perished,
   count how many young men were killed."
And Mikhail, a boyar of Moscow replied:
  "Our lord, Great Prince Dmitry Ivanovich,
   we are missing forty boyars from Moscow,
   twelve princes from Belozersk,
   thirty *posadniks* from Novgorod,
   twenty boyars from Kolomna,
   forty boyars from Serpukhov,
   thirty magnates from Lithuania,
   twenty boyars from Pereslavl,
   twenty-five boyars from Kostroma,
   thirty-five boyars from Vladimir,
   eight boyars from Suzdal,
   forty boyars from Murom,
   seventy boyars from Riazan,
   thirty-four boyars from Rostov,
   twenty-three boyars from Dmitrov,
   sixty boyars from Mozhaisk,
   thirty boyars from Zvenigorod,
   and fifteen boyars from Uglich.
   And altogether 253,000 Russian men were
   cut down by the infidel Emperor Mamai.[8]
   But God was merciful to the Russian land,
   and still more Tatars fell on the battlefield."
And then Prince Dmitry Ivanovich addressed the dead:
  "Fellow princes, boyars, and sons of boyars,
   you have found peace everlasting here, between
   the Don and the Dnieper, on the field of Kulikovo.
   Here you gave your lives for the holy Church,
   for the Russian land and for the Christian faith.
   Forgive me, brethren, and give me your blessing
   for this life and for the life everlasting."

And then Prince Dmitry Ivanovich addressed his brother:
  "Let us go, my brother, Vladimir Andreevich,
   back to the Russian land,
   back to the glorious city of Moscow.
   And let us rule there on our throne,
   for we have won glory and veneration.
   Glory be to God!"

---

[8] Actually, the Russian casualties were barely higher than 100,000.

HOMILETIC WORKS

25. *Serapion of Vladimir*

SERAPION of Vladimir is one of the outstanding Russian writers of the first century under the Tatar yoke. Probably of southern origin, Serapion was abbot of the Kievan Crypt Monastery at the time of the Tatar invasion, and later became Bishop of Vladimir, the capital city of the Vladimir-Suzdal principality. After the invasion, Vladimir became a new nucleus for Russian national life and culture. Bishop Serapion died in 1275.

The eloquent homilies of Serapion are distinguished by their highly rhetorical style, and are composed principally of short, rhythmic sentences. Very often these sentences are rhymed and show repetition of an initial word or syllable through several lines. These characteristics tend to convey a sense of poetic unity.

The first sermon is entitled *Sermon on the Merciless Heathens.* By the term "merciless heathens" Serapion refers to those Christians who do not follow the commandments of God and are not charitable to their fellowmen. In the second sermon, *Sermon on Omens*, Serapion speaks of God's wrath, which has manifested itself in earthquakes, conflagrations, and the Tatars' invasion of the Russian land.

The old Russian texts used as the basis for this translation can be found in *Serapion Vladimirskii, russkii propovednik XII veka* by E. V. Petukhov, St. Petersburg, 1888.

❖   ❖   ❖

SERMON ON THE MERCILESS HEATHENS

Let us contemplate, brethren, our Lord's love for men.
How does he try to bring us to himself?
What commandments does he place upon us?
What words does he chastise us with?
Yet, in spite of this, we do not turn to him.

He has seen our trespasses multiply.
He has seen us forsake his commandments.
Many admonitions have we heard from him.
Many fears has he inspired in us.

Many of his servants has he enlightened,
Yet what man has become the better for all this?

Then he released upon us the merciless heathens,
violent heathens, people having mercy neither
for the young,
for the weak and aged,
nor for infants.
The wrath of the Lord has descended upon us
even as David said: "He cast upon them the fierceness of his
   anger."

The sacred churches were destroyed.
The sacred vessels were defiled.
The saints were trodden upon.
The prelates were victims of the sword.
The bodies of holy monks became food for birds.
The blood of our priests and brothers,
as if it were water, soaked into the earth.
The strength of our princes and voevodas has disappeared.
Our valiant warriors, seized with great fear, have fled.
Many of our brothers and our children
have been led into captivity.
Weeds overgrow our villages.
Our pride has been humbled.
Our serenity has vanished.
Our wealth was taken from us by the heathens,
inheriting the fruits of our labors.
Our land has become the property of foreigners.
Our land taken from us,
we became the objects of the jibes
of those who live beyond our lands.

Then we realized that
God's wrath is like a torrent from heaven.
Yet we brought his anger upon ourselves.
His favor abandoned us,
and we became deprived of his merciful vigilance.
And now there is no misfortune which will pass us by.
And now we are punished without surcease.
Yet we do not turn to God.
We do not rue our trespasses.
We do not forsake our malevolent ways.
We do not cleanse ourselves of sin,

forgetting the awesome castigation meted out upon our land.
Being reduced to paucity, we act grandiosely.
And therefore evil forces will not cease to torment us.
Envy has increased and wickedness has overcome us.
Pride has turned our heads.
Hatred for friends has taken root in our hearts.
Avarice for possessions has enslaved us
and does not permit us to have mercy upon orphans,
nor does it permit us to be human beings.
We are predatory beasts desiring flesh to appease their
  hunger.
Nothing would prevent us from seizing the possessions of
  others,
even if it came to killing.
But even the beasts are satiated, after having eaten,
but we cannot appease our hunger,
for, when we have gained one thing,
we desire only another.

For wealth rightly come by, God will not be angered,
but as the prophet said:
  "The Lord looked down from heaven
  to see if they were any that did
  understand and seek God."
And he saw that they had all gone astray.
  "Have they no knowledge,
  these evildoers who eat up my people
  as if they eat bread?"

And Apostle Paul unendingly admonished:
  "Brothers, refrain from evil and dark deeds,
  for usurer-robbers will be judged with the idolaters."
And what did God say to Moses?
  "You shall not afflict any widow or orphan.
  If you do afflict them, and they cry out to me,
  I will surely hear their cry;
  and my wrath will burn,
  and I will kill you with the sword."

And now that prophecy has been fulfilled,
for didn't we perish by the sword
and not once, but twice?
What can we do to end the evils which oppress us?
Remember the words of the Holy Scriptures:

to love each other,
to be charitable to all men,
to love thy neighbor as thyself,
to keep the body pure
so that it will not be defiled by lechery;
to cleanse the body with penitence,
if it has been defiled,
to be free of haughtiness,
to render good for evil.

No one does the Lord hate more than the rancorous,
for they will say: "Our Father, forgive us our trespasses,"
yet they themselves will not forgive others.
It is clearly written: "And with what measure you mete,
so shall it be measured to you again."

SERMON ON OMENS

The blessing of the Lord be with you!
Brethren, you have heard what the
Lord himself said in the Gospel:
  "And there shall be signs in the sun,
    and in the moon, and in the stars,
    and there will be earthquakes in many places,
    and famines."

This prophecy of our Lord
has now been fulfilled in our days.
Many times have we seen the sun extinguished,
the moon darkened,
and the stars disquieted.
And recently with our own eyes
have we seen the quaking of the earth.[1]
Now the earth, firm and immovable from time immemorial
by the will of God,
is today moved, quaking because of our sins,
unable to withstand our evil ways.

We have obeyed neither the Gospel
nor the Apostles,
nor the prophets,
nor those enlightened in God's ways:

[1] According to the chronicles, an earthquake occurred in 1230,
just six years before the Tatar invasion of Russia.

Basil and Gregory the Theologians,
John Chrysostom,
and the other blessed fathers
by whom the Faith was upheld,
the heretics were driven out,
and God made known to all the lands.
They have taught us without surcease,
but we are living in evil ways.

For this does God punish us,
bringing upon us calamities and earthquakes.
He no longer chastizes us with words,
but punishes us with afflictions.
God has castigated us in all ways,
yet he has not dispelled our evil ways.
Now he shakes the earth and makes it quake,
wishing to shake, like leaves from a tree,
our evil ways from the earth.
If any should declare that there have been earthquakes
    before,
I should not deny it.
But what has happened to us after the earthquakes?
Were there not famines, plagues, and numerous wars?
But we did not repent.
Thus, by the will of God,
there fell upon us a merciless people
who devastated our land,
took entire cities off to captivity,
destroyed our holy churches,
put our fathers and brothers to death,
and defiled our mothers and sisters.
Now, brethren, that we have experienced such calamities,
let us pray to the Lord, and repent,
lest we incur the wrath of God even more,
and thus bring upon us an even greater castigation.

Much is still wanting in our repentance and contrition.
If we turn from dissolute and merciless judgments,
if we turn from bloody usury,
and from greed, thieving, blasphemy, lies,
slander, malediction, denunciations, and other diabolical ways;
if we turn away from all these,
I know full well that good times will come to us,
both in this life and the next.

For the Lord himself has said:
  "Turn unto me, and I will turn to you.
  Refrain from all evil things,
  and I will keep all afflictions from you."
When will we turn from sins?
Let us spare ourselves and our children.
When have we seen so many deaths?
Many were taken away before they could care for their
  houses.
Many lay down to sleep in the evening,
never to rise again.
Be fearful of such a sudden death, brethren.
If we follow the ways of God,
He will comfort us with his solace,
He will cherish us as his own children,
He will remove the burden of our earthly grief,
He will give us peace in the next life,
where we shall know elation and unending joy
with those who do the will of God.

I have told you many things, brethren and children,
but I perceive that our afflictions will neither lessen
nor change, for many take no heed,
acting as if they deemed themselves immortal.
I am afraid that the prophecy of the Lord
will come to pass for such people.
If I had not told them of God's ways,
they would not have sinned in their ignorance,
but I have told them, and now
there can be no pardoning of their sins.
And so I repeat again to you
that if we do not change our ways,
we shall have no pardoning before God.

I, your sinful pastor,
have followed the command of the Lord
in giving his word to you.

LIVES OF SAINTS AND
BIOGRAPHICAL TALES

26. *Epiphanius the Wise*

THE names of Epiphanius the Wise, St. Stephen of Perm, St. Sergius of Radonezh, and the great painter Andrey Rublev signify the Russian spiritual and cultural revival of the late fourteenth and early fifteenth centuries. St. Sergius, and to some extent St. Stephen, gave a new impetus to Russian monasticism. St. Sergius became the holy patron of Muscovite Russia. His spirit of humility, his contemplation and unending prayers inspired and comforted the Russian people of the late Middle Ages. The wonderful icons and frescoes of Andrey Rublev offered a harmonius and colorful expression of the spirit of complete serenity and humility. For the Russian people these icons became the finest achievement of religious art and the highest expression of Russian spirituality. A contemporary of Andrey Rublev, Epiphanius the Wise, described the lives of St. Sergius and St. Stephen. In these works he made wide use of new literary devices, and perfected a completely new style of writing. Thus a new page in Russian literary history appeared.

Epiphanius gives a consistent, detailed, and well-organized account of the lives of these two saints. His main purpose in writing these biographical works was not to give an account of the life and deeds of each saint, but to portray an ideal type of sanctity. He endowed the heroes of his *vitae* with a number of general traits that he describes in lengthy panegyrics, containing a great number of epithets. The literary style that Epiphanius the Wise perfected was termed "weaving of words" (*pletenie sloves*, in Russian). In this style sentences are nearly deprived of verbs, consisting almost entirely of the adjectives and nouns that characterize the deeds and humility of the saints. Another feature of Epiphanius' "word-weaving" is the abundance of neologisms formed by nouns or combinations of nouns and adjectives, such as "songbeautifier," rather than "beautifier of songs."

Particularly representative of this style is the *Panegyric to St. Stephen of Perm*. Stephen of Perm was a well-known fourteenth-century missionary who converted the Finnic tribe of Permians to Christianity. He also created a Permian alphabet, thus becoming the founder of the Permian written tradition. The text of the present translation is based on the Russian text of the *Life of St. Stephen of Perm* published by V. G. Druzhinin in *Zhitie sv. Stefana episkopa Permskago, napisannoe Epifaniem Premudrym*, St. Petersburg, 1897.

The life of St. Sergius, which likewise abounds in epithets and lengthy panegyrics, was reworked in the fifteenth century by Pachomius the Serb. The present translation is taken from the work *St. Sergius, Builder of Russia* by Nicholas Zernov, and is based upon the simplified Russian text of G. P. Fedotov, who removed the panegyrics and especially cumbersome passages. Even though there have been some stylistic deletions, the overall meaning and continuity of the work remain.

◆ ◆ ◆

PANEGYRIC TO ST. STEPHEN OF PERM

My father, lord, and bishop, although you have passed away, I should like to sing your praises with my heart, with my tongue, and with my mind. When you were alive, I often was your annoyance, but now I am your panegyrist; and sometimes I would argue with you about happenings and works, about some verses or some lines, but now, remembering your enduring patience, your great reasoning, and your blessed humility, I humble myself; I cry, shedding tears.

And now, how shall I call you, my bishop?

> How shall I name you?
> How shall I appeal to you?
> How shall I announce you?
> How shall I regard you?
> How shall I proclaim you?
> How shall I praise you?
> How shall I esteem you?
> How shall I gratify you?
> How shall I present you?
> How shall I weave lauds to you?

> Shall I call you a prophet,
> since you prophesied prophetic prophecies,
> and, like a prophet, explained the hopes of the prophets,
> and among the people, faithless and unlearned,
> you were a prophet?

Shall I call you an Apostle,
since you performed apostolic deeds
and, acting like an Apostle, following the examples of
    Apostles,
acted, following in the steps of the Apostles?

Shall I call you a lawgiver or a lawmaker,
since you gave the law to the lawless,
brought faith to the lawless,
and established the law among them?

Shall I call you the Baptist,
since you baptized many
who came to you to be baptized?

Shall I call you a preacher, since,
like a herald who announces in the town square,
you loudly preached the word of God to the heathens?

Shall I call you an evangelist,
since you proclaimed grace to them
and the Holy Evangel of Christ,
and performed many deeds of the annunciator of grace?

Shall I call you bishop,
since you were the great archbishop and the eldest
    bishop,
since you consecrated priests in your land,
and since you were above all other priests?

Shall I call you a teacher,
since you taught the heathens who had gone astray,
since you brought the faith to the heathens
and taught men who were unlearned?

Shall I call you a sufferer or a martyr,
since, like a martyr, you surrendered yourself
into the hands of men who were cruel in torturing,
since you were as a sheep among wolves,
since you accepted martyrdom, suffering, and torment?

And I, a great and unlearned sinner,
following the words that eulogize you,
do knit words and create words,

attempting to glorify you with words.
Gathering the words of praise,
and adding and weaving words,
I ask: How shall I eulogize you?
Shall I call you
    the pastor of those who have gone astray,
    the redeemer of those who have perished,
    the teacher of those who were enticed,
    the leader of those whose sight has been darkened,
    the cleanser of those who have been defiled,
    the guardian of the soldiers,
    the consoler of those who are afflicted,
    the nourisher of those who hunger,
    the provider for those in need,
    the punisher of those who are simpleminded,
    the sustainer of the offended,
    the one who prays for others fervently,
    the intercessor for the faithful,
    the savior of the heathen,
    the curser of demons,
    the breaker of idols,
    the destroyer of graven images,
    the servant of God,
    the upholder of wisdom,
    the lover of philosophy,
    the protector of chastity,
    the defender of the truth,
    the writer of books,
    the creator of Permian letters?

Many epithets have you received, O Bishop!
Many titles have you won!
Many gifts have you deserved!
Many blessings have enriched you!

THE LIFE, ACTS, AND MIRACLES OF OUR REVERED AND HOLY FATHER ABBOT SERGIUS

I. CHILDHOOD

Our holy Father Sergius was born of noble, Orthodox, devout parents. His father was named Cyril and his mother Mary. They found favor with God; they were honorable in the sight of God and man, and abounded in those virtues which are well-pleasing unto God.

Cyril had three sons, Stephen, Bartholomew, and Peter, whom he brought up in strict piety and purity. Stephen and Peter quickly learned to read and write, but the second boy did not so easily learn to write, and worked slowly and inattentively; his master taught him with care, but the boy could not put his mind to his studies, nor understand, nor do the same as his companions who were studying with him. As a result he suffered from the many reproaches of his parents, and still more from the punishments of his teacher and the ridicule of his companions. The boy often prayed to God in secret and with many tears: "O Lord, give me understanding of this learning. Teach me, Lord, enlighten and instruct me." His reverence for God prompted him to pray that he might receive knowledge from God and not from men.

One day his father sent him to seek for a lost foal. On his way he met a monk, a venerable elder, a stranger, a priest, with the appearance of an angel. This stranger was standing beneath an oak tree, praying devoutly and with much shedding of tears. The boy, seeing him, humbly made a low obeisance, and awaited the end of his prayers.

The venerable monk, when he had ended his orisons, glanced at the boy and, conscious that he beheld the chosen vessel of the Holy Spirit, he called him to his side, blessed him, bestowed on him a kiss in the name of Christ, and asked: "What art thou seeking, or what dost thou want, child?"

The boy answered, "My soul desires above all things to understand the Holy Scriptures. I have to study reading and writing, and I am sorely vexed that I cannot learn these things. Will you, holy Father, pray to God for me, that he will give me understanding of book-learning?"

The monk raised his hands and his eyes toward heaven, sighed, prayed to God, then said, "Amen."

Taking out from his satchel, as it were some treasure, with three fingers, he handed to the boy what appeared to be a little bit of white wheaten bread of the Holy Sacrament, saying to him: "Take this in thy mouth, child, and eat; this is given thee as a sign of God's grace and for the understanding of Holy Scriptures. Though the gift appears but small, the taste thereof is very sweet."

The boy opened his mouth and ate, tasting a sweetness as of honey, wherefore he said, "Is it not written, How sweet are thy words to my palate, more than honey to my lips, and my soul doth cherish them exceedingly?"

The monk answered and said, "If thou believest, child, more

than this will be revealed to thee; and do not vex thyself about reading and writing; thou wilt find that from this day forth the Lord will give thee learning above that of thy brothers and others of thine own age."

Having thus informed him of divine favor, the monk prepared to proceed on his way. But the boy flung himself, with his face to the ground, at the feet of the monk, and besought him to come and visit his parents, saying, "My parents dearly love persons such as you are, Father."

The monk, astonished at his faith, accompanied him to his parents' house. At the sight of the stranger, Cyril and Mary came out to meet him, and bowed low before him. The monk blessed them, and they offered him food, but before accepting any food, the monk went into the chapel, taking with him the boy whose consecration had been signified even before birth,[1] and began a recitation of the Canonical Hours, telling the boy to read the Psalms.

The boy said, "I do not know them, Father."

The monk replied, "I told thee that from today the Lord would give thee knowledge in reading and writing; read the Word of God, nothing doubting."

Whereupon, to the astonishment of all present, the boy, receiving the monk's blessing, began to recite in excellent rhythm; and from that hour he could read. His parents and brothers praised God, and after accompanying the monk to the house, placed food before him. Having eaten, and bestowed a blessing on the parents, the monk was anxious to proceed on his way. But the parents pleaded, "Reverend Father, hurry not away, but stay and comfort us and calm our fears. Our humble son, whom you bless and praise, is to us an object of marvel. While he was yet in his mother's womb three times he uttered a cry in church during holy Mass. Wherefore we fear and doubt of what is to be, and what he is to do."

The holy monk, after considering and becoming aware of that which was to be, exclaimed, "O blessed pair, O worthy couple, giving birth to such a child! Why do you fear where there is no place for fear? Rather rejoice and be glad, for the boy will be great before God and man, thanks to his life of godliness."

Having thus spoken the monk left, pronouncing a dark saying that their son would serve the Holy Trinity and would lead

---

[1] According to an introductory passage here omitted, the future spiritual life of St. Sergius was revealed to his mother shortly before his birth.

many to an understanding of the divine precepts. They accompanied him to the doorway of their house, when he became of a sudden invisible. Perplexed, they wondered if he had been an angel, sent to give the boy knowledge of reading. After the departure of the monk, it became evident that the boy could read any book, and was altogether changed; he was submissive in all things to his parents, striving to fulfill their wishes, and never disobedient. Applying himself solely to glorifying God, and rejoicing therein, he attended assiduously in God's church, being present daily at Matins, at the Mass, at Vespers. He studied holy scripts, and at all times, in every way, he disciplined his body and preserved himself in purity of body and soul.

Cyril, devout servant of God, led the life of a wealthy and renowned boyar, in the province of Rostov, but in later years he was reduced to poverty. He, like others, suffered from the invasions of Tatar hordes into Russia, from the skirmishes of troops, the frequent demands for tribute, and from repeated bad harvests, in conjunction with the period of violence and disorder which followed the great Tatar war. When the principality of Rostov fell into the hands of the Grand Duke Ivan Danilovich of Moscow, distress prevailed in the town of Rostov, and not least among the princes and boyars.[2] They were deprived of power, of their properties, of honors and rank, of all of which Moscow became the possessor. By order of the Grand Duke they left Rostov, and a certain noble, Vassili Kotchev, with another called Mina, were sent from Moscow to Rostov as voevodas. On arrival in the town of Rostov these two governors imposed a levy on the town and on the inhabitants. A severe persecution followed, and many of the remaining inhabitants of Rostov were constrained to surrender their estates to the Muscovites, in exchange for which they received wounds and humiliations, and went forth emptyhanded and as veriest beggars. In brief, Rostov was subjected to every possible humiliation, even to the hanging, head downward, of their governor, Averky, one of the chief boyars of Rostov. Seeing and hearing of all this, terror spread among the people, not only in the town of Rostov but in all the surrounding country. Cyril, God's devout servant, avoided further misfortune by escaping from his native town. He assembled his entire household and family and with them

[2] Grand Duke Ivan Danilovich of Moscow (1301–1341), called Kalita ("Moneybag"), was the actual founder of the Muscovite state. He spread his reign over a considerable part of the land between the Oka and Volga rivers. Rostov was an important city of the Volga.

removed from Rostov to Radonezh,[3] where he settled near the church dedicated to the Birth of Christ, which is still standing to this day.

II. The Hermitage

Cyril's two sons, Stephen and Peter, married, but his second son, Bartholomew, would not contemplate marriage, being desirous of becoming a monk. He often expressed this wish to his father, but his parents said to him, "My son, wait a little and bear with us; we are old, poor and sick, and we have no one to look after us, for both your brothers are married." The wondrous youth gladly promised to care for them to the end of their days, and from henceforth strove for his parents' well-being until they entered the monastic life and went one to a monastery, and the other to a convent. They lived but a few years and passed away to God. Blessed Bartholomew laid his parents in their graves, mourned for them forty days, then returned to his house. Calling his younger brother Peter, he bestowed his share of his father's inheritance on him, retaining nothing for himself. The wife of his elder brother, Stephen, died also, leaving two sons, Clement and Ivan. Stephen soon renounced the world and became a monk in the Holy Mother of God Monastery at Khotkov.

Blessed Bartholomew now came to him, and begged him to accompany him in the search for some desert place. Stephen assented, and he and the saint together explored many parts of the forest, till finally they came to a waste space in the middle of the forest, near a stream. After inspecting the place they obeyed the voice of God and were satisfied. Having prayed, they set about chopping wood and carrying it. First they built a hut and then constructed a small chapel. When the chapel was finished and the time had come to dedicate it, Blessed Bartholomew said to Stephen, "Now, my lord and eldest brother by birth and by blood, tell me, in honor of whose feast shall this chapel be, and to which saint shall we dedicate it?"

Stephen answered: "Why do you ask me, and why put me to the test? You were chosen of God while you were yet in your mother's womb, and he gave a sign concerning you before ever you were born, that the child would be a disciple of the Blessed Trinity, and not he alone would have devout faith, for he would

[3] Radonezh was a village that belonged to St. Sergius' family and after which his family was named. This village, some nine miles from the Monastery of St. Sergius, is the present-day industrial city of Zagorsk.

lead many others and teach them to believe in the Holy Trinity. It behooves you, therefore, to dedicate a chapel above all others to the Blessed Trinity."

The favored youth gave a deep sigh and said, "To tell the truth, my lord and brother, I asked you because I felt I must, although I wanted and thought likewise as you do, and desired with my whole soul to erect and dedicate this chapel to the Blessed Trinity, but out of humility I inquired of you." And he went forthwith to obtain the blessing of the ruling prelate for its consecration. From the town came the priest sent by Theognost, Metropolitan of Kiev and all Russia, and the chapel was consecrated and dedicated to the Holy Trinity in the reign of the Grand Duke Simon Ivanovich,[4] we believe in the beginning of his reign. The chapel being now built and dedicated, Stephen did not long remain in the wilderness with his brother. He realized soon all the labors in this desert place, the hardships, the all-pervading need and want, and that there were no means of satisfying hunger and thirst, nor any other necessity. As yet no one came to the saint, nor brought him anything, for at this time, nowhere around was there any village, nor house, nor people; neither was there road or pathway, but everywhere on all sides were forest and wasteland. Stephen, seeing this, was troubled, and he decided to leave the wilderness, and with it his own brother the saintly desert-lover and desert-dweller. He went from thence to Moscow, and when he reached this city he settled in the Monastery of the Epiphany, found a cell, and dwelt in it, exercising himself in virtue. Hard labor was to him a joy, and he passed his time in ascetic practices in his cell, disciplining himself by fasting and praying, refraining from all indulgence, even from drinking beer. Alexis, the future metropolitan, who at this time had not been raised to the rank of bishop, was living in the monastery, leading a quiet monastic life. Stephen and he spent much time together in spiritual exercises, and they sang in the choir side by side. The Grand Duke Simon came to hear of Stephen and the godly life he led, and commanded the Metropolitan Theognost to ordain him priest and, later, to appoint him abbot of the monastery. Aware of his great virtues, the Grand Duke also appointed him as his confessor.

Our saint, Sergius, had not taken monastic vows at this time

[4] Grand Duke Simon Ivanovich the Proud (1323–1353) was the son of Ivan Kalita. Metropolitan Theognost, the former Metropolitan of Kiev, lived in Moscow and was one of the upholders of the rise of Muscovy.

for, as yet, he had not enough experience of monasteries, and of all that is required of a monk. After a while, however, he invited a spiritual elder, who held the dignity of priest and abbot, named Mitrofan, to come and visit him in his solitude. In great humility he entreated him, "Father, may the love of God be with us, and give me the tonsure of a monk. From childhood have I loved God and set my heart on him these many years, but my parents' needs withheld me. Now, my lord and father, I am free from all bonds, and I thirst, as the hart thirsteth for the springs of living water."

The abbot forthwith went into the chapel with him, and gave him the tonsure on the 7th day of October on the feast day of the blessed martyrs Sergius and Bacchus. And Sergius was the name he received as monk. In those days it was the custom to give to the newly tonsured monk the name of the saint whose feast day it happened to be. Our saint was twenty-three years old when he joined the order of monks. Blessed Sergius, the newly tonsured monk, partook of the Holy Sacrament and received grace and the gift of the Holy Spirit. From one whose witness is true and sure, we are told that when Sergius partook of the Holy Sacrament the chapel was filled with a sweet odor; and not only in the chapel, but all around was the same fragrant smell. The saint remained in the chapel seven days, touching no food other than one consecrated loaf given him by the abbot, refusing all else and giving himself up to fasting and prayer, having on his lips the Psalms of David.

When Mitrofan bade farewell, St. Sergius in all humility said to him: "Give me your blessing, and pray regarding my solitude; and instruct one living alone in the wilderness how to pray to the Lord God; how to remain unharmed; how to wrestle with the evil and with his own temptations to pride, for I am but a novice and a newly tonsured monk."

The abbot was astonished and almost afraid. He replied, "You ask of me concerning that which you know no less well than we do, O Reverend Father." After discoursing with him for a while on spiritual matters, and commending him to God, Mitrofan went away, leaving St. Sergius alone to silence and the wilderness.

Who can recount his labors? Who can number the trials he endured living alone in the wildnerness?

Under different forms and from time to time the devil wrestled with the saint, but the demons beset St. Sergius in vain; no matter what visions they evoked, they failed to overcome the firm and fearless spirit of the ascetic. At one moment it was Satan who laid his snares; at another, incursions of wild beasts took place, for many were the wild animals inhabiting this wilderness. Some of these remained at a distance; others came near the saint, surrounded him and even sniffed him. In particular a bear used to come to the holy man. Seeing the animal did not come to harm him, but in order to get some food, the saint brought a small slice of bread from his hut, and placed it on a log or stump, so the bear learned to come for the meal thus prepared for him, and having eaten it went away again. If there was no bread, and the bear did not find his usual slice, he would wait about for a long while and look around on all sides, rather like some moneylender waiting to receive payment of his debt. At this time Sergius had no variety of foods in the wildnerness, only bread and water from the spring, and a great scarcity of these. Often, bread was not to be found; then both he and the bear went hungry. Sometimes, although there was but one slice of bread, the saint gave it to the bear, being unwilling to disappoint him of his food.

He diligently read the Holy Scriptures to obtain a knowledge of all virtue, in his secret meditations training his mind in a longing for eternal bliss. Most wonderful of all, none knew the measure of his ascetic and godly life spent in solitude. God, the beholder of all hidden things, alone saw it.

Whether he lived two years or more in the wilderness alone we do not know; God knows only. The Lord, seeing his very great faith and patience, took compassion on him and, desirous of relieving his solitary labors, put into the hearts of certain god-fearing monks to visit him.

The saint inquired of them, "Are you able to endure the hardships of this place, hunger and thirst, and every kind of want?"

They replied, "Yes, Reverend Father, we are willing with God's help and with your prayers."

Holy Sergius, seeing their faith and zeal, marveled, and said: "My brethren, I desired to dwell alone in the wildnerness and, furthermore, to die in this place. If it be God's will that there shall be a monastery in this place, and that many brethren will be gathered here, then may God's holy will be done. I welcome you with joy, but let each one of you build himself a cell. Furthermore, let it be known unto you, if you come to dwell in the wilderness, the beginning of righteousness is the fear of the Lord."

To increase his own fear of the Lord he spent day and night in the study of God's word. Moreover, young in years, strong and healthy in body, he could do the work of two men or more.

The devil now strove to wound him with the darts of con-
cupiscence. The saint, aware of these enemy attacks, disciplined
his body and exercised his soul, mastering it with fasting, and
thus was he protected by the grace of God. Although not yet
raised to the office of priesthood, dwelling in company with the
brethren, he was present daily with them in church for the reciting of the offices, Nocturnes, Matins, the Hours, and Vespers.
For the Mass a priest, who was an abbot, came from one of
the villages. At first Sergius did not wish to be raised to the
priesthood and especially he did not want to become an abbot;
this was by reason of his extreme humility. He constantly remarked that the beginning and root of all evil lay in pride of
rank, and ambition to be an abbot. The monks were but few in
number, about a dozen. They constructed themselves cells, not
very large ones, within the enclosure, and put up gates at the
entrance. Sergius built four cells with his own hands, and performed other monastic duties at the request of the brethren; he
carried logs from the forest on his shoulders, chopped them up,
and carried them into the cells. The monastery, indeed, came to
be a wonderful place to look upon. The forest was not far distant from it as now it is; the shade and the murmur of trees
hung above the cells; around the church was a space of trunks
and stumps; here many kinds of vegetables were sown.

But to return to the exploits of St. Sergius. He flayed the
grain and ground it in the mill, baked the bread and cooked the
food, cut out shoes and clothing and stitched them; he drew
water from the spring flowing nearby, and carried it in two
pails on his shoulders, and put water in each cell. He spent the
night in prayer, without sleep, feeding only on bread and water,
and that in small quantities; and never spent an idle hour.

III. THE HUMBLE ABBOT

Within the space of a year the abbot who had given the tonsure to St. Sergius fell ill, and after a short while, he passed out
of this life. Then God put it into the hearts of the brethren to
go to blessed Sergius, and to say to him: "Father, we cannot
continue without an abbot. We desire you to be our abbot, and
the guide of our souls and bodies."

The saint sighed from the bottom of his heart, and replied,
"I have had no thought of becoming abbot, for my soul longs
to finish its course here as an ordinary monk." The brethren
urged him again and again to be their abbot; finally, overcome
by his compassionate love, but groaning inwardly, he said:
"Fathers and brethren, I will say no more against it, and will

(*Above*) St. Sergius. A portrait worked in embroidery of about 1450. (*Below*) St. Sergius and his monks build a fence around the monastery. A sixteenth-century miniature from the *Life of St. Sergius.*

submit to the will of God. He sees into our hearts and souls. We will go into the town, to the bishop."

Alexis, the Metropolitan of all Russia, was living at this time in Constantinople, and he had nominated Bishop Athanasius of Volynia in his stead in the town of Pereiaslavl. Our blessed Sergius went, therefore, to the bishop, taking with him two elders; and entering into his presence made a low obeisance. Athanasius rejoiced exceedingly at seeing him, and kissed him in the name of Christ. He had heard tell of the saint and of his beginning of good deeds, and he spoke to him of the workings of the Spirit. Our Blessed Father Sergius begged the bishop to give them an abbot, and a guide of their souls.

The venerable Athanasius replied, "Thyself, son and brother, God called in thy mother's womb. It is thou who wilt be father and abbot of thy brethren." Blessed Sergius refused, insisting on his unworthiness, but Athanasius said to him, "Beloved, thou hast acquired all virtue save obedience."

Blessed Sergius, bowing low, replied: "May God's will be done. Praise be the Lord forever and forever." They all answered, "Amen."

Without delay the holy bishop, Athanasius, led blessed Sergius to the church, and ordained him subdeacon and then deacon. The following morning the saint was raised to the dignity of priesthood, and was told to say the holy liturgy and to offer the bloodless Sacrifice. Later, taking him apart, the bishop spoke to him of the teachings of the Apostles and of the holy fathers, for the edification and guidance of souls. After bestowing on him a kiss in the name of Christ, he sent him forth, in very deed an abbot, pastor, and guardian, and physician of his spiritual brethren. He had not taken upon himself the rank of abbot; he received the leadership from God; he had not sought it, nor striven for it; he did not obtain it by payment, as do others who have pride of rank, chasing hither and thither, plotting and snatching power from one another. God himself led his chosen disciple and exalted him to the dignity of abbot.

Our revered father and abbot Sergius returned to his monastery, to the abode dedicated to the Holy Trinity, and the brethren, coming out to meet him, bowed low to the ground before him. He blessed them, and said: "Brethren, pray for me. I am altogether ignorant, and I have received a talent from the Highest, and I shall have to render an account of it, and of the flock committed to me."

There were twelve brethren when he first became abbot, and he was the thirteenth. And this number remained, neither increasing nor diminishing, until Simon, the archimandrite of Smolensk, arrived among them. From that time onward their numbers constantly increased. This wondrous man, Simon, was chief archimandrite, excellent, eminent, abounding in virtue. Having heard of our Reverend Father Sergius' way of life, he laid aside honors, left the goodly city of Smolensk, and arrived at the monastery where, greeting our Reverend Father Sergius with the greatest humility, he entreated him to allow him to live under him and his rules in all submission and obedience: and he offered the estate he owned as a gift to the abbot for the benefit of the monastery. Blessed Sergius welcomed him with great joy. Simon lived many years, submissive and obedient, abounding in virtue, and died in advanced old age.

Stephen, the saint's brother, came with his younger son, Ivan, from Moscow and, presenting him to Abbot Sergius, asked him to give him the tonsure. Abbot Sergius did so, and gave him the name of Theodore; from his earliest years the boy had been taught abstinence, piety, and chastity, following his uncle's precepts; according to some accounts he was given the tonsure when he was ten years old, others say twelve. People from many parts, towns and countries, came to live with Abbot Sergius, and their names are written in the book of life. The monastery bit by bit grew in size. It is recorded in the *Paterikon* —that is to say, in the book of the early fathers of the Church— that the holy fathers in assembly prophesied about later generations, saying that the last would be weak. But, of the later generations, God made Sergius as strong as one of the early fathers. God made him a lover of hard work, and to be the head over a great number of monks. From the time he was appointed abbot, the holy Mass was sung every day. He himself baked the holy bread; first he flayed and ground the wheat, sifted the flour, kneaded and fermented the dough; he entrusted the making of the holy bread to no one. He also cooked the grains for the "kutia," and he also made the candles. Although occupying the chief place as abbot, he did not alter in any way his monastic rules. He was lowly and humble with all people, and was an example to all.

He never sent away anyone who came to him for the tonsure, neither old nor young, nor rich nor poor; he received them all with fervent joy; but he did not give them the tonsure at once. He who would be a monk was ordered, first, to put on a long, black cloth garment and to live with the brethren until he got accustomed to all the monastic rules; then, later, he was given full monk's attire of cloak and hood. Finally, when he was deemed worthy, he was allowed the "schema," the mark of the ascetic.

After Vespers, and late at night, especially on long dark nights, the saint used to leave his cell and go the round of the monk's cells. If he heard anyone saying his prayers, or making genuflections, or busy with his own handiwork, he was gratified and gave thanks to God. If, on the other hand, he heard two or three monks chatting together, or laughing, he was displased, rapped on the door or window, and passed on. In the morning he would send for them and, indirectly, quietly and gently, by means of some parable, reprove them. If he was a humble and submissive brother he would quickly admit his fault and, bowing low before St. Sergius, would beg his forgiveness. If, instead, he was not a humble brother, and stood erect thinking he was not the person referred to, then the saint, with patience, would make it clear to him, and order him to do a public penance. In this way they all learned to pray to God assiduously; not to chat with one another after Vespers, and to do their own handiwork with all their might; and to have the Psalms of David all day on their lips.

In the beginning, when the monastery was first built, many were the hardships and privations. A main road lay a long way off, and wilderness surrounded the monastery. Here the monks lived, it is believed, for fifteen years. Then, in the time of the Grand Duke Ivan Ivanovich,[5] Christians[6] began to arrive from all parts and to settle in the vicinity. The forest was cut down; there was no one to prevent it; the trees were hewn down, none were spared, and the forest was converted into an open plain as we now see it. A village was built, and houses; and visitors came to the monastery bringing their countless offerings. But in the beginning, when they settled in this place, they all suffered great privations. At times there was no bread or flour, and all means of subsistence was lacking; at times there was no wine for the Eucharist, nor incense, nor wax candles. The monks sang Matins at dawn with no lights save that of a single birch or pine torch.

One day there was a great scarcity of bread and salt in the

[5] Grand Duke Ivan Ivanovich, son of Ivan Kalita and brother of Simon the Proud, reigned from 1353–1359. His son, Dmitry, was the hero of the Battle of Kulikovo.

[6] The word "Christians" here refers to the Russians themselves; surrounded by Moslem, pagans, and unorthodox Christians, the Russians called themselves Christians. This is reflected in the Russian word for peasant—krest'ianin.

whole monastery. The saintly abbot gave orders to all the brethren that they were not to go out, nor beg from the laity, but to
remain patiently in the monastery and await God's compassion.
He himself spent three or four days without any food. On the
fourth day, at dawn, taking an ax, he went to one of the elders,
by name Danila, and said to him: "I have heard say that you
want to build an entrance in front of your cell. See, I have come
to build it for you, so that my hands shall not remain idle."

Danila replied, "Yes, I have been waiting it for a long while,
and am awaiting the carpenter from the village; but I am afraid
to employ you, for you will require a large payment from me."

Sergius said to him: "I do not require a large sum of money.
Have you any mildewed loaves? I very much want to eat some
such loaves. I do not ask from you anything else. Where will
you find another such carpenter as I?"

Danila brought him a few mildewed loaves, saying, "This is
all I have."

Sergius said: "That will be enough, and to spare. But hide it
until evening. I take no pay before work is done."

Saying which, and tightening his belt, he chopped and worked
all day, cut planks and put up the entrance. At the close of day,
Danila brought him the sieveful of the promised loaves. Sergius,
offering a prayer and grace, ate the bread and drank some water.
He had neither soup nor salt; the bread was both dinner and
supper.

Several of the brethren noticed something in the nature of
a faint breath of smoke issuing from his lips, and turning to one
another they said, "Oh, brother, what patience and self-control
has this man!"

But one of the monks, not having had anything to eat for
two days, murmured against Sergius, and went up to him and
said: "Why this moldy bread? Why should we not go outside
and beg for some bread? If we obey you we shall perish of
hunger. Tomorrow morning we will leave this place and go
hence and not return; we cannot any longer endure such want
and scarcity."

Not all of them complained, only one brother, but because of
this one, Sergius, seeing they were enfeebled and in distress,
convoked the whole brotherhood and gave them instruction from
Holy Scriptures: "God's Grace cannot be given without trials;
after tribulations comes joy. It is written, at evening there shall
be weeping but in the morning gladness. You, at present, have
no bread or food, and tomorrow you will enjoy an abundance."

And as he was yet speaking there came a rapping at the gates.

The porter, peeping through an aperture, saw that a store of provisions had been brought; he was so overjoyed that he did not open the gates but ran first to St. Sergius to tell him. The saint gave the order at once, "Open the gates quickly, let them come in, and let those persons who have brought the provisions be invited to share the meal"; while he himself, before all else, directed that the *bilo* should be sounded,[7] and with the brethren he went into the church to sing the *Te Deum*. Returning from church, they went into the refectory, and the newly arrived, fresh bread was placed before them. The bread was still warm and soft, and the taste of it was of an unimaginable strange sweetness, as it were honey mingled with juice of barley and spices.

When they had eaten, the saint remarked: "And where is our brother who was murmuring about moldy bread? May he notice that it is sweet and fresh. Let us remember the prophet who said, 'Ashes have I eaten for bread and mixed my drink with tears.'" Then he inquired whose bread it was, and who had sent it. The messengers announced, "A pious layman, very wealthy, living a great distance away, sent it to Sergius and his brotherhood." Again the monks, on Sergius' orders, invited the men to sup with them, but they refused, having to hasten elsewhere.

The monks came to the abbot in astonishment, saying, "Father, how has this wheaten bread, warm and tasting of butter and spices, been brought from far?" The following day more food and drink were brought to the monastery in the same manner. And again on the third day, from a distant country. Abbot Sergius, seeing and hearing this, gave glory to God before all the brethren, saying, "You see, brethren, God provides for everything, and neither does he abandon this place." From this time forth the monks grew accustomed to being patient under trials and privations, enduring all things, trusting in the Lord God with fervent faith, and being strengthened therein by their holy Father Sergius.

According to an account by one of the elders of the monastery, Blessed Sergius never wore new clothing, nor any made of fine material, nor colored, nor white, nor smooth and soft; he wore plain cloth or caftan; his clothing was old and worn, dirty, patched. Once they had in the monastery an ugly, stained, bad bit of cloth, which all the brethren threw aside; one brother had it, kept it for a while and discarded it, so did another, and a third and so on to the seventh. But the saint did not despise it,

---

[7] Bilo: a wooden or iron rod used to beat a gong, gongs being used in Russia instead of bells.

he gratefully took it, cut it out and made himself a habit, which he wore, not with disdain but with gratitude, for a whole year, till it was worn out and full of holes.

So shabby were his clothes, worse than that of any of the monks, that several people were misled and did not recognize him. One day a Christian from a nearby village, who had never seen the saint, came to visit him. The abbot was digging in the garden. The visitor looked about and asked, "Where is Sergius? Where is the wonderful and famous man?"

A brother replied, "In the garden, digging; wait a while, until he comes in."

The visitor, growing impatient, peeped through an aperture, and perceived the saint wearing shabby attire, patched, in holes, and face covered with sweat; and he could not believe that this was he of whom he had heard. When the saint came from the garden, the monks informed him, "This is he whom you wish to see."

The visitor turned from the saint and mocked at him: "I came to see a prophet and you point out to me a needy-looking beggar. I see no glory, no majesty and honor about him. He wears no fine and rich apparel; he has no attendants, no trained servants; he is but a needy, indigent beggar."

The brethren, reporting to the abbot, said, "We hardly dare tell you, Reverend Father, and we would send away your guest as a good-for-nothing rude fellow; he has been discourteous and disrespectful about you, reproaches us, and will not listen to us."

The holy man, fixing his eyes on the brethren and seeing their confusion, said to them: "Do not do so, brethren, for he did not come to see you. He came to visit me." And, since he expected no obeisance from his visitor, he went toward him, humbly bowing low to the ground before him, and blessed and praised him for his right judgment. Then, taking him by the hand, the saint sat him down at his right hand, and bade him partake of food and drink. The visitor expressed his regret at not seeing Sergius, whom he had taken the trouble to come and visit; and his wish had not been fulfilled. The saint remarked, "Be not sad about it, for such is God's Grace that no one ever leaves this place with a heavy heart."

As he spoke a neighboring prince arrived at the monastery, with great pomp, accompanied by retinue of boyars, servants, and attendants. The armed attendants, who preceded the prince, took the visitor by the shoulders and removed him out of sight of the prince and of Sergius. The prince then advanced and, from a distance, made a low obeisance to Sergius. The saint gave him his blessing and, after bestowing a kiss on him, they both sat down while everyone else remained standing. The visitor thrust his way through, and going up to one of those standing by, asked, "Who is the monk sitting on the prince's right hand? Tell me."

The man turned to him and said, "Are you then a stranger here? Have you indeed not heard of Blessed Father Sergius? It is he speaking with the prince."

Upon hearing this, the visitor was overcome with remorse, and after the prince's departure, taking several of the brethren to intercede for him, and making a low obeisance before the abbot, he said: "Father, I am but a sinner and a great offender. Forgive me and help my unbelief."

The saint readily forgave, and with his blessing and some words of comfort, he took leave of him. From henceforth, and to the end of his days, this man held a true, firm faith in the Holy Trinity and in St. Sergius. He left his village a few years later, and came to the saint's monastery, where he became a monk, and there spent several years in repentance and amendment of life before he passed away to God.

IV. The Miracles

We shall now turn to the miracles God performs through his elect. Owing to lack of water near the monastery, the brotherhood suffered great discomfort, which increased with their numbers and having to carry water from a distance. Some of the monks even complained to the abbot, "When you set out to build a monastery on this spot, why did you not observe that it was not near water?" They repeated this query with vexation, often.

The saint told them: "I intended to worship and pray in this place alone. But God willed that a monastery such as this, dedicated to the Holy Trinity, should arise."

Going out of the monastery, accompanied by one of the brethren, he made his way through a ravine below the monastery, and finding a small pool of rainwater, he knelt down and prayed. No sooner had he made the sign of the cross over the spot, than a bubbling spring arose, which is still to be seen to this day, and from whence water is drawn to supply every need of the monastery.

Many cures have been granted to the faithful from the waters; and people have come from long distances to fetch the water and carry it away and to give it to their sick to drink. From the time it appeared, and for a number of years, the spring was called after Sergius. The wise man, not seeking renown, was displeased, and remarked: "Never let me hear that a well is called by my name. I did not give this water; God gave it to us unworthy men."

A certain devout Christian living close by the monastery, who believed in St. Sergius, had an only son, a child, who fell ill. The father brought the boy to the monastery, and entreated the saint to pray for him: but while the father was yet speaking the boy died. The man, with his last hope gone, wept and bemoaned, "It would have been better had my son died in my own house." While he went to prepare a grave, the dead child was laid in the saint's cell. The saint felt compassion for this man, and falling on his knees prayed over the dead child. Suddenly the boy came to life, and moved. His father, returning with preparations for the burial, found his son alive, whereupon, flinging himself at the feet of God's servant, he gave him thanks. The saint said to him, "You deceive yourself, man, and do not know what you say. While on your journey hither your son became frozen with cold, and you thought he had died. He has now thawed in the warm cell, and you think he has come to life. No one can rise again from the dead before the Day of Resurrection."

The man however insisted, saying, "Your prayers brought him to life again."

The saint forbade him to say this; "If you noise this abroad you will lose your son altogether." The man promised to tell no one and, taking his son, now restored to health, he went back to his own home. This miracle was made known through the saint's disciples.

Living on the banks of the Volga, a long distance away from the Lavra,[8] was a man who owned great possessions, but who was afflicted incessantly, day and night, by a cruel and evil spirit. Not only did he break iron chains, but ten or more strong men could not hold him. His relatives, hearing tell of the saint, journeyed with him to the monastery, where dwelt the servant of the Lord. When they came to the monastery the madman broke loose from his bonds, and flung himself about, crying, "I will not go, I will not. I will go back from whence I came." They informed the saint, who gave the order to sound the *bilo,* and when the brethren were assembled they sang the *Te Deum*

---

[8] Lavra was the name given a monastery which was independent of local bishops, being under the direct authority of the head of the Russian Church. There were four such monasteries in Russia.

for the sick. The madman grew calmer little by little, and when he was led into the monastery, the saint came out of church, carrying a cross, whereupon the sufferer, with a loud cry, fled from the spot, and flung himself into a pool of rainwater standing nearby, exclaiming, "O horrible, O terrible flame." By the grace of God and the saint's prayers he recovered, and was restored to his right mind. When they inquired what he meant by his exclamation, he told them, "When the saint wanted to bless me with the cross, I saw a great flame proceeding from him, and it seized hold of me. So I threw myself into the water, fearing that I should be consumed in the flame."

One day the saint, in accordance with his usual rule, was keeping vigil and praying for the brotherhood late at night when he heard a voice calling, "Sergius!" He was astonished, and opening the window of the cell he beheld a wondrous vision. A great radiance shone in the heavens; the night sky was illumined by its brilliance, exceeding the light of day. A second time the voice called: "Sergius! Thou prayest for thy children; God has heard thy prayer. See and behold great numbers of monks gathered together in the name of the Everlasting Trinity, in thy fold, and under thy guidance."

The saint looked and beheld a multitude of beautiful birds, flying, not only on to the monastery, but all around; and he heard a voice saying, "As many birds as thou seest by so many will thy flock of disciples increase; and after thy time they will not grow less if they will follow in thy footsteps." Anxious to have a witness of this vision the saint called aloud for Simon, he being the nearest. Simon ran to him with all haste, but he was not found worthy to behold this vision; he saw no more than a ray of its light, but even so was greatly astonished. Filled with awe and wonder at this glorious vision, they rejoiced together.

V. The Patriarchal Charter

One day some Greeks arrived from Constantinople, sent by the patriarch to visit the saint. Making a deep obeisance they said to him, "The all-powerful Patriarch of Constantinople, Philotheus, sends you his blessing," and they presented him with gifts from the patriarch, a cross and a "paramand," and also handed him a letter from him.

The saint asked: "Are you sure you have not been sent to someone else? How can I, a sinner, be worthy of such gifts from the most illustrious patriarch?"

They replied, "We have indeed been sent to you, holy

Sergius." The elder went then to see the metropolitan, Alexis,[9] and took with him the missive brought from the patriarch. The metropolitan ordered the epistle to be read to him. It ran: "By the Grace of God, the Archbishop of Constantinople, the Ecumenical Patriarch Philotheus, by the Holy Spirit, to our son and fellow servant Sergius. Divine grace and peace, and our blessing be with you. We have heard tell of your godly life dedicated to God, wherefore we greatly praise and glorify God. One thing, however, has not been established: you have not formed a community. Take note, Blessed One, that even the great prophet and our father in God, David, embracing all things with his mind, could not bestow higher praise than when he said, 'But now, however good and however perfect, yet, above all, is abiding together in brotherly love.' Wherefore I counsel you to establish a community. That God's blessing and his grace be always upon you." The elder inquired of the metropolitan, "Revered teacher, what would you have us do?" The metropolitan replied, "With all our heart we approve, and return thanks."

From henceforth life on the basis of community was established in the monastery. The saint, wise pastor, appointed to each brother his duties, one to be cellarer, others to be cooks and bakers, another to care for the sick, and for church duties, an ecclesiarch, and a subecclesiarch, and sacristans, and so forth. He further announced that the ordinances of the holy fathers were to be strictly observed; all things were to be possessed in common, no monk was to hold property of his own.

His community having been established with much wisdom, the numbers of his followers soon increased. Also, the larger the supply of offerings to the monastery, the more hospitality was extended. No person in need ever left the monastery emptyhanded; and the saint gave orders that the poor and all strangers were to be allowed to rest in the monastery, and no suppliant to be refused, adding, "If you will follow my precepts and continue in them faithfully, God will reward you, and when I leave this life our monastery will prosper and continue to stand with the Lord's blessing for many years." And to the present day it has remained standing.

[9] Metropolitan Alexis (1353–1378), the son of a boyar from Chernigov in southern Russia, was an outstanding Russian Church leader. He became adviser to Prince Ivan II and Prince Dmitry. Following the policy set by Metropolitan Peter and Theognost, he supported Moscow as the main center of Russian political and spiritual life, and fostered the unification of all Russian lands around Moscow.

VI. The Dissensions

Before long dissension arose; the devil, hating goodness, put about the idea of disputing the authority of Sergius.[10] One Saturday, while Vespers were being sung, and the Abbot Sergius, wearing his vestments, was at the altar, his brother, Stephen, who was standing by the choir, on the left, asked the canonarch, "Who gave you that book?" The canonarch replied, "The abbot gave it to me." The other said, "What has the abbot to do with it? Did not I sit in that place before?" and adding other silly remarks.

Although the saint was standing by the altar, he heard what was said, but he kept silence. When they all came out of church he did not go to his cell; he walked away from the monastery, unknown to all. When he arrived at the monastery of Makrisch,[11] he asked the abbot, Stephen, if one of his monks could lead him to some desert place. Together they searched and finally discovered a beautiful spot close to a river called the Kerzhach. The brotherhood, hearing about the saint, took to visiting him, in twos and threes, and more. Our Father Sergius sent two of his followers to the Metropolitan Alexis, with the request for his blessing and permission to erect a church. Aided by divine favor, a church was erected in a short while, and many brethren gathered there.

Soon several monks from the Holy Trinity, unable any longer to bear the separation from their spiritual father, went to the metropolitan and said: "Holy Lord, we are living like sheep without a shepherd. Command our abbot to return to his monastery, that he may save us from perishing and dying of grief without him."

The metropolitan dispatched two archimandrites, Gerasim and Paul, to the abbot with the message: "Your father, Alexis the Metropolitan, sends you his blessing. He has rejoiced exceedingly to hear that you are living in a distant wilderness. But, return now to the monastery of the Holy Trinity; those persons who were dissatisfied with you shall be removed from the monastery."

Whereupon, hearing this, the saint sent reply, "Tell my lord

---

[10] These dissensions were apparently caused by St. Sergius' desire to introduce a more disciplined and strictly enforced communal life in the monastery, which was in disagreement with earlier Russian monastic tradition.

[11] Makrisch was another monastery situated about twenty miles from the Monastery of St. Sergius.

the metropolitan, all from his lips, as from those of Christ, I receive with joy and do disobey in nothing."

The metropolitan, glad at his prompt obedience, instantly dispatched a priest to consecrate the church to the Annunciation of the Immaculate and Blessed Virgin, Mother of God. Sergius selected one of his followers, called Romanus, to be the abbot of the new monastery, and sent him to the metropolitan to be raised to the priesthood. The saint then returned to the monastery of the Holy Trinity.

When the news reached the monastery that the saint was returning, the brethren went out to meet him. On beholding him it appeared as if a second sun were shining; and they were so filled with joy that some of the brethren kissed the father's hands, others his feet, while others seized his clothing and kissed that. There were loud rejoicing and glorifying God for the return of their father. And what of the father? He rejoiced with his whole heart at seeing this gathering of his flock.

VII. St. Stephen of Perm

Now Bishop Stephen,[12] a god-fearing and devout man, had for St. Sergius a deep spiritual affection. One day he was travelling from his episcopacy of Perm to the capital, Moscow. The road along which the bishop journeyed lay about seven miles from St. Sergius' monastery. When the godly bishop came opposite the saint's monastery, he stopped and said, bowing low toward the direction of the saint, "Peace be with thee, brother in God!" The saint, at this hour, was seated at table with his brethren. Perceiving in spirit what Bishop Stephen was doing, he rose from the supper table, stood for an instant in prayer, then bowing said aloud, "Be joyful, thou shepherd of Christ's flock; the peace of God be always with thee." At the end of supper his disciples inquired of him what he meant. He openly told them, "At that hour Bishop Stephen, going on his way to Moscow, did reverence to the Holy Trinity, and blessed us humble folk." He pointed out to them, also, where this had taken place.

One time, when Theodore,[13] son of Stephen, was with Blessed Sergius in the monastery, he was taking part in the divine liturgy which was being sung by the saint, and with aforenamed

---

[12] Bishop Stephen: refers to St. Stephen of Perm (see introductory commentary).

[13] Theodore was the son of Sergius' brother, Stephen. He later became the bishop of Rostov.

Stephen, the saint's brother. Of a sudden Isaac, who had taken the vow of silence, saw a fourth person serving at the altar with them, of a bright, shining appearance, and in dazzling apparel. Isaac inquired of Father Macarius, who was standing by his side, "What miraculous apparition is this?" Macarius replied: "I do not know, brother; I see a fearful and ineffable vision. But I think, brother, that someone came with the prince." (Prince Vladimir was at this time in the monastery.) One of the prince's attendants was asked whether a priest had come with him; but, no, they knew of no one.

When the divine Mass was at an end, seizing a favorable moment, one of the brethren approached St. Sergius and questioned him. But he, anxious not to disclose the secret, asked, "What wonder did you see, brother? My brother, Stephen, was saying the Mass; also his son, Theodore and I, unworthy as I am. No other priest whatever was serving with us." His disciples insisted, entreating the saint to reveal the mystery to them, whereupon he said, "Beloved brethren, what the Lord God has revealed can I keep secret? He whom you beheld was an angel of the Lord, and not only this time but every time I, unworthy as I am, serve with this messenger of the Lord. That which you have seen tell no one, so long as I am on this earth." And his disciples were astonished beyond measure.

VIII. St. Sergius and Russia

A rumor spread that Khan Mamai was raising a large army as a punishment for our sins and that with all his heathen Tatar hordes he would invade Russian soil. Very great fear prevailed among the people at this report. The puissant and reigning prince, who held the scepter of all Russia, great Dmitry,[14] having a great faith in the saint, came to ask him if he counseled him to go against the heathen. The saint, bestowing on him his blessing, and strengthened by prayer, said to him: "It behoveth you, Lord, to have a care for the lives of the flock committed to you by God. Go forth against the heathen; and upheld by the strong arm of God, conquer; and return to your country sound in health, and glorify God with loud praise."

The grand duke replied, "If indeed God assist me, Father, I will build a monastery to the Immaculate Mother of God." And with the saint's blessing he hurriedly went on his way. As-

[14] Grand Duke Dmitry, reigned 1363–1385, was the hero of *Zadonshchina*, and the first Russian prince to defeat the Tatars in a major battle.

sembling all his armies, he marched against the heathen Tatars; but, seeing the multitudes of them, he began to doubt; and many of his followers, not knowing what to do, were overwhelmed with fear. Of a sudden, a courier from the saint arrived, in all haste, with the message. "Be in no doubt, Lord; go forward with faith and confront the enemy's ferocity; and fear not, for God will be on your side." Forthwith, the Grand Duke Dmitry and all his armies, were filled with a spirit of temerity; and went into battle against the pagans. They fought; many fell; but God was with them, and helped the great and invincible Dmitry, who vanquished the ungodly Tatars. In that same hour the saint was engaged with his brethren before God in prayer for victory over the pagans. Within an hour of the final defeat of the ungodly, the saint, who was a seer, announced to the brotherhood what had happened, the victory, the courage of the Grand Duke Dmitry, and the names, too, of those who had died at the hands of the pagans; and he made intercession for them to all-merciful God.

The Grand Duke Dmitry returned to his country with great joy in his heart, and hastened to visit holy, venerable Sergius. Rendering thanks for the prayers of the saint and of the brotherhood, he gave a rich offering to the monastery and, in fulfillment of his vow, expressed his wish to build at once the monastery of the Immaculate Mother of God. After searching for a favorable place, venerable Sergius fixed upon one by the banks of the river Dubenka, and with the consent of the grand duke a church to the Assumption of our Blessed Virgin Mother of God was consecrated by St. Sergius. As abbot, the saint appointed one of his followers, Sabbas by name, a man of exceeding great virtue. A community was formed, and many brethren joined it.

Once again the Grand Duke Dmitry entreated St. Sergius to come to Kolomna, to consecrate a site for the building of a monastery to be dedicated to the Holy Epiphany. It was the saint's custom to go everywhere on foot. Obedient to the grand duke, he went to Kolomna, consecrated the site, and a church was erected and, at the grand duke's request, he sent him one of his disciples for the founding of the monastery, a priest-monk, Gregory, a devout man and of great virtue. In time a stone church was built, which is standing to this day.

Another time the illustrious Prince Vladimir begged St. Sergius, likewise, to come to his part of the country, to the town of Serpukhov, and consecrate a place by the river Nar, and dedicate a church to the Conception of the Immaculate Mother of God. Once again the saint obeyed the request. This god-fearing

prince also begged him to send one of his disciples, Athanasius
by name. Although the saint found it hard to grant this request,
love prevailed, and he consented. Athanasius being a man of
rare virtue, exceedingly learned in Holy Scriptures—many valuable writings by his hand bear witness to him to the present
day—the saint loved him dearly. To him the saint entrusted the
founding of the monastery, and the forming of the community.
Aided by the prayers of the saint, the monastery was built, wonderful and beautiful, and named "On the Height."

But why pursue further the saint's planting of ecclesiastical
fruit? It is well known how many monasteries were founded by
God's own chosen servant. And, offspring of his offspring, burning bright as stars, they are everywhere radiating a serene and
wondrous life, and a blessing to all.

The Metropolitan Alexis, being old, and seeing his weakness
increasing, sent for St. Sergius. While they conversed, the metropolitan asked to have the cross with the "paramand" adorned
with gold and precious stones brought to him, to give it to the
saint; but he, bowing low in great humility, refused it, saying,
"Forgive me, Lord, I have worn no gold ornaments since childhood, wherefore all the more do I wish in old age to continue
in poverty." The bishop insisted, and said, "I know, beloved,
that thou art fulfilling a vow, but be obedient, and take this
which we offer thee with a benediction." Further, he said to
the saint: "Dost know why I sent for thee? I desire, while I yet
live, to find a man able to feed Christ's flock. I have doubted of
them all; thee alone have I chosen as worthy. I know with all
certainty that, from the puissant prince to the lowliest of his
people, thou art the one they want."

On hearing this the saint was deeply grieved, regarding honor
for himself as a thing of naught, and he pleaded with the
bishop: "Forgive me, Lord, but this of which you speak is beyond my powers, and you never will find it in me. What am I
but a sinner, and the least of men?" The bishop quoted many
sayings from Holy Scriptures, but the saint, unyielding in his
humility, said, "Gracious Lord, if you do not wish to drive away
my poverty from your Holiness, speak no more about my poor
self, nor permit anyone else, for no one can make me otherwise."

The bishop, understanding that the saint would not yield,
allowed him to return to his monastery. Before long the Metropolitan Alexis left this life, in the year 1378 (6885); and once
more the princes implored the saint to accept the rank of bishop;
but, firm as adamant, he would in no way consent. Then a
certain archimandrite, Michael, was raised to the bishopric; but

this man, with great presumption, not only invested himself with the episcopal robes but also proceeded to plot against the saint, in the belief that the venerable Sergius would put a check on his audacity, wishing to occupy the episcopal throne himself. Blessed Sergius, hearing of Michael's threats against him, remarked to his disciples that Michael, vaunting himself of his sacred appointment, would not obtain his wish, for, overcome by pride, he would not reach the imperial city. The saint's prophecy was fulfilled. On his way by boat to Constantinople,[15] Michael fell ill and died. Thereupon everyone regarded St. Sergius as one of the prophets.

IX. THE LAST MIRACLES AND THE PASSING AWAY OF ST. SERGIUS

One day the blessed father was praying, as was his wont, before the image of the Mother of our Lord Jesus Christ. Having sung the "Magnificat" of the Blessed Virgin, he sat down to rest a while, saying to his disciple, Micah, "Son, be calm and be bold, for a wonderful and fearful event is about to happen." Instantly a voice was heard, "The Blessed Virgin is coming." Hearing this the saint hurried from his cell into the corridor. A dazzling radiance shone upon the saint, brighter than the sun, and he beheld the Blessed Virgin, with the two Apostles Peter and John, in ineffable glory. Unable to bear so resplendent a vision, the saint fell to the ground. The Blessed Virgin, touching the saint with her hand, said: "Be not afraid, mine own elect, I have come to visit thee. Thy prayers for thy disciples for whom thou prayest, and for thy monastery, have been heard. Be not troubled; from henceforth it will flourish, not only during thy lifetime but when thou goest to the Lord, I will be with thy monastery, supplying its needs lavishly, providing for it, protecting it."

Having thus spoken, she vanished. The saint, in ecstasy, stood in trembling awe and wonder. Returning slowly to his senses, he saw his disciple, terror-struck, lying on the ground, whereupon he raised him up; but the other flung himself down at the feet of the elder, saying, "Tell me, Father, for God's sake what miraculous vision was this? For my spirit almost loosed its bonds with the flesh from so resplendent a vision."

[15] From the beginnings of the Russian Church until 1448, the head of the Russian Church, who was first the Metropolitan of Kiev and later the Metropolitan of Moscow, was consecrated by the Patriarch of Constantinople. After 1448, the year the Byzantine Church concluded its union of short duration with the Church of Rome, the Russian Church broke away and became independent.

The saint, so filled with ecstasy that his face glowed there-
with, was unable to answer other than a few words, "Wait a
while, son, for I, too, am trembling with awe and wonder at this
miraculous vision." They continued in silent adoration until,
finally, the saint said to his disciple, "Son, call hither Isaac and
Simon." When these two came, he recounted to them all that
had happened, how he had beheld the Blessed Virgin with the
Apostles, and what a wonderful promise she had given him.
Hearing this their hearts were filled with indescribable joy, and
they all sang the "Magnificat," and glorified God. All night long
the saint remained in meditation on this ineffable vision.

After a while, a Greek bishop came from Constantinople to
Moscow, but, although he had heard a great deal about the
saint, his doubt about him prevailed, for, he reasoned, "How can
such a light have appeared in this savage land, more especially
in these latter days?" He therefore resolved to go to the monastery and see the saint. When he drew near to the monastery,
fear entered his soul, and as soon as he entered the monastery
and beheld the saint, blindness fell upon him. The venerable
Sergius took him by the hand and led him to his cell. The
bishop, with tears, confessed his doubts to the saint, and prayed
for the recovery of his sight. The gentle lover of humility
touched his blinded pupils, and, as it were, scales fell from his
eyes, and instantly he recovered his sight. The bishop proclaimed to all that the saint was indeed a man of God and that
in God's mercy he himself had been deemed worthy to behold a
celestial man and an earthly angel.

A moneylender, living near the saint's monastery, and who,
like the strong in all ages, oppressed the poor, ill-treated a certain poor orphan, and, moreover, carried off his pig which was
being fattened, and without paying for it had it killed. The ill-
used orphan went to the saint in great distress and, weeping,
begged for help. The saint, moved by compassion, sent for the
offender, convicted him of wrongdoing, and said, "My son, do
you believe that God is a judge of the righteous and of sinners;
a father to widows and orphans; that he is quick to avenge and
that it is a fearful thing to come under the wrath of God?"
Having reproached him and told him he must pay what he owed
to the orphan, he added, "Above all, do not oppress the poor."
The man, overcome by fear, promised to amend and to pay the
orphan, then returned to his own house. Little by little the effect
of the saint's rebuke grew faint, and he decided not to pay his
debt to the orphan. And, thinking it over in his mind, he went
as usual into his larder, where he found the pig half devoured

and swarming with maggots, although it was midwinter. He was stricken with fear, and without delay paid the debt; and ordered the pig to be thrown to the dogs and birds to eat, but they would not touch it and clear the usurer of his offense.

Now, again, one day, the saint was reciting the divine liturgy with one of his disciples, venerable Simon, the ecclesiarch, of whom we have already spoken, when a wonderful vision was vouchsafed to Simon. While the saint was saying the liturgy, Simon saw a flame pass along the altar, illuminating it and surrounding the holy table; as the saint was about to partake of the Blessed Sacrament the glorious flame coiled itself and entered the sacred chalice; and the saint thus received Communion. Simon, who saw this, trembled with fear. The saint, when he moved away from the altar, understood that Simon had been deemed worthy of this miraculous vision, and telling him to approach, asked, "Son, why are you fearful?" The other replied, "Master, I beheld a miraculous vision; the grace of the Holy Spirit operating with you." The saint forbade him to speak of it: "Tell no one of this which you have seen, until the Lord calls me away from this life."

The saint lived a number of years, continually chastening himself with fasting, and working unceasingly. He performed many unfathomable miracles, and reached an advanced age, never failing from his place at divine service; the older his body grew, the stronger grew his fervor, in no way weakened by age. He became aware of his approaching end six months before, and assembling the brotherhood he appointed his dearest disciple to take his place, one perfect in all virtue, following his master in all things, small of stature, but in mind a continual blossoming, whose name was Nikon. The saint exhorted him to guide Christ's flock with patient care and justice. The great ascetic soon began to lose strength and in September was taken seriously ill. Seeing his end, he again assembled his flock and delivered a final exhortation. He made them promise to be steadfast in orthodoxy and to preserve amity among men; to keep pure in body and soul; to love truth; to avoid all evil and carnal lusts; to be moderate in food and drink; above all, to be clothed with humility; not to forget love of their neighbor; to avoid controversy, and on no account to set value on honor and praise in this life, but rather to await reward from God for the joys of heaven and eternal blessings. Having instructed them in many things, he concluded, "I am, by God's will, about to leave you, and I commit you to Almighty God and the Immaculate Virgin, Mother of God, that they may be to you a refuge and rock of defense against the snares of your enemies." As his soul was about to leave his body, he partook of the sacred Body and Blood, supported in the arms of his disciples and, raising his hands to heaven, with a prayer on his lips, he surrendered his pure, holy soul to the Lord, in the year 1393 (6900), September 25th, probably at the age of seventy-eight. After his death an ineffable sweet odor flowed from the saint's body.

The entire brotherhood gathered around him and, weeping and sobbing, laid on its bier the body of him who in life had been so noble and unresting, and accompanied him with psalms and funeral orisons. The saint's face, unlike that of other dead, glowed with the life of the living, or as one of God's angels, witnessing to the purity of his soul, and God's reward for all his labors. His body was laid to rest within the monastery of his own creation. Many were the miracles that took place at his death and after, and still are taking place, giving strength to the weaker members of the community, deliverance from the crafts and wiles of evil spirits, and sight to the blind. The saint had no wish during his life for renown, neither in death, but by God's Almighty Power he was glorified. Angels were present at his passing into the heavens, opening for him the gates of paradise and leading him toward the longed-for blessings, into the peace of the righteous, the ever-looked-for glory of the Blessed Trinity.

27. *Peter and Fevronia of Murom*

In Russian medieval literature the tale of *Peter and Fevronia of Murom* is a unique instance of a work in which some romantic elements are presented. The love between Peter and Fevronia is considerably spiritualized, however, emphasizing their faithfulness to each other both in this life and in life after death. In this respect, the story of Peter and Fevronia resembles that of Tristan and Iseult, although deprived of any amorous background. This tale can be divided into composite segments, as has been done in this translation. The first, and the most fantastic, part, "The Story of the Evil Serpent," echoes the widely spread motif concerning the effect of the blood of an evil serpent, a motif which can be found in the *Nibelungenlied*. The second section treats the miraculous healing of Prince Peter by a wise and fair maiden, a theme also to be found in both Eastern and European legends and fairy tales. The third part, "The Intrigues of the Boyars," unlike the preceding sections, contains a political polemic attempting to prove that the autocratic rule of a prince is superior to the rule of an aristocracy that leads to its own self-destruction through dissension. The conclusion of this work has hagiographic colorations. Peter and Fevronia appear here as devout and just rulers who care for their subjects, helping the poor and supporting the Church.

Unusual for a work describing the lives of saints—Peter and Fevronia actually were venerated as the saintly patrons of the city of Murom—is their last testament: to remain together in the same casket after death. Here, the elements of the purity and sanctity of the family supersede the usual ascetic tradition of hagiographic works.

Peter and Fevronia, in its language, symbolism, and its use of riddles (as in the speech of Fevronia), clearly reflects a folklore origin. The name Agrica itself plainly shows this influence, for Agrica was an invincible mythological warrior of Russian folk epics who possessed a magic sword with which he slew evil serpents and monsters.

The exact background of this story is not well known. Peter and Fevronia had been venerated in Murom since the middle of the fifteenth century, and they were both canonized in 1547 by an All-Russian Church Council in Moscow. However, this narrative has never been included in the official collection of *vitae* nor was it read in the Church. There are some indications that the life of Prince David of Murom, who ruled there from 1203 to 1228, was the historical source for this work.

This translation is based upon the Old Russian text prepared by Professor M. O. Skripil and published in the collection *Russkie povesti XV–XVI vekov*, Moscow, 1958, pages 108–115.

◆ ◆ ◆

I. The Evil Serpent

There is in the Russian land a city called Murom. I was told that this city was once ruled by a good prince named Paul. The devil, hating everything good among men, sent a serpent to the palace of Prince Paul's wife to seduce and debase her. And when the princess was with the serpent, she saw him as he really was, while it seemed to others who visited the princess's palace that not a serpent, but Prince Paul himself was with the princess. Time passed, and the wife of Prince Paul decided that she could no longer hide her secret. She revealed what had happened to her husband, for the serpent had already debased her.

Prince Paul tried to think of what to do with the serpent, and finally he told his wife: "I cannot discern how I am to deal with this evil spirit. I don't know any means of killing it. But we shall do the following. When you talk with him, ask him cleverly whether he knows how he is destined to die. And when you learn this, tell me, and you will not only be rid of this evil spirit and its debauchery, of which it is disgusting even to speak, but also in the next life you will gain the mercy of our righteous Judge, Jesus Christ."

The princess became gladdened by her husband's words, and thought, It would be good if it would only happen so. And when the serpent came, she began to converse slyly and cleverly with it about various things, keeping in mind her intentions. When it began to brag, she asked humbly and with respect, "You certainly know everything, and so you must certainly know to what kind of death you are destined."

And the great deceiver was himself deceived by the deception of the faithful wife and unknowingly betrayed his secret, saying, "My death will come from Peter's hand and Agrica's sword." The princess, hearing this, concealed it firmly in her heart. After the departure of this evil being, she told her husband, the prince, what the serpent had said. The prince, hearing this, was unable to understand what was meant by the words "My death will come from Peter's hand and Agrica's sword." But, since he had a brother named Peter, he summoned him and told him what his wife had learned from the evil serpent. Prince Peter, learning from his brother that the serpent gave his namesake as the cause of his death, began to think bravely of how to kill this serpent. Yet he was confused by the fact that he did not know what was the sword of Agrica.

Prince Peter had the custom of going alone to church to pray. Once he came to the Church of the Elevation of the Holy Cross which belonged to a convent beyond the city wall. There he was approached by a youth who asked the prince if he wished to see the sword of Agrica. The prince, desirous of fulfilling his desire to kill the serpent, answered, "Certainly! Where is it?" And the youth asked Prince Peter to follow him, and he showed him a niche in the bricks of the altar in which a sword was lying. Faithful Prince Peter took the sword and went to his brother, Prince Paul, and told him everything. And from that moment Prince Peter began to wait for the opportunity to kill this evil serpent.

Each day he visited his brother and his sister-in-law. One day, after he had visited his brother, he went to the room of his sister-in-law, and there he once again found his brother, sitting with the princess. Leaving her room, he met a man from Prince Paul's retinue, and he asked him: "I was just in my brother's room and found him there. Then I went directly to my sister-in-law's room and once again I found him there. How is this possible?"

And the man answered: "It is not possible, my lord. Prince Paul has not left his room since you left him." He went to his older brother's room and asked him: "When did you return to your room? When I left you, I went to the chambers of the princess without losing any time. And yet, when I came there, I found you next to her. I can't understand how you could get there before me. Therefore, I left there, came back here, and now once more I see that you were faster than I in getting here. I don't understand it."

Then Prince Paul explained to Peter that he had not left his room nor had he been with the princess during this time. Then Prince Peter understood what had happened. "All this is the witchcraft of this evil serpent. In my presence he assumes your image for his own so that he would not be killed by me. Brother, do not leave this room, for I am now going to your wife's chambers to fight the evil serpent. I hope that I will be able to slay it with the help of God."

Prince Peter then took Agrica's sword and went to the princess's chambers, where he again found the serpent in the form of his brother. He struck it with the sword, and the evil spirit returned to its true form and died in convulsions. Before it died, however, its blood spilled on Prince Peter. The body of Prince Peter became covered with sores and ulcers from this blood, and the prince became gravely ill. He was attended by many physicians, but none were able to cure him.

II. THE HEALING OF PRINCE PETER

Having heard that there were many physicians in the region of Riazan, Prince Peter told his servants to convey him there. Weakened by his illness, Prince Peter was no longer able to mount his horse. When he arrived in the land of Riazan, he sent all the men of his retinue to look for physicians.

One of the young men of his retinue came accidentally to a village called Charity. In this village he approached the gate of a house in which apparently no one was at home. He entered the house and found no one. Finally, he entered a room in which

he found a beautiful maiden who was weaving. Before her a
hare was jumping and playing about. The maiden said to the
young soldier, "It is indeed unfortunate when the yard is without ears and the house without eyes."

The young man didn't understand the meaning of these words,
but asked where the master of the house was. The maiden answered, "My father and mother have gone alone to weep so as
to pay their debt in advance, and my brother has gone to view
death between his feet."

Once more the young soldier did not understand the maiden's
words, and things appeared to be strange to him. He again spoke
to the maiden: "I came to your place and I saw you weaving
and a hare jumping about before you. Now I hear strange words
from your lips which I cannot understand. First you told me
that it is unfortunate when a yard is without ears and a house
without eyes. Then you told me that your mother and father
have gone to weep alone so as to pay their debt in advance and
that your brother has gone to view death between his feet. I
have not understood a word that you have told me."

The maiden smiled, and said: "Well, it is not too difficult to
understand. You came into the house and found me sitting here
weaving and dressed in house clothes. If we had a dog, it might
have heard you and started barking. In such a case the yard
would have had ears. If my brother were at home, he might
have seen you coming here and warned me. In this case the
house would have eyes. I told you that my parents went to weep
alone so as to pay their debt in advance. Actually, they went to
a burial and wept there. Once death has come to them, others
will weep after them, and therefore they weep now to pay their
debt in advance. As for my brother, I told you that he had gone
to view death between his feet. Actually, he and my father
climb trees and collect pitch. He went just now to climb trees,
and when he does so, he must watch his feet so that he will not
fall. If he should fall, it would be his death. Therefore I said
that my brother had gone to view death between his feet."

The young soldier then said to the maiden: "I see that you
are very wise. Please tell me your name." Upon learning that
the maiden's name was Fevronia, the young soldier explained
why he had come there: "I have come here on behalf of my
lord, Prince Peter of Murom. My prince is sick and covered with
sores and ulcers. He received these afflictions from the blood of
an evil serpent which he killed with his own hands. Since that
time many doctors have treated him, but none have been able

to cure him. Therefore, he ordered us to bring him to this land, for he heard that there are many physicians here. But we know neither where they live nor what are their names."

Fevronia answered, saying, "The only one who can cure the prince is the one who would order that your prince be brought to this place."

"Who would that be? What do you mean by these words?" the young man inquired. "The prince will lavishly reward the physician who will cure him. Tell me the name of such a physician—who he is and where he lives."

The maiden then told him: "Bring your prince to this place. If he is kind of heart and not proud in answering my questions, he will be cured." The young soldier listened to these words and then returned to Prince Peter and told him in detail all that he had seen and heard.

Prince Peter then enjoined his retinue to take him immediately to this wise maiden. And they took him to the house wherein lived the maiden. The prince sent a page to the maiden asking: "Tell me, maiden, who is the man who can cure me? Let him cure me, and he will receive a large part of my wealth!"

Without hesitation the maiden answered the page: "I am the physician who is able to cure your prince, but I do not desire any part of his wealth. However, if I do not become his wife, I shall have no reason to cure him."

The page returned to the prince and repeated to him the words of Fevronia. Prince Peter did not take her words seriously, thinking that it would be impossible for a prince to marry the daughter of a man whose station in life was as low as that of one who collects pitch. And he instructed his page to tell the maiden that she must cure him, and that if she did, she would become his wife. The page repeated these words to the maiden. She then took a small pitcher and scooped up some leaven from a barrel and told the page: "Prepare a steambath for your prince, and, after the bath, spread this leaven over the sores and ulcers on his body. But you must take care not to cover all of the scabs, but leave one uncovered. And then your prince will return to good health." The young man brought the ointment made from leaven to the prince, and the servants immediately prepared the steambath.

While the servants were preparing the steambath, the prince decided to learn how wise this maiden really was, for he had only the word of his servant in this matter. To this end he sent her a small bundle of linen, asking that she make him a shirt, towel, and pants from this linen while he was in the steambath, and if she were successful, she would thereby prove her wisdom.

A servant brought the bundle of linen to Fevronia and repeated the command of Prince Peter. Fevronia, without any hesitation, ordered the man to climb up on the stove and fetch down a piece of dry wood. When the servant gave her the piece of wood, she marked off a piece one foot in length and ordered the man to cut off this piece. When the servant had done so, she told him to take the block to his master and ask him to make from it a spinning wheel and a loom, while she was combing the linen in preparation for making the shirt, pants, and towel.

The servant took the block of wood to Prince Peter and repeated Fevronia's request. The prince laughed, and said: "Go to Fevronia and tell her that it is not possible to prepare so many things from so small a block in so short a time."

Fevronia had anticipated this answer, and told the servant: "Well, if your prince is unable to make a spinning wheel and a loom from such a small piece of wood in so short a time, how can I, in return, weave a shirt, pants, and a towel for him from such a small bundle of linen, while he takes a steambath?" When the page returned to the prince, he was astounded by the wisdom of her answer.

Then Prince Peter went into the steambath, and his servants applied the ointment over the sores and ulcers, leaving only one scab uncovered, as was ordered by Fevronia. When Prince Peter left the steambath, his pains left him, and the next morning all his body was clear and healed excepting the one scab that had been left uncovered. He marveled at the curing powers of Fevronia. However, since Fevronia was the daughter of one of lowly birth, Prince Peter did not wish to marry her. He did, however, send her luxurious gifts, but Fevronia would not accept them.

Peter returned to his native city of Murom with his body completely healed excepting the single scab. Soon afterward, however, more sores and ulcers began to spread from the single scab which had not been covered by the ointment. And then his whole body was once again covered with sores and ulcers. Seeing that his affliction had returned, Prince Peter decided to return to Fevronia once again to undergo the proven treatment.

He returned to Riazan and to Fevronia's house, and despite the fact that he was ashamed for not having kept his promise to marry her, he asked her to treat him once more. Fevronia was not the least bit angry, but said that she would treat him only if he decided to be her husband. This time the prince firmly promised that he would take her as his wife.

The maiden then prescribed the same treatment as before. And when he was healed again, Prince Peter took Fevronia for his wife. And in this way did Fevronia become a princess. And both of them went to Peter's native city of Murom, and there they lived extremely piously, closely obeying the commandments of God. Soon after their arrival in Murom, Prince Paul died, and Prince Peter became the sole ruler of the city.

III. THE INTRIGUES OF THE BOYARS

The boyars of the city of Murom did not find Princess Fevronia to their liking. They, under the influences of their spouses, resented the princess because of her common origin. However, because of her charitable deeds, she was extremely popular among the simple people, and they prayed to God for her. Once, one of the courtiers, wanting to bring strife between Peter and Fevronia, came to the prince and told him: "The princess usually gets up from the table when she is not supposed to do so. Moreover, before leaving the table, she picks up the crumbs as if she were hungry."

Prince Peter decided to see if these accusations were true. He ordered that Princess Fevronia sit beside him at the table. When dinner was over, Fevronia picked up all the crumbs and kept them in her hand as she was accustomed to doing since her childhood. Seeing this, Prince Peter caught her by the hand and told her to open her fist, but when she did so they found fragrant myrrh and incense in the palm of her hand. And from that day on, Peter never attempted to question his wife's deeds.

Many years later the resentful boyars came once again to Peter and said: "Our lord, we want to serve you honestly and want you as our ruler, but we do not want Princess Fevronia as our princess, nor do we want her to rule over our wives. If you are to remain, our lord, you must take another for princess. Fevronia may take her wealth and go away anywhere she may wish to go."

Blessed Prince Peter was of gentle nature and did not become angry, but promised to talk to Princess Fevronia to learn what she would say of this. The shameless courtesans then decided to organize a banquet. They became drunk at this banquet and began to talk arrogantly like loudly barking dogs. And they began to deny Fevronia's miraculous gift of healing, which she had received from God not only for this life but even for after death.

They began talking: "Our lady, Princess Fevronia, the whole
city and all the boyars ask you to give back to us Prince Peter,
because we want him."

Fevronia answered: "You can have him. Only speak with him."

Then the boyars all spoke at once, saying: "Our lady, all of us
want Prince Peter to rule over us, but our wives do not want
you to rule over them. Please, take as much wealth as you desire and go wherever you like."

Hearing these words, Princess Fevronia told them that she
would do as they desired but that now she must ask them to do
one thing that she desired. The boyars, who were not very
clever, rejoiced, and thought that they would easily rid themselves of her. So they pledged to do as she asked. And Princess
Fevronia said, "I want nothing from you but my husband,
Prince Peter."

The boyars deliberated for a short while and then said, "If
Prince Peter will have it this way, we will not contradict him."

They hoped that they would be able to choose another ruler
if Prince Peter did not wish to break the divine commandment,
for it is written in the Gospel of Apostle Matthew: "But I say
unto you, that whosoever shall put away his wife, saving for the
cause of unchastity, makes her an adulteress." And Prince Peter,
following the commandment of Jesus, gave up his rule over the
city of Murom.

The evil lords prepared boats for Peter and Fevronia, for the
city of Murom was situated on the river Oka. And so they went
down the river in these vessels. On the princess' boat was a
courtier who, despite the fact that he was accompanied by his
wife, was tempted by evil spirits and began to stare at Princess
Fevronia with shameful thoughts. The princess immediately discerned his evil thoughts and exposed them to the man. Approaching him, she ordered him to scoop up water from the
river on one side of the boat and drink it. When the man had
done so, she ordered him to go to the other side of the ship and
do the same. When the man had drunk the water, Fevronia
approached him, and asked, "Tell me, did you find that the
water tastes the same on both sides of the ship, or was it perhaps sweeter on one side than on the other?"

The man answered: "No, my lady. The water tasted the same
on both sides."

Then she replied: "And so is the nature of all women. Why
then do you want to leave your wife and think about another
woman?" The courtier then realized that the princess possessed

the gift of reading the minds of men. Becoming afraid, he gave up his evil intentions.

In the evening the boats docked, and when the travelers were disembarking, Prince Peter became seized with doubts as to whether he was right in giving up his rule in the city of Murom. His sagacious wife perceived his doubts, and comforted him, saying: "Do not grieve, my Prince, for merciful God, our Creator, who directs our life, will never forsake us to misfortune."

That same evening the servants began to prepare dinner for the prince. They cut down branches of some trees and, making a spit, put the kettle on. Princess Fevronia, who was walking along the shore, came upon these branches that had been cut from the trees. Seeing them, she said, "Bless them, for before morning these branches will grow into great trees with rich foliage." And so it happened, for when the travelers got up in the morning they found that these branches had grown into great trees with rich foliage.

And when the servants began to load the boats, there came a lord from the city of Murom, saying: "My lord, Prince Peter, I come to you in behalf of all the courtiers of the city of Murom. They ask that you do not desert them, your poor orphans, but that you return as ruler to your native land. Many lords of the city have perished by the sword. Each, wanting to become ruler of the city, killed the other. Those lords who have survived and all the rest of the people beg you to come back, my lord, and rule over us. And we will neither anger nor irritate you again. Some of our ladies did not wish to be ruled by Princess Fevronia, but now these ladies have perished in the feud. Those of us who remain alive do love her, and we beg you not to leave us alone, your humble servants."

Thus Prince Peter and Princess Fevronia returned to the city of Murom, and they ruled according to the commandments of God.

IV. THE PASSING AWAY OF PETER AND FEVRONIA

Peter and Fevronia always helped their people with alms and prayers. They treated all as if they were their own children. They loved everyone equally, and disliked only those who were proud or who exploited the people. Peter and Fevronia lay up their treasures, not on earth, but in heaven. They were real pastors of their city. They always ruled with truth and humility, and never with anger. They gave shelter to pilgrims, fed the hungry, and clothed the naked. And they helped the poor in their misfortune.

When death was nearing, Peter and Fevronia prayed to God that they both might die in the same hour. And they requested that they be buried in the same tomb and in a common coffin in which their bodies would be separated only by a partition. And together they took monastic vows, Prince Peter becoming Brother David, and Princess Fevronia, Sister Euphrosinia.

And it happened that, shortly before her death, Princess Fevronia was embroidering a figure of the saints on a coverlet for the chalice of the cathedral. And a messenger came from Prince Peter, now Brother David, saying, "Sister Euphrosinia, I am ready to die, and wait only for you, so that we may die together."

But Princess Fevronia, now Sister Euphrosinia, answered, "You should wait, my lord, until I finish the coverlet for the chalice of the holy cathedral."

Then Brother David sent another messenger, who announced, "I can wait for you only a short time." Shortly after, another messenger arrived, saying: "I shall soon depart this world. There is no time left for waiting."

Princess Fevronia was just finishing the embroidering of the coverlet, but, hearing these words, she placed the needle in the coverlet and wound up the thread she had been using. Doing so, she sent a message to Brother David saying that they would now die together. And, having prayed, they offered up their souls to God on Friday, the 20th day of June.

After their deaths, some of the people decided that Prince Peter should be buried in the Cathedral of the Holy Virgin, which was within the walls of the city of Murom, and that Princess Fevronia should be buried in the Church of the Elevation of the Holy Cross, which was outside the walls of the city. And they actually did so, saying that it was not becoming for a man and woman who had taken monastic vows to be buried in the same casket. The body of Prince Peter was put in a casket and was placed in the cathedral, where it was left overnight. The body of Princess Fevronia was put in another casket and placed in the church outside the city walls. A tomb, which had been carved from a huge rock as a resting-place for Peter and Fevronia, remained empty in the yard of the Cathedral of the Holy Virgin.

The next morning the people went to the caskets of Peter and Fevronia and found them empty. The bodies of the holy prince and princess were found together in the tomb of stone, which

they had ordered prepared for them. The people, not understanding the meaning of this event, once more placed the bodies
in separate caskets. On the following day the bodies of Prince
Peter and Princess Fevronia were once again found together in
the tomb of stone. Since that time no man has dared to disturb
their holy bodies, but left them in their common tomb in the
yard of the Cathedral of the Holy Virgin, which is located in
the city of Murom. And whoever touched with contrition the
tomb wherein lie the holy relics of Peter and Fevronia always
received comfort and healing.

28. *The Life of St. Michael, A Fool in Christ*

THE life of Michael of Klopsko was one of the most popular
hagiographic works of northern Russia in the fifteenth and sixteenth centuries. Some seventy ancient manuscripts containing
different versions of this *vita* have been preserved, and they
have been rewritten, re-edited, and expanded upon by various
medieval writers. Michael of Klopsko was an actual historical
person, known not only from his *vita* but also from chronicles
and documents. He lived in the first half of the fifteenth century,
came to the Monastery of the Holy Trinity in Klopsko, near the
city of Novgorod, between 1408 and 1412, and died there between 1453 and 1458. This was a period of intense struggle
within the Muscovite ruling dynasty—specifically, between the
Grand Prince of Moscow, Vasily III (or the "Blind"); his cousin,
Prince Dmitry Shemiaka; and the latter's brother, Vasily the
"One-Eyed." The epithets "the Blind" and "the One-Eyed"
indicate the cruelty of this struggle, as each cousin was responsible for the other's mutilation. Shemiaka's memory has become
notorious because of his cruelty and perfidy; in fact, the name
Shemiaka has become a synonym for injustice. His story will be
found in the tale of *Shemiaka's Judgment*. In addition to the
struggle for power among these cousins, the *Life of St. Michael*
also reflects the desire of the Muscovite princes to unify Russia
under their leadership and to incorporate the Novgorodian Republic into the Russian state.

Michael of Klopsko was one of the first Russian *yurodivy*, or
"fools in Christ," as certain people were called who devoted
themselves entirely to the service of God. They accepted voluntarily the role of a fool in order to be able to teach people the
truth of Christ and also to speak the truth to the powerful
princes and lords. These "fools in Christ" usually wore coarse

linen frocks throughout the whole year, ate the barest minimum of food, and walked barefoot, even in winter. In their prophecies they often spoke truths in the forms of parables, and interesting examples of such can be found in this work.

This *vita* consists of a number of episodes that have been placed under subtitles for easier reading. The style of this work clearly recalls the simple, clipped language of the *Novgorodian Chronicle*. Many sentences are so curt that they often require additional words for comprehension, and any such added words have been placed in parentheses. Similar also to the *Novgorodian Chronicle* is the use of "in this same year" to introduce a new topic or episode. The style of "Michael's Advice to the Novgorodian Republic," however, differs considerably from the anecdotal manner and abrupt, curt style of the rest of the story. One can surmise that this section was a late addition to this work and was of a political nature—that is, it was intended to show the people of Novgorod that God himself, speaking through the mouth of Michael, wished Novgorod to become incorporated into the Muscovite realm.

Some of these episodes are presented in the form of anecdotes, and are among the earliest examples of Russian satirical writing. Their language resembles that of later Muscovite satirical tales of adventure, especially *Shemiaka's Judgment*. Michael's *vita* offers an interesting instance of primitive biography written in simple, naïve language and consisting of disconnected episodes from the life of the saint.

This translation is based upon version B of the earlier text of the *Life of St. Michael of Klopsko* to be found in L. A. Dimitrieva's *Povesti o zhitii Mikhaila Klopskogo*, published by the Academy of Sciences of the U.S.S.R., Moscow and Leningrad, 1958, pages 99–110. The subtitles for the various episodes have been supplied by the translator.

◆ ◆ ◆

I. MICHAEL'S ARRIVAL IN KLOPSKO

St. Michael, a fool in Christ, came to the Church of the Holy Trinity in Klopsko in the time of Abbot Theodosius who later became archbishop of Novgorod.

St. Michael came to the monastery on the eve of St. John's Day. The priest Ignatius, who was officiating in the church, began to cense it during the ninth hymn. Then he went to cense the cells (wherein resided the monks). When the priest entered one cell, the door of which was open, he found there Monk Michael who was sitting in a chair before a burning taper. He was writing *The Acts of the Apostles*. Ignatius became alarmed (at the presence of this unknown monk), and returning to the church, informed Abbot Theodosius and the other monks of this. The abbot then took the cross and the censer and himself went to the same cell and found that the door of the porch of this cell was closed. Therefore the abbot went to the window and, looking in, also saw a monk who was sitting and writing inside the cell. The abbot then began to pray, saying: "O Lord, Jesus Christ, Son of God, be merciful unto us."

After he had said his prayers, the abbot addressed the monk: "Who are you, my son, a man or a devil?"

And Michael answered with the same words, "Are you a man or a devil?"

The alarmed abbot then ordered the tearing down of the porch roof and the door to gain entrance to the cell. When Abbot Theodosius entered the cell, he began to cense the icon and the monk with thyme; and the monk, attempting to protect himself with his hand from the incense, made the sign of the cross. Theodosius once more asked him: "Who are you? Why did you come to us? Where are you from? What kind of man are you?"

But Michael, instead of answering, only repeated the words of the abbot: "Who are you? Why did you come to us? Where are you from? What kind of man are you?" And so the abbot did not learn the name (of the newcomer).

A short time later, before the day of Christ's Transfiguration, Prince Constantine and his wife came to the monastery to take Holy Communion and to present a gift to the monastery on the occasion of the holy day. On that occasion Michael was asked to read from the Book of Job during the dinner given in the refectory. Hearing his voice, Prince Constantine turned toward him and, recognizing him, said, "Oh, is it you Michael, the son of Maxim?"

But Michael countered, "God alone knows who I am."

Then Abbot Theodosius questioned the monk: "Well, my son, why won't you reveal your name to us?"

But Michael simply replied, "God alone knows who I am." But then he revealed his name as being Michael, and so he was called by all from that day on. Prince Constantine, however, asked the abbot and the monks to care for Michael because he was his relative. From that time the abbot and the monks began to care for Monk Michael.

II. MICHAEL PREDICTS THE EVERLASTING SPRING

In this same year and in the three that followed, there was a great drought and the river Veriazh was entirely dried up. Toward the end of these years of drought Abbot Theodosius went to this dried up river and noticed the following words written in the sand of the riverbed: "In this place will be the spring of everlasting water." Seeing this, the abbot asked Michael, who was accompanying him, "Tell me, son, what is that which is written here?"

And Michael answered: "Here will be the spring of water everlasting." And both Abbot Theodosius and Michael addressed their prayers of thanksgiving to God. And then they began to dig, and immediately water gushed forth from the earth. And since that time there has been a well in that place, and it still exists. As soon as the inhabitants of that region learned of it, they began to use it, and do so until this day.

III. MICHAEL PREDICTS THE TONSURING OF PROKHOR

A short time later, Michael told Abbot Theodosius, "We shall have guests."

And Theodosius asked Michael, "Son, what kind of guests shall we have?" But Michael did not explain who the guests would be. But when Abbot Theodosius and Michael left the church, they found three men standing in the monastery yard.

Michael told the abbot, "Invite them to the refectory, Father, that they might break bread with us."

And Theodosius told the strangers, "Let us go, my children, into the refectory that we may break bread."

One of the strangers answered, "Father, there are other friends with us."

And Theodosius told the man, "One of you must go and invite your other friends to have the meal with us."

One of the strangers then went for their friends, and he returned with thirty men who were in armor and with weapons and javelins. And they entered the refectory to break bread.

Theodosius and Michael addressed them: "Sit down, children, and break bread." All but two began eating.

Then Michael addressed those who were not eating. "It will not come to pass as you believe it will."

Actually, almost immediately after, both strangers who were not eating became ill. After the meal everyone who had eaten got up from the table, glorifying God and the Holy Trinity. And one of the strangers gave the monastery one hundred squirrel furs[1] (for the meal). And he said the following: "Father, care for our ill comrades. We leave you in peace."

And the two strangers remained ill for five days. One of them wanted very much to become a monk, and since Theodosius hesitated to tonsure him, Michael said to the abbot, "Tonsure him, Father, and he will be our brother." And so he took monastic vows and received the name of Prokhor. And the other stranger recovered, and left the monastery.

IV. The Miracle of the Filled Granary

In this same year there was a famine throughout the land of Novgorod. And Theodosius and all his brothers became saddened, but Michael said to Abbot Theodosius: "Don't grieve, Father, but remember that our Lord fed forty thousand men, besides the women and children, in the wilderness." And he convinced Abbot Theodosius that the monks should commence cooking rye in kettles and distribute it to pilgrims and travelers. But the monks began to grumble about this, being dissatisfied with Abbot Theodosius and with Michael. But Theodosius and Michael suggested to the monks, "Let us visit our granary."

And they learned that the granaries were overflowing and that the amount of grain did not diminish (even though many were fed from this grain). And they ordered that more rye be prepared so that they might continue to distribute it to the people without hesitation. And they glorified God, the Holy Trinity, and the blessed saints.

V. The Building of the Church of the Holy Trinity

On the Saturday of St. Lazarus, Prince Constantine arrived at the Monastery of the Holy Trinity in Klopsko greatly saddened. And he told Abbot Theodosius and Monk Michael, "I am very sad now because my brothers do not wish to give me my share of the patrimony."

And Michael answered him: "Prince, don't grieve. You will yet come in possession of your estate. In a short time your brother will send for you. Pray to the Holy Trinity and build a stone church in its name, and in return the Lord will reserve a temple in heaven for you."

And then the prince asked Abbot Theodosius: "Do you have any craftsmen? I want to build a church of stone in honor of

---

[1] Squirrel furs, or, as they are sometimes called, vairs, were a monetary unit in ancient Russia.

the Holy Trinity, the source of all life, to commemorate the memory of my parents and myself."

Theodosius sent for craftsmen, and there came craftsmen by the names of John, Clement, and Alexis. And the prince ordered these master craftsmen: "Build a church of stone in the honor of the Holy Trinity, the source of all life, and embellish it in the manner of the Church of St. Nicholas in Latki."

And the craftsmen answered: "We can do so, Lord Prince. And we are ready to serve you if God and the Holy Trinity will aid us." And they laid the foundation of the church on the day of the Commemoration of our holy Father Theodore Sekiot, April 22, 1423 (6931). And they began bringing the stone, but a mighty storm hindered them in their work, and they were able neither to bring the stones by the river nor to work on the walls of the church.

Then Michael said to the masters, "Pray to God for help, because the invisible power of God builds churches." And even as Michael spoke, God sent a helpful wind to fill their sails as they were going for the stone and when they returned with the stone.

For the consecration of the church, Prince Constantine came with his princess and the boyars and brought plenty of food and drink, because he was very glad. And, on the Day of the Holy Martyr Tekla, September 24, 1425 (6932), this Church of the Holy Trinity was completed, thanks to the blessings of Abbot Theodosius and the prayers of St. Michael. And Prince Constantine said to Theodosius and Brother Michael, "Father, thanks to your prayers I received the news from my older brothers that they will give me my patrimony."

And Theodosius and Michael answered: "Go in peace, our child, and they will meet you with friendship. Only, don't forget, our child, this house of God, the Church of the Holy Trinity, the source of all life, as well as ourselves, your poor servants."

And the prince promised: "All my life I shall never forget this House of God, the monastery, the Church of the Holy Trinity, and you, my poor brothers, who have prayed for me."

VI. Michael Predicts Abbot Theodosius' Election
to the Archbishopric

This same year Simon, Archbishop of Novgorod, passed away. And Michael predicted to Abbot Theodosius, "You will be elected to the chair of the archbishop and will rule for three years, but you will also be deposed before you have become consecrated."

VII. MICHAEL'S MIRACULOUS APPEARANCES

On Tuesday of Holy Week during Matins the brethren found that Michael was missing from the monastery. And at that very time he appeared during Matins in the sacristy of the Cathedral of Holy Sophia of Novgorod, and he was there recognized after Matins by Gregory, the *posadnik*, who addressed him, saying, "Come and break bread with us," and he ordered one of his men to attend him. And suddenly Michael was no longer there. But when in Klopsko the priest went that day to celebrate the liturgy in the monastery, Michael was already in the church. When the brothers left the church for the refectory, there arrived a man who was sent by the *posadnik* to inquire the whereabouts of Michael. And Michael was already there.

VIII. MICHAEL PREDICTS ALFIRY'S MISFORTUNES

This very day there was an argument between Alfiry, son of John, and Ivan Loshinsky, son of Simon, over the possession of land. And Michael predicted to Alfiry, "You will remain without hands and feet and you will become mute." And when Alfiry came to the Church of the Holy Virgin in Kurechka, he met Ivan, and said, "Brother Ivan, this land is mine," and he clapped his hands and his gloves dropped to the floor. When he bowed down to pick them up, a stroke hit him. His hands, feet, and tongue became paralyzed, and he could no longer speak.

IX. MICHAEL AND PRIEST NICEPHORIUS

And there was another prophecy made by Michael concerning a certain priest, Nicephorius, who had secretly stolen the venerable icon of the archbishop. And Michael said to this priest, "You will be dishonored." And from that time the priest lost his mind. And Michael ordered that they look in the stove, and there they found the venerable icon that had been stolen.

X. THE PROPHECY TO THE ARCHBISHOP

Archbishop Euthemius received the taxes due him from the monastery, but he wanted additional collections. And so he took a horse as black as a raven from the monastery. And Michael told the archbishop, "You will live but a short time, and you will leave everything behind." And soon the archbishop fell ill and passed away.

XI. MICHAEL AND ARCHBISHOP EUTHEMIUS II

In this same year, another Euthemius was elected to the archbishopric. For the three years that followed he was not consecrated. Once, the bishop came to Klopsko to help the monastery. During the meal at the table the archbishop asked Michael, "Dear Michael, pray to God for me that I should be invested by Great Prince Vasily."

The archbishop had a kerchief in his hand, and Michael snatched it suddenly from the bishop and placed it on the bishop's head, and said, "You will go to Smolensk and you will be consecrated to the archbishopric." And actually, the bishop did go to Smolensk and was there consecrated.

The bishop returned to Michael, and said, "God and the metropolitan of Moscow gave me their blessing."

And Michael once again spoke to the archbishop: "You will be summoned to Moscow, and you will go there and you will submit yourself to the Great Prince and to the metropolitan.

XII. THE PUNISHMENT OF POSADNIK GREGORY

And the Monastery of the Holy Trinity at Klopsko was heavily oppressed by *Posadnik* Gregory. Once, on Easter Sunday, this Gregory came to Mass at the Church of the Holy Trinity of this monastery. When the abbot finished celebrating the Mass, he and the *posadnik* left the church. The *posadnik* stopped the abbot and the monks in the monastery, and addressed them: "Abbot, do not let your horses and cows into the meadows in the summer, for that is my land. Also, don't hunt or fish along river Voriazh, or in the marshes, or in the vicinity of my estates. And if your people come there, I shall order that their arms and legs be broken."

And Michael replied to the *posadnik*, "You yourself will lose your arms and legs, and, more than that, you will nearly drown in the river."

Once the abbot and Michael sent their men to the river and to the marshes. As the men of the monastery were pulling in the nets, the *posadnik* went to the river. He went up to the men of the monastery and followed them into the water. Chasing the fishermen, he hit one of them with his fist, and wanted to hit another one, but he missed and fell in the water, and nearly drowned. When his people came, he was nearly drowned, and they carried him home because he was unable to use his arms and legs, as was predicted by Michael.

Early in the morning he was brought to the monastery, but Michael forbade him to enter it and he forbade the monks to pray for him, to light a candle for him, or to mention his name in the liturgy. And Michael added, addressing the *posadnik*, "Don't bring us any food or drink; only leave us in peace."

The abbot and the monks were afraid that they had made a mistake by not praying for the *posadnik* or by not mentioning his name in the liturgy. In the meantime the *posadnik's* men decided to complain, and said: "We are going to complain to the bishop and to the authorities of the city of Novgorod, for you would neither pray for the *posadnik* nor mention his name during Mass." And they went to the bishop and to the authorities of the city of Novgorod—to Jacob Andreianov, Fefilat Zakharin, and John Vasiliev to lodge their complaint. And the bishop sent his archpriest and his archdeacon to Michael and Abbot Theodosius, saying, "Do pray for the *posadnik* during Mass, and celebrate special services for his recovery."

But Michael replied to the archpriest and the archdeacon: "We pray to God for the entire world, and not only for Gregory." (And then he addressed Gregory:) "Go to the other monasteries and ask there God's forgiveness."

And the *posadnik* began his pilgrimages to the monasteries, and he began to make gifts to them, as well as to the churches in the cities. His pilgrimages to monasteries lasted a year and one and one-half months. But nowhere, in any of these monasteries, did he find God's forgiveness.

Thereafter (returning to Novgorod), he sent a man to the bishop, saying, "My lord and my father, nowhere in the monasteries could I find help."

(The bishop answered:) "Go now, my child, to the Monastery of the Holy Trinity, and ask there the mercy of the Holy Trinity and of Monk Michael." And the bishop sent a priest (to Michael), and the *posadnik* went there personally. It was decided to hold a special service to the Holy Trinity and to celebrate the Mass. The *posadnik* was brought into the church in a carpet, but he was not even able to make the sign of the cross. The celebration of the service to the Holy Trinity began. And when they began to sing the hymn, the *posadnik* was able to move his hands, even though he had not been able to move his hands and feet for one year and one and one-half months. When the priest began reading the Gospel, the *posadnik* was already able to make the sign of the cross and to sit down. In the middle of the service he was able to stand, and so he remained standing until the end of the service. After Mass, everyone went to the refectory, and the *posadnik* addressed the monks during the meal, "Holy brothers, I wish you health and appetite."

But Michael countered: "Those who live by the sword shall perish by the sword." In such manner did Michael teach a lesson to Gregory the *posadnik*. And Michael added, "My child, be good to Michael and to the monastery."

XIII. MICHAEL AND DMITRY SHEMIAKA

A short time afterward Prince Dmitry Shemiaka visited Novgorod, and he came to the monastery in Klopsko that he might receive Michael's blessing. (And he said to Michael:) "Dear Mikhailushka, I was chased away from my patrimony, and my enemies have driven me from the throne of the great prince."[2]

And Michael replied, "Every power is given by God."

"My dear Mikhailushka, pray to God to help me get back my patrimony, and to become once more the great prince," Shemiaka once again said to Michael.

But Michael answered only, "Prince, all you will get is a three-foot coffin." But Prince Dmitry, paying no heed to Michael's words, decided to begin another campaign to become great prince. But Michael said, "It is in vain, Prince, for you cannot receive that which God does not wish you to have." And God did not help Shemiaka, and he escaped once more to Novgorod.

On Friday of the week of Pentecost, Prince Shemiaka returned to the monastery at Klopsko to bring gifts. He gave the brothers much food and drink. And to Michael he gave his own fur coat. When Prince Dmitry, accompanied by the abbot and the monks, returned to his boat, Michael patted the prince's head, and said, "The damp earth is already awaiting you." And he repeated these words thrice.

And the prince said, "My dear monk, I want to return to the city of Rzhev to my patrimony in Konstantinov."

But Michael added: "Prince, your desire will not be fulfilled." And so it came to pass, for the prince died soon afterward.

XIV. MICHAEL ADDRESSES THE NOVGORODIAN REPUBLIC

Once, *Posadnik* John Nemir came to the monastery, and he asked the *posadnik*, "Why do you travel?"

The *posadnik* answered, "I have been at my wife's grandmother, Euphrasinia, and now I come to you to receive your blessing."

And Michael asked, "Well, my child, what kind of problems do you try to solve with women?"

John Nemir answered: "We expect that that great prince (of Moscow) will start a campaign against us. But we expect help from Prince Michael of Lithuania."

[2] Shemiaka led a revolt against his cousin, the Great Prince of Moscow, and for a short time became the ruler of Muscovy.

But Michael retorted: "Your Lithuanian prince will not be a help, but worse than nothing at all. Send your envoy to the Great Prince of Moscow right now, and sue for peace. If you don't come to an agreement with the Great Prince of Moscow, he will come with all his forces to Novgorod, and you will have no divine help. And the Great Prince of Moscow will camp at Bureguy. He will display his army along the river Shelon, and he will jail many citizens of Novgorod. Some will be sent to Moscow, some will be executed, and some will be forced to pay tribute. And the Lithuanian prince will not fight for you, and you will receive no help from him. Better that you send your archbishop and *posadniks* to Moscow with a petition for peace to the Great Prince. Better to pay him tribute; otherwise the Great Prince of Moscow will return here, will take your city, and will deprive you of liberty, and God will help him."

And so it came to pass as Michael said.

XV. MICHAEL'S DEATH

Michael had a simple way of living. He lived alone in his cell and had neither a headboard and pillow nor a bed; neither sheets nor covers, but he slept on the earth. He heated his cell with dried horse manure and lived in the monastery for forty and four years. The entire week he ate only break and water.

Once Abbot Theodosius called Michael for Communion, and after it Michael said, "Father, I would receive the Divine Sacrament from you."

And the abbot answered, "Have it, my child, and once more take Holy Communion."

And all were astounded by these words. And Michael took the censer and thyme and went to his cell. When everyone went to the refectory, the abbot had food sent to Michael's cell. And when the monks came to his cell and entered in, they found the holy man lying as if asleep. And the fragrance of the thyme from the censer near Michael was rising from the earth to the heavens. On January 11th, the Day of Our Father, Theodosius of Jerusalem, Michael was buried in the Monastery of the Holy Trinity, the source of all life.

Glory be to God, now and forever more.

29. *The Heroic Deeds of Mercurius of Smolensk*

AFTER having conquered central and northern Russia, the Mongolian commander, Batu, began his advance into western Russia in 1237. However, because of the spring floods he was unable to take the city of Novgorod, and thus turned southward to the city of Smolensk. For some reason that remains indiscernible from historical writings, the Tatar troops were unable to capture Smolensk. From this event developed the charming legend of St. Mercurius of Smolensk, the heroic defender of his city. Written in a simple style characterized by redundancy, this is probably the most "medieval" of Russian legends. Contrary to this narrative, however, upon leaving the region of Smolensk Batu marched into southern Russia, where he devastated Kiev and other cities, and in 1241 he invaded Hungary. Defeating the Hungarians, he left Hungary so that he might return to Mongolia and participate in the selection of a new khan. The killing of Batu by King Stephen of Hungary, as mentioned in this tale, is the product of the writer's imagination.

The subject of *The Heroic Deeds*—the fight of a pious Russian knight against the nomadic invaders—was a common theme in Russian medieval epics, and various details have been supplied from early Christian and Byzantine hagiography. Very likely this legend grew out of the life of Mercurius of Caesarea (now Kaisaria, Turkey) and from the writings of Dionysius Pseudo-Areopagite. It was probably written in the late fourteenth century, and absorbed a considerable amount of Russian folklore elements.

This translation is based on the Old Russian text, edited by Professor M. O. Skripil, found in *Russkie povesti XI–XVI vekov*, Moscow, 1958, pages 106–107.

◆   ◆   ◆

There used to live in the city of Smolensk a young man called Mercurius who was very pious, who studied God's commandments both day and night, who distinguished himself by his holy life, and who, because of his fasting and prayers, shown like the star which announced the birth of Christ to the entire world. He had a contrite soul and the gift of tears.[1] Often he would pray before the cross of our Lord for the whole world, and he lived in the St. Peter's part of the city.

At that time the evil emperor Batu had conquered the Russian land, had shed rivers of innocent blood, and had tortured the Christians. This emperor came with a great army to the pious city of Smolensk, camped at a distance of twenty miles, burned

---

[1] Eastern Christianity considered the capacity for incessant tears during prayers to be a divine gift.

many holy churches, killed many Christians, and began to prepare for the assault of the city. The people of the city were deeply grieved, and remained incessantly in the Cathedral of the Holy Mother of God. From all their hearts they prayed and worshiped. And, shedding tears, they asked Almighty God, the Holy Mother of God, and all the saints to preserve their city from evil. And God decided to preserve the city and its people.

In the Crypt Monastery, which was located in the vicinity of the river Dnieper outside the city, the sexton of the church had a vision of the most Holy Mother of God. And she addressed him, saying: "O servant of God! Go at once to the cross where my servant, Mercurius, prays. And tell him, 'The Mother of God beckons you to come.'"

The sexton, going there and finding Mercurius praying to God before the cross, called to him by name, "Mercurius."

Mercurius answered, "What do you wish, my lord?"

And the sexton replied: "Go at once, brother. The Mother of God beckons you to the Crypt Monastery."

And when Mercurius, who was made wise by God, entered the holy church, he saw the Most Holy Mother of God sitting on the golden throne with the Christ Child in her arms and surrounded by the host of angels. Seized by awe, he fell at her feet and genuflected low before her.

And the Holy Mother of God raised him, and said: "Mercurius, my chosen one, I send you to take revenge immediately for the Christian blood which has been spilled. Go and defeat the evil-doing emperor Batu and all his armies. Afterward, there will come to you a man with a handsome face. Give him all your arms, and he will decapitate you. Then take your head in your hands and return to your city. And there you will pass away and will be buried in my church."

Mercurius was saddened by these words, and, beginning to weep, he said: "O Most Holy Mother of God. How can I, a poor sinner and undeserving servant, be strong enough for such a deed? Is it possible, my Lady, that the heavenly hosts are not enough to defeat this evildoing emperor?"

Thereafter, Mercurius received her blessing, took up weapons and, bowing to the earth, went from this church. Outside the church he found a spirited steed and, mounting it, he left the city. With the help of God and his Holy Mother, he came to the regiments of the evildoing emperor, defeated the enemy, gathered together the Christian prisoners and, sending them back to his city, he courageously galloped over the regiments of

Batu even as an eagle soars through the air. The evildoing emperor, seeing such a rout of his men, and being seized by great awe and fright, rapidly fled with a small retinue, not having achieved the smallest success in battle. From Smolensk, Batu fled to Hungary, and there this evildoer was killed by King Stephen.

And the handsome warrior appeared before Mercurius. The latter gave all his arms to him and bowed deeply before him. And the warrior severed his head from the body. Then the Blessed One took his head in one hand and, leading his horse with the other hand, returned to the city decapitated. The people of the city, seeing this, were astounded by God's design. And when Mercurius came to the Molokhov Gate, he met there a certain maiden who was going to fetch water. When she saw the Blessed One walking without his head, she began to abuse him vilely. But he lay down at this gate and offered up his most contrite soul to God. And his steed, at that moment becoming invisible, disappeared.

The archbishop of the city came with a large number of people carrying crosses and hoping to take the honorable body of this saint to the church, but they were unable to lift his body from the ground. Then there began a great wailing and weeping among the people because it was impossible to raise the body of the saint. Even the archbishop became greatly bewildered and began to pray to God. And there came a voice to him that announced: "O servant of God! Do not grieve. He will be buried by the Same who sent him to victory."

And the body of the saint remained there unburied for three days. In the meantime, the archbishop remained all these nights praying to God to explain to him this mystery. And he remained without sleep. Praying, he looked out through the window that faced the cathedral, and there he saw a great light as if it were the rising of the sun. And in this light the Most Holy Mother of God and the Archangels Michael and Gabriel came from the church. And, coming to the place where the body of St. Mercurius was lying, the Most Holy Mother of God raised the venerable body of the saint and brought it to her cathedral and placed it in a casket. And this body can still be seen there, attesting to the miracle and glory of Christ, our God, and spreading the fragrance of cedar.

The next morning, when the bishop went to Matins in the cathedral, he saw there the wondrous miracle, the body of the saint lying in its place. And the people flocked to the cathedral, and, seeing this miracle, they glorified God.

30. *The Story of Great John, Archbishop of Novgorod the Great; How, in One Night, He Was Taken from Novgorod to the City of Jerusalem, and Then Returned to Novgorod the Great That Same Night*

THIS is one of the oldest Novgorodian legends. Bishop John was a very popular Church leader in the middle of the twelfth century, and around him there arose a number of stories. When Novgorod was threatened with incorporation into the Muscovite realm in the middle of the fifteenth century, Bishop Euthemius II (1430–1458) began collecting the legends and tales concerning the city's history and the deeds of its most outstanding leaders. Most likely this account of Great John was re-edited by Pachomius the Serb after discovery of Bishop John's relics in 1439. Pachomius, one of the innovators of the literary style known as "weaving of words" (*pletenie sloves*), embellished this text with more biblical words, difficult and complex sentences, and its stylistic redundancy.

The motif of a demon confined in a vessel is found both in tales from the East, as for instance in *Tales of the Arabian Nights*, and in early Russian hagiography.

The story is not presented here in its entirety. It ends with an account of the procession of the people and clergy to the St. George Monastery to ask Bishop John to return. Bishop John forgives the people and returns to his see.

This translation is based on the text published by N. K. Gudzy in *Khrestomatiia po drevnei russkoi literature*, Moscow, 1955, pages 207–209.

◆ ◆ ◆

FATHER, MAY YOUR BLESSING BE WITH US

This story should not lapse into oblivion, for God Almighty, who placed John in the bishopric, permits people to be overcome by temptation. He does this to sanctify and glorify them, testing their mettle as one might test gold. God has said, "I will glorify those who glorify me." Wondrous is God among the host of his saints, and God himself glorifies them.

And Christ said, "I give you power over evil spirits."

Once, in the evening, John, Archbishop of Great Novgorod,

went to recite his evening prayers, as was his custom. At that time there was a vessel filled with water near his cell, and the Reverend Father used it for his oblations. Suddenly he heard someone struggling in the water of this vessel. Coming closer to the vessel, and realizing that this was the design of the devil, he read a prayer so as to confine the demon in the vessel. The devil wished to frighten the holy father, but he was defeated in this purpose by the firm adamant.[1] The devil wanted to get out of the vessel, but could not overcome this power. A short time later, the demon could no longer endure and so began to shriek: "Oh, what a miserable plight! I am burned by fire and cannot resist any longer. Let me go at once, O servant of God."

The bishop answered: "And who are you? How did you get in this vessel?"

This devil answered: "I am an evil demon and came to this place so that I might corrupt you, hoping that you would become frightened and cease your praying. But you confined me so cruelly in this vessel, and here I am burned terribly by the fire. O woe is me, a cursed one! How could I become tempted? How could I get in this vessel? I am bewildered! Release me now, you servant of God. I shall not return to this place again!"

And the evil demon shrieked so, that finally the bishop spoke, saying: "For your daring I order that you this very night take me from Novgorod the Great to the city of Jerusalem. And place me before the church wherein is the Lord's Sepulcher. And this very night you must bring me back to my cell, which you have dared to enter. And only then shall I release you."

The demon promised to comply with the will of the bishop, and said, "Please, only release me from confinement, you servant of God."

Without releasing the demon from the power of the cross, the holy bishop let the devil out of the vessel and said to him: "Ready yourself and appear before me as a horse. Then I will mount you and you will fulfill my request."

The devil, like a cloud of darkness, left the vessel and appeared as a horse before the cell door. The bishop went from his cell and, having armed himself with the cross and grace, mounted the demon and that very night arrived in the city of Jerusalem in which is located the Holy Sepulcher of the Lord and the Tree of Life. Retaining his power over the demon, the bishop forbade it to move from the spot where it stood. And

---

[1] Adamant was often used in Russian medieval literature as a symbol of firm strength, and in this case refers to the power of the cross.

the demon, remaining under the power of the cross, was unable to move away.

In the meantime the Reverend Father went to the Church of the Holy Resurrection and, standing before the door of this church, knelt and prayed. And the doors of the church opened of their own accord, while the tapers and censers of the Lord's Sepulcher began to burn. The bishop, shedding tears, thanked God. And he venerated and kissed the Holy Sepulcher and the Tree of Life and the other shrines. Then he left the church, having fulfilled his longing. And the church doors closed after him of their own accord.

The bishop found the demon standing in the form of a horse and in the same place, as he had been ordered. And mounting the demon, the bishop found himself that very night in his cell, in the city of Novgorod the Great.

Leaving the saint's cell, the devil said: "Oh, John, you forced me to labor, carrying you in one night to Jerusalem and that very same night carrying you back to Novgorod the Great. I was bound to do so, by the power of the cross, as if I were bound by shackles. I had to undergo many calamities. Reveal to no one what has happened this night. If you do, I will lead you into temptation. You will be tried and sentenced for lechery, abused, and put on a raft in the river Volkhov.[2]

To prevent the abuse of the demon, Bishop John made the sign of the cross.

The bishop had the custom of discussing problems of the spirit with the honorable abbots, most learned priests, and God-abiding men, since he considered it a necessity that he share his wisdom with others and open to them the sublimity of the Holy Trinity. He never tired of teaching men, and he often told to them the occurrences of his own life, describing them as those of another man. "I know," he told them once, "a certain man who happened to go from Novgorod to the city of Jerusalem in one night, worshiped there at the Lord's Sepulcher, and returned that very night to Novgorod the Great." The abbots and the others were astounded.

But from that time on, and with the permission of God, the demon began to lead the bishop into temptation. The people had the vision many times of a harlot leaving the cell of the bishop. Many officials of the city, who used to come to the bishop's cell to receive his blessing, would see there a woman's

---

[2] Novgorod was situated on the river Volkhov, and the placing of convicts on a raft in the middle of the river was a common punishment.

necklace of coins and also a woman's robe and sandals. And they felt sore offended, and wondered what to say of this. But all this was the design of this demon who expected that the people would rise up against the bishop, would speak unjustly of him, and would drive him from their midst.

The people took council with the officials, and declared: "It is unjust for such a bishop, who is a whoremonger, to occupy the apostolic seat. Let us go and drive him from our midst, for about such people King David said: 'And words will pour forth from the mouth of the flatterer and they will speak of righteousness, lowliness, pride, and destruction. This they do for they worship the devil, even before the assembly of Jews.'"

But let us return to the narration. When the people came to the cell of the bishop, the demon walked among the people, and they saw him as a girl, leaving the cell of the saint. And the people began to exclaim that she should be seized, but they could not do so, although they followed her for a long time.

The bishop heard the cries of the people and came out to them and said, "What has happened, my children?" But the citizens paid no heed to these words, and told him what they had seen, condemned him as a whoremonger, abused him, and, after wondering what should be done with him, they decided, "Let us put him on a raft in the middle of the river Volkhov so that he may float down the river and away from our city."

And so they took the ascetic, holy, and great bishop of God, John, to the great bridge which spanned the river Volkhov, led him down to the river, and put him on a raft. And so the dream of the evil demon was fulfilled. However, God's grace shone on the face of the bishop, and his prayers to God overcame the demon's design. The demon had begun to rejoice, but when John, the bishop of God, was put on the raft in the middle of the river Volkhov, the raft immediately began to move upstream, although it was not driven by anyone. The raft on which the bishop was sitting was pushed upstream from the great bridge to the Monastery of St. George, and against a strong current. The bishop was praying for the people on the raft, saying, "O Lord, forgive them this sin, for they know not what they do."

And seeing this, the demon was abashed, and began to weep.

The people of Novgorod, seeing this miracle, rent their garments, returned, and said: "We have sinned; we have committed an injustice to this father, and we have condemned our pastor. We now know that this has happened through the designs of a demon."

IDEOLOGICAL WRITINGS

31. *The Tale of the White Cowl*

THE *Tale of the White Cowl*, which was to become the corner-
stone of Russian national ideology, was written toward the end
of the fifteenth century in Novgorod, apparently by Archbishop
Genady and his co-worker and interpreter, Dmitry Gerasimov.
The tale was conceived with the purpose of defending the
sovereignty of the Novgorodian Church, in particular, and the
Russian Church, in general, from encroachment by the Grand
Duke of Muscovy, but the tale grew into an ideological work
that glorified the prestige of Russian Orthodox Christianity.
Later, in the sixteenth century, after the fall of Constantinople to
the Turks, there developed from this work the theory of Moscow
being the Third Rome, which theory was clearly and concisely
formulated by Monk Philotheus (*circa* 1510–1540) when he
wrote: "All Christian realms will come to an end and will unite
into the one single realm of our sovereign, that is, into the
Russian realm, according to the prophetic books. Both Romes
fell, the third endures, and a fourth there will never be."[1] This
theory defined Moscow as the sole staunch defender of the
Eastern Orthodox Faith, which, in the minds of Greeks, Russians, Southern Slavs, and other Eastern Europeans, was the
only true Christian Church.

The background of this concept is a rather eclectic one, and
can be traced to the Book of Daniel (VII, 27), in which the
prophet announced that the final kingdom of the one true faith
will come about and will never be destroyed. This concept of
Daniel's was taken up by the Chiliasts (from the Greek, *chiliad*,
meaning "a thousand"), who proclaimed the forthcoming Kingdom of Christ which would last a thousand years.

In the Middle Ages the Irish philosopher John Scotus Erigena
(ninth century) and the Italian theologian Joachim de Fiore
(twelfth century) modified Daniel's original concept into the
theory of the "three kingdoms," that is, the Kingdom of the
Father who gave the Law (Old Testament), the Kingdom of

[1] The best discussion of the works of Monk Philotheus can be
found in V. Malinin's *Starets Eleazarova Monastyria Filofey i ego
Poslaniia*, Kiev, 1901. This quotation is to be found on page 45 in the
appendix of Malinin's work.

the Son who brought Grace, and the final Kingdom of the Holy Spirit, of which the Apostles said: "Where there is the spirit of God, there is freedom." The theory of the final Kingdom of the Holy Spirit became known in Russia, and later formed the basis for both the *Tale of the White Cowl* and the Third Rome theory.

In the eyes of Archbishop Genady and Dmitry Gerasimov, Russia was predestined by God to be revealed as this last kingdom, the Kingdom of the Holy Spirit, which will endure until the Last Judgment. The authors of the *Tale of the White Cowl* combined this theocratic, utopian tenet with the Roman Catholic legend of the gift of the city of Rome to Pope Sylvester by Emperor Constantine (Emperor of Rome, 306–337). This legend lay the foundation for the secular power of the Pope of Rome and also for the independence of the pope from the emperor.

The *Tale of the White Cowl* underwent many revisions and is extant in several versions; however, its central theme remains the same in all: the White Cowl, the symbol of the radiant Resurrection and Orthodox Christianity, remained in Rome as long as the popes preserved the original teachings of Christ. But when the popes broke with the Eastern Church and developed their "Latin heresies,"[2] divine power gave the White Cowl to the patriarch of Constantinople, which the Greeks of that time called the "Second Rome." When the Greeks began to "multiply their sins" and even began negotiating with the Pope of Rome, God punished them by letting their land be overrun by Turks.[3] The tale states that a century before the fall of Constantinople, God, who had predestined the last Orthodox nation, after the fall of Byzantium, to be Russia, commanded that the White Cowl be taken to the Archbishop of Novgorod, Vasily.

The present translation is based on the Russian text published by G. Kushelov-Bezborodko in *Pamiatniki starinnoi russkoi literatury*, Volume I, St. Petersburg, 1860, pages 287–303.

Since the translation given here is not the complete tale, it is essential to present a synopsis of the narrative up to the point where the translation begins.

[2] The Byzantines, and later the Russians, called the teachings of the Western Church "Latin Heresies," since Rome proclaimed the primacy of the pope and used the Latin tongue exclusively for liturgical purposes.

[3] The actual conquest of Constantinople by the Turks took place in 1453, some thirty or forty years before the *Tale of the White Cowl* was written in Novgorod.

SYNOPSIS

The *Tale of the White Cowl* opens with the story of Emperor Constantine's illness, which could be cured neither by physicians nor by magicians. One such magician, who was violently opposed to Christianity, advised the emperor that in order to be cured he must bathe in the blood of three thousand infants killed expressly for that purpose. However, at the last minute Emperor Constantine, moved by the tears and wailings of the mothers of the children who were to be slain, canceled his plan, preferring to die rather than to kill children in order to restore his health. That very night the emperor had a vision of the Apostles Peter and Paul, who told him that Pope Sylvester, who was in hiding from his persecutors at that time, could show him a font of salvation, bathing wherein would cure him of this affliction. In recompense, the emperor was to grant new rights to the Christian Church and to support it as the national religion.

The tale continues that the emperor was cured, ended the persecutions of Christians, and even wished to grant the imperial crown to the pope. The pope most humbly refused to accept it. So the emperor gave him a white cowl, the symbol of the primacy of spiritual power over secular power and of the Resurrection, the color white representing the radiance of the Resurrection of Christ. Having given the supreme power in the city of Rome to the pope, Emperor Constantine then left the Eternal City and went to the ancient city of Byzantium, which was later renamed the "city of Constantine," or Constantinople. Thus did the Eastern, or Byzantine, Roman Empire come into being.

After the death of Pope Sylvester, the tale goes on to say, the White Cowl was highly revered by the popes of Rome. However, in the ninth century, when the West was ruled by Emperor Charlemagne and the papal see was ruled by Pope Formosus,[4] a schism arose between the Eastern and Western Churches. The Western Church, under the leadership of the pope, developed new teachings and doctrines that the Eastern Church considered to be "Latin heresies," particularly the doctrine of the primacy of the Pope of Rome over the entire Church. From that time on the popes ceased to revere the White Cowl, and finally decided to profane and destroy it. However, a miraculous power saved the White Cowl, and the pope was

[4] Pope Formosus reigned from 891 to 896. During his reign there began the first conflicts between Rome and Constantinople over the jurisdiction of the two branches of the Church.

forced to send it to the patriarch of Constantinople, the capital of the still-extant Eastern Roman Empire, or, as it is more often called, Byzantium.

The translation begins at this point in the tale—that is, with the arrival of the White Cowl in Constantinople.

❖ ❖ ❖

At that time the Patriarch of Constantinople was Philotheus,[5] who was distinguished by his strict fasting and his virtuous ways. Once, he had a vision in the night of a youth from whom emanated light and who told him:

"Blessed teacher, in the olden times the Roman Emperor, Constantine, who, through the vision of the Holy Apostles Peter and Paul, was enlightened by God, decided to give Blessed Pope Sylvester the White Cowl to glorify the Holy Apostolic Church. Later, the unfaithful popes of the Latin heresies wanted to profane and destroy this cowl, but I appeared to the evil pope, and now this pope has sent this cowl to you. When the messengers arrive with it, you must accept it with all honors. Then send the White Cowl to the Russian land, to the city of Novgorod the Great with your written blessing. And there this cowl will be worn on the head of Vasily, Archbishop of Novgorod,[6] so that he may glorify the Holy Apostolic Cathedral of Holy Sophia and laud the Orthodox. There, in that land, the faith of Christ is verily glorified. And the popes, because of their shamelessness, will receive the vengeance of God." And having spoken these words, the youth became invisible.

The patriarch awoke filled with awe and joy, and was unable to sleep throughout the remainder of the night. And he contemplated this vision. In the morning he ordered that the bells should sound the Matins, and when day came he summoned the Church council and revealed his vision. And all praised God, perceiving that a holy angel had appeared to the patriarch. Yet they did not fully understand the meaning of the message. When they were still in council and were filled with awe due to their great joy, there arrived a servant of the patriarch, and he announced to them that messengers had arrived from the Pope of Rome. The patriarch ordered that they be brought

[5] Philotheus was patriarch of Constantinople from 1353 to 1355, and from 1364–1376.

[6] Vasily was archbishop of Novgorod from 1330 to 1342. In 1946 his grave was discovered and opened. In it were found both the White Cowl and the vestments embroidered with crosses which are mentioned in this tale.

before him. The messengers came, bowed lowly to the patriarch, and gave him the message. The patriarch read the message and pondered it, praising God. He announced its contents to Emperor John who was reigning at that time and whose name was Kantakuzen.[7] And then he went with the entire council to meet the bringers of the divine treasure which lay in an ark. He accepted it with all honors, broke the seal, and took from the ark the Holy White Cowl. He kissed it with reverence, and looked upon it with wonderment both for its creation and for the wonderful fragrance that emanated from it.

At that time the patriarch had diseased eyes and constant headaches, but when he placed the White Cowl upon his head, these afflictions immediately ceased to be. And he rejoiced with great joy and rendered glory to Christ, our Lord, to Constantine's blessed memory for his creating this wonderful cowl for Blessed Pope Sylvester. And he put the Holy Cowl on the golden salver that was also sent by the pope. He placed them in the great church in an honorable place until he could make a decision with the emperor's counseling.

After the White Cowl was sent from Rome, the evil pope, who was counseled by heretics, became angered against the Christian faith and was driven to a frenzy, extremely regretting his allowing the White Cowl to be sent to Constantinople. And he wrote an evil letter to the patriarch, in which he demanded the return of the White Cowl on the golden salver. The patriarch read this letter and, understanding the pope's evil and cunning design, sent him a letter in return that was based on Holy Scripture, and in it he called the pope both evil and godless, the apostate and precursor of the Antichrist. And the patriarch cursed the pope in the name of our Lord, Jesus Christ, the Holy Apostles, and the Church Fathers. And this letter came to the pope.

When the pope had read the letter and learned that the patriarch intended to send the White Cowl with great honor to the Russian land, to the city of Novgorod the Great, he uttered a roar. And his face changed and he fell ill, for he, the infidel, disliked the Russian land and could not even bear to hear of this land where the Christian faith was professed.

Patriarch Philotheus, having seen that the White Cowl was illumined with grace, began to ponder how he might keep it in

---

[7] John VI Kantakuzen (or Cantacuzene) was Emperor of Byzantium from 1347 to 1354.

Constantinople and wear it on his own head. He consulted with the emperor about the matter several times, and wanted to write to the other patriarchs and metropolitans to summon them to a council. After Matins one Sunday, the patriarch returned to his chambers and, after the usual prayers, lay down to rest. But he slept but lightly, and in this sleep he saw that two men, who were unknown to him, came through the door. And from them there emanated light. One of them was armed as a warrior and had an imperial crown upon his head. The other wore a bishop's vestments and was distinguished by his venerable white hair.

The latter spoke to the patriarch, saying: "Patriarch! Stop pondering your wearing of the White Cowl on your own head. If this were to be, our Lord, Jesus Christ, would have so predestined it from the founding of this city. And for a long time did divine enlightenment come from heaven, and then God's voice came to me and I learned that Rome had to betray God and embrace their Latin heresies. That is the reason I did not wish to wear this cowl upon my head, and thus I instructed other popes not to do so. And this imperial city of Constantinople will be taken by the sons of Hagar[8] because of its sins, and all holy shrines will be defiled and destroyed. Thus has it been predestined since the founding of this city.

"The ancient city of Rome will break away from the glory and faith of Christ because of its pride and ambition. In the new Rome, which will be the City of Constantinople, the Christian faith will also perish through the violence of the sons of Hagar. In the third Rome, which will be the land of Russia, the Grace of the Holy Spirit will be revealed. Know then, Philotheus, that all Christians will finally unite into one Russian nation because of its orthodoxy. Since ancient times and by the will of Constantine, Emperor of the Earth, the imperial crown of the imperial city is predestined to be given to the Russian tsar.[9] But the White Cowl, by the will of the King of Heaven, Jesus Christ, will be given to the archbishop of Novgorod the Great. And this White Cowl is more honorable than the crown of the tsar, for it is an imperial crown of the archangelic spiritual order. Thus, you must send this Holy White Cowl to the Russian land,

---

[8] Both the Byzantines and the Russians called all nomads, whether they were Turks, Mongols, or Arabs, the sons of Hagar. "Hagar" refers to the handmaid of the biblical patriarch Abraham.

[9] The Russians of that time used only one word, "tsar," for the English words "king," "King of Heaven," "emperor," and even "kahn." Equally, the word "tsarstvo" was used to mean "realm," "empire," "tsardom," and the "Kingdom of God."

to the city of Novgorod the Great, as you were told to do in the vision of the angel. You should believe and trust in what I say. And when you send it to the Russian land, the Orthodox Faith will be glorified and the cowl will be safe from seizure by the infidel sons of Hagar and from the intended profanation by the Latin pope. And the grace, glory, and honor which were taken from Rome, as well as the Grace of the Holy Spirit, will be removed from the imperial city of Constantinople after its capture by the sons of Hagar. And all holy relics will be given to the Russian land in the predestined moment. And the Russian tsar will be elevated by God above other nations, and under his sway will be many heathen kings. And the power of the patriarch of this imperial ruling city will pass to the Russian land in the predestined hour. And that land will be called Radiant Russia, which, by the Grace of God, will be glorified with blessings. And its majesty will be strengthened by its orthodoxy, and it will become more honorable than the two Romes which preceded it."

And saying this, the man of the vision who was dressed in a bishop's vestment wished to leave, but the patriarch, seized by great awe, fell before the bishop and said: "Who are you, my lord? Your vision has seized me with great awe; my heart has been frightened by your words, and I tremble to my very bones."

The man in the bishop's vestments answered: "Don't you know who I am? I am Pope Sylvester, and I came to you because I was ordered by God to reveal to you the great mystery which will come to pass in the predestined time." Then, pointing to the other man in the vision, he added: "This is blessed Emperor Constantine of Rome to whom I gave rebirth in the holy font and whom I won over to the faith of our Lord, Jesus Christ. He was the first Christian emperor, my child in Christ, who created and gave me the White Cowl in place of the imperial crown." And saying this, he blessed the patriarch, and became invisible.

Waking up, the patriarch was seized with awe, remembering the words about the White Cowl and the conquest of Constantinople by the pagan sons of Hagar. And he wept for a long time. When the hour of the divine Mass arrived, the patriarch went to the church, fell before the icon of the Holy Mother of God, and remained lying there for some time. Then he arose, took the White Cowl with great reverence, kissed it piously, placed it upon his head, and then put it to his eyes and his heart. And his adoration for this cowl increased even more. And doing this, he wept. His clerics, who were around him and saw that he wept inconsolably, did not dare to inquire as to why he was weeping. Finally the patriarch ceased crying and told his clerics in detail of the vision of Pope Sylvester and Emperor Constantine. Having heard these words, the clerics wept sorrowfully, and exclaimed, "Thy will be done!"

The patriarch, mourning the forthcoming misfortunes of the city of Constantinople and fearing to trespass the divine will, told them that he must fulfill the will of the Lord and do with the White Cowl as he was commanded to do. After having deliberated with blessed Emperor John, he took the White Cowl and the golden salver, put them in the aforementioned ark, sealed it with his seal, and, as he was commanded by the holy angel and Blessed Pope Sylvester, put in his epistle with his blessings, and in it he commanded Archbishop Vasily and all other bishops who would follow Vasily to wear the White Cowl upon their heads. He added many other honorable and marvelous gifts from his clergy for the bishopric of Novgorod the Great. And he also sent vestments with their embroidered crosses[10] for the glorification of the Holy Apostolic Church. And all this was placed in another ark. And he gave these arks to a bishop named Eumeny, and sent him forth with both joy and sorrow.

In the bishopric of the city of Novgorod the Great was Archbishop Vasily who distinguished himself by his fasting and virtuous ways. Once, in the night, he prayed to God and then lay down to rest, but he slept but lightly, and had a dream in which he saw the angel of God. This angel of God, who had a handsome appearance and radiant face, appeared before him in the garb of a monk and with the White Cowl upon his head. With his finger he pointed to his head and in a low voice announced: "Vasily! This White Cowl which you see on my head is from Rome. In olden times the Christian Emperor Constantine created it in honor of Sylvester, Pope of Rome. He gave it to this pope to wear upon his head. But God Almighty did not permit the White Cowl to remain there because of their Latin heresies. Tomorrow morning you must go from the city with your clergymen and meet the bishop and messengers sent by the patriarch. And they will bring an ark, and in this ark you will find the White Cowl upon a golden salver. Accept it with all honors, for this White Cowl symbolizes the radiant Resurrec-

---

[10] See footnote 4.

tion which came to pass on the third day. And from now, you and all other archbishops of this city will wear it on your heads. And I have come to you to assure you before hand that all is as God wills it and to assuage any doubts you may have." And saying this, the angel became invisible.

Waking up, Archbishop Vasily was seized with awe and joy, pondering the meaning of the vision. The next morning he sent his clerics outside the city, to the crossroads, to see whether the messengers really would appear. In the vicinity of the city the servant of Archbishop Vasily met a Greek bishop who was unknown to him and who traveled to the city of Novgorod. They made a low obeisance and returned to the archbishop and told them all they had seen. The bishop then sent his messenger into the city to summon the clerics and the entire population. And he ordered the tolling of the bells, and both he and his clerics donned their vestments.

The procession had not gone far from the Cathedral of Holy Sophia when they met the aforementioned bishop, sent by the patriarch and bearing the ark that had been sealed by the patriarch, and which contained the venerable gifts, came to Archbishop Vasily, made a low obeisance before him, and gave him the epistles of the patriarch. They blessed and greeted each other in Christ's name. Archbishop Vasily accepted the epistles of the patriarch and the arks bearing the venerable gifts. And he went with them to the Cathedral of Holy Sophia, the Wisdom of God. There he put them in the middle of the church in an honorable place, and ordered that the patriarchal epistles be read aloud. When the Orthodox people, who were in the cathedral, heard these writings read aloud, they rendered glory to God and rejoiced with great joy. Archbishop Vasily opened one of the arks and removed the cover. And a wonderful fragrance and miraculous radiance spread through the church. Archbishop Vasily and all present were in wonderment, witnessing these happenings. And Bishop Eumeny, who was sent by the patriarch, wondered about these blessed deeds of God that he had witnessed. And they all rendered glory to God, and celebrated the service of thanksgiving.

Archbishop Vasily took the White Cowl from the ark and saw that it appeared exactly like the one he had seen on the angel's head in his vision. And he kissed it with reverence. At that same moment there came a sonorous voice from the icon of the Lord, which was in the cupola of the church, saying, "Holy, holy." And after a moment of silence there came the

same voice, which thrice announced, "Ispola eti despota."[11] And
when the archbishop and all those present heard these voices,
they were seized with awe and joy. And they said, "The Lord
have mercy upon us!" And the archbishop then ordered that all
present in the church be silent, and he revealed to them his
vision of the angel and his words concerning the White Cowl.
And he told of his vision as it had happened and in detail, even
as it was told to him by the angel in the night.

Giving thanks to God for sending this cowl, the archbishop
went forth from the church, preceded by the deacons in holy
vestments carrying tapers and singing hymns. And they proceeded with serenity and piety. And the people crowded round,
jostling each other and jumping so that they might see the White
Cowl on the archbishop's head. And all were in wonderment.
Thus, in this way, thanks to the Grace of our Lord, Jesus Christ,
and to the blessing of his Holiness Philotheus, Patriarch of
of Constantinople, the White Cowl became a symbol upon the
heads of the archbishops of Novgorod. And Archbishop Vasily
was overcome with great joy, and for seven days he feasted all
priests, deacons, and clerics of the city of Novgorod the Great.
And he also offered food and drink to the poor, to monks, and
to prisoners. And he asked that the prisoners be released. During
the divine service he placed the holy and venerable gifts of the
patriarch in the Cathedral of Holy Sophia and with the blessings
of all clerics. And the golden salver, on which the White Cowl
was placed, was also deposited in the Cathedral of Holy Sophia
during the Mass.

The messengers of the patriarch who brought the Holy White
Cowl were also shown great honor and they received many gifts.
The archbishop sent gifts to the Emperor and Patriarch of
Constantinople and sent the messengers forth with great honors.
Thereafter, multitudes arrived from many cities and kingdoms
to look upon, as if it were a miracle, the archbishop in the White
Cowl. And they were in wonderment about it, and told of it in
many lands. This Holy White Cowl was created by the first
pious Christian Emperor, Constantine, for Blessed Pope Syl-
vester in the year 297 (5805). And this is the history of the
Holy White Cowl up to this day.

---

[11] *Ispola eti despota* is Greek for "Many years to the lord," or,
more loosely translated, "Long live the bishop." The Russians used
this expression during the Church service, and it was always pronounced in Greek.

the muscovite period

(1478–1700)

Russia Toward 1660 A.D.

32. The Story of Stephen Bathory's Campaign Against Pskov

FOR almost two centuries the primary objective of Muscovite Russia's foreign policy was to gain free access to the Baltic Sea in order to establish direct contact with the West and put an end to Russia's political and cultural isolation. On many occasions Russian armies had tried to capture the Baltic shores, which had been in the hands of the Teutonic Knights of the Livonian Order since the thirteenth century. In 1558 Ivan IV began a military campaign against this Order, and at first he was successful. When Sweden and the Polish-Lithuanian Empire came to the help of the Livonian Order, however, the Russian advance lost momentum. The war then became an exhausting, indecisive undertaking that lasted some twenty-five years. In its final stages Russia had to face the powerful coalition of Sweden, Denmark, Poland, Lithuania, and Hungary, the last three countries being united under the scepter of the energetic King of Hungary, Stephen Bathory.[1] After 1578 Russia lost most of the lands she had conquered earlier, and by 1581 King Stephen Bathory was able to begin an invasion of Russian territory. Polish, Lithuanian, and Hungarian troops, supported by some German mercenaries, invaded Russia and advanced on the city of Pskov, Russia's principal stronghold in the northwest. After a long siege and many attempts to subdue the city, King Stephen Bathory was forced to abandon his plans for conquest, for the heroic defense of Pskov and his failure to take the city had undermined both the strength and morale of his Polish-Lithuanian forces.

The *Story of Stephen Bathory's Campaign Against Pskov* was written in the form of an epic in the late sixteenth century by a talented and erudite anonymous writer who displays an excellent command of the traditional, ornamental stylistics of his

[1] Stephen Bathory was also elected King of Poland and Lithuania in 1575. His wife was Anna, the last princess of the Polish dynasty of Jagellons. The author of this work refers to Stephen as "King of Lithuania," although Poland, Lithuania, and Hungary were all united under his scepter.

time. His account is at once dramatic and ironic, picturesque, and varied. His metaphors and literary devices ideally serve his purpose to present a solemn account of the heroism of the Russian soldiers. With considerable mastery and pointed irony, the author describes King Stephen Bathory's campaign, his courageous, boastful courtiers and knights who, long before the final outcome of the battle was in sight, bragged that they would capture Princes Vasily and Ivan Shuysky, the valiant defenders of Pskov. This tale betrays the strong national fervor of the writer, who was firmly convinced that God would help the "only truly Christian" Russian army, and grant it final victory over the "infidel" invaders.

The excerpts that follow were taken from the early seventeenth-century Russian text published by V. I. Malyshev in *Povest o prikhozhdenii Stefana Batoriia na grad Pskov*, Academy of Sciences of the U.S.S.R., Moscow and Leningrad, 1952, pages 56, 57, 59, 60, and 65–78.

◆ ◆ ◆

Dreadful and cruel times have come. The Polish and Lithuanian king, Stephen Bathory, approached the borders of the Russian land with numerous forces. The rumor has spread to Pskov that this Lithuanian king has already invaded the land of Pskov and has occupied the city of Voronoch, located sixty miles from the city of Pskov.

Similar to insatiable hell which opens its jaws to swallow its victim, so also did the Polish-Lithuanian king prepare to take the city of Pskov in the pincers of his regiments. Always livelier and swifter, this king's army, like an ominous and great serpent wriggling from its cave, moved in columns to Pskov, and threatened the Russians with its campfires, guns, and smoke. The Lithuanian king boasted that he would swallow Pskov, even before he reached it. He boasted that he would satiate all the reptiles, snakes, and scorpions of his army with the rest of the booty. This ominous serpent leaped at Pskov, wanting to hurl it to the earth with its wings and to sting the Pskovian men to death with its stinger. He boasted that he would plunder all the spoils of Pskov and take them to Lithuania and that he would swallow up the Pskovian land, dragging on its tail all those who remained alive to the Lithuanian land. The serpent already flattered itself with thoughts of victory over Pskov.

Dark smoke rose from south of the God-protected city of

Pskov. The Lithuanian armies approached Pskov, and their black shadows, like a cloud, fell over the white stone walls of Pskov. Still, the whole Lithuanian land could not make the city black. Smoke began to rise from the enemy camp, which was three miles away from the city, on the river Cherekh. The tsar's officers, who scouted at this river, rushed to Pskov to inform the tsar's boyars and voevodas that the first Lithuanian troops were already at the river Cherekh. The tsar's boyars and voevodas ordered the tocsin sounded, and gave the command to burn the settlement beyond the Velikaia[2] River in order not to leave behind any quarters for the enemies. And so, on the day of the Holy Martyrs Frol and Lavr, on August 18, 1581 (7189), the siege of the God-protected city of Pskov began. The Lithuanian troops began crossing the river Cherekh, and soon afterward their regiments appeared at the gates of the city. The boyars and voevodas lead their men in a sortie against the enemy troops. But the enemy demonstrated their weakness in this skirmish, beginning the siege with methods of flight, and not daring to approach the city. And for them this was a bad omen. . . .

On Friday, September 8th, the day of the birth of the Holy Virgin, at five o'clock in the afternoon, the Polish and Lithuanian voevodas, captains, storm troops, and gaiduks[3] hurried joyfully and hopefully to storm the city of Pskov. The tsar's boyars and voevodas,[4] all warriors, and the citizens of Pskov saw from their walls that a large number of regiments were leaving the king's camp and moving toward the city with banners. The gaiduks were entering the trenches and tunnels, and the Russians understood that they were moving to storm the breaches in the fortress wall. The voevodas ordered that the tocsin, which was located on the city wall in the vicinity of the Church of Vasily the Great on the hill, be sounded to warn all people of Pskov that the Poles and Lithuanians had begun the storming of the city. The boyars and voevodas of the tsar, with all their warriors and streltsi, were ordered to their places, and stood in preparedness while the artillery received the command to open fire on the enemy regiments. The artillery fired incessantly on the enemy, destroyed many regiments, and killed many Lithuanians and Poles. And their corpses were covering the ground. Still the enemy was advancing to the fortress, fight-

[2] The city of Pskov is located on the Velikaia (Great) River.
[3] The Gaiduks were mercenary infantry and shock troops.
[4] The city of Pskov was under the command of Princes Ivan and Vasily Shuysky, and Prince Andrew Khvorostinin.

ing fiercely, daringly, and hopefully. The enemy advanced as if it were a great stream flowing toward the city. The enemy troops looked as terrifying as the waves of the sea. And an endless number of their sabers were glinting at the city as if they were lightning bolts.

In the Cathedral of the Life-Giving Trinity the clergy began the service, praying to God with tears and appealing to God for the deliverance of the city. The Pskovian men took leave of their wives and children, and hurried to the breaches of the fortress wall, prepared to stave off the enemy, and in their hearts they pledged to God that they would defend the Christian faith and die for each other, for the city of Pskov, for their homes, for their wives and children, and never surrender. And they did as they promised.

At six o'clock of this same day they heard a noise comparable to that of approaching gigantic waves or of powerful thunder. And the entire enemy army howled and ran to the breaches in the fortress wall, covering themselves with their shields, rifles, muskets, lances, and other weapons, and thus appearing to be under a roof. The tsar's boyars and voevodas appealed to God for help, encouraged the Russian warriors with their battle cries, and began fighting the enemies on the fortress walls. The innumerable Lithuanian troops rushed to the fortress wall like a rampaging stream. But our Christian warriors remained as firm as the stars in the sky, and did not permit the enemy to scale the walls. Like powerful thundering, there arose a din of shouts, noises of the shooting of artillery and gunfire, and battle cries of the great multitude of warriors from both armies.

The Pskovian army barred the way of the Lithuanian army, but these lawless Lithuanian warriors fiercely and daringly scaled the wall. The enemy artillery made such large breaches in the wall that even the cavalry could go through them. And at the Virgin's Veil and the Hog Gates there was not a single place safe from the enemy's artillery and guns. The Russians had begun building new wooden walls of many stories for artillery, but they could not complete them because of the heavy enemy artillery barrage. And only their foundations were completed. Thus many enemy warriors were able to climb the city walls. Many of their captains and gaiduks scaled the Virgin's Veil and Hog Towers with their banners, shooting at our defenders from the tower windows and from behind their shields. The first to scale the wall and to remain on it were the enemy's veteran soldiers who were clad in steel armor and armed with the best of weapons. The tsar's boyars and voevodas and the entire

Orthodox army resisted them firmly and unbendingly, fighting bravely and skillfully, and not letting the enemy into the city.

When the most glorified King Stephen saw that his choicest storm troops were on the walls of the city, that his captains and gaiduks had unfurled the banners of the Lithuanian army over the Virgin's Veil and Hog Towers, and that they opened fire against the city and against the Russian artillery to open the way for the taking of the city, his heart was filled with indescribable joy. And he looked hopefully forward to the taking of the fortress. He moved his headquarters closer to the city, into the church of Christ's great martyr, Nikita, which was situated one-half mile from the wall of Pskov.

His retinue, councilors, and beloved foremost aristocrats approached the king and spoke words of hope and praise to him: "Our lord and sovereign, you have done it. You are the conqueror and victorious ruler of the city of Pskov. Glory be to you. We beg you, extend your kindness to us and allow us to proceed to the fortress of Pskov, so that not only your captains and gaiduks will know the glory of having taken Pskov."

When the king heard how joyfully his noblemen and councilors expressed their readiness to fulfill his plans, joy overcame him. With a gay face and happy heart he told them, as if they were his brothers, "Well, my friends, if you show such intentions to fight, I shall also go with you and not stay behind, my friends."

But they answered: "Oh, our sovereign, King Stephen! You will make your triumphant and glorious entry into this great city of Pskov, in the same way as the great king, Alexander the Great, made his glorious and triumphant entry into the city of Rome.[5] And in the same way as Alexander's courtiers met him in the city, so also shall we, your servants, meet you in the city of Pskov with a hymn of glory. And we will prepare for you the spoils of the city. And we will meet you with the Russian commanders of Pskov, whom we shall capture! And for a particularly cherished treasure, we shall meet you with the two captured boyars and voevodas: the first commander of Pskov, Prince Vasily Shuysky, and the glorious, strong, invincible, great, and courageous second commander, Prince Ivan Shuysky. And we shall put them both in irons before you. And you, our sovereign, will do what you please with them in order that they be punished for their unruly resistance to you."

[5] Either the Polish nobles erred in their speeches or the author of this tale did, for Alexander the Great certainly was never at war with Rome.

Hearing this, the king permitted them to go to the walls of the fortress of Pskov with joy, telling them the following: "I knew, friends, that it always would happen as you used to predict, and so it will happen now. And you will accomplish what you intend to, for no one can resist you and your brilliant mind." And two thousand selected storm troops and personal guards of the king began the assault of the Hog Tower, which was already destroyed on their side, and they began shooting through the windows of the wall at the Christian people and at the Russian militia. Their bullets fell like drops of rain from a storm cloud, and flooded the Russian warriors. These bullets were killing the Christian people as if they were the stings of serpents. Other enemy troops stormed through the break in the Virgin's Veil Tower, and cleared the tower of Russian warriors, preparing the way for the final taking of the city.

The Russian voevodas, their soldiers, and the Pskovian militia firmly and courageously stood their ground. Some waited for the enemy with lances at the foot of the wall. The streltsy shot at the Poles with their muskets. Some of the noblemen shot with their bows, while still others hurled rocks or defended the city of Pskov in other ways. The artillery shot at the Russian army from the walls and the towers and, relieving tired ones with fresh troops, they shot incessantly and shouted, "Let's take the city of Pskov!"

The king often sent his messenger to them, inquiring whether the city had been taken, and ordered the commanders, captains, and the entire army to speed the taking of the city.

In the God-protected city of Pskov the voevodas and boyars of the tsar, with kindness and tears, urged their Christian warriors to fight heartily, and they, themselves, fought unyieldingly at the side of their troops. It was sad to see the heads of the Christian warriors falling to the earth like the ears of wheat torn from the ground and lying in one heap. Many soldiers fell from the many wounds inflicted by the enemy's weapons, from exhaustion, and from the incessant fighting. During the day it was extremely hot because of the burning sun. Only faith in God's protection and deliverance gave strength to the warriors.

In the city itself and in the Cathedral of the Life-Giving Trinity the clergy incessantly prayed with tears and moaning for deliverance of the city. When the clergy of the cathedral learned the news that the Lithuanians were already on the walls and in the towers, and that they had unfurled their banners and were shooting from the walls into the city, preparing their way, then Tikhon, the abbot of the Caves Monastery, and archpriest Luka, and all the deacons of the city began to weep with loud voices, extending their arms to the most holy icon. They fell to their knees. Like the streams of many rivers their tears covered the marble steps of the altar, and they began to pray with more fervor, asking the Holy Virgin to protect the city and its inhabitants. The noble ladies, who had gathered in the cathedral for the service, beat their breasts and prayed to God and the most Pure Virgin; they fell on the floor, beating the ground with their heads and crying for divine help. And in every house of the great and God-protected city of Pskov the women, infants, and children who remained at home fervently cried and prayed before the holy icons, beating their breasts and asking the Holy Virgin and all saints for help, and begging God for the forgiveness of their sins and deliverance of the city. And in all the streets of the city there was crying, moaning, and indescribable wailing.

The enemy troops were incessantly and steadily advancing. "Forward, friends!" shouted their officers. "Let us slay all the people of Pskov for their unsubmissiveness. Not even a memory of the Christian inhabitants of Pskov will remain. The shadow of death will engulf them, and nothing will be able to aid them in escaping from our hands."

But who can speak of the power of God? Who can praise his glory?

Blessed are those that fear God and follow his righteous ways,

and who honestly enjoy the fruits of their labors.

Listen, all people of the universe.

Listen all sons of man.

Listen all rich and poor.

Come all saints of Russia to the Christian land to aid the city of Pskov.

You have prayed for us and have helped us through your prayers to God.

You protected the city of Pskov,

which verily I say unto you is the God-protected city.

Let us glorify and declare together the power of the Holy Trinity.

God is our protection and power; God is our aid in the sorrow befallen us.

Therefore, I verily say unto you,

that we have no fear, as the voice of the prophet announced it.

Great is God and greatly is he glorified in this city of God.
We recognize God, who is on his holy mountain,
when we are in misfortune and when he intercedes for us.
For our humility God did not forsake us
when the kings of the earth gathered to march on Pskov,
    saying:
"God has abandoned that city. Let us hurry and take it."

O Lithuanian commander, Stephen Bathory!
Your tongue is cursed, and both you and your army are in-
    sanely proud.
How can you say that no one will deliver this city?
The power of God is with us!
Our Protector is the God of Jacob, the God of the Glorified
    Trinity,
the One God who has three names, but whom we worship
    as One,
the Father, the Son, and the Holy Ghost.
We place our hope in him and we rely upon him.
But you, Bathory, do not know him with your lawless
    Latin Heresies.
And you, Bathory, who place your own majesty before that
    of Heaven,
hope to conquer the city of Pskov, relying on your multi-
    tude of forces.
Wait, accursed one! You will see what happens to your
    forces!
You will see whether there is One who can deliver us!
And what is the worth of all your proud bragging about
    the taking of Pskov?
Because of your pride, you will now experience humiliation.
And from the heights of arrogance, you will descend to the
    hell of shame.
And so will it happen to your army,
for the Lord has remembered us for our humility
and has delivered us from our enemies.
And the Lord has heard the prayers of his servants
and through the miracle of his unfathomable compassion,
his mercy was revealed,
and he delivered his people and showed clemency to his
    servants.

  A bomb from the great gun called the Leopard, which was
placed upon the Praise Bastion, hit the Hog Tower squarely.

And the bomb killed a great many Polish and Lithuanian warriors. At about the same time, the tsar's boyars and voevodas ordered the exploding of a large quantity of black powder under this Hog Tower. And the overproud knights, courtiers, and nobles of the king, who had begged their king for permission to take the city of Pskov and bring in the Russian boyars and voevodas in irons, as it was previously mentioned, were blasted into the air according to God's design, and were thus slain by these Russian boyars and voevodas. And the corpses were so numerous that another tower might have been built with them. And the best of the royal nobles, who had boasted that they would bring the imprisoned Russian commanders to their king, remained under the ruins of the Hog Tower, prisoners of death until the Last Judgment. And the deep Pskovian moat was overflowing with their bodies.

The king learned this, when he asked, "Are my noblemen already in the castle?"

And his courtiers told him: "No, sire, they are under the walls of the castle."

And then the king asked, "Do my nobles fight behind the walls of the city and destroy the Russian forces?"

And they answered, "Sire, all your nobles have been killed in the Hog Tower or lie burned in the moat."

And the king was so bereaved that he wanted to run on his sword, as the pagans used to do, for his heart was bursting with sorrow. And he became wroth, and ordered his captains and storm troops who were fighting at the Virgin's Veil Tower to stand firm and take by any and all means the city of Pskov.

The tsar's boyars and voevodas, seeing the heavy and uninterrupted bombardment, the incessant storming, and realizing that many of their warriors had been killed or wounded, relied only upon the help of God. They sent for the holy and miracle-working icons and for the miracle-working relics of the faithful and great Prince Gabriel[6] who had once delivered the city of Pskov from the enemy. And they ordered that the icons be brought to the breach which had been made in the wall by the Poles. Once the holy icon of the Holy Virgin of Vladimir had protected the city of Moscow at the time of Tamerlane's invasion. Now another icon was brought to Pskov because of the invasion of King Stephen Bathory. Once the icon of the Virgin

[6] Prince Gabriel, as well as Prince Dovmont, mentioned in the following paragraph, were rulers of Pskov in the thirteenth and fourteenth centuries, and became known for their courageous defense of Pskov against the Teutonic Knights of the Livonian Order.

protected the city of Moscow from the infamous lame man
[Tamerlane]. Now another icon of the Virgin, which had been
brought from the Crypt Monastery,[7] helped and protected
Pskov. At that time the holy icon of Vladimir was brought to
Moscow on the day of the Assumption of the Holy Virgin, and
Tamerlane was defeated because he became afraid of this icon
of the Pure Virgin, and fled with all his army from Moscow and
from Russia. This time the miracle happened in the glorious city
of Pskov, on the very day of the venerable and glorious holy day
of her birth.

When the holy, miracle-working icon of the Assumption of
the Holy Virgin of the Crypt Monastery was brought from the
Cathedral of the Holy Trinity with other icons, relics of Prince
Gabriel, and other holy relics, divine protection invisibly appeared over the breach in the wall.

The Poles and Lithuanians were fiercely fighting against the
Russians in the breaches of the wall and in the Virgin's Veil
Tower. Together with the warriors, the Russian officers and
commanders were fighting, preventing the enemy from breaking
through into Pskov. And when the church procession moved
from the cathedral with the icons, at the head of the procession,
black-robed heralds rushed on their steeds; they were not
soldiers, but the warriors of Christ. Among them were the cellarer of the Crypt Monastery, whose name was Arseny Khvostov;
the treasurer of the Monastery of the Birth of the Holy Virgin
in Snetegorsk, Jonah Naumov; and the abbot, Mantiry, who was
known to everyone in Pskov. All three of these monks were
aristocrats by birth and, before becoming monks, had been great
warriors. Seeing the bloody battle, they rushed to the breach
and, for the sake of God and their holy faith, called out in strong
voices. And it seemed as if these voices were coming from the
icons. They called to the commanders and to the whole Christian army: "Be not afraid. Let us stand firm. Let us charge
against the Polish and Lithuanian forces. The Holy Virgin has
come to our aid with all her mercy and protection, and with all
the saints."

As soon as the words were heard that the Holy Virgin had
come with all the saints to help the Russian commanders and
warriors, they felt that the Holy Virgin really did give them her
blessing and protection, and thus their weakening hearts became

---

[7] The Crypt Monastery mentioned here is west of the city of Pskov,
and has preserved to the present its fortifications built by Ivan IV.
The name of the monastery was apparently taken from the Kievan
Cave (or Crypt) Monastery.

firm and they became ready for heroic deeds. In their hearts they accepted the aid of the Holy Virgin, and all commanders, warriors, and the aforementioned monks cried out in unison: "Oh, friends, let us die this day at the hands of the Lithuanians for the sake of Christ's faith and for our Orthodox tsar, Ivan of all the Russias! Let us not surrender to the Polish king, Stephen!" And they appealed also for the intercession of the holy protectors of Pskov, late Prince Gabriel, late Prince Dovmont, and Nicholas, the fool in Christ. And in their hearts they accepted their help, and the entire Russian Christian army stormed the enemy together, and they were fighting in the breach of the wall.

Thus, with God's and the Holy Virgin's help, and with the intercession of the holy miracle workers, the Russians expelled the Polish-Lithuanian forces from the breach and, where recently stood the feet of the enemy, now stood the firm feet of the Christian warriors. And they continued to defeat the enemy, going beyond the walls of the city, while others fought with the Lithuanian troops who remained in the Virgin's Veil Tower.

When the Lord demonstrated the Christian victory over Paul the Lithuanian, and when the Russian troops repulsed the Lithuanian warriors, captains, and gaiduks from the breach in the wall, this news of the blessing of Christ spread throughout the entire city of Pskov, and reached the women who had been left at home. And the word that the enemy had been stopped through divine help spread from house to house. And the women were ordered to go take the Lithuanian artillery and the remnants of the Lithuanian and Polish troops that remained in the city, and then to gather at the breach. And all the women of Pskov, who had remained in their homes in great sorrow, were seized with joy, forgot their womanly weaknesses, and gained the strength of men, hurried to the breach, and took from their homes weapons according to their strengths. Even before, at the beginning of the assault, some strong young women had been fighting against the enemy with arms. Now all, the young, the strong, and the weak, were running with ropes to pull the artillery pieces left by the enemy into the city. All of them rushed to the breach. And each woman wanted to surpass the others in her speed. A multiude of women gathered at the breach, and they were great help for the Christian warriors. Some of them, as I mentioned above, who were young and strong, fought with masculine courage against the Polish and Lithuanian forces, demonstrating their superiority over them. The others brought rocks so that the soldiers might hurl them at the Lithuanians both within and outside of the fortress. Others helped the warriors, and brought them water to quench their thirst, thus bringing back courage to their brave hearts.

This happened on Friday, on the holy day of the Holy Virgin's Birth. It was already evening, but the Polish and Lithuanians were still fighting in the Virgin's Veil Tower and were shooting against the Christian warriors in the city. Then the tsar's boyars and voevodas appealed to God for succor, called their troops together, and began the storming of the Virgin's Veil Tower. Men and women hurled themselves against the remaining enemy troops in the tower, fighting with all the arms given to them by God. Some shot muskets, while others were trying to smoke out the enemy from their hiding places. Others threw rocks at the Poles and Lithuanians, while still others poured boiling water upon them. Finally they put black powder under this tower also, and with God's help they blasted the remaining Lithuanians and Poles from the Virgin's Veil Tower. In this way, with the Grace of Christ, the stone wall of Pskov was cleansed of the evil Lithuanian feet. When night came, God sent light, and the remainder of the enemy was driven out from under the walls.

And then the Lithuanians and Poles began to flee from the fortress back to their camps. The Christian Russian warriors made sorties from the fortress, pursued them, cut them to pieces, and chased the others away. Those who remained in the moat were destroyed. Many were taken prisoner and brought back to the city, to the tsar's boyars and voevodas to be interrogated. Many enemy warriors were taken with banners, drums, and weapons. And many Russians returned to the city uninjured, and brought back with them enemy arms, special muskets, guns, and endless booty.

Thus, with God's blessing, through the infinite mercy of the Divine Trinity, and the prayers and intercession of the Holy Virgin, and in the honor of her glorious birth, and for the sake of the holy, great miracle workers, the great city of Pskov was delivered from the Poles and Lithuanians. And at three o'clock in the night the Lord gave a great victory to the Christian army over the proud and lawless enemy.

[The final part of this work describes the fighting around Pskov until February 4, 1582, the day when King Stephen Bathory lifted the siege of this fiercely embattled Russian fortress.]

EPISTOLARY POLEMICS

33. *Prince Andrew Kurbsky: First Epistle Written to the Tsar and Grand Prince of Moscow in Consequence of His Fierce Persecution*

PRINCE Andrew Kurbsky's first epistle to Ivan IV is a strong protest against Tsar Ivan's autocratic rule. Wishing to destroy the old feudal system of Russia, by which the princes were practically independent rulers of their appanages, Ivan IV began a systematic purge of the aristocracy in the late 1550's and many nobles died on the scaffold or in prison.

An outstanding statesman and military leader, Prince Kurbsky was a close friend and adviser of Tsar Ivan IV until the latter began his cruel struggle against the Russian feudal aristocracy. Kurbsky then broke with the tsar and fled to Lithuania, where he settled for the rest of his life. Kurbsky had belonged to the intellectual elite of sixteenth-century Moscow and had been a pupil and friend of the famous and erudite scholar-monk, Maxim Trivolis, called Maxim the Greek, who had come to Russia in the early years of the sixteenth century. Living in Lithuania, Andrew Kurbsky became a writer and translator and participated in the revival of Russian Orthodox literature in the Russian parts of Poland and Lithuania. His best-known work is his correspondence with Ivan IV, in which he sharply criticized the tsar's autocratic policies and his persecution of the aristocracy.

This translation of the letter was made by J. L. I. Fennell and was published in *The Correspondence Between Prince A. M. Kurbsky and Tsar Ivan IV of Russia, 1564–1579*, Cambridge University Press, 1955, pages 3, 5, 7, 9, and 11.

✦ ✦ ✦

To the tsar, exalted above all by God, who appeared (formerly) most illustrious, particularly in the Orthodox faith, but who has now, in consequence of our sins, been found to be the contrary of this. If you have understanding, may you understand this with your leprous conscience—such a conscience as cannot be found even amongst the godless peoples. And I have not let my tongue say more than this on all these matters in turn; but because of the bitterest persecution from your power, with much sorrow in my heart will I hasten to inform you of a little.

Wherefore, O tsar, have you destroyed the strong in Israel
and subjected to various forms of death the *voevodas* given to
you by God?[1] And wherefore have you spilled their victorious
holy blood in the churches of God during sacerdotal ceremonies,
and stained the thresholds of the churches with their blood of
martyrs?[2] And why have you conceived against your well-
wishers and against those who lay down their lives for you
unheard-of torments and persecutions and death, falsely accusing the Orthodox of treachery and magic and other abuses, and
endeavoring with zeal to turn light into darkness and to call
sweet bitter? What guilt did they commit before you, O tsar,
and in what way did they, the champions of Christianity, anger
you? Have they not destroyed proud kingdoms and by their
heroic bravery made subject to you in all things those in whose
servitude our forefathers formerly were? Was it not through the
keenness of their understanding that the strong German towns
were given to you by God?[3] Thus have you remunerated us
[your] poor [servants], destroying us by whole families? Think
you yourself immortal, O tsar? Or have you been enticed into
unheard-of heresy, as one no longer wishing to stand before the
impartial judge, Jesus, begotten of God, who will judge according to justice the universe and especially the vainglorious tor-
mentors, and who unhesitatingly will question them "right to the
hairs [roots?] of their sins," as the saying goes? He is my Christ
who sitteth on the throne of the Cherubims at the right hand of
the power of the Almighty in the highest—the judge between
you and me.

What evil and persecution have I not suffered from you!
What ills and misfortunes have you not brought upon me! And
what iniquitous tissues of lies have you not woven against me!
But I cannot now recount the various misfortunes at your hands

[1] The expression "the strong in Israel" echoes the current panegyrical political literature of the sixteenth century, extolling the
absolution of the grand prince and the supremacy of Moscow, "the
Third Rome," "the new Israel."

[2] A reference to the first wave of Ivan's persecutions which, according to Kurbsky (Skazaniia Kn. A. M. Kurbskogo, ed. N. Ustrialov
[St. Petersburg, 1842], "Istoria . . ." Chapter VI, page 90) began
"shortly after the death of Alexis Adashev and the banishment of
Priest Sylvester," i.e., in 1560.

[3] The "proud kingdoms" destroyed by the "strong in Israel" in the
fifties of the sixteenth century were the Tatar Khanates of Kazan
(captured in 1552) and Astrakhan (captured in 1556). The "strong
German towns" are the Baltic towns captured during the first three
years of the Livonian War (1558–1560): Narva, Neuhausen, and
Dorpat (1558); Marienburg, Ermes, and Fellin (1560).

which have beset me owing to their multitude and since I am still filled with the grief of my soul. But, to conclude, I can summarize them all [thus]: of everything have I been deprived; I have been driven from the land of God without guilt [*lit.* in vain], hounded by you. I did not ask [for aught] with humble words, nor did I beseech you with tearful plaint; nor yet did I win from you any mercy through the intercession of the hierarchy. You have recompensed me with evil for good and for my love with implacable hatred. My blood, spilled like water for you, cries out against you to my Lord. God sees into [men's] hearts—in my mind have I ardently reflected and my conscience have I placed as a witness [against myself], and I have sought and pried within my thoughts, and, examining myself [*lit.* turning myself around], I know not now—nor have I ever found—my guilt in aught before you. In front of your army have I marched—and marched again; and no dishonor have I brought upon you; but only brilliant victories, with the help of the angel of the Lord, have I won for your glory, and never have I turned the back of your regiments to the foe. But far more, I have achieved most glorious conquests to increase your renown. And this, not in one year, nor yet in two—but throughout many years have I toiled with much sweat and patience; and always have I been separated from my fatherland, and little have I seen my parents, and my wife have I not known; but always in far distant towns have I stood in arms against your foes and I have suffered many wants and natural illnesses, of which my Lord Jesus Christ is witness. Still more, I was visited with wounds inflicted by barbarian hands in various battles and all my body is already afflicted with sores. But to you, O tsar, was all this as nought; rather do you show us your intolerable wrath and bitterest hatred, and, furthermore, burning stoves.[4]

And I wanted to relate all my military deeds in turn which I have accomplished for your glory by the strength of my Christ, but I have not recounted them for this reason, that God knows better than man. For he is the recompenser for all these things, and not only for them, but also for a cup of cold water; and I know that you yourself are not unaware of them. And furthermore may this be known to you, O tsar; you will, I think,

---

[4] Evidently one of the commonest forms of torture employed by Ivan IV. Kurbsky speaks of Ivan's torture in his *History:* "Are not the various instruments of torture of the ancient torturers the same as those used by our new torturer [i.e. Ivan]? Pans and stoves? Cruel flogging and sharp nails? Red-hot pincers for lacerating human bodies? Needles to drive under the fingernails . . . ?" (p. 145)

no longer see my face in this world until the glorious coming of
my Christ. Think not that concerning these things I will remain
silent before you; to my end will I incessantly cry out with tears
against you to the everlasting Trinity, in which I believe; and
I call to my aid the Mother of the Lord of the Cherubims, my
hope and protectress, Our Lady, the Mother of God, and all the
Saints, the elect of God, and my master and forefather, Prince
Fedor Rostislavich, whose corpse remains imperishable, preserved throughout the ages, and emits from the grave sweet
odors, sweeter than aromatics, and, by the grave of the Holy
Ghost, pours forth miraculous healing streams, as you, O tsar,
know well.[5]

Deem not, O tsar, and think not upon us with your sophistic
thoughts, as though we had already perished, massacred [though
we are] by you in our innocence and banished and driven out
by you without justice; rejoice not in this, glorying, as it were,
in a vain victory; those massacred by you, standing at the throne
of our Lord, ask vengeance against you; while we who have
been banished and driven out by you without justice from the
land cry out day and night to God, however much in your pride
you may boast in this temporal, fleeting life, devising vessels of
torture against the Christian race, yea, and abusing and trampling on the Angelic Form,[6] with the approbation of your flat-
terers and comrades of the table, your quarrelsome boyars, the
destroyers of your soul and body, who urge you on to erotic
deeds and, together with their children, act more [viciously]
than the priests of Cronus. So much for this. And this epistle,
soaked in my tears, will I order to be put into my grave with
me, when I [shall be about to] come with you before the judgment of my God, Jesus Christ. Amen.

Written in Wolmar, the town of my master, King Augustus
Sigismund, from whom I hope to receive much reward and com-

---

[5] Fedor Rostislavich, prince of Yaroslavl, Andrew Kurbsky's
paternal grandfather to the ninth degree, ruled in Mozhaisk at the
end of the thirteenth century. In 1294 he received the principality of
Yaroslavl after marrying the daughter of Vasily Vsevolodovich, prince
of Yaroslavl. He died in 1299 and was canonized in 1463.

[6] The Russian expression "to accept the Angel's form" is the
equivalent of "to take monastic vows." In certain copies of the text
there exists the following marginal note: "That is to say, he abuses
the Angelic Form when he flies into a rage with certain people and
then forces them to accept the monastic tonsure together with their
wives and children, and condemns them to everlasting imprisonment
in strong monasteries and dark cells, making the holy places fortresses
of hell with the approbation of certain accursed and cunning monks."

fort for all my sorrow, by his sovereign grace, and still more with
God's help.

I have heard from sacred writings that a destroyer will be
sent by the devil against the human race, a destroyer conceived
in fornication, the Antichrist, hostile to God; and now I have
seen a counselor, known to all, who was born in adultery and
who today whispers falsehoods in the ears of the tsar and sheds
Christian blood like water and has already destroyed the strong
and noble in Israel, as one in agreement with the Antichrist in
deed.[7] It is not befitting, O tsar, to show indulgence to such
men! In the first law of the Lord it is written: "A Moabite and
an Ammonite and a bastard to the tenth generation shall not
enter into the congregation of the Lord."[8]

34. Ivan IV: Epistle of the Tsar and Sovereign to All His Russian Tsardom Against Those Who Have Broken the Pledge of Allegiance, Against Prince Andrew Kurbsky and His Comrades, Concerning Their Treacheries

THE epistle of Ivan IV, the Terrible, to Prince Andrew Kurbsky
is one of the most impressive works defending the Byzantine-
Russian concept of autocracy, which accepted the tsar as ruler
by divine right. Ivan IV thus claimed the exclusive right to
command the destinies of the state and his subjects, while considering himself responsible only to God for the fate of the state
and its people. (Concerning Prince Andrew Kurbsky and the
roots of this conflict, see the introduction to Prince Kurbsky's
letter to Ivan.)

A cruel tyrant who was merciless to his enemies, Ivan IV was
at the same time a great ruler whose policies helped determine
the future of Russia. By breaking the power of the aristocracy
he ended the feudal system of medieval Russia and thus laid
the foundation for a unified Russian state. His successes against
the Tatars opened to Russia the nearly limitless territories of the

[7] This is probably a reference to Fedor Alekseevich Basmanov, who
was a favorite of Ivan's at that time. He was, indeed, renowned for
his cruelty, and is alleged by Kurbsky to have murdered his father.
There is, however, no confirmation of his illegitimacy.

[8] See Deuteronomy, 23: 2-3.

Tsar Ivan IV (the Terrible).
A late sixteenth-century Russian portrait.

Volga-Ural region and northern Asia, thus paving the way for future Russian expansion. Some one hundred and fifty years before Peter the Great, Ivan IV tried to open a window to Europe and to end Russia's isolation by winning an area on the Baltic shore from the Order of Livonian Knights.

Ivan IV was very well educated, was a forceful polemicist and writer, and even composed music. His style of writing is not restrained, but fierce, stinging and merciless, and he did not hesitate to insult his enemies.

These excerpts from Tsar Ivan's letter to Prince Kurbsky, which grew into a rather lengthy treatise, have been translated by Leo Wiener.

◆ ◆ ◆

Our God, the Trinity, who has existed since eternity but now as Father, Son and Holy Ghost, has neither beginning nor end; through him we live and move about, through him kings rule and the mighty write laws. By our Lord Jesus Christ the victorious standard of God's only Word and the blessed Cross, which has never been vanquished, have been given to Emperor Constantine, first in piety, and to all the orthodox tsars and protectors of orthodoxy, and insofar as the Word of God has been fulfilled, they, in eagle's flight, have reached all the godly servants of God's Word, until a spark of piety has fallen upon the Russian realm. The autocracy, by God's will, had its origin in Grand Prince Vladimir, who had enlightened all Russia through the holy baptism, and the great Tsar Vladimir Monomakh, who had received memorable honors from the Greeks, and the valiant great Tsar Alexander Nevsky, who had obtained a great victory over the godless Germans, and the praiseworthy great Tsar Dmitry, who had obtained a great victory over the sons of Hagar beyond the Don, then it passed to the avenger of wrongs, our ancestor, the great Tsar Ivan, the gatherer of the Russian land from among the ancestral possessions, and to our father of blessed memory, the great Tsar Vasily until it reached us, the humble scepter-bearer of the Russian empire.[1]

[1] Roman Emperor Constantine (306–337) granted the rights to the Christians, and summoned the first Ecumenical Council of the Christian Church. Prince Vladimir Christianized Russia in 988 or 989. Vladimir Monomakh was the last prince of Kiev (1112–1125) to be recognized as Grand Prince by all Russian princes of the Kievan era. Dmitry, Grand Prince of Muscovy, was the victor over the Tatars in 1380. "The great Tsar Ivan" is Ivan III, unifier of northern Russia (1462–1505) and grandfather of Ivan IV. Vasily—Vasily III (1505–1533)—was father to Ivan IV.

But we praise God for the great favor he has shown me in
not permitting my right hand to become stained by the blood of
my race: for we have not snatched the realm from anyone, but
by the will of God and the blessing of our ancestors and parents,
were we born in the realm, were brought up there and enthroned, taking, by the will of God and the blessing of our ancestors and parents, what belonged to us, and not seizing that
which was not ours. Here follows the command of the orthodox,
truly Christian autocrat, the possessor of many kingdoms—our
humble Christian answer to him who was an orthodox, true
Christian and a boyar of our realm, a councilor and a general,
but now is a criminal before the blessed, vivifying cross of the
Lord, a destroyer of Christians, a servant of the enemies of
Christianity, who has departed from the divine worship of the
images and has trodden underfoot all sacred commands, destroyed the holy edifices, vilified and trampled the holy vessels
and images, who unites in one person Leo the Isaurian, Constantine Kopronymos and Leo of Armenia—to Prince Andrew
Mikhailovich Kurbsky, who through treachery wanted to become
a ruler of Yaroslavl.[2]

Wherefore, O Prince, if you regard yourself to have piety,
have you lost your soul? What will you give in its place on the
day of the terrible judgment? Even if you should acquire the
whole world, death will reach you in the end! Why have you
sold your soul for your body's sake? Is it because you were afraid
of death at the false instigation of your demons and influential
friends and counselors? . . .

Are you not ashamed before your slave Vaska Shibanov,[3] who
preserved his piety and, having attached himself to you with a
kiss of the cross, did not reject you before the tsar and the
whole people, though standing at the gate of death, but praised
you and was all too ready to die for you? But you did not emulate his devotion: on account of a single angry word of mine,
have you lost not only your own soul, but the souls of all your
ancestors: for, by God's will, had they been given as servants to
our grandfather, the great tsar, and they gave their souls to
him and served him up to their death, and ordered you, their
children, to serve the children and grandchildren of our grand-

---

[2] Leo III the Isaurian (717–741), Constantine V Kopronymos
(741–755), and Leo V, the Armenian, were Byzantine emperors who
supported the heresy of the iconoclasts and were posthumously condemned by the Orthodox Church.

[3] Vaska (Vasily) Shibanov, a faithful servant of Prince A. M.
Kurbsky who delivered his master's letter to Ivan IV, and died after
long tortures without betraying the prince.

father. But you have forgotten everything and traitorously, like a dog, have you transgressed the oath and have gone over to the enemies of Christianity, and, not considering your wrath, you utter stupid words, hurling, as it were, stones at the sky. . . .

We have never spilled blood in the churches. As for the victorious, saintly blood—there has none appeared in our land, as far as we know. *The thresholds of the churches:* as far as our means and intelligence permit and our subjects are eager to serve us, the churches of the Lord are resplendent with all kinds of adornments, and through the gifts which we have offered since your satanic domination, not only the thresholds and pavements, but even the antechambers shine with ornaments, so that all the strangers may see them. We do not stain the thresholds of the churches with any blood, and there are no martyrs of faith with us nowadays. . . . Tortures and persecutions and deaths in many forms we have devised against no one. As to treasons and magic, it is true, such dogs everywhere suffer capital punishment. . . .

It had pleased God to take away our mother, the pious Tsarina Helen, from the earthly kingdom to the kingdom of heaven. My brother George, who now rests in heaven, and I were left orphans and, as we received no care from anyone, we laid our trust in the Holy Virgin, and in the prayers of all the saints, and in the blessing of our parents. When I was in my eighth year, our subjects acted according to their will, for they found the empire without a ruler, and did not deign to bestow their voluntary attention upon us, their master, but were bent on acquiring wealth and glory, and were quarreling with each other. And what have they not done! How many boyars, how many friends of our father and generals they have killed! And they seized the farms and villages and possessions of our uncles, and established themselves therein. The treasure of our mother they trod underfoot and pierced with sharp sticks, and transferred it to the great treasure, but some of it they grabbed themselves; and that was done by your grandfather Mikhaylo Tuchkov. The Princes Vasily and Ivan Shuysky took it upon themselves to have me in their keeping, and those who had been the chief traitors of our father and mother they let out of prison, and they made friends with them. Prince Vasily Shuysky with a Judas crowd fell in the court belonging to our uncle upon our father confessor Fedor Mishurin, and insulted him, and killed him; and they imprisoned Prince Ivan Fedorovich Byelsky and many others in various places, and armed themselves against the realm; they ousted metropolitan Daniel from the metropoli-

tan see and banished him: and thus they improved their opportunity, and began to rule themselves.

Me and my brother George, of blessed memory, they brought
up like vagrants and children of the poorest. What have I not
suffered for want of garments and food! And all that against my
will and as did not become my extreme youth. I shall mention
just one thing: once in my childhood we were playing, and
Prince Ivan Vasilievich Shuysky was sitting on a bench, leaning
with his elbow against our father's bed, and even putting his
foot upon it; he treated us not as a parent, but as a master . . .
who could bear such presumption? How can I recount all the
miseries which I have suffered in my youth? Often did I dine
late, against my will. What had become of the treasure left me
by my father? They had carried everything away, under the
cunning pretext that they had to pay the boyar children from it,
but, in reality, they had kept it back from them, to their own
advantage, and had not paid them off according to their deserts;
and they had also held back an immense treasure of my grandfather and father, and made it into gold and silver vessels, in-
scribing thereupon the names of their parents, as if they had
been their inheritance. . . . It is hardly necessary to mention
what became of the treasure of our uncles: they appropriated it
all to themselves! Then they attacked towns and villages, tortured the people most cruelly, brought much misery upon them,
and mercilessly pillaged the possessions of the inhabitants. . . .

When we reached the age of fifteen, we, inspired by God,
undertook to rule our own realm and, with the aid of almighty
God, we ruled our realm in peace and undisturbed, according
to our will. But it happened then that, on account of our sins, a
fire having spread, by God's will, the royal city of Moscow was
consumed. Our boyars, the traitors whom you call martyrs,
whose names I shall purposely pass over in silence, made use of
the favorable opportunity for their mean treachery, whispered
into the ears of a stupid crowd that the mother of my mother,
Princess Anna Glinsky, with all her children and household, was
in the habit of extracting men's hearts, and that by a similar
sorcery she had put Moscow on fire, and that we knew of her
doings.[4] By the instigation of these our traitors, a mass of in-
sensate people, crying in the manner of the Jews, came to the
apostolic cathedral of the holy martyr Dmitry of Saloniki,
dragged out of it our boyar Yury Vasilevich Glinsky, pulled him

[4] Princes Shuyskys were members of an influential and wealthy
aristocratic family who actually ruled in Moscow during Ivan IV's
childhood.

inhumanly into the cathedral of the Assumption, and killed the innocent man in the church, opposite the metropolitan's place; they stained the floor of the church with his blood, dragged his body through the front door, and exposed him on the market-place as a criminal—everybody knows about this murder in the church. We were then living in the village of Vorobievo; the same traitors instigated the populace to kill us under the pretext, and you, dog, repeat the lie that we were keeping from them Prince Yury's mother, Princess Anna, and his brother, Prince Mikhail. How is one not to laugh at such stupidity? Why should we be incendiaries in our own empire? . . .

You say that your blood has been spilled in wars with foreigners, and you add, in your foolishness, that it cries to God against us. That is ridiculous! It has been spilled by one, and it cries out against another. If it is true that your blood has been spilled by the enemy, then you have done your duty to your country; if you had not done so, you would not have been a Christian but a barbarian—but that is not our affair. How much more ours, that has been spilled by you, cries out to the Lord against you! Not with wounds, nor drops of blood, but with much sweating and toiling have I been burdened by you unnecessarily and above my strength! Your many meannesses and persecutions have caused me, instead of blood, to shed many tears, and to utter sobs and have anguish of my soul. . . .

You say you want to put your letter in your grave: that shows that you have completely renounced your Christianity! For God has ordered not to resist evil, but you renounce the final pardon which is granted to the ignorant; therefore it is not even proper that any Mass shall be sung after you. In our patrimony, in the country of Lifland, you name the city of Volmir as belonging to our enemy, King Sigismund: by this you only complete the treachery of a vicious dog![5] . . .

Written in our great Russia, in the famous, imperial, capital city of Moscow, on the steps of our imperial threshold, in the year from the creation of the world 1564 (7072), the fifth day of July.

[5] The city of Volmir, actually Volmar, was conquered by Ivan IV during the first phase of the Livonian War (see introduction to Selection 32, the *Story of Stephen Bathory's Campaign Against Pskov*), and later was claimed by the Polish King Sigismund.

HISTORICAL WORKS FROM THE
TIME OF TROUBLES

35. *Avraamy Palitsyn: Pseudo-Dmitry*

Soon after the death of Ivan IV, the Rurik dynasty, which had presided over Russia's destiny for seven hundred years, came to its end. Ivan had accidentally killed his eldest and favorite son, Tsarevich Ivan, and the throne was inherited by the physically and mentally debile Fedor. After reigning fourteen years, 1584 to 1598, Tsar Fedor died without leaving an heir to the throne. The dynastic crisis was aggravated by the fact that Ivan's youngest son, Dmitry, mysteriously perished in 1591. Rumors circulated that he had been slain at the order of Boris Godunov, Tsar Fedor's brother-in-law, a brilliant but ruthless statesman who wanted the throne for himself. Indeed, the Land Assembly, which was manipulated by Boris, elected him as Tsar of all the Russias in 1598. His reign was not a happy one, however, for Russia was plagued by famines and epidemics. Moreover, in 1602 a mysterious impostor appeared who claimed that he was Tsarevich Dmitry, the son of Ivan IV, declaring that he had escaped the knives of Boris' henchmen in 1590. The Poles, the age-old rivals and enemies of Russia, supported Dmitry and his claim to the Russian throne. He also received the blessing of the Pope of Rome, and in return Pseudo-Dmitry promised the Holy See that he would convert all Russia to the Roman Catholic faith. In 1604 he began his campàign against Tsar Boris, leading both Russian and Polish troops. Upon the unexpected death of Boris Godunov, Dmitry entered Moscow and became tsar in 1605. Hated by the boyars because of his sympathy for the Poles and by the Russian clergy for his rapprochement with the Catholic Church, Pseudo-Dmitry was murdered in the following year. For the next seven years anarchy reigned while Polish and Swedish armies occupied a good deal of Russian territory. Even Moscow fell to the Poles, in September of 1610. Only in 1613, after the election of Michael, the first tsar of the Romanov dynasty, did Russia begin its rehabilitation under a stable and legal government.

These nine years, 1604 to 1613, years of crisis, great unrest, and foreign intervention, are usually called the "Time of Troubles," and they left a deep and indelible impression on the mind

of Russia. Many writers who lived through these dramatic events
left memoirs and analyses concerning this period. In most of
them can be found a feeling of offended nationalism and fierce
hatred toward the foreigners who had invaded the Russian land
during these turbulent years. These writers are especially bitter
toward the Poles and Catholics, who supported Pseudo-Dmitry,
hoping, through him, to dominate all of Russia.

Among such writers Avraamy Palitsyn, a monk and cellarer
of the powerful Holy Trinity-St. Sergius Monastery, left one of
the best accounts of the events of the time. A member of a
wealthy aristocratic family, Averky (Avraamy was his monastic
name) was born about 1555, and, like many aristocrats of the
day, served both in the civil service and in the army. In 1588
the anti-Godunov faction forced him to take monastic vows, thus
excluding him for a time from political activity. As cellarer of
the Holy Trinity-St. Sergius Monastery he participated in the
patriotic and counterrevolutionary revival of 1610 to 1613, and
as an influential leader he wrote his history (*skazanie*), which
became one of the most popular accounts of the Time of Troubles, surviving in over one hundred extant manuscripts from the
seventeenth century alone. Palitsyn died in the Solovki Monastery on September 13, 1627.

The translations of Chapters V and VI of his work, *A Concise History Written in Memory of Past Generations*, are given
here. These translations follow the text of *Skazanie Avraamiia
Palitsyna*, edited by O. A. Derzhavina and E. V. Kolosova,
Academy of Sciences, Moscow and Leningrad, 1955, pages
110–115.

◆ ◆ ◆

ABOUT THE DEFROCKED MONK GREGORY AND
THE DEATH OF TSAR BORIS

In the year 1605 (7113) a certain monk, whose name was
Gregory and who was a scion of the Otrepiev[1] family, and who
had been an addict of occult books and other evils, left Russia
and went to the Polish Kingdom. Living there, he began to
write subversive proclamations, sending them to all parts of
Russia, in which he declared that he was the real Dmitry, son of

---

[1] Pseudo-Dmitry remains one of the great enigmas of Russian history. His actual identity has remained unknown to this day. However,
the government of Boris Godunov, as well as other opponents of the
pretender, identified him as being Gregory Otrepiev, a scion of a
wealthy and noble Muscovite family.

the tsar. He would go from city to city, hiding himself and causing disturbances among the people of both realms. Then he was joined by fugitives from western Russian and Polish cities, by serfs whose time had arrived according to the will of the evil spirit, and by one village after another, and by one city after another, and finally all were tempted. However, his scheme was evident to many. Yet, what a great amount of evil did they cause! And until this day Russia is unable to be rid of this yoke. He and his followers in evil have done so many base deeds in Russia that no one could describe them all, even if he wrote for many years. In two years this unfrocked monk Gregory succeeded in winning over one-quarter of the entire universe, the entirety of Europe; and even the Pope of Rome wrote on his behalf to the entire West, presenting Gregory as an exile from his fatherland. And the Pope ordered the Polish king, Sigismund III, to start a campaign against Russia in order to take revenge for the impostor. Gregory joined the Catholics, that eternal enemy of Christians, and he gave them a written promise that he would bring entire Russia under the blessing of the Antichrist,[2] thus delivering all Russians to eternal death through the abomination of the Catholic Communion. And he would have done this, if the Lord hadn't overthrown his evil design. To him refer the prophecies of Ezekiel, for it is written, "You shall be fuel for the fire and your blood shall be in the midst of the land" (21: 32).

Although Tsar Boris was not killed by this impostor, he died a sudden death in the summer of 1605 (7113) during the revolt brought about by Gregory, and all those upon whom Boris relied were dispersed along with his household.[3]

After Boris' death, this monk ascended the throne and called himself Tsar Dmitry. But from many witnesses we know that this Gregory was a simple monk, despite the fact that he wanted to become the Tsar of Russia. And he gathered together all the relatives of the murdered Tsarevich Dmitry[4] and many other people who had been deported by Tsar Boris. And those who

[2] In the sixteenth and seventeenth centuries the Protestant West and the Orthodox East often called the Pope of Rome the Antichrist, and they claimed that the Pope served Satan. The Catholics, in turn, called the Protestants the servants of Satan and the Antichrist.

[3] When Tsar Boris Godunov died, his son, Fedor II, became Tsar of Russia. However, he was soon murdered by the impostor's supporters, and Pseudo-Dmitry ascended to the throne of Muscovy.

[4] Maria Nagoy was the last wife of Ivan IV. After the killing of her son, Tsarevich Dmitry, Boris Godunov forced her to take monastic vows. She did so under the name of Marfa (Martha).

did not wish to join him, he won over through his gifts. In such manner did he win over the nun Marfa, the mother of Tsarevich Dmitry and the wife of Tsar Ivan Vassilevich, Tsar of all the Russias. And so she called this impostor her son. And many of the people of Uglich[5] who could have exposed him and even his real mother, Barbara, the wife of Bogdan Otrepiev, his brother's widow and son, and his uncle, Smirny-Otrepiev, did not. Therefore his uncle was sent to Siberia, and underwent many tribulations there. And there appeared many new martyrs: the nobleman Peter Turgenev, and Fedor Kolachev, who fearlessly exposed him, were beheaded in the central square of the imperial city of Moscow, after having undergone many tortures. When this Fedor Kolachev was led to the scaffold, he shouted to the crowd, saying: "You have accepted this servant of the Antichrist and you worship this messenger of Satan. But you won't understand this until you have perished because of it."

But the Muscovites only abused him and answered that he well deserved his execution. They paid no more heed to the execution of Peter Turgenev. Soon after these executions, Prince Vasily Shuysky[6] was also condemned to death on the scaffold for his exposures and intrigues, but the Poles, fearing his execution, asked the impostor to pardon him.

Soon after, following the evil impostor's advice, all metropolitans, archbishops, bishops, abbots, and all the leading clergymen with Patriarch Ignaty, as well as the princes and boyars with all the army commanders, obeyed him and signed the petition and sent ambassadors to the Polish Kingdom to ask the Lord of Sandomir to give his daughter to this impostor for his wife.[7] And all of them gave witness in their message that he was Dmitry, the real son of Tsar Ivan IV.

And even those who knew that he was Monk Gregory gave witness to this. Among them were Pafnuty, the Metropolitan of Krutitsa. When Pafnuty was abbot of the Miracle Monastery, this Gregory used to sing in his choir and then remained at the court of the Patriarch Job for one year, where he worked as a clerk. Soon after, he ran away to Lithuania because his heretical intrigues were exposed. And like a chariot of the pharaoh, he

[5] Tsarevich Dmitry was killed in the city of Uglich in 1591, so it is quite natural that in 1605 many inhabitants of this city could have testified that Pseudo-Dmitry was an impostor.

[6] After Pseudo-Dmitry's death, Prince Vasily Shuysky became Russia's tsar, ruling from 1606 to 1610.

[7] Marina Mnishek, a daughter of a voevoda of Sandomir, became the impostor's wife in 1606 in Moscow.

became involved in a plot, and after him the entire Russian state became insane, giving in to his temptations.

Now involved in this plot, this accursed, defrocked impostor got into a conspiracy with the voevoda of Sandomir when he lived at his house in Poland. And, following an evil path, this voevoda decided to give his own daughter, Marina, in marriage [to this pretender, and took her to Moscow] to the lawless celebration of her wedding, taking with him some six thousand selected troops. For the quartering of these Polish knights, not only were the houses of simple people taken, but even those of officials, courtiers, and the Nagoy family, the so-called relatives of the impostor. And in all good and noble places and houses heretical joy and violence spread.

This defrocked impostor, who was himself a sponsor of the crooked faith, feared that the same fate that befell Tsar Boris would befall himself. And therefore, coming and leaving the tsar's palace, and going to walk about the city, he surrounded himself with many guards. Before him and behind him there were marching armed soldiers with arquebuses, halberds, and other weapons. And this impostor would always walk in the center of them, while Russian courtiers and boyars had to follow far behind. Indeed, it was terrifying to behold so many glinting arms and shining armor. He selected his personal guardsmen, as well as the guards of his palace, only from among the Polish and German mercenaries. He permitted gamblers to gamble and cheat even in the tsar's palace. All his retinue and his common servants were clothed in finery as if they were bridegrooms, though no one knew what they had to celebrate. They loitered from street to street searching for pleasure and bedecked in purple finery and with gold and silver accouterments. And when they served the impostor, they adorned themselves with precious stones and pearls. And they did not want to look upon anyone who was humble. In such a way, the Poles were squandering the ancient treasures of Russia. And they used the silver vessels for carrying water and even in the bath, while they used silver and gold vessels for washing. And besides all this, they spread the seeds of the heretical dogma of Luther.

And no one dared to pronounce a word in the presence of the evil and fiercesome Cossacks.[8] And many an aristocrat shed tears, seeing the arrogance shown them by their serfs. The serfs could always claim that their masters had called Dmitry "an

[8] Many Don and Dnieper Cossacks, among whom were many runaway serfs, joined with Pseudo-Dmitry.

unfrocked impostor," and then such masters would always disappear. In all the Russian cities and in the venerated monasteries many laymen and monks perished. Some of them were imprisoned, while others were drowned, and the belly of a huge fish became their tomb. The impostor permitted both Jews and heretics to visit the holy and divine churches, and foreigners dared to enter the Cathedral of the Assumption of Our Holy and Honored Lady and to profane the miracle-working relics of the holy metropolitans, Peter and Jonas, leaning upon the reliquaries. And the unholy Poles entered the churches even with their weapons, but no one dared tell them a word, since resisting one of them could mean death.

Soon after, the accursed Roman pope sent a missal to the impostor reminding him of his promise to introduce into Russia the Roman Catholic form of Holy Communion and fasting on Saturday. This cursed, defrocked monk attempted to do as he was ordered, but when he wed his heretical bride, they were married in a divine Orthodox Church. But before marrying her, this cursed man corrupted many virgin nuns and even pious monks. And both he and the Poles were committing many shameful deeds. And the rebels and Cossacks who brought him to the throne enjoyed the fall of Christian virtues, seeing those shameful acts. And they offended people who were sad and grieved sorrowfully, calling them Jews and saying, "The tsar does as he wants, but, like Jews, you only complain about it." Even the Muscovites trod the path of perdition, did not repent before God, but enjoyed the gains from their speculations and, although bemoaning much, still cared primarily for the accumulation of wealth.

Becoming insanely proud, this defrocked monk and impostor ordered that his title be, "The most illustrious, invincible Caesar." This accursed man believed that by bearing the name of the Tsar he could win the highest and most sought-after of honors.

There was a high official at the court, whose name was Timothy Osipov, who was a person of pious behavior and disposition, and who gave little heed to this impostor's ambitions. This virtuous man saw that much harm was being done by this defrocked monk and his councilors. Seeing the unnatural and high title the impostor had given himself, this man realized that each man is mortal and possessed by passions and therefore should not call himself an "invincible Caesar," since only God is invincible. This Timothy Osipov was a man devoted to God, and he prayed piously and the fasts were strictly kept in his house. Once, after he had received the most wonderful and life-giving Communion—the pure flesh and blood of Christ, Our Lord, he went to the tsar's palace and daringly exposed the defrocked monk before the people, saying: "Verily, verily thou art Grishka Otrepiev, a defrocked monk, and not an 'invincible Caesar.' Thou art not Dmitry, the son of the tsar, but a slave to sin, and a heretic."

The defrocked impostor could not stand such a denunciation and shame, but ordered the man immediately executed. So ended the life and the heroic deed of this worthy martyr.

Once the impostor sent to the Khan of Crimea the most dishonorable of gifts. He ordered a fur coat made of swines' skins for the khan, and wrote him that he was preparing a campaign against the Crimea, the land of the southern sun, and that he himself would appear there soon to plunder the Crimean homes. And he ordered all Russians, as well as the Poles, to his service and to prepare the campaign against the city of Azov.[9] And he immediately sent a large corps of selected artillerymen to the city of Elets. He ordered that the army prepare to advance either by boats on the river Don or on land across the prairie. Rumors about these military moves spread to Constantinople, and the Turks began to prepare for the spilling of Christian blood. Some people claimed, I do not know whether it is true or not, that this defrocked monk wanted to arouse the Crimean Khan and the Turks, so that many Christian Russians would fall on the battlefield. It does appear that he was not really interested in victory over the sons of Hagar, but wanted rather to withdraw the Orthodox Russians in order that he might afterward settle the Muscovite realm with Poles. But the Lord himself did not allow this ambitious man's plan to come to fruition.

HOW THE DEFROCKED MONK PREPARED A PLOT WITH THE POLES TO KILL MUSCOVITES, BUT WAS HIMSELF KILLED BY THE MUSCOVITE BOYARS

This enemy, the defrocked monk, plotted with the heretics [the Poles] to massacre the Russian people of all ranks, beginning with the courtiers and ending with common officers. And he intended to have a great celebration with the shooting of artillery in the Pond Field at the Strelets Gate. And when the people went to this celebration, then he would order the gate to be closed and all would be slain.

[9] The city of Azov, located at the mouth of the river Don not far from the Azov Sea, was an important Turkish-Tatar fortress at that time.

But this base plot did not come to fruition because two days before the celebration was to have taken place, and ten days after his improper wedding, this accursed man died an evil death, having reigned for one year. He used to say of himself that he was thirty-four years of age, but his friends, the demons, didn't give him many more years of life. And so the writing of St. John Chrysostom, "Such is the honor which demons render to those who love them," was fulfilled.

After his death, the people of Moscow gave themselves to drinking in their joy, instead of rendering thanks to God. And everyone bragged about his deeds in murdering the impostor, Pseudo-Dmitry, and all boasted about their courage. But the people forgot to give thanks through prayer in the Church of the Holy Virgin for this most glorious victory. Once, a great miracle was performed by the Most Pure Holy Virgin in Constantinople, but this miracle against the Persians and the Scythians occurred on the sea and beyond the walls of the city, and not within the city walls.[10] In Moscow, however, the miracle occurred within the city. This accursed heretic was able to keep everyone firmly in tow, and he was loved by everyone. And yet, on that day, by the command of God, everyone rose against him. And a great amount of heretical [Polish] blood was spilled in the streets of Moscow. But, instead of rendering thanks to the Righteous Avenger, the people were seized by insanity and pride. And therefore the wrath of God did not subside; but we the Russians did not recognize the divine plan and designs, and were not able to realize from what evils the Lord had delivered us.

36. Avraamy Palitsyn: Answer of the Defenders of the Holy Trinity—St. Sergius Monastery to the Polish Request of Surrender

ONE of the most dramatic events of the Time of Troubles was the besieging of the Holy Trinity—St. Sergius Monastery by Polish and Lithuanian troops in 1609. After a long siege and many attempted stormings of the well-fortified monastery-fortress, the commanders of the Poles and Lithuanians, John Peter Paul Sapieha and John Alexander Lisowski, demanded

[10] The author refers to the so-called Miracle of the Holy Virgin's Veil which, according to the legend, protected the city of Constantinople against a Russian attack.

the monastery's surrender. The commanders of the Russian
troops defending the monastery, Prince Gregory Dolgorukov and
Alexis Golokhsvastov, together with Abbot Ioasaf and the leading elders, refused to capitulate, and answered the Polish and
Lithuanian commanders in a letter that well reflects the bitter-
ness, hatred, and fierce national feeling that reigned in both
camps. For the defenders of this monastery, surrender to the
Poles would not only have meant betrayal of the national cause
but also betrayal of the Orthodox Faith. There are reasons to
believe that the letter was written by Avraamy Palitsyn himself,
as he was certainly the most skillful writer in the monastery at
that time.

The present translation follows the text of the letter contained
in *Skazanie Avraamiia Palitsyna* edited by O. Derzhavina and
E. V. Kolosova, Academy of Sciences of the U.S.S.R. Moscow
and Leningrad, 1955, pages 110–115.

✦ ✦ ✦

To the proud commanders Sapieha and Lisowski! Your dark
majesties and your warriors are the opposers of God, the abomination of dissolution, and know that you attempt in vain to lead
us, a flock of Orthodox Christians, into temptation. You should
know that even a ten-year-old Christian youth from the Holy
Trinity–St. Sergius Monastery would laugh at your request. And
as far as your letter is concerned, we spit on it upon receiving
it. What man would, at the expense of his soul, prefer darkness
to light, a lie to the truth, honor to dishonor, and freedom to
bitter slave labor? How could we forsake our eternal, holy, and
true Orthodox Christian Faith of the Greek confession and submit ourselves to the new heretical law which betrays the Christian Faith and which was cursed by the four ecumenical patriarchs.[1] What would be our gain and honor in betraying our
Orthodox sovereign and tsar[2] and submitting ourselves to our
enemy, the impostor and rebel?[3] And you, people of the Latin
faith, have become like Jews, and even worse, for the Jews
didn't recognize the Lord and consequently crucified him. Yet
how can we, who know our Orthodox sovereign, concede to your

---

[1] The four patriarchs refers to the four patriarchs of the cities of
Constantinople, Antioch, Jerusalem, and Alexandria who broke with
the Pope of Rome owing to the latter's claim for primacy.

[2] Sapieha and Lisowski fought in the name of the second impostor,
that is, the second Pseudo-Dmitry, while the monastery refused to
capitulate in the name of Tsar Vasily Shuysky (1605–1610).

[3] This refers to the second Pseudo-Dmitry.

request to forsake our Christian tsar despite the fact that our
grandfathers were born in the vineyard of our true pastor Christ
and under the rule of a Christian tsar? And how can you attempt to tempt us with false kindness, vain flattery, and ill-
gained wealth. We shall remain faithful to the pledge we gave
on the cross, for we do not care for all the wealth in the entire
world.

37. Prince Ivan M. Katyrev-Rostovsky
A Description of the Tsars and Their Families

The Book of Annals, written by Prince Ivan M. Katyrev-
Rostovsky, gives one of the best accounts of the Time of Troubles. Others who wrote about this first great national crisis in
Muscovite Russia followed both the basic outline and the literary
style found here. Since it gives a vivid description of this difficult time, the author remaining quite unbiased and keeping to
the historical truth, it is an important source for historians. *The
Book of Annals* is also significant for several innovations, such
as the first literary portraits of the heroes of the narrative, especially of the tsars and their families. *The Book of Annals* was
as well one of the first Russian works to describe nature and the
changes of the seasons superbly; the account of the coming of
spring is particularly noteworthy. The author often used rhymed
passages, and there are many rhymed couplets to be found
throughout the text.

The reader will find in this selection from *The Book of
Annals* the portraits of the tsars and their families. The translation follows one of the earliest extant manuscripts, published in
Russkaia istoricheskaia biblioteka, Volume 13, St. Petersburg,
1912.

◆ ◆ ◆

A SHORT DESCRIPTION OF THE MUSCOVITE TSARS,
THEIR PHYSICAL APPEARANCES, STATURES,
AND TEMPERAMENTS

[TSAR IVAN IV (THE TERRIBLE), REIGNED FROM 1533 TO 1584]

Tsar Ivan was physically unattractive, had gray eyes, a
hooked and long nose, and was tall, lean, and with broad shoulders and chest. He had great physical prowess and was a person

of great acumen, being well read, erudite, and very eloquent.
He was fearsome to the enemy, and was always prepared to
fight for the fatherland. He was cruel to his subjects given to
him by the Lord, being always ready to spill their blood, and
both merciless and daring at killing. He ordered that many people be slain, from infants to the aged; he laid waste to many of
his own cities; and many clergymen were thrown into prisons
and mercilessly executed at his orders. He committed many
other evil deeds to his own people, deflowering many girls and
women in his lust. This Tsar Ivan did many good things, however, and he cared very much for his armies, generously reward-
ing them from his treasury. Such was Tsar Ivan.

[TSAR FEDOR (IVAN'S SON) REIGNED FROM 1584 TO 1598]

Tsar Fedor was short of stature, and appeared as a man who
constantly fasted. He was most humble, and greatly cared after
his soul, standing before the icons and praying endlessly. He
generously gave alms to the poor. He was not taken up with
worldly matters, but concerned himself only with the salvation
of his soul. And so, from his infancy to the very end of his days,
his life was dedicated to matters of salvation; and thus God
gave peace to his reign, brought his enemies in tow, and granted
him a blessed epoch. Such was Tsar Fedor.

[TSAR BORIS (GODUNOV, BROTHER-IN-LAW OF TSAR FEDOR) REIGNED
    FROM 1598 TO 1605]

Tsar Boris shone in the full bloom of his handsome appearance, and he surpassed many people in his attractiveness. He
was of average stature. He was a man of great intelligence, had
a marvelous power of reasoning, and was a clever polemicist
and eloquent orator. He was a faithful Christian, gave generously to the poor, and was a great builder. He spent much time
on state affairs and he performed a great many marvelous deeds.
He had, however, two great shortcomings, for he was not
granted a certain virtue by God: he used to go too much to
doctors, and he was obsessed by an insatiable desire for power.
And he dared to slay those who should have been tsars before
himself. And for such deeds he received divine retribution.

[TSAR FEDOR II, THE SON OF BORIS, WHO REIGNED SOME WEEKS
    IN 1605]

Tsar Fedor, the son of Tsar Boris, was a marvelous youth.
He was so handsome that he blossomed like a flower in the
meadow, having been created by God like a lily blooming in the

fields. His eyes were large and black; his complexion was light and white as milk; his stature was average; and his body was slightly stout. He was brought by his father to the learned books, and he was clever and eloquent in polemics. And never did any senseless or coarse words come from his lips, but he was devoted to the faith and to the reading of books.

[TSAREVNA XENIA (DAUGHTER OF BORIS AND SISTER OF TSAR FEDOR II)]

Tsarevna Xenia, Tsar Boris's daughter, was a maiden of wonderful spirit, physically very attractive, of light complexion, and had beautiful rosy cheeks, red lips, and big black eyes. From her there radiated graciousness. Being sad and shedding tears, her graciousness would become particularly radiant. Her eyebrows were thick and joined, and her body was supple, while her skin was as white as milk. She was neither too tall nor too short; her hair was black and long, covering her shoulders. She was the most distinguished among maidens, and she was accustomed to reading books. She shone by her forceful and distinguished speech, and she did well in whatever she attempted. She had a fondness for beautiful voices, and loved to listen to church music.

[PSEUDO-DMITRY, REIGNED FROM 1605–1606]

This defrocked impostor was of very short stature, but was powerfully built and of great physical strength. His face did not have the distinction of a tsar, but it was very common and his body was covered with dark spots. But he was very witty and was rather learned. He was a daring and eloquent speaker, loved horseracing, was courageous in fighting the enemy, was brave and strong, and cared greatly for warriors.

[TSAR VASILY SHUYSKY (THE HEAD OF THE POWERFUL AND ARISTOCRATIC FAMILY OF BOYARS, HE ORGANIZED THE MURDER OF THE PRETENDER, PSEUDO-DMITRY, AND WAS THEREAFTER ELECTED BY THE BOYARS TO SUCCEED HIM) REIGNED FROM 1606 to 1610]

Tsar Vasily was short of stature, physically very unattractive, and had eyes that were dull, as if he were blind. He was rather cultured, and his reasoning was sound and pointed. He cared only for those people who brought him gossip and rumors about people, and he used to receive such persons with a joyful face, and with sweet pleasure, did he listen to them. He was given to sorcery, and cared little for the military.

BIOGRAPHICAL WORKS

38. K. Druzhina-Osoryin
The Life of Yuliania Lazarevskaia

THE *vita* of Yuliania Osoryin, called Lazarevskaia after the village of Lazarevo, where she lived and died, was written in the first quarter of the seventeenth century by her son, Kallistrat Druzhina-Osoryin. Although written with the purpose of glorifying her holy life, this work is very different from the typical *vitae* of saints of medieval Russia. With the exception of the descriptions of some miracles and the appearances of demons, Yuliania's biography much more resembles a narrative from a family chronicle than a hagiographic work. The biographer gives a detailed account of the domestic relations of Yuliania's family, and often remarks that the author, himself, and his family, witnessed her works and life. Yuliania was neither a nun who spent her life in a convent, nor a princess whose Christian charity and works gave her the halo of a saintly protectoress. She spent all her life with her family, and her biography is filled with the details of every-day events. While her life was one of prayer and Christian piety, the fact that she remained all her life with her husband and children as a devoted wife, mother, and daughter-in-law distinguishes this *vita* from the usual hagiographies dealing with heroes who performed miraculous deeds or defended the Orthodox Faith, and who were usually either hermits, church leaders, or pious rulers. With this *vita* there began to appear in Russia a realistic, secular biography.

This narrative is written in plain language, completely devoid of the panegyrics, lengthy epithets, and stylistic embellishments that characterize Russian lives of saints. The present translation follows an early seventeenth-century text published by M. Skripil in *Russkaia provest XVII veka*, Moscow, 1954, pages 39–47.

◆ ◆ ◆

In the days of the pious Tsar and Great Prince Ivan Vasilievich[1] of all Russia, there was at his imperial court a good and

[1] Ivan IV, or Ivan Vasilievich, usually called the Terrible or Dread, reigned over Russia from 1530 to 1584.

charitable man by the name of Yustin Nediurev, a housekeeper by rank.[2] He had a wife named Stefanida, equally devout and compassionate, daughter of a certain Gregory Lukin from the city of Murom. They led a pious and virtuous life, had several sons and daughters, and possessed considerable wealth and many serfs. To them was born this blessed Yuliania.

Her mother died when she was six years of age, and Yuliania was taken to the lands of Murom by her grandmother, who raised her in piety for six years. When the grandmother died, Yuliania's aunt, Natalia, wife of Putila Arapov, took, at the grandmother's behest, the young girl to her house. As the blessed Yuliania had loved God and the Holy Virgin since her very youth, she respected and honored her aunt and her aunt's daughters. She was humble and obedient, assiduous in prayer and fasting. Because of her fasting, she was much berated by her aunt and ridiculed by her cousins, who said, "O insane one! Why dost thou exhaust thy flesh and so ruin thy beauty, while thou art so young?" They urged her to take food and drink every morning, but she did not yield to them; rather she withdrew in silence, even though she accepted everything with gratitude and was obedient to all. She also refrained from laughter and games, as from her very childhood she was meek, silent, and obedient, and never rude or haughty. Although frequently urged by her companions to take part in games and frivolous songs, she did not comply, pretending confusion in order to conceal her virtues. Instead, she applied herself with great diligence to spinning and hoop embroidery, working late into the night. She also did all the sewing for orphans and ailing widows in the village, and supplied the sick and needy with all kinds of goods. Everyone admired her wisdom and devotion.

The fear of God dwelt in her. There was no church in the village, nor any closer than within two miles; so Yuliania had no chance to go to church in her maidenhood. Neither did she ever hear the reading of the Holy Scriptures, nor any preacher teaching salvation, but God himself instructed her in virtuous ways. When she was in her sixteenth year she was given in marriage to a virtuous and wealthy man, named Georgii Osoryin. They were married by a priest, Potapy, in the church of the righteous Lazar, in her husband's estate. This priest instructed them in the law of God according to the rules of the holy fathers, and she carefully listened to the teaching and instructions, carrying them out in her deeds. Her parents-in-law were

[2] The names of the relatives and other people mentioned in this *vita* are the names of real historical personages.

still alive and, when they saw her of mature age and accomplished in virtue, they commanded her to take charge of the
whole household. She humbly obeyed them in all things, never
contradicting them, but respecting them and fulfilling all their
orders without fail, so that all marveled at her. Many people
tested Yuliania in conversation and she gave a seemly and rea-
sonable reply to every question, so that all wondered at her
good sense, and glorified God. She prayed much every evening,
and made one hundred and more genuflections. Upon arising
each morning, she did the same, together with her husband.
When her husband would be away in the tsar's service in
Astrakhan[3] for a year or two, and sometimes even for three
years, she went without sleep all night, praying or working,
weaving or embroidering. She would sell her work and give the
price to the poor or for the building of churches; she gave many
alms in secret by night. During the day she managed the household and cared for widows and orphans as a true mother, min-
istering to them with her own hands and giving them to drink
and to eat. She provided the serfs, both men and women, with
food and clothing, and assigned them work according to their
strength. She called no one a rude name, nor did she command
anyone to pour water while she washed her hands, or to take
off her shoes, but did all this herself. She instructed and corrected foolish serfs with meekness and humility, taking the
blame upon herself and denouncing no one, but placing all her
hopes in God and the Holy Virgin, She called for help upon
the great wonder-worker Nicholas, and he assisted her.

One night in her husband's absence, as Yuliania arose for
prayer, as was her wont, she was seized with fear and great
terror by the attack of demons. Being young and inexperienced,
she was frightened, lay down on the bed, and fell fast asleep.
Then she saw many demons coming at her with weapons, saying, "If thou wilt not cease thy efforts, we will straightway
destroy thee." She prayed to God and to the Most Holy Virgin
and to St. Nicholas the wonder-worker. And St. Nicholas appeared to her, holding a large book; he dispersed the demons,
so they disappeared like smoke. Lifting up his right hand, he
blessed her, saying: "My daughter, take courage and stand firm
and do not be afraid of the demons' threats! For Christ hath

[3] All Russian nobles were supposed to serve either with the army or
in the civil service. This service was not a permanent one, but each
noble could be summoned into the service as soon as the necessity
arose. The city of Astrakhan, where Yuliania's husband served, is
located at the delta of the Volga in the vicinity of the Caspian Sea.

commanded me to guard thee from demons and from evil men." Then she straightway awoke from sleep and clearly saw the holy man leaving the chamber through the door, quick as lightning. Rising promptly, she followed him, and forthwith he became invisible; yet the anteroom of the chamber was securely locked. Taking this as a message, Yuliania rejoiced, praising God, and was more diligent in good works than before.

In a short time, for our sins God's wrath fell upon the Russian land, and a great famine occurred, and many starved to death. Yuliania gave many alms in secret; she began to accept food from her mother-in-law for morning and midday meals, and gave all to the poor and hungry. So her mother-in-law said to her: "How comes it that thou hast changed thy custom? When there was an abundance of bread, I was not able to make thee eat early and midday meals, and now, when there is a dearth of food, thou eatest!" Wishing to keep her secret, Yuliania answered, "When I did not bear children, I did not want to eat, but when I started to bear them I grew weak and I cannot eat my fill. Not only in the daytime, but many times in the night as well I am hungry, but I am ashamed to ask." The mother-in-law was glad to hear it, and sent her enough food not only in the daytime but also at night, for in their house there was an abundance of bread and of everything. However, while receiving food from her mother-in-law, Yuliania did not partake of it herself, but gave all to the poor. When anyone would die, she hired women to cleanse him, gave sheets to wrap the bodies, and money for the burial. When any deceased whatever were buried in their village, she prayed for the remission of their sins.

In a short time, there was a severe pestilence among the people and many died from the plague. Many locked their doors so that those who were afflicted would not enter their homes; and they would not even touch the garments of the ill. Yet, secretly away from her parents-in-law, Yuliania healed many of the afflicted, washing them in the bathhouse with her own hands; she prayed to God for their recovery, and if they died she prayed for their salvation, hired men to bury them, and ordered the forty days' prayer.[4] When her parents-in-law, after having been tonsured,[5] died in extreme old age, Yuliania buried them with honor: she gave many alms in their memory, and

---

[4] In the Orthodox Church special prayers are required for the dead for forty days after their death.

[5] It was the custom in medieval Russia, especially among the aristocracy, to take monastic vows shortly before the approach of death.

ordered many forty days' prayers. She also had the Mass celebrated for them and had meals served at her house for the
priests, monks, and beggars every day during the forty days,
and sent alms to the prisons. At that time her husband was
serving for three years in Astrakhan, and she spent a great part of
their wealth in almsgiving, not only in those days, but throughout these years, honoring the memory of her dead parents-in-
law.

Having thus lived with her husband for many years in great
virtue, according to God's commandments, Yuliania gave birth
to sons and daughters. The devil, who hateth all good, sought
to cause her strife, arousing frequent discord among the children and the serfs. Reasoning sensibly and wisely, Yuliania restrained them all, but the devil provoked a serf to slay the
eldest son; then another son was killed in the service. Although
she grieved, it was for their souls, and not because of their
deaths. And she honored them with memorial Masses, prayers,
and almsgiving. Then Yuliania begged her husband to give her
leave to go to a nunnery. He did not let her go, but they agreed
to live together yet have no bodily intercourse. She continued
to prepare his bed as usual, yet she herself, after long evening
prayers, would lie down on the stove without any bedding. She
lay on firewood with the sharp edges against her body, and she
put iron keys under her ribs, and on these she took little sleep
until her serfs fell asleep. Then she would rise to pray throughout the night, until daylight, when she went to church for
Matins and Mass. She occupied herself diligently with handiwork and managed her house in a manner pleasing to God. She
provided her serfs with sufficient food, and appointed each of
them a task according to their strength. She cared for widows
and orphans, and helped the poor in all things.

Ten years after their bodily separation, Yuliania's husband
passed away, and she buried him reverently, honoring him with
memorial Masses, prayers, the forty-day service, and alms. From
then on, she rejected even more all worldly things that she
might better care for her soul and emulate the holy women of
old and, in this way, to please God. She prayed and fasted, went
every day to church, gave unending alms, so that ofttimes not a
silver coin remained in her house and she had to borrow in
order to give alms to the poor. When winter came, Yuliania
borrowed silver from her children for warm clothing, but gave
even this money to the poor and she herself passed the winter
without any warm clothes. She wore her shoes over bare feet,

using nutshells and sharp potsherds instead of inner soles so as to mortify the flesh.

Once the winter was so cold that the ground cracked from the frost, and for some time Yuliania did not go to church but prayed at home. It came to pass that once the local priest came alone to church very early and heard a voice from the icon of the Holy Virgin, which said: "Go and ask merciful Yuliania why she does not come to church and pray? Her prayers at home are also pleasing to God, but not so much as her prayers in church. However, let her be venerated, for she is already no less than sixty years of age, and the Holy Spirit resides within her!" The priest, being seized by awe, came forthwith to Yuliania, fell at her feet, asked her forgiveness, and told her of the vision. She treated him severely because he spoke of it in the presence of others. And she said, "Thou hast been tempted when thou spake of it; for how may I, a sinner, be worthy of such heavenly intervention?" And she adjured him not to tell anyone. Yet she herself went to church, prayed with warm tears, and venerated the icon of the Holy Virgin.

From then on, Yuliania even more devoted herself to God, going to church and praying every evening in the porch of the church, where there were icons of our Lady and of St. Nicholas. One evening she entered it to pray, as was her wont, and suddenly the chamber was filled with demons who wanted to kill her with various weapons. But she prayed to God with tears, and St. Nicholas appeared to her. He carried a club and chased the demons away, so that they disappeared like smoke. Yet he caught one of them, and tormented it. He blessed St. Yuliania with a cross, and forthwith became invisible. Still the demon screamed, crying: "I have always made trouble for thee: I have aroused strife amongst thy children and slaves. Yet I did not dare to come close to thee because of thy charity, humility, and prayer." (For Yuliania incessantly said Jesus' prayer with beads in her hands; and whether she was eating or drinking, or doing anything, she said the prayer incessantly; even when she was asleep, her lips moved and her soul was aroused to the praise of God; many times we saw her asleep, and her hand was moving the beads.) The demon ran away from her, screaming, "A great disaster befell me now because of thee, but I will make trouble for thee in thy old age: thou wilt starve, instead of feeding others!" But she blessed herself with the sign of the cross, and the demon disappeared. She came to us sore afraid and changed in the face. Seeing her perturbed, we questioned her, but she did not tell us anything. Yet, not too long later, she told us secretly, and bade us to tell no one.

Yuliania lived as a widow for nine years and showed great goodness to everyone. She gave away much property as alms, retaining only the essential for home needs; she rationed food year after year and gave all surplus to the needy. She lived even until the reign of Tsar Boris.[6] At that time there was a great famine in the whole land of Russia—such that, in dire need, many partook of unclean meats and of human flesh, and untold numbers starved to death. In Yuliania's house there was great scarcity of food and of all necessary supplies, for the sown spring rye never sprouted, and both horses and cattle died. She implored her children and serfs that they in no way touch anything belonging to others, nor steal, and whatever cattle and clothes and vessels were left, she sold for rye to feed the servants. She also gave considerable alms, for even in destitution she did not discontinue her customary charity, but let no one asking for help go away empty-handed. She herself came to extreme need, and not a grain was left in her house; yet she was not alarmed but placed all hope in God.

That year Yuliania moved to another village, called Vochnevo, in the confines of Nizhny-Novgorod, where there was no church closer than within two miles. Being afflicted with old age, and destitute, she did not go to church but prayed at home. That grieved her sorely, yet she remembered St. Kornily and other saints, and knew that praying at home did not harm them. When destitution increased in her house, she set the serfs free so they would not be exhausted by hunger. Those of them who were virtuous promised to endure with her, while others left, and she let them go with her blessing and prayers, being not the least angered. Then Yuliania commanded the remaining slaves to gather goosefoot and wood bark and, making bread therefrom, she lived on it with her children and the serfs. And through her prayers that bread was sweet. She continued to give to the poor and let no pauper go without; at that time the poor were innumerable. Her neighbors said to the beggars, "Why do you go to Yuliania's house? For even she herself is starving!" And the beggars told them, "We have walked through many villages and have received pure bread, but we did not relish it so much, for sweet is the bread of this widow." They called her this, for many did not know her name. And the neighbors, who

[6] Tsar Boris, brother-in-law of the last representative of the dynasty of Rurik, Tsar Fedor, ruled from 1598–1605. During his reign there were both plagues and great famines in Russia.

had plenty of bread, sent to Yuliania's house to ask for some of hers, to try it, and they also witnessed that her bread was very sweet. They marveled, saying to themselves, "Her servants are good at baking bread," for they did not understand that the bread was sweet through Yuliania's prayer. Yuliania endured this destitution for two years, and she neither grieved nor was troubled, nor complained, and did not sin with her lips, neither did she charge God foolishly. And she was not broken by poverty, but was more cheerful than in earlier years.

As her righteous passing drew near, Yuliania became ill on the twenty-sixth day of December and stayed abed for six days. In daytime she prayed as she lay in bed, and at night she arose to pray to God, standing without assistance and supported by no one, for, as she said, "Even from the sick God demands prayer." At daybreak on the second day of January, she summoned her confessor and received the last rites. Then, sitting up, she summoned her children and serfs and instructed them in love, prayer, charity, and in the other virtues. She added this also: "Since my youth and with all my heart I have desired to take monastic vows, but because of my sins and wretchedness this was not granted to me. I was not worthy, being a wretched and lowly sinner, God willing it so; glory be to His righteous judgment." She commanded that a censer be prepared and that incense be put in it; she kissed all those present and bade them peace and forgiveness. She lay down, crossed herself thrice, and, having wound the beads around her arm, she spake her last, saying, "Praise God in all things! Into Thy hands, O Lord, I commend my spirit. Amen!" And she surrendered her soul into the hands of God, whom she had loved since her youth. And all saw a golden halo around her head, such as is painted around the heads of the saints on icons. Having washed her, they laid her out in a storeroom, and that night they saw there light and burning candles, and a strong fragrance wafted from that storeroom. Having put her into an oaken coffin, they took her back to the confines of Murom, and buried her beside her husband at the wall of the church of the righteous Lazar, in the village of Lazarevo, which was three miles from the city. And this came to pass in the year 1604 (7112), on the tenth day of January.

They later erected over Yuliania a church in the name of Archangel Michael. A stove happened to be over her grave and, through the removal of ashes, the earth above her became thicker through the years. In the year 1615 (7123), on the eighth day of August, her son Georgii passed away, and they

started to dig a grave for him in the porch between the church
and the stove, for that porch had no floor. They found Yuliania's
coffin intact and on top of the earth. It was in no way damaged,
and they wondered whose it was, as for many years no one had
been buried there. On the tenth day of the same month they
buried her son Georgii next to her coffin, and went to his house
to offer refreshments to the burial attendants. But the women
who attended the funeral opened the coffin and saw it to be
full of fragrant myrrh. Being seized with awe at that time, they
did not reveal anything, but after the departure of the guests
they related what had happened. Having heard this, we marveled. And when we opened the coffin, we saw even as the
women had told us. We ladled out a small vessel of that myrrh
and took it to the cathedral church of the city of Murom. In
the daytime that myrrh looked like beetroot kvass, and at night
it thickened, looking like crimson oil. We did not dare to open
the grave and to view all the body. We saw only her legs and
thighs intact, yet her head we did not see, because a log from
the oven lay on the end of the coffin.

Next to the coffin there was an opening under the stove. In
the night the coffin, by itself, moved toward the east. And,
having gone the distance of two yards, it stopped at the church
wall. This same night many people heard the ringing of the
church bell. When they arrived, they saw nothing; only a fragrance emanated. Many people heard of it and came there to
anoint themselves with the myrrh. And they received relief from
various diseases. When all the myrrh had been distributed, a
dustlike sand began to issue near the coffin. Those suffering of
various ailments came and rubbed themselves with this sand
and received relief. And even to this day they do so. And we
would not dare to write this if there had been no witnesses.

39. *The Life of Archpriest Avvakum by Himself*

A SIMILAR fate befell the most unusual literary works of both
the Kievan and Muscovite eras of Russian literature. Because of
their nonconformity with the spirit of the Russian Church, both
the *Lay of Igor's Campaign* and the *Life of Archpriest Avvakum
by Himself* remained unavailable to the general reader, and
therefore did not have a considerable influence on the further

development of Russian literature. Once discovered, however, they fascinated the Russian reading public.

Born in 1621, Avvakum became a priest at the age of twenty. In the early 1640's he joined the revival movement of the Zealots of Piety, or Seekers After God (Bogoliubtsy), which attracted many representatives of the Russian Church at that time and which tried to breathe new life into Russian Orthodoxy. For several years both the government and the Church leaders supported this movement, but when the authoritarian and unbending Nikon became patriarch in 1652, he moved against this revival because he saw in its activities a threat to the authority of the hierarchy. Officially, the conflict arose over the re-editing of the missal and changes in the ritual, both of which Nikon revised to conform to those of the contemporary Greek Church. Avvakum and his followers advocated the ancient texts and rites which had originally been introduced into Russia from Greece, some seven centuries earlier. The real core of the conflict, however, was different. Nikon sought the unquestioning submission of the Church to the authority of the patriarch, and received the support of Tsar Alexis and the state, since they also desired stronger controls over the Church by both the central ecclesiastic offices and the state itself. Avvakum and his followers, who represented the lower clergy and their parishioners, felt that the parish priests and local laity should have a greater voice in Church affairs. Moreover, in opposition to domination and disciplining of the Church from above, they proposed a genuine religious regeneration of the Church on the local level.

In 1653 Patriarch Nikon succeeded in deporting Avvakum, Ivan Neronov, and other leaders of the reform movement, and thus Avvakum spent some nine years in Siberia. He was permitted to return to Moscow in 1662, but his fierce defense of his principles led once more to his deportation to northern Russia and, finally, to his censure by the Church council. In 1666 he was condemned for his opposition to the ecclesiastic authorities and for upholding the ancient traditions of the Russian Church. The next year this condemnation was reaffirmed by a larger Church council, in which not only the Russian hierarchs participated but also the Greek patriarchs of Alexandria, Antioch, and Jerusalem. This time Avvakum and his followers, Deacon Fedor (Theodore), the monk Epiphany, and the priest Lazar, were deported to Pustozersk, a small settlement and fort in the extreme northeast of European Russia, about a hundred miles from the Arctic Ocean. They remained there some fifteen years, and during that time Pustozersk became the spiritual center of the Old Believer movement, as it was called. It was there that Avvakum's autobiography and his many treatises and epistles were written. In 1682 the government, which was unable to curb the spread of this movement, ordered that Avvakum and his three comrades should be burned at the stake.

The autobiography of Avvakum is certainly not the first Russian work in which an author describes his own life and deeds, but it is the most important one in old Russian literature. Avvakum uses a simple but vigorous, clear, and laconic style in which there are hardly any of those stylistic devices of ornamentation which so characterized the literary works of his predecessors and contemporaries. His narration is dynamic, and reflects the active, unbending nature of the author. Avvakum rarely used the solemn Church Slavonic literary language, but turned to colloquial Russian. He does not hesitate to use crude folk sayings that lend expressiveness to his style. A keen observer and penetrating psychologist, he gives short, pointed, sometimes ironic portrayals of his contemporaries, among which perhaps the best are those describing his wife, Nastasia Markovna, and Tsar Alexis.

The *Life of Archpriest Avvakum by Himself* is given here in the translation by Jane Harrison and Hope Mirrlees, published by Leonard and Virginia Woolf at the Hogarth Press, London, 1924. This work is given in its entirety except for the introduction, which does not deal at all with Avvakum's life but consists rather of theological arguments and considerations, and also excepting the final section describing "The Healing of Those Possessed." For the convenience of the reader, the work has been divided into chapters by the editor of this anthology. The editor has also made some minor changes in personal and place names, and occasionally in wording, for a better understanding.

✦ ✦ ✦

I. FAMILY BACKGROUND

I was born in the Nizhny country, beyond the River Kudma, in the village of Grigorovo.[1] My father was given to strong drink; but my mother was given to fasting and prayer, and did most constantly instruct me in the fear of God. Now one day at a neighbor's I saw a dead ox, and that night, rising from my

[1] The village of Grigorovo is in the Nizhny-Novgorod (presently Gorky) region on the right shore of the Volga.

bed, I wept abundantly for my soul before the holy icons, pondering mortality and how I too must surely die; and from that day it became my custom to pray every night. Then my mother was left a widow, and I, young that I was, an orphan, and we were driven out by our kinsmen. My mother resolved that I should marry. And I prayed to the Mother of God that she would give me such a wife as should help me to win salvation. And in that village there was a maiden, she too was an orphan, who was wont to go continually to church, and her name was Anastasia. Her father was the blacksmith Marko, exceedingly rich, but when he died all his substance was wasted. So she lived in poverty and she would pray to God that he might so compass it that she should be joined to me in matrimony; and he willed that it should be so. At that same time my mother went to God, having first taken the veil, and died in the odor of sanctity. And I, because of persecution, moved to another place, and at the age of twenty I was ordained deacon and, after two years, priest. When I had been a priest eight years, I was raised to the rank of archpriest by Orthodox bishops, and this was twenty years ago. And it is thirty years in all that I have been in Holy Orders.

II. The Years of Mission with "Seekers After God" and Clashes with the Administration (1640–1652)

And when I was still but a parish priest I had many spiritual children—it would be five or six hundred souls in all. And never resting, I, miserable sinner, in churches and houses and at crossways, by towns and hamlets, even in the city of the tsar and in the country of Siberia, was diligent during a period of some thirteen and a half years in teaching and preaching the Word of God.

And in these days of my ministry a young woman came to confess to me, burdened with many sins, guilty of fornication and of all the sins of the flesh, and, weeping, she began to acquaint me with them all, leaving nothing out, standing before the Gospels. And I, thrice-accursed, though a leech, fell sick myself. I inwardly burned with a lecherous fire, and that hour was bitter to me. I lit three candles and fixed them to the lectern and placed my right hand in the flame, and held it there till the evil passion was burned out and, when I had dismissed the young woman and laid away my vestments, I prayed and went to my house, grievously humbled in spirit.

The time must have been midnight, and when I reached my house I wept before the icons so that my eyes swelled; and prayed diligently that God might remove from me my spiritual children, in that the burden was too heavy for me. And I threw myself upon the ground face downwards, sobbing bitterly. And as I lay I swooned and wist not how I was weeping, and in my fancy I was transported to the banks of the Volga and gazed at it with the eyes of my heart; and this is what I saw: On it were sailing two stately ships of gold, and their oars were of gold, and their masts were of gold and all was of gold; at the helm of each was sitting a man, and I said: "Whose are these ships?" They answered: "Luke's and Laurence's." Now these had been two of my spiritual children, and they had set me and my house on the path of salvation, and their end had been pleasing to God. And after that I saw a third ship, not adorned with gold, but pied with many and varied hues, red and white, and blue and black and ash, so that the mind of man would be hard put to grasp at the same time all its loveliness and excellence. And a young man, all shining, sat at the helm, to the right, and I called out to him: "Whose ship?" and he who was on her answered: "Thine. Sail away on her with thy wife and children, if thou wilt persist." And I was troubled not a little, and sitting there I pondered the meaning of the vision and of the sailing.[2]

And but a little time after this—as it has been written—*the sorrows of death compassed me, and the pains of hell gat hold upon me: I found trouble and sorrow.* A headman abducted her daughter from a widow, and I besought him to return the orphan to her mother; he scorned our prayers and raised up storms against me; he came to the church with a band of followers, and they crushed me to death. And I, having lain dead for half an hour and more, was brought to life by a wave of God's hand, and he was sore afraid and renounced the girl for my sake. Then the Devil prompted him: he came to the church, he beat me and dragged me, clad in my vestments, along the ground by the legs, and while he did it I was praying.

And likewise another headman at another time became as a wild beast against me. Breaking into my house, he beat me and gnawed the fingers of my hand, like a dog, with his teeth; and when his throat was full of blood, then he loosened his teeth from my hand, and, throwing me aside, went to his house. But I, blessing God, wrapped up my hand in a cloth, and started for vespers; and on the way he leaped out on me again with two small pistols and, standing close to me, fired from one of

[2] The symbol of the ship is very common in Russian literature, and usually symbolized the life of a man. It has a biblical origin.

them and, by God's will, the powder exploded in the pan and
the pistol missed fire. So he flung himself on the ground and in
the same manner fired from the other, and God willed it should
be in the same sort, for that pistol also missed fire. But I, praying diligently, with one hand signed him with the Cross and
bowed low before him; then began he to snarl imprecations,
but I said to him: "Out of thy mouth, Ivan Rodionovich, let
blessings proceed." And next he took from me my homestead
and drove me out with violence, seizing all my goods, leaving
me not even a morsel of bread to eat on the road.

During that time my son Prokopy was born, the same that
today lies a prisoner with his mother dug into a pit in the earth.
So I took my staff and his mother took the unbaptized infant,
and we set off on our wanderings, whither God should lead us,
and on the way we baptized our son, even as Phillip of old baptized the eunuch.[3] And when in my wanderings I reached Moscow, I made straight for the tsar's chaplain, the Archpriest
Stephen, and for Neronov, the Archpriest John, and they informed the tsar concerning me, and from that time began my
acquaintance with the tsar.[4] And the reverend fathers sent me
back whence I had come with royal mandates, and wearily I
dragged myself home; but the walls of my house had been
pulled down and I set to to rebuild them, and once again the
Devil raised up a storm against me. There came to my village
dancing bears with drums and lutes, and I, though a miserable
sinner, was zealous in Christ's service, and I drove them out and
I broke the buffoons' masks and the drums, on a common outside
the village, one against many, and two great bears I took away—
one I clubbed senseless, but he revived, and the other I let go
into the open country. And after that Vasily Petrovich Sheremetiev,[5] who was sailing up the Volga to Kazan to take over the
Governorship, took me on board, and he sternly reprimanded me
and ordered me to bless his son who had a shaven face.[6] And
when I saw that image of shame I would not bless him, but
condemned him from the Scriptures. So my lord waxed terribly
wrath and ordered that I should be flung into the Volga and,

[3] The episode described in the Acts of the Apostles, 8, 27-38.
[4] Archpriest Stephen Vonifatiev was the confessor of the tsar. He
and Archpriest Ivan Neronov were the leaders of the Zealots of Piety.
[5] The Zealots of Piety energetically fought these buffoons, or
skomorokhs, traveling actors, singers, and bear trainers whose per-
formances and songs strongly reflected the pre-Christian mentality.
[6] The shaving of a beard was considered sinful in Muscovite
Russia. Vasily Sheremetiev was a wealthy and influential aristocrat
and high official.

having inflicted on me many hurts, they cast me aside, but in
later years their rough handling turned to friendliness, for we
were reconciled one to another in the antechamber of the tsar,
and my youngest brother was his lady's confessor. Thus does
God fashion the lives of his people.

Let us return to earlier days: again another headman became
as a wild beast against me; he arrived with his folk at my
homestead and attacked me, shooting from bows and muskets;
and I, the while, prayed to the Lord, calling to him in a loud
voice: "Lord God! Make his heart gentle, and reconcile him to
me by whatsoever means thou choosest." And he fled from my
yard, driven out by the Holy Ghost. And that very night his folk
came running and they called out to me with many tears: "Little
father! Euphemy Stepanovich is near his end and he is most in-
conveniently screaming; he strikes himself and groans, and of
his own accord he says: 'I want parson Avvakum, God will
punish me because of him.'" And I felt it to be a trap. And
terror seized on the spirit within me and I prayed to God thus:
"Thou, O Lord, who broughtest me out of my mother's womb,
and out of nothing didst create me, if they are about to strangle
me, then count me with Phillip, the Metropolitan of Moscow[7];
and if they are about to stab me, count me with the Prophet
Zachariah[8]; and if they are about to drown me, then deliver me
from their hands, as thou didst Stephen of Perm."[9] And praying
the while I betook myself to the house, even to the house of
Euphemy. And when they had led me into the yard, out rushed
his wife, Neonila, and seized me by the hand, and she said:
"Come in then, dearie, my lord, my father! Come in then, light
of our eyes!" And I answered: "Strange! Before it was 'Son of
a whore'! and now it's 'My Father!' Christ wields a crueler
scourge than he. Your good man has not taken long to own himself in fault." She led me into the bedroom. Euphemy leaped
out of the feather bed, fell down at my feet, and howled and
blubbered confused words: "Forgive me, my lord! I have sinned
before God and before thee"; and he was all of a tremble. And I
said in reply: "Dost thou wish to be healed?" and he, lying on
the ground, answered: "Aye, good father!" And I said: "Stand
up, God pardons thee." But he, sorely stricken, could not rise
by himself, so I lifted him and laid him on his bed, and con-

---

[7] Phillip, Metropolitan of Moscow, was imprisoned and then slain
by the order of Ivan IV.

[8] According to biblical tradition, Prophet Zachariah was slain in
520 by his enemies whose immorality he denounced.

[9] For Stephen of Perm, see introduction to Selection 26.

fessed him and anointed him with sacred oil, and his sickness departed. So Christ willed it. And the next morning they sent me back with honor to my home, and he and his wife became my spiritual children, excellent servants of Christ. Thus doth the Lord harden his heart against the proud, but he showers blessings on the meek.

And but a little time after this I was once again driven out of this place, so I betook me to Moscow and by God's will the tsar was pleased to appoint me Archpriest of Yurievets-on-the-Volga.[10] But I did not stay there long, but a matter of eight weeks. The Devil prompted the priests and the peasants and the good wives; and they came to the patriarch's chancellery where I was occupied in business of the church and dragged me out of the chancellery (there would be nigh two thousand of them), and in the middle of the street they beat me with cudgels and stamped on me, and the good wives beat me with shovels; and, for my sins, they flung me into a corner of a house. The captain of the troops came rushing up with his soldiers, and seizing me they galloped on their horses to my little home; and the captain placed the soldiers round the house. But the folk came up to it, and raised an outcry through the town, especially the Jack priests and their Jills, whom I had rated for their whoring ways, and they howled: "Death to the thief, to the son of a whore, and we'll fling his body into the ditch, for the dogs." And, on the third day, by night, not having closed an eye, I left my wife and children and with two others made for Moscow by way of the Volga; I would have taken refuge in Kostroma,[11] but, lo! there too they had driven away their Archpriest, Daniel. Ah, lack-a-day! The Devil leaves no man in peace! I reached Moscow; and went to Stephen, the tsar's chaplain; and he grumbled at me: "Why," says he, "have you abandoned your minster church?" And more trouble was awaiting me. In the middle of the night the tsar came in to his chaplain for his blessing and he saw me there;—more vexation: "And why have you abandoned your town?" And there were my wife and children and household (some twenty souls in all) left behind in Yurievets and I not knowing if they were alive or dead—yet another burden on my heart!

[10] Yurievets-on-the-Volga used to be an important market city in the province of Nizhny-Novgorod.

[11] Kostroma was an important merchant city on the Volga. Archpriest Daniel was the leading member of the Zealots of Piety in that city, and he met with considerable difficulties there because he denounced the morality of the city's people.

III. Conflict with Nikon, and the Rout of the "Seekers After God" (1652–1653)

After that, Nikon, our friend, brought down the relics of the Metropolitan Phillip from the Solovki Monastery,[12] and before his arrival, Stephen, the chaplain, with the brotherhood[13] and I with them, passed a week in prayer and fasting, concerning the patriarchate, even that God might give us a shepherd fitted to the saving of our souls. And the Metropolitan of Kazan and I, we signed our names to a petition and gave it to the tsar and the tsarina, concerning the chaplain Stephen, that he might be made patriarch. But he did not wish it for himself and named the Metropolitan Nikon. And the tsar hearkened to him and wrote to Nikon to greet him on his arrival. "To Nikon, the Right Reverend Metropolitan of Novgorod and Velikie Luki and of all Russia, greetings,"[14] and so forth. And when he arrived he played the fox with us, and it was bowings and scrapings and "Good morrow to you!" For he knew that he was to be patriarch and wished to remove all obstacles thereto. But I'll not waste my time telling all these cunning machinations. And when he became patriarch he would not so much as allow his friends into the room of the Cross,[15] and now at last belched forth his venom.

In Lent he sent a pastoral letter to St. Basil's Church, to John Neronov. Now the latter was my spiritual father and I was lodging in his presbytery; and when he was absent I took the services; and at the time there was some talk of making me the successor to Silas, God rest his soul, at St. Saviour's, but God willed not that it should be so and I myself was not over eager concerning it; I was well content to continue at St. Basil's: I used to read godly books to the flock, and they would come in great numbers. Nikon inscribed his letter with the year and the date, "According to the tradition of the holy Apostles and the Fathers, it is not seemly to make obeisance in church to the knee, it should be no lower than the girdle, and moreover it behooves you to sign yourselves with three fingers."[16] We met

---

[12] In 1652 Tsar Alexis sent Nikon to bring the relics of Metropolitan Phillip from the Solovki Monastery to Moscow.

[13] When speaking of brotherhood, Avvakum refers to the main group of the Zealots of Piety in Moscow.

[14] Before becoming patriarch, Nikon was Metropolitan of Novgorod and Velikie Luki.

[15] Room of the Cross—the official reception room in the patriarchal palace.

[16] As previously mentioned, the conflict between the Zealots of

together and took counsel. It was as if winter was of a mind to come; our hearts froze, our limbs shook. Neronov entrusted his church to me and shut himself up in the Miracle Monastery, and he spent a week praying in a cell, and one day a voice came from the icon of the Saviour: "The hour of tribulation has come; it behooves you to suffer and be strong." And, weeping, he recounted these words to me and to Paul, the Bishop of Kolomna, the same that afterwards Nikon was to burn in the Novgorod country[17]; and then to Daniel the Archpriest of Kostroma, and also to all the brothers. Together with Daniel I wrote out excerpts from the Fathers concerning the manner to be used in crossing oneself and making obeisances, and we gave them to the tsar. And many were the excerpts we had made. But he hid them, we know not where; I am of opinion that he gave them to Nikon.

And a little later Nikon seized Daniel in the monastery outside the Tver Gates, and sheared him monk in the presence of the tsar, and tearing off his cassock and insulting him the while, had him taken to the Miracle Monastery and put in the bakehouse, and when he had suffered grievously there, he sent him to Astrakhan; and there they placed a crown of thorns on his head and cast him into a dungeon, where he died. After the shearing of Daniel, they seized another Daniel—he also was an archpriest, of Temnikov—and they confined him in the monastery of New St. Saviour's. And in the same way with the Archpriest Ivan Neronov, Nikon took off his biretta in church and had him confined in the monastery of Simon, and later banished him to Vologda, to the walled monastery of St. Saviour's, then to the fortress of Kola,[18] and in the end, after having suffered exceedingly, he recanted—poor soul; he signed himself with three fingers, and so died a heretic. Woe is me! Let every man stand firm and be ever on the watch lest his foot shall stumble. In the words of the Scriptures, these are surely evil days when even the elect yield to the blandishments of Antichrist. It behooves us to be exceeding strong in prayer to God, and he will save us and help us, for he is merciful and loves mankind.

Piety, which was later to grow into the movement of Old Believers, and Patriarch Nikon originally grew out of the latter's changes in the Russian rites and missals. One of the most controversial changes was that of the two-fingered sign of the cross to a three-fingered one.

[17] Bishop Paul of Kolomna was a staunch upholder of old traditions and a resolute enemy of Nikon. Nikon deported him to the Novgorod region, and, according to rumor, had him burned.

[18] The city of Vologda is located in northern Russia. The fortress Kola is located in the extreme north not far from the Arctic Ocean.

And I, too, while I was celebrating vespers, was arrested by
Boris Neledinsky and his musketeers, and together with me they
arrested nigh on sixty souls and took them off to prison, and me
they fastened with a chain for the night in the patriarch's court.
And when the Sabbath dawned they placed me in a cart and
stretched out my arms and drove me from the patriarch's court
to the monastery of Andronicus, and there they put chains on
me and flung me into a black dungeon, dug into the earth, and
there I lay for three days, and I had nothing to eat or to drink
in the darkness, as I sat there bowing myself to the earth against
my chains, though I knew not, as I made my obeisances, which
was east and which was west. No one came to me but mice and
black beetles, and the crickets chirped, and of fleas there was
abundance. And on the third day I was famished, that is to say,
I wanted to eat, and after vespers someone was standing before
me, I knew not whether he was man or angel, and to this day I
know not. I only know this that he said a prayer in the darkness
and, taking me by the shoulder, led me on my chain to a bench
and seated me on it and put a spoon into my hands and gave
me a little bread and some cabbage soup to sup—Oh, but it was
tasty!—and he said to me: "Enough, let that serve you as restora-
tive." And, lo, he was gone! The door had not opened and yet
he was gone! Were he a man, it were a miracle; but were he
an angel? Then were there no cause for wonder, because for
such as he there are no barriers. In the morning came the archimandrite[19] with the brothers, and they led me away; they spoke
to me coaxingly, that I should yield to the patriarch, but I
thundered against them from the Scriptures and snarled at them.
They took off the big chain and put a small one on me in its
place, and set a monk as jailer over me; they ordered that I
should be dragged to church. In church they pulled my hair and
poked my ribs and pulled at my chain, and spat in my eyes.
May God forgive them in this life and the next! It was not they
themselves that did it, but Satan in his malice. I remained there
four weeks.

After me they next seized Login, the Archpriest of Murom. In
the monastery church, in the presence of the tsar, they sheared
him monk at mass. At the time of the carrying round of the
Host, the patriarch seized the paten from the head of the Archdeacon and placed it on the altar, together with Christ's body
and the chalice. Meanwhile, Therapont, the archimandrite of
the Miracle Monastery, was standing outside the choir before

[19] This refers to Therapont, the archimandrite, or abbot, of the
Miracle Monastery.

the King's Gates. Woe is me that Christ's body should be
sundered, more impiously than ever by the Jews! When they
had shorn him they tore from him his kaftan and his outer garment. But Login was consumed with the zeal of God's fire; and
he defied Nikon and spat across the threshold to the altar
straight into his eyes; loosening his girdle, he tore off his shift
and flung it into the altar, into Nikon's face, and, oh, wondrous
to tell, the shift spread itself out and fell on the altar in such
way that it covered the paten as though it had been the corporals. And the tsarina was in church at the time. They put a
chain on Login and, dragging him from the church, beat him
with brooms and whips to the monastery of the Epiphany, and
thrust him into a dungeon for the night and set musketeers to
guard him strictly. But lo! in the night God gave him a new fur
cloak and a biretta; and in the morning they told Nikon, and
he, laughing, said: "I know that breed of sham saint!" and he
took from him the hat, but left him the fur coat.

At that time they led me again from the monastery on foot
to the court of the patriarch's palace; and then again, spreading
out my arms and wrangling much with me, they took me away
from there also. And on St. Nikita's day there was a procession
with crosses, and as they were driving me in a cart we met the
crosses. And they drove me to the monastery church, that they
might shear me, and during Mass they kept me for a long time
on the threshold. The tsar rose from his place and going up to
the patriarch entreated him that he should not shear me, and
they took me away to the Siberia Office and handed me over to
the scribe, Tretiak Bashmakov, the same that today is suffering
for Christ—the elder Savvaty (for he took the cowl), he lies in
the monastery of New St. Saviour's in a dungeon dug into the
earth: may God have mercy on his soul! and even in these days
he entreated me kindly.

IV. Deportation to Tobolsk (1653–1655)

So they sent me then to Siberia with my wife and children,
and of the many and great privations on the way, had I the
time there would be much to tell. Dame Avvakum bore a sickly
child in the cart and we brought it as far as Tobolsk; it was a
journey of 3,000 versts, and for some thirteen weeks we dragged
along in carts and by water and half of the way in sledges.[20]

The archbishop got me a church in Tobolsk. And there in

[20] One verst is about five-eighths of a mile. The city of Tobolsk is
located in western Siberia.

that church great afflictions found me out; in half a year five times were the *Tsar's Words*[21] called out against me, and a certain member of the archbishop's household, the scribe Ivan Struna, outraged me. The archbishop was away in Moscow, and in his absence he, taught by the Devil, fell on me. He was minded to torment without cause Anthony, the clerk of my church. He, Anthony, gave him the slip and fled to me, in church. But this Ivan Struna, having collected some others, came to me that same day in church—I was singing vespers— and came leaping into the church and seized Anthony in the choir by the beard. I, in the meantime, had shut the church doors and would let no one in, so Struna was alone and kept twirling round like an imp of hell; and I, when I had finished vespers sat him down, Anthony lending a hand, in the middle of the church on the floor and thrashed him soundly with a leather strap for having made a riot in church; and the other rogues, some twelve in number, fled, every man of them, driven away by the Holy Ghost. And Struna having declared that he repented, I let him go in peace. But Struna's kinsmen among the priests and monks raised the whole town against me, so that they might compass my death. And in the middle of the night they drove up in sledges to my homestead and broke into my house, being of a mind to take and drown me; but a terror from God fell upon them and drove them hence, and they fled away. For a month was I tormented by their tricks, for they would attack me in secret; and sometimes I would take refuge by night in the church, and sometimes with the governor, and I would beg that for safety I might be put in prison—but this they would not do. Matthew Lomkov—the same that as a monk was called Mitrophan, and later in Moscow was apparitor to the Metropolitan Paul—he kept close to my side; it was he that afterwards sheared me in the monastery church together with the deacon Afanasy: but at that time he was a just man, though the Devil has now swallowed him. Then the archibishop returned from Moscow, and, as was but meet considering his offense, thrust Struna into prison with chains on him. For a certain man had lain with his own daughter, and he, Struna, had accepted fifty kopeks from the fellow and had let him go without punishment. And the lord bishop ordered him to be fettered, and he bethought him of that affair with me. For he, Struna, went to the

---

[21] The expression "Tsar's Words" meant that one person accuses another and, pointing to him, claimed he was involved in a conspiracy against the tsar. It always led to the arrest of the accused man.

governor and his men in their office, and said the *Tsar's Words* against me. And the captain allowed a petty squire, Peter Beketov, to go bail for him. Woe is me! Misfortune entered the gates of Peter's dwelling place, and it grieves my soul. The archbishop took council with me, and, in accordance with the rubric, on the first Sunday in Lent he started cursing Struna for the sin of incest in the great church. And that same Peter Beketov came to church, and rated the archbishop and myself, and within an hour, on his way home from church, he went mad, and he died a bitter and an evil death. And his grace and I, we ordered his body to be flung into the street to the dogs, and the townsfolk mourned him and his sin; for three days they importuned God diligently that on the Day of Judgment he might be pardoned. Through pity for Struna he had brought this dire calamity upon himself, and on the third day his grace and I read the office over his body. But enough of this woeful business!

V. THE HARDSHIPS OF TRAVELING TO DAURIA (1655)

At this time an edict arrived, ordering that I should be taken from Tobolsk to the Lena, in that I had condemned Nikon from the Scriptures and pronounced him a heretic.[22] At that time a letter came from Moscow telling how two brothers, who lodged in the tsarina's apartments at the top of the palace, had both of them died of the plague, together with their wives and children, and many also of their friends and kinsfolk; God was pouring forth the vials of his wrath on the kingdom. But they, wretched men, knew not this and continued making disturbance in the church. Then Neronov spoke to the tsar, saying: "The visitation for schism is threefold: plague, the sword, and division." And thus has it come to pass in our days, even now; but the Lord is merciful. When he has punished us to bring us to repentance, than has he mercy on us and, driving away the ills of our souls and bodies, he giveth quietness. I preach Christ and my hope is in him; I confidently await his mercy and I believe in the Resurrection of the Dead.

So once more I got into the boat that had been assigned me —as I have said before—and sailed towards the Lena. And when I reached Eniseysk I was met by another edict, wherein I was ordered to get me to Dauria[23]—it would be more than twenty thousand versts from Moscow—and to give myself over to

[22] This was the result of Struna's *Tsar's Words* against Avvakum.
[23] Dauria was a region in eastern Siberia in the vicinity of Lake Baikal and which the Russians intended to conquer.

Afanasy Pashkov as chaplain to his troops that numbered six hundred men, and, for my sins, he was a fierce hard man, and it was ever his custom to burn folk and torture them, and beat them, and many times did I try to persuade him to desist, and now I was in his hands, and from Moscow came an order from Nikon that I was to be tormented.

On our journey from Eniseysk, it would be on the great Tunguska River, a storm sank my raft. It foundered completely in midstream and it was full of water and its sail was in tatters, only the deck remained above water, all the rest was under water. My wife, bareheaded[24] as she was, managed, I know not how, to drag the children out of the water on to the deck, but I, looking up at the sky, cried out: "O Lord! Save us! O Lord! Help us!" And by God's will we were driven to the shore; but why multiply words?

From another raft two men were wrenched away and drowned in the water. After that, when we were come to ourselves, we set out once more on our way.

VI. First Difficulties with Pashkov (1655–1656)

When we came to the Shaman rapids, diverse folk came sailing out to meet us, and with them were two widows; one of them was aged about sixty; and the other was older, and they were traveling by boat to a nunnery where they were to take the veil. And this Pashkov was minded to send them back, and to give them by force in marriage; and I said to him: "It is against the canons of the church to give such women in marriage." And in lieu of heeding my words and letting the widows go, he waxed angry and devised how he might torment me.

In other rapids—called the long rapids—he set about driving me from the raft. "You bring bad luck," says he, "to the raft. You're a heretic," says he; "off with you to the mountains! It is not for such as you to keep company with Cossacks." Alackaday! The mountains were high, the ravines impassable, there was a stone crag that stood there like a wall—you'd crick your neck before you saw its top. In these mountains great serpents were to be found, and in them dwelt geese and ducks with red feathers, and black crows, and grey jackdaws; in these mountains were also eagles, and hawks, and gerfalcons and guinea fowl and pelicans, and swans and other wild things in plenty, every variety of bird. Moreover, on these mountains many wild

[24] It was unseemly for a married woman to be without a kerchief on her head.

beasts wandered at liberty: wild goats, and deer and bison, and elk, and boars, and wolves, and wild sheep—clearly to be seen but not to be caught.

Pashkov was of a mind to turn me out into these mountains to live with beasts and birds, and I wrote him a little letter that began thus: "O man! Fear God who sits on the Cherubim and gazes into the abyss; before him tremble the celestial powers and every creature including man; thou alone despisest him and doest things that are not seemly," and so forth. It was a long letter; and I sent it to him. And some fifty men rushed on me; they seized my raft and hastened towards him, who was distant some three versts; and I stood there, boiling some porridge for the Cossacks and I fed them with it; and they, poor souls, ate of it and trembled, and some of them, looking at me, began to weep for me. They dragged up the raft; the executioners seized me and led me before him. He was standing with drawn sword, shaking with rage; he began to speak to me, saying, "What are you? A parson, or an unfrocked one?" And I answered, "I am Avvakum, the archpriest; speak! what is your business with me?" Then he roared like a wild beast, and struck me a great blow first on one cheek and then on the other, and then again on the head, and knocked me off my feet; and seizing his leather sword-strap struck me, where I lay, thrice on the back, and then, tearing off my shift, gave me seventy-two strokes on my naked back with the knout. And I kept saying, "O Lord Jesus Christ, Son of God! Help me!" And this I kept repeating without pause, so that it was bitter to him, in that I did not say, "Have mercy." At each stroke I said a prayer, but in the middle of the flogging I screamed to him, "You've beat me enough, I say"; so he ordered that it should stop. And I said to him, "Why do you beat me—do you know?" And he ordered them to beat me again on the ribs; and then they stopped; and I was trembling all over, and I fell. And he ordered them to drag me off to the raft that carried the money bags: they put fetters on my hands and feet and flung me on to the deck. It was autumn, the rain fell on me all night, and there was a pool where I was lying. When they were beating me it did not hurt because of the prayers I was saying; but now, as I lay, the thought came to me: "Son of God, why didst thou permit them to beat me so sorely? Look thee, Lord, I was championing the widow, consecrated to thee. Who shall judge between thee and me? When I was living as an evil man, thou didst not chastise me thus; but now I know not in what I have sinned." Ay! There was a righteous man for you, another dungfaced Pharisee, wishing,

forsooth, to judge the Almighty! If Job spoke in that fashion it
was because he was a perfect and an upright man; and, moreover, he knew not the Scriptures, for he dwelt outside the Law
in a barbarian land, and it was through Creation, not through
Revelation, that he learned to know God. But I, in the first
place, was a sinful man, and, in the second place, I was learned
in the Law and the Prophets and was fortified by the Scriptures
in all my goings: "*We must, through much tribulation, enter
into the Kingdom of God*"; and yet had I reached such a pitch
of folly. Woe is me! How came it that the raft did not founder
with me in the water? Then my bones began to ache, my veins
to grow rigid, my heart to palpitate, verily, I was dying; the
water began to splash into my mouth, then I heaved a sigh,
yea, I repented before the Almighty, for, verily, the sweet Lord
of compassion remembers not against us our former transgres-
sions when once we have repented of them; and once more I
ceased to feel the pain.

In the morning they flung me onto a small craft and carried
me away. Then we came to the great rapids of the Padun,
where the river is a verst in breadth, and there are three exceeding steep reefs stretching across the whole of the river, and,
except you find the passages between them, your boat will be
shattered into splinters. They brought me into the rapids: above
was rain and snow, and they flung over my shoulders nought but
a mangy little kaftan; the water flowed over my belly and my
spine—my poor body was in sorry plight. The took me out of
the raft and, skirting the rapids, they dragged me over the
stones in fetters. Verily I was in a sad plight, but with my soul
it was well; I was no longer peevish with God. Once again there
came into my head the words spoken by the Prophets and the
Apostles: "*My son, despise thou not the chastening of the Lord,
nor faint when thou art rebuked of him.*

"*For whom the Lord loveth he chasteneth, and scourgeth
every son whom he receiveth. If ye endure chastening, God
dealeth with you as with sons; for what son is he whom the
father chasteneth not?*"

And with these words I comforted myself.

And after that they brought me to the fortress of Bratsky, and
flung me into a dungeon, and gavè me straw to lie upon. And
there I lay till Advent, in a freezing tower; these are the seasons
when winter reigns, but God kept me warm, and that without
garments. Like a poor dog I lay on the straw; and sometimes
they fed me, and sometimes they did not; there were many mice
and I would strike at them with my biretta—the fools had not

given me a stick; I lay all the time on my belly, my back was covered with sores, and of fleas and lice there was abundance. I would fain have cried on Pashkov to pardon me; but it would have been contrary to God's will, it was ordained that I should endure. Then they moved me to a warm hut, and there I dwelt in fetters with hostages and dogs the whole winter; and my wife had been sent with the children some twenty versts away. And all the winter her serving-wench, Xenia, tormented her with her tantrums and complaints. After Christmas my son Ivan, who was still but a little lad, stole away from home that he might dwell with me; and Pashkov ordered him to be flung into the freezing dungeon where I lay; dear little lad, he spent the night there and was nigh froze to death; and in the morning Pashkov ordered him back to his mother and I saw him no more; it was all he could do to drag himself home to his mother from the frostbite on his hands and feet.

VII. THE DAURIA CAMPAIGN (1656–1662)

In spring we set out once more. There remained but scant provision, for the first store had all been robbed—books and garments and other sundries had all been taken; but the second store remained. I came near again to drowning on the lake of Baikal; I was made to pull a towing rope on the Khilok River, and upstream it was mighty hard going. And there was no time for eating nor for sleeping; for a whole year I suffered from the hardships of water-travel; the folk kept dying, and my feet and belly were blue. For two summers we journeyed by water and in the winter we were towed along by haulage. And, as I have said, on this same Khilok for the third time I came nigh to drowning. My boat was sucked by the current from the shore, and the boats of the other folk stayed where they were, but mine was caught up and carried away. My wife and children had remained on shore, and the boat bolted with the steersman and me! she was pitched and tossed on the swirling water, but I climbed onto her and cried out, "Help, Blessed Virgin! Thou art our Hope and Defense. Let me not be drowned!" Sometimes my feet would be in the water and sometimes I would scramble to the top; she was carried on for a verst and more, and then the folk stopped her and she was shattered to fragments. Ay, what could one do if Christ and the Immaculate Mother of God so willed it? And I climbed out of the water laughing, but the folk were weeping, and they spread out my garments on the bushes—cloaks of satin and taffetas, and sundry trifles: for I still had a store of such things in chests and coffers, but from that day they were rotted. But Pashkov was fain to give me another flogging. "You're making yourself a laughingstock," said he. And once again I importuned the sweet Mother of God: "Our Lady! Soothe thy fool!" And she, our Hope, did soothe him, and he began to concern himself about me.

Our next stage was the Lake of Irgen. There is there a haulage and in the winter we began hauling; he took from me my workmen, and would not permit me to hire others, and we had small children—many mouths and none to fill them; this poor hapless wretch of an archpriest set to fashion a dog-sleigh for himself and started hauling. That spring we began to sail down the Ingoda River—it was the fourth summer of my journey from Tobolsk. They were floating logs for the building of houses and towns. There began to be nothing to eat, the folk began to die of hunger and from ceaseless working in the water; shallow was the river, heavy were the rafts, merciless were the taskmasters, stout were the sticks, gnarled were the cudgels, cutting were the knouts, cruel were the sufferings—fire and rack; the folk were so spent with hunger that let him, Afanasy, but start tormenting one of them, and lo! he was dead on his hands. Ah, me! What a time! It would almost seem that he was out of his mind. There remained to Dame Avvakum one Moscow gown that had not been rotted with damp. It would have fetched twenty-five rubles and more in Moscow; but in these parts they gave us four sacks of rye for it, and we dragged on for another year, living on the Nercha River, and keeping ourselves alive with the roots and herbs that grew on the banks. One after another the folk died of hunger, and he saw to it that none of them ran away, and they were circumscribed within a small space, and they would wander over the steppes and fields, digging up grasses and roots, and we with them. And in winter we would live on fir cones, and sometimes God would send mare's flesh, and sometimes we found the bones of stinking carcasses of wild beasts left by the wolves, and what had not been eaten up by the wolves that did we eat; and some would eat frozen wolves and foxes—in truth, any filth that they could lay their hands on. A mare foaled, and, in secret, the starving folk devoured the foal together with the caul. And Pashkov got wind of it, and he flogged them with his knout to the point of death. And another mare died, and desperation seized them all, inasmuch as they had pulled the foal out of her, stealing a march on nature. When nought but the head had as yet emerged from the womb, they tore it out, yea, and they began to eat the blood that came away with it. Ah, me! What a time! And two of my little sons died from these sore straits, and roaming the hills and the sharp rocks with my children that survived, naked and barefoot, living on grass and roots, what did I not endure? And I, sinful man, partook willy-nilly of mare's flesh and foul carrion and the flesh of birds. Woe for my sinful soul! Who will pour water on my head and unseal for me the fountain of tears, even that I may weep for the poor soul that is mine, which I have been destroying with my daily appetites? But in Christ's name a great lady helped us, the captain's daughter-in-law, Eudokia Kirilovna, and also his, Afanasy's, wife, Thekla Semenovna; in secret they would give us some comfort against a death from starvation. Without his knowledge they would sometimes send us a piece of meat, sometimes a circular loaf, sometimes flour and oats, as much as ever they could, and sometimes one of them would save up ten pounds of flour and some coins and sometimes twenty pounds and hand it over to us, and sometimes she would rake out the chicken's food from the trough. My daughter, the hapless lass Agraphena, would go in secret under her window. And it was both pitiful and laughable! Sometimes, without the lady's knowledge, they would chase the child from the window, and sometimes she would come home burdened with a nice little store; at that time she was still but a child, but now she is twenty-seven. My poor little maid! She dwells unwed with her younger sisters by the Mezen, living from hand to mouth and weeping; and their mother and brothers lie buried in a dungeon in the earth. But what would you? Let every man endure great tribulation for Christ's sake! With God's help let even that which has been ordained come to pass, and let us suffer tribulation for the sake of the Christian faith. The archpriest used to love keeping company with the great but love in place of that, poor wretch, to endure even to the end; for it is written: *"Better is the end of a thing than the beginning thereof."* Enough of this: let us return to the previous matter.

We continued in the land of Dauria in dire straits some six or seven years, but during some of these years there would at times be some little balm, and he, Afanasy, slandering me, ceaselessly sought my death. And during these lean years he sent me of his own accord two widows—they were servants in his house and dear to him—Mary and Sophia, clothed about with an unclean spirit; many times had he tried spells and incantations upon them, but it had availed him nought; and tongues had begun to wag concerning the matter, whereupon the imp of hell would start tormenting them most cruelly, and they would twist themselves and shriek. He summoned me and,

bowing to me, said, "I pray you take them home with you and
physick them with prayer to God; God will hearken to you."
And I answered him, "My Lord! What you ask of me is beyond
my powers. By the prayers of the holy Fathers of our Church
all things are possible to God." So I took the poor souls home—
if it was presumptuous in me may I be forgiven. I had had some
experience in such matters in Russia. Three or four persons possessed by an unclean spirit had, in former times, been brought
to my house, and with the prayers of the holy Fathers I had
cast out the imps of hell by the action and will of the living
God and of our Lord Jesus Christ, Son of God, Light of the
World. I had sprinkled them with tears and with water and
anointed them with oil, chanting prayers the while, in the name
of Christ, and the holy magic of these things had driven the
imps out of these persons, and they had been healed—not by
any virtue in me—by no means; but by their own faith. Of old
time an ass was made the instrument by which a blessing came
to Balaam,[25] and by a lynx a blessing came to Julian the martyr,
and by a stag to Sisinius: they spoke with a human voice. God
whensoever he chooses triumphs over Nature's laws. Read the
life of Theodore of Edessa; there will you find that a harlot
raised a man from the dead; in the *Christian's Pilot*[26] it is
written: *"Not for all men are the gifts of the Holy Ghost, but
all men can he leaven, excepting only heretics."*

So they brought me these two women that were possessed;
and I, as the custom is, myself fasted and would not let them
eat, and I prayed and anointed them with oil and tried every
remedy I knew. And the good wives returned to health and to
their right minds; and I confessed them and administered the
Sacrament to them; and they tarried in my house, praying to
God, for they loved me and would not go home. And it came to
his knowledge that they had become my spiritual daughters;
and he was angered against me, more fiercely than before, and
he was fain to burn me alive. "You have wormed out of them
in the confessional," said he, "private matters concerning me."
And how, forsooth, can one administer the Sacrament to a man
if one has not first confessed him? And if you do not administer
the Sacrament to the possessed, you'll in no wise succeed in
casting out of them the imps of hell. A devil is not a mujik, forsooth, that he should fear the stick; what he fears is the Cross
of Christ, and holy water and holy oil, but before the Body of

[25] See the Book of Numbers, Chapter 22.
[26] The *Christian's Pilot* was a Byzantine codex of canon law.

Christ he flies. Without the Blessed Sacrament I cannot heal; in our Orthodox faith there is no Communion without Confession; in the Roman faith they pay no heed to Confession; but to us, the Orthodox observers, this is not seemly, and for us the Sacrament of Penance must ever first be sought. And if in your need you cannot have a priest, then confess your sins to some discreet brother, and, beholding your contrition, God will pardon you; and then, having read through the Canon of the Mass before communicating, keep by you some reserved sacrament. And, whensoever you are away on a journey or engaged in traffic or whatever it may be that takes you far from a church, if you have first given sighs of contrition to the Lord and have confessed to your brother, as has been said above, then may you partake with a clear conscience of the Blessed Sacrament and all will be well, if you have first fasted and read through the Canon of the Mass: take then a little casket and spread a napkin in it, and light a candle, and pour a little water into a cup, and ladle some out in a spoon, and place with prayer a portion of Christ's Body in the water in the spoon, and sense it all with a censer; and weeping say out loud the whole of the prayer that begins: "O Lord! I believe and confess that thou art Christ, the son of the living God." (It is written in the Canon of the Mass.) Then, throwing yourself on the ground before the icon, ask for forgiveness and, standing up, kiss the holy image; and, having signed yourself, communicate with prayer, and drink a little of the water and pray again to God, saying, "Now glory to Christ!" Even if you die the minute after, it will be well with you. Enough of that matter, you yourselves know that it is good counsel. Now I shall go on with the story of the women.

Pashkov took the poor widows away from me, and in lieu of gratitude he gave me harsh words. He hoped that Christ had settled the matter once and for all; but they began to rave worse than before. He shut them up in an empty outhouse and allowed no one access to them; then he summoned a monk to them, but they flung logs at him, and he scuttled away. I sat at home weeping, and I knew not what to do. I did not dare to go up to the big house, for he was mighty wroth with me; so in secret I sent them holy water, and told them to wash themselves and drink a little of it, and, poor souls, their sufferings were eased a little. And in secret they stole off to me, and I anointed them with oil in the name of Christ, and once again God granted that they should be healed, and they returned home; and by night they would escape to me in secret to pray to God. And they became exceeding good churchwomen; they put aside vanities and began to follow all the observances of the Church; and afterwards in Moscow they went with their lady to dwell in the nunnery of the Ascension. Glory to God for them!

And then from the Nercha River we began to journey back to Russia; for five weeks we traveled on the naked ice in sledges. I was given two sorry nags for my children and my baggage, while myself and Dame Avvakum, we made our way on foot, stumbling over the ice. The country was barbarous, the natives were hostile, so we feared to get separated from the others, and yet we could not keep up with the horses—for we were a hungry, weary pair; and my poor old woman tramped along, tramped along, and at last she fell, and another weary soul stumbled over her, and he fell too; they both screamed, and were not able to get up. The man cried out, "Oh, good wife! Oh, my lady! Your pardon!" and my old woman answered, "Fie, gossip! Would you crush me to death?" And I came up, and she, poor soul, began to complain to me, saying, "How long, arch-priest, are these sufferings to last?" And I said, "Markovna! till our death." And she, with a sigh, answered, "So be it, Petro-vitch; let us be getting on our way."

VIII. The Story of the Black Hen

And we had a pet, a black hen, and she laid two eggs a day to feed the children, by God's will, helping us in our need; it was God's doing. But when they were carrying out the baggage to the dog sledge, she was crushed to death, for our sins, and to this day whenever I think of that hen my heart aches for her. I know not if it were a hen or miracle: all the year round she laid two eggs a day, and we would not have taken a hundred rubles for her—nay, we would have spat on them! mere dross! And that hen, God's living creature, fed us, and she would take her meals with us, pecking at the porridge of fir cones in the caldron, and pecking at the fish, and in exchange she gave us two eggs a day. Glory to God, who fashions all things well! And we had come by her in no ordinary way. My lady's hens had one after another turned blind, and they began to die, whereupon she gathered them into a basket and sent them to me. "And may it please you, Father," said she, "to pray over the hens." And I considered: she was a lady bountiful to us, she had children, and she had need of the hens. So I chanted a prayer and blessed some water and sprinkled the hens and censed them. Then I went to the forest and fashioned them a trough from which to eat, and sprinkled it with holy water, and sent the whole baggage back to her. And by a wave of God's hand the hens were healed, because of her faith. And it was from that same brood that our hen came; but enough of this matter; it was not the first miracle that Christ had brought to pass. Already Kosma and Damian had blessed and healed both men and cattle in the name of Christ.[27] God has a use for everything: cattle and fowls —they were created for the glory of his pure majesty, and also for the sake of mankind.

IX. AT LAKE IRGEN

So we made our way back to Lake Irgen. My lady had pity on us and sent us a little basket of wheat, so we had our fill of frumenty. Eudokia Kirilovna was a lady bountiful to me, but the Devil set her quarreling with me in this manner: she had a son whose name was Simeon; he had been born in that place. It was I that had churched the mother and baptized the child, and every day they would send him to me for my blessing and I, having signed him with the Cross and sprinkled him with holy water, would kiss him and send him home; he was a fine healthy child and I loved him like my own. But the little lad began to ail, and I was away from home. And in a moment of pettiness of spirit she was vexed with me and sent the child to a medicine man. And I, when I learned of it, was angry with her, and a wide breach came between us; the little boy began to ail still more, and his right hand and foot dried up, so they were like little sticks. She grew ashamed; but she knew not what to do, and God oppressed her still further. The little one became sick unto death, and the nurses came to me weeping and I said to them, "If the goodwife is a baggage, then let her keep herself *to* herself." For I was waiting that she should repent. I saw that the Devil had hardened her heart, and I bowed down before the Lord God, praying that he might bring her to her right mind. And the Lord, the God of Mercy, softened the rich soil of her heart, and early next morning she sent to me her second son, Ivan; with tears he begged forgiveness for his mother, walking round the stove and bowing before me; and I was lying on the stove, naked, under a covering made from birch-bark, and Dame Avvakum was lying within the stove, and the children anywhere. It was raining at the time; we had no covering, and our winter quarters were dripping, so we were in sorry straits. And I said to him, bringing him low, "Tell your mother that she must ask forgiveness of Aretha, the medicine

---

[27] Kosma and Damian were considered the saintly protectors of men and cattle, and possessing miracle-working powers for healing.

man." Then she brought the sick child to me and I ordered her to lay him before me, and they were all weeping and bowing themselves. And I arose and got me my stole out from the mess and dirt and found some holy oil, and, praying to God, I censed the boy and signed him with the sign of the Cross. And God granted that the child was healed, both in his hand and foot. And I sprinkled him with holy water and sent him to his mother. Consider, thou who hearkenest to my story, what great things were compassed by a mother's penitence; it both physicked her own soul and healed her child. What then? It is not only today that God is with penitents. On the morrow she sent us fish and pies; and they were apt to our need, for we were starving; and that day we made our peace, she and I. When we had journeyed back from Dauria, she, sweet lady, died in Moscow, and I buried her in the nunnery of the Ascension.

And Pashkov himself learned of the affair with the boy, for she told him. I went to him and, bowing low before me, he, Pashkov, said, "God bless you! You have acted like a true priest; remember not our sins against us." And at that time he sent us no small store of food.

X. The Tribulations of the Mongolian Expedition (1661)

But in a very short space he was minded to torture me—hearken how it came about. He was sending his son, Eremy, off to fight in the kingdom of the Mongols, and with him some seventy-two Cossacks and some twenty natives. And he made a native to *"shamanit'*,"[28] that is to say, to tell their fortune, as to whether they would prosper and return home victorious. And in the evening that wizard—it was near my winter quarters—brought a live sheep and began to work magic over it: he rolled it to and fro for a long space and then he twisted its head and flung it away. Then he began to jump and dance, and invoke devils, and, giving great screams the while, he flung himself upon the earth, and foamed at the mouth; the devils were pressing him, and he asked them, "Will the expedition prosper?" And the devils said, "It will return with much booty, having gained a great victory." And the captains were glad; and all the folk, rejoicing, cried, "We will come home rich!" Oh, lackaday! It was bitter then, and even now it is not sweet to think upon. I, a bad shepherd, made my sheep to perish; from vexation of

[28] *Shamanit':* the Shamans were Siberian pagan priests and medicine men. Avvakum gives to this word a verbal infinitive ending, thus *shamanit'* means to perform pagan rites.

spirit I forgot the words of the Gospel, when the Sons of Zebedee counseled our Lord concerning the stubborn villagers, saying:—

"Lord, wilt thou that we command fire to come down from heaven and consume them, even as Elias did?"

But He turned and rebuked them, and said, Ye know not what manner of spirit ye are of.

For the Son of Man is not come to destroy men's lives, but to save them. And they went to another village.

But I, accursed, did not so. In my poor room I cried with a great cry to the Lord, "Hearken to me, my God! Hearken to me, King of Heaven! Sweet Lord! Hearken to me! Let not one of them return home; and dig a grave for every one of them yonder! Lay on them an evil fate, O Lord! Bring them to destruction, so that the Devil's prophecy may not be fulfilled." And many like words did I say, and in secret I prayed to God concerning it. They told him that I was praying thus, but he did but snarl abuses at me. Then he sent off his son with the captain; they rode off at night, directing their course by the stars. And I was seized with pity for them, for my soul foresaw that they would perish; nevertheless, I continued praying for their destruction, and some of them, as they passed, called out goodby to me, and I called back, "You will die yonder." And, as they rode off, the horses under them began to whinny, and the cows that were there to low, and the sheep and goats to bleat, and the dogs to howl, and the natives to howl, like the dogs. Terror seized them all. With tears Eremy sent me word, "that it may please my lord and spiritual father to pray for me." And I was seized with pity for him, for he had been my secret friend and had suffered for my sake. When his father was flogging me with the knout, he had tried to dissuade him, so that his father had chased him with drawn sword. And when they arrived after me, at other rapids, those of the Pandun, forty rafts all got through the straits in safety; but his, Afanasy's own raft, though her rigging was excellent and six hundred Cossacks had been set to build her, yet were they not able to get her through: the waters overcame them, or rather God was punishing him: all the crew were sucked into the water, and the raft was hurled against a rock; the waters splashed up against it, but did not flow into it. It is marvelous to watch God's lessons to the foolish! He himself was on the shore, and his lady was on the raft, and Eremy began to speak, saying, "Father! God will punish you for your sins; you flogged the archpriest with that knout unjustly; it is time to repent, my lord!" But he roared at him, like a wild beast, and Eremy, dodging behind a fir, clasped his hands and repeated the *Lord have mercy upon us*. But Pashkov, having seized a ringed musket, one that never missed, from an attendant, took aim at his son and pulled the trigger, and by God's will the weapon missed fire. Then, having adjusted the powder, he fired again, and again it missed fire. And he did the same a third time, and the third time, also, it missed fire. So he flung it on the ground, and the attendant picked it up and threw it out of the way, and it went off of its own accord.

And Pashkov sat him down on a chair and, leaning on his sword, he came to his right mind, and beginning to weep, he said, "I have sinned, accursed that I am, I have spilled innocent blood, I flogged the archpriest unjustly, God will punish me." It was strangely, strangely in accord with the words, *God is slow to anger and swift to hearken*. For because of his repentance the raft floated away from the reef; its prow was toward the water; and they pulled it from the shore and it leapt out into a lower level of the water. Then Pashkov called his son to him, and entreated him, saying, "Forgive me, Eremy, you spoke truly!" and he, running up, and bowing before his father, said, "It is God, my lord, that will forgive you; for I myself am guilty before God and before you." And he took his father's hand, and led him away. Eremy was a righteous-minded man, and a virtuous one; already was his own beard grey, and yet he honored his father exceedingly, and feared him, and according to the Scriptures it is seemly so to do, for God loves the children that honor their fathers. Come then, hearkener to my story! Is it not true that Eremy had suffered for my sake, and for the sake of Christ and his Law?

And all this was recounted to me by the helmsman of his, Afanasy's raft, by name Gregory Tielnoy. Let us return to the previous matter.

They went away, then, from me, and rode off to the wars; and pity seized me for Eremy, and I began to importune God Almighty that he might protect him. Time passed and they were expected home from the wars, and the day came fixed for their return, but they came not; and during three days Pashkov refused me admittance to his house. And at last he prepared a torture chamber, and had a fire kindled; he wished to torture me. And I was repeating prayers for my latter end, for I knew what manner of cook he was and that few came out alive from his roasting. And I sat waiting in my house, and I said to my wife, who was weeping, and to my children, "God's will be done! For whether we live, we live unto the Lord; and whether we die, we die unto the Lord." And lo! at that moment I saw two executioners come hurrying in to seize me. Marvelous are the acts of the Lord, and unspeakable the counsels of Almighty God! Suddenly Eremy himself, wounded, comes riding along by the little path that goes past my house and garden, and he calls out to the executioners, and makes them turn back with him; and he, Pashkov, left the torture chamber and came toward his son, staggering like a drunk man from grief. And Eremy, bowing low to his father, acquainted him with all that had taken place: how all his troops had been slaughtered, no single man surviving; and how a native had led him, through wild and lonely places, away from the Mongolian people; and how, without food, they had wandered over stony mountains and through the forest for seven days, having nought to eat but one squirrel; and how a man in my image had appeared to him in a dream and had shown him the path, and whither he must journey; and how he had leaped up and gone on his way rejoicing. When he had recounted all to his father, then I came in to greet him. But Pashkov rolled his eyes at me—the very spit of a white polar bear, and he would have gobbled me up alive, only the Lord did not grant that it should be so—and, drawing in his breath, he said, "What think you of your handiwork? How many men, think you, have you caused to perish?" But Eremy said to me, "Father Avvakum! for Christ's sake, get thee gone, and do not bandy words with him." And I went.

For ten years he had tormented me, or I him—I know not which. God will decide on the Day of Judgment.

A change of post came for him, and for me a letter; we were ordered back to Russia. He went away and did not take me with him, for in his heart he was saying, "If he travels back alone, then surely the natives will slay him." He and his guns and his folk, they sailed away on rafts, and, on my own journey back, I learned from the natives that they were a timid, trembling crew. And I, a month afterwards, having assembled the aged, and the sick, and the wounded, whatever there was there of useless folk (there would be ten of them, and I with my wife and children would bring it to seventeen), got into a boat, and, putting our trust in Christ and fixing the Cross to our prow, we started on our way, wherever God should lead us, fearing nothing. I gave the book, the *Christian's Pilot*, to the clerk, and he gave me a fellow for steersman in exchange; and he manumitted my friend Basil, the same that was wont to denounce folk to Pashkov and was the cause that much blood was shed, and he sought my life also. And at one time, having flogged me, he fastened me to the stake, but once again God kept me safe; and when Pashkov was gone the Cossacks wished to flog him to death, but I begged him off for Christ's sake and gave the money for his manumission to the clerk, and carried him back to Russia, from death to life. Poor soul, may he repent his sins! Ay, and I took back with me another lousy spy of the same kidney; him they did not wish to give up to me, and he fled from death to the forest, and, coming upon me on the path, he flung himself into my boat, for he was pursued and had nowhere to turn. And I, forgive me, acted cunningly. As Rahab, the harlot of Jericho, hid Joshua the son of Nun, so did I hide him, making him lie down at the bottom of a chest, and I flung a coverlet over him, and ordered my wife and daughter to lie on the top of him; they sought him high and low, but they would not disturb my wife from her place, and all they said was, "Rest in peace, Mother Avvakum! You have had enough to endure, as it is, my lady." And I—for God's sake forgive me—I lied that day, and I said, "He is not here"—I was loth to give him up to be slain. And when they had searched they went away empty-handed, and I carried him back to Russia. Elder and servant of Christ![29] Forgive me, then, in that I lied that day. How think you, it may be that it was not a very grievous sin? It would seem that Rahab the harlot did likewise, and the Scriptures praise her for it; give judgment, then, for God's sake: and if I acted sinfully, then pardon me; but if I acted in accordance with the traditions of the Church, then is it well. See, I have left a space for you, and do you, with your own hand, write in either forgiveness or penance for me and my wife and my daughter, for we all three shared in the cheat—we saved a man from death that he might repent before the Lord. Judge us then so that we shall not be judged for it by Christ on the Day of Judgment; write in a few words, I pray you:—

God pardons thee and blesses thee in this life and the life to come, together with thy helpmeet Anastasia, and thy daughter, and all thy house: thou hast acted rightly and justly. Amen.[30]

So be it then, my elder. God bless you for your graciousness. But enough of this.

The clerk gave us sacks of corn to the value of thirty silver pieces, and a cow, and five or six sheep, and dried meat, and

[29] These words are addressed to Avvakum's cellmate and spiritual father, Epiphany.

[30] This last passage is written into the manuscript by Epiphany, who read the manuscript and made some addenda.

this we fed on for the summer, as we sailed on our way. The clerk was a good soul; he had been sponsor to my daughter Xenia, who had been born in the days of Pashkov, but Pashkov would not give me myrrh and oil, so she had to stay long un-christened; but when he was gone I christened her (I myself churched my wife and baptized my children),[31] and the clerk and my eldest daughter were the gossips, and I was the parson. In this manner, then, I also christened my son Afanasy, and both confessed my own children and administered the Sacra-ment to them during the Mass I said at Mezen, and I myself communicated, but I did not administer it to my wife: there are instructions concerning this in the rubric, wherein we are bade so to do. But as to my excommunication, it came from heretics and, in Christ's name, I trample it under foot, and the curse written against me—why, not to mince my words, I wipe my arse with that; if the heretics curse me, the saints of Moscow—Peter, and Alexis, and Jonah, and Phillip—*they* bless me; and in accordance with their books, with a clear conscience I believe in and serve my God; but the apostates I loathe and curse: they are God's enemies and, living in Christ, I do not fear them. Were they to heap stones on me then, secure in the tradition of the Fathers, I would lie in peace beneath these stones—how much more so beneath the thorny, knavish curses of Nikon! Tush! Why multiply words? All we need do is to spit on their doings and their ritual, and on their newfangled books, then all will be well. Our following discourse will be pleasing to Christ and the Immaculate Mother of God, so enough of their knavery. Pardon me, good Nikonites,[32] for having abused you; live as ye will. As for me, I am now about to take up again my tale of woe, so go your ways in peace. For twenty years God has willed that I should be tormented by you, and should it be for twenty more, then will I endure it, in the name of the Lord our God and of our Saviour Jesus Christ. Enough of this. I have wandered, as it is, far enough from my story—let us return to it.

So I left Dauria; the food began to grow scarce, so I prayed together with my company, and Christ gave us a roebuck, a huge beast, and on him we lived till we reached Baikal. There, by the lake, we came on Russian folk—a settlement of sable-hunters and of fishermen; they were right glad to see us, dear souls, and we them, and they dragged us and our boat to shore, and led us far inland to the hills. There was a dear lad called

[31] Under ordinary circumstances, it was prohibited by the canons of the Orthodox Church to baptize one's own children.
[32] Nikonites: refers to the supporters of Nikon.

Terenty, and he and his comrades gazed on us, and we on them
—dear souls—with tears of joy. And they snowed meat and drink
on us, as much as ever we needed. They brought me some forty
freshwater sturgeons, saying, "There, Father! God sent them
into our fishery for you. Take them all." I, bowing to them,
blessed the fish and bade them take them back, saying, "What
need have I of so many?" They entertained me there and, from
dire need, I accepted from them some provision. Then, having
repaired our boat, we let out our sails, and prepared to cross the
lake. But the lake grew rough, so we took to our oars. In that
place the lake is very broad—it must be a hundred or at least
eighty versts. When we stood to the shore there sprang up a
tempest and we were forced to find a shelter from the waves
on the shore. The place was surrounded by high mountains: I
have wandered over the face of the earth 20,000 versts and
more, but never have I seen their like. On their summit are
tents and earthen huts, portals and towers, stone walls and
courts, all neatly fashioned. Onions grow of them and garlic,
bigger than the Romanov onion, and exceeding sweet to the
taste; there also grows wild hemp, and in the gardens fine grass
and exceeding fragrant flowers, and there is great quantity of
birds—geese and swans that fly over the lake like snow. And
there are fishes—sturgeon and trout, sterlet and salmon-trout and
whiting and many other kinds; it is fresh water and in that
mighty ocean lake there are sea-calves and great sea-hares. I
saw none such during all the time that I was living on the
Mezen,[33] and the fish in it are of a great weight, the sturgeon
and salmon-trout are exceeding fleshy—they are not for frying,
for it would be naught but fat. And all this has been fashioned
by our sweet Christ for man, so that, with a mind at last at
rest, he might give praise to God. But such is man that he is
given to vanity, and his days go by like a shadow: he leaps,
like a goat; he blows himself out, like a bubble; he rages, like
a lynx; he seeks to devour, like a serpent; when he looks on the
comeliness of his neighbour he neighs like a foal; he is crafty,
like a fiend; when he has eaten his fill then, like an heathen, he
falls asleep, without saying his prayers; he puts off repenting
till his old age and then he vanishes; we know not where,—
whether it be to light of darkness: it will be shown on the Day
of Judgment. Forgive me; I myself have sinned more than other
men.

[33] Mezen was a small city in northern Russia to which Avvakum
was deported in 1664, remaining there until 1665.

XI. THE STAUNCH PROTOPOPITSA[34]

So we reached Russian settlements, and I was informed concerning the Church, and like Pilate, I saw that I *"could prevail nothing, but that rather a tumult was made."* My mind was troubled and, sitting down, I began to ponder what I should do —should I continue preaching God's Word or should I hide myself? For I was tied by my wife and children. And seeing that I was troubled, my wife came up to me, timidly, delicately, and said, "How comes it, my lord, that you are troubled?" And I acquainted her with all my thoughts. "Wife! What must I do? The Winter of Heresy is at the door; am I to speak or to hold my peace? I am tied by you!" And she said to me, "Lord have mercy! What are you saying, Petrovitch? Have I not heard, have you not read, the words of the Apostle: *Art thou bound unto a wife? seek not to be loosed. Art thou loosed from a wife? seek not a wife.* I and the children, we give you our blessing, continue preaching the Word of God as heretofore, and take no thought for us until such time as shall seem good to God; when that times comes, remember us in your prayers; Christ is strong and he will not abandon us. Get thee gone, get thee gone to church, Petrovitch! Unmask the Whore of Heresy!" And I bowed myself to the earth before her, and shook myself free from the blindness of a troubled mind and began once more to preach and teach God's Word in the towns and in all places until such time as I could boldly tear the mask from the heresy of Nikon.

In Yeniseisk[35] I wintered, and having sailed through the summer again I wintered in Tobolsk; and on my way as far as Moscow I cried aloud in every town and in every village, in churches and in marketplaces, preaching the Word of God and teaching and laying bare the snares of the ungodly. And thereon I came to Moscow. Three years was I in coming from Dauria, and it took me five years traveling upstream. We journeyed ever eastward amid native tribes and habitations. Much might be said of that. Sometimes we fell into the hands of the natives; at Ob, the mighty river, in my presence they put to death twenty men who were Christians. And they were minded to do the like to me, but they let me go altogether. And again on the Irtysh River there was standing a company of them—they were lying in ambush for our men of Berezov to slay us—but I knew it not and I went up toward them. And when I was come up to

---

[34] Protopopitsa: the wife of a protopope, or archpriest.
[35] Yeniseisk: a Russian outpost and merchant city in central Siberia on the Yenisei River.

them I put in to the bank. In a moment they were round about
me with their bows, and I, I tell you, went forth to embrace
them as though they were monks and I spoke and said, "Christ
be with me and with you too." And they entreated me kindly
and they brought their wives to my wife. And my wife dis-
sembled with them, as in the world they are wont to employ
flattery; and the womenfolk were kindly and we felt it: when
the womenfolk are good, then under Christ all is well. The men
hid their bows and arrows. I bought some bear's flesh from them
and they let me go free. As I was saying, I was come to Tobolsk.
And the folk were astonished thereat, for Bashkirs and the
Tatars were scouring all Siberia. But I, trusting in Christ, went
through their midst. And when I had reached Verkhoturie,[36]
Ivan Bogdanovitch, my friend, was astonished at me. "How did
you ever get through, archpriest?" And I made answer, "Christ
brought me through, and the all pure Mother of God brought
me through. I fear no man, only Christ do I fear."

XII. BACK IN MOSCOW: JOYS AND DISPUTES (1664)

Thus did I come to Moscow, and as though I were an angel
of God the tsar and all his boyars received me gladly. I went
to see Theodore Rtishchev,[37] he came himself from his tent,
received my blessing and began to speak of many things: for
three days and three nights he suffered me not to go home, and
thereafter he informed the tsar concerning me. His Majesty
gave command to place me at his side and spake kindly to me.
"Art thou well in health, archpriest?" said he. "God bade me
see thee again." And I in answer kissed his hand and pressed it,
and myself said, "God lives and my spirit lives, your Majesty!
but for what is before us that God will ordain." And he sighed
softly and went whither he had need. And other things happened, but what need to speak of it? That too passed by. He
bade them place me in the guesthouse of a monastery in the
Kremlin, and when he passed my door going out on expeditions
he often gave me greeting, bowing low, and himself would say,
"Bless me," said he, "and pray for me"; and one time he took

[36] Verkhoturie was a Russian city in western Siberia almost in the
foothills of the Ural Mountains.
[37] Theodore (Fedor) Rtishchev was a statesman and personal
friend of Tsar Alexis. He actively participated in church affairs and
from 1645 to 1653 was a member of the Zealots of Piety. He remained faithful to Nikon after the latter's break with this movement.
He was well known for his support of the arts, learning, and charitable activities.

his fur cap from his head and let it fall as he was riding on horseback. He used to slip out of his carriage to come to me and all his boyars kept bowing and scraping, crying, "Archpriest, bless us and pray for us." How shall I not grieve for such a tsar and such boyars? It grieves me to think how good they were, they gave me place wheresoever I wished, and they named me their confessor, that I might be made one with them in the faith. But I held all these things to be but vanity. And I gained Christ and was mindful of death, how all these things pass away.

And this was revealed to me in Tobolsk when I was half asleep. "Watch, I bid thee, that thou be not a branch cut off." I leaped up and fell before the icon in great terror, and I spake and said, "Lord, I will not go when they chant in newfangled fashion; my God." I was at early Mass in the cathedral on the name day of the tsarina. I was jesting with them in that Church in the presence of the officials, and from the moment of arrival I took notice whether they mixed the elements in triple or in twofold wise, and standing at the altar by the sacrificial table I abused them, and with time I got used to them, so I ceased from abusing them. Such was the bitter spirit of Antichrist that stung me.

Thus did our sweet Christ make me afraid and said to me, "After so great suffering wilt thou perish? Watch, lest I hew thee off as a dry branch." I went not to Mass, but I went to sup with the prince, and I told him all, every word. A kind boyar prince, Ivan Andrew Chelkov, began to weep. Woe is me, accursed one, that I forget so great mercy of God!

When I was at Dauria and I labored as a fisherman, I went in the winter to my children, and I went along the lake on snowshoes; there was no snow but great frosts, and the ice froze well-nigh the thickness of a man. I began to want to drink, and I suffered much from thirst. I couldn't go on, I was midway in the lake, I couldn't get to the water; the lake was eight versts. I began to look up to heaven and to say, "O Lord, thou didst cause water to flow in the desert for the thirsty people of Israel, then and now art thou; give me to drink by whatever means seem good to thee. O Lord my God! Woe is me. I know not how to pray, forgive me for the Lord's sake. Who am I, a dead dog?" The ice gave a crack beneath me and split up to either side across the whole lake and came together again, and a great mountain of ice rose up, and while this was going on I stood in my accustomed place, and looking toward the east, I bowed twice or thrice, pronouncing the name of the Lord in a loud voice from the depths of my heart. God had left me a small hole in the ice, and I, falling down, slaked my thirst. And I wept and was glad, praising God. After that the hole in the ice joined up and I, rising up, bowed down to the Lord and then again ran along the ice whither I must needs go to my children. And in my other wanderings it often happened to me like this. I was either walking along, dragging my sledge or catching fish or cutting wood in the forest, or whatsoever I might be doing, I always recited my office at the regular time, whether it was morning Mass or evening, at the hours it was the custom; if I chanced to be among other people none could hinder me, but I would stand upright and none of my companions with me, for they did not love my office, and when they were there it was impossible for me to carry it out, and I, going away from among men, would go through it in a shortened form, either under a hill or in a wood, beating with my head against the earth, and sometimes I would weep and feel wounded. But if there should be people with me I would place the icon on the sledge-rail and I would recite the office right through, and some would pray with me, but others would cook their porridge; and when I am going in my sledge on Sundays to the guesthouses I sing the whole church service, and on festival days when I am driving in a sledge I will sing, and often on Sundays as I go along I would sing. And when I do it very persistently, sometimes I would grumble though only a little, for my body was ahungered and would fain eat, and was athirst and would fain drink, and likewise my spirit, O Father Epiphany, desires spiritual food: It is not the hunger for bread that destroys a man nor the thirst for water, but the great hunger of a man when he lives without praying to God.[38]

If thou art not weary of listening to this thy servant of Christ, I, a sinner, will make known to thee this too, how often in the land of Daur, from loss of strength and from hunger I could not keep my rule, only a little of it could I keep, only the evening psalms and the midnight office at the first hour, but more than that I could not: I dragged myself about like a poor beast. I was grieved about that office of mine, but I could not take it up. You see by now I had got so weak. But sometimes I went to the forest for wood, and while I was away my wife and children would sit on the ground by the fire, my daughter with her mother, and they would both cry. Agraphena, my poor unhappy one, was then not yet grown up. I came back from the wood—

---

[38] Another direct address to Epiphany, Avvakum's confessor and fellow inmate in Pustozersk.

the child was sobbing hard. She could not speak for her tongue was fast bound, but she sat there and whimpered to her mother, and the mother looked at her and cried. But I breathed heavily and came near to the child with a prayer and said, "In the name of the Lord I bid thee speak to me and tell me why thou weepest." And she jumped up and bowed before me and began to speak clearly thus, "I do not know who it is, my Lord father, but there is a Shining One within me and he held me by my tongue and he would not let me speak to mother, and because of it I cried. But he said to me, 'Tell your father that he should recite his office as he used to do, and then ye all go forth again to Russia, but, if he does not keep his rule, about which he is himself troubled, then in this place ye shall all die, and he shall die with you.' " At that time another thing of that sort was said to her, that there would be an edict to fetch us, and how that many of our friends had perished in Russia; all this came to pass. I was to say to Pashkov that if he sang the morning and evening office then God would give fair weather, and the corn would grow and there would be constant rain, and they sowed wheat on a small plot a day or two before Peter's day, and immediately it sprouted and was all but rotted by the rains. I spoke to him about the evening and morning office and he set to do this. God sent fair weather, and the corn ripened immediately. What a miracle! It was sown late but it ripened early.

And again, poor man, he began to practice cunning arts about God's doings—the following year he sowed much, but an unwonted rain poured down, and the water overflowed from the river and drowned the plowed fields and washed everything away, and it washed away our hut, and until that time there had never been water there, and the natives wondered. Mark you, as he went his way, so God moved in his mysterious way. At first he laughed at the news, but afterward, when the child wanted to eat, he betook him to tears—and then I sought not to slacken about my office. Enough of this have I spoken; let us return to our first subject. We must needs remember all these things and not be forgetting them, so as not to lay aside any of God's doings in negligence and waste and not to alter them for the pleasure of this age of vanity.

Now I will tell of what was done at Moscow. They said that I was not at one with them. His Majesty bade Rodion Streshnev[39] persuade me that I should hold my peace. And I did his

[39] Rodion Streshnev: a relative of the tsar's wife and his councilor in Church affairs.

bidding. The tsar is set over us by God, and at this moment was
kindly disposed towards me. So I hoped that little by little he
would come to a better mind. They promised me on Simeon's
day to place me at the printing office to correct books, and I
was exceedingly glad, for that pleased me better than to be the
tsar's confessor. I wanted something better than the confessional.
I waited on him. He sent me ten rubles and the tsarina sent me
ten. Luke, the confessor, sent me ten, and Rodion Streshnev also
ten, and our old friend Theodore Rtishchev then ordered them
to slip into my hat sixty rubles from his official salary, but about
that I was to say nothing! Each man put his hand in his pocket
and brought out every manner of thing. I lived in the house of
my dear one, Theodosia Prokofievna Morozova,[40] and didn't go
out inasmuch as she was my spiritual daughter. And her sister,
Princess Eudoxia Prokofievna, was my daughter also. My dear
ones, martyrs for Christ! And I was ever in the house of Anna
Petrovna Miloslavskaia.[41] God rest her soul! And I went to
Theodore Rtishchev's house to dispute with the apostles, and
so lived about the space of half a year. And I saw that I prevailed nothing but that rather a tumult was made; again, I
began to grumble, and I wrote to the tsar many things to the
effect that he should earnestly seek for the ancient piety and
defend from heresy our common mother holy Church, and on
the patriarchal throne he should place a shepherd of the orthodox faith in place of the wolf and apostate Nikon, him that was
an evildoer and a heretic. And when I had got ready the letter
I had no more strength left in me: and I sent it forth on the
journey to the tsar by my spiritual son Theodore, the Fool in
Christ, which Theodore they strangled at Mezene, hanging him
upon the gallows-tree. Now he in all boldness approached the
tsar's carriage, and the tsar bade him sit down with the letter
near the great entrance: he did not perceive that the letter was
from me. And afterward, having the letter from him he bade
let him go. And he—God rest his soul!—after staying a while
with me again went into the church in the presence of the
tsar and began to play the fool as though he was half-witted.
The tsar was angry and bade them send him away to the

[40] Theodosia Morozova—a lady-in-waiting to the tsarina, and
widow of an influential boyar. She remained a faithful supporter of
Avvakum. She and her sister, Eudoxia Urusova, were arrested in
1670 for their support of the Old Believer movement, and both died
in prison in 1672.
[41] Anna Miloslavskaia: a relative of the tsarina, and an influential
supporter of Avvakum.

Miracle Monastery, There Paul the archimandrite bade them put fetters on him, and by the will of God the fetters brake to pieces upon his legs before the people. But he, God rest his soul! my friend! crept into the burning stove in the bakehouse after the loaves and sat on the grating with his naked rump and picked up the crumbs in the stove to eat of them. Then the monks were affrighted and told the archimandrite Paul that was now metropolitan. He acquainted the tsar with this, and the tsar came to the monastery and ordered them to let him go with honor. He again came to me, and from that day on the tsar began to look askance at me. He was ill pleased that I began again to speak. He would have liked me to hold my peace but that was not my way. And the bishops, like goats, began to leap up against me, and they plotted to send me in banishment from Moscow, for many of the Christians had come to me and perceiving the truth they would not walk in the service of a lie. And from the tsar there came to me the accusation, "They tell me that the bishops bring complaint against thee; they say because of thee the churches are empty. Go again," said he, "into banishment." Thus spake the boyar Peter Mikhailovich Saltykov.[42] And they brought me to Mezen, and many good people gave me this and that in the name of Christ. And everything remained, only they took me with my wife and my children and my household. From town to town I taught the people of God and denounced them, the spotted beasts. And they brought us to Mezen.

Having endured for half a year, they took me again without my wife to Moscow, and my two sons journeyed with me, Ivan and Prokopy. But my wife and the rest were all left at Mezen. And having brought us to Moscow they took us at first away to the Pafnutiev Monastery,[43] and there they sent us a letter, and they spake thus and thus: "Wilt thou so long vex us? be reconciled to us, dear old Avvakum!" But I refused as though they were devils. And they flew in my face.

Then I wrote them an answer with much violence of words, and I sent it by Kosma, a deacon of Yaroslavl, by the subdeacon of the patriarchal court—Kosma in public tried to overpersuade me, but in private he upheld me, speaking thus, "Archpriest, do not desert the ancient rites; a mighty man wilt thou be with Christ if thou wilt endure to the end—do not look to us for we

[42] Peter Saltykov was a boyar who energetically opposed Avvakum and his movement.

[43] Pafnutiev Monastery: a monastery in the vicinity of Moscow that often served as a prison for clergymen.

are ruined." And I to him made answer that he should again stand for Christ. And he said, "I cannot. Nikon has led me astray." And to speak shortly, he had denied Christ before Nikon, in that he had no strength to stand firm, my poor Kosma. I fell to crying; I blessed him, unhappy one—after that I had no more dealings with him; let God deal with him as seems good to him.

XIII. PREPARATIONS FOR THE TRIAL (1664–1666)

Thus having remained ten weeks in Pafnutiev in chains, they took me again to Moscow, and in the room of the Cross the bishops held disputation with me. They led me to the Cathedral church, and after the Elevation of the Host they sheared me and the deacon Theodore, and then they cursed us and I cursed them back. And I was heavy at heart for the Mass. And after I had stayed for a time at the patriarchal court, they took us by night to Ugresha,[44] to the monastery of St. Nicholas—and the enemies of God shaved off my beard. What would you? It is like unto wolves not to pity the sheep; they tore at my hair like dogs and only left one forelock—such as the Poles wear on their foreheads. They did it carrying me not along the road to the monastery but by the marshes and the quagmires that people might not see me. They themselves saw that they were behaving as fools but they did not wish to cease from their folly; the devil had darkened their minds, why should one reproach them? It was not them or they would have been otherwise. The time had come spoken of in the Gospel. *"It must needs be that offences must come,"* and another Evangelist saith: *"It must needs be that offences come, but woe unto him by whom offence cometh."* Look thou that readest! Our misery was of necessity, we might not escape it! For this cause God doth let loose offenses and even that the elect may be inflamed and that they may be made white, even that temptations be made manifest in us. Satan has asked and obtained from God our bright shining Russia, that he might purple it with martyr's blood. Well, hast thou imagined this, O devil, and to us it is sweet to suffer for our Sweet Lord.

They kept me at Nikolas's in a cold room for seventeen weeks. There I had a visitation from God; read of it in the letter to the tsar. And the tsar came to the monastery and paid a visit to my prison cell and gave a groan and then left the monastery; it seems from that that he was sorry for me, the will of God lay in that. When they had shorn me there was a very great dis-

---

[44] Ugresha: a village in the vicinity of Moscow.

turbance among them with the tsarina, God rest her soul! She, sweet lady, detected me at that time and asked to have me released from prison, as to which there is much to be said; God forgive them! As to my sufferings I do not hold them answerable, neither now nor hereafter; it sufficeth me to pray for them, be they alive or be they dead. The devil set discord between us but they were ever good toward me. Enough of this.

And poor Prince Ivan Vorotynsky[45] came there without the tsar to pray, and he asked to be admitted to my prison cell. But they would not let the hapless man in. I could only, looking through the window, weep over him. My sweet friend feared God, he was Christ's orphan. Christ will not cast him away. Thus always was Christ on our side, and all the boyars were good to us, only the devil was malicious and what could we have done if Christ had left us? They beat my dear Prince Ivan Khovansky[46] with rods and they burnt Isaiah,[47] and the lady Theodosia Morozova they brought to ruin, and they killed her son and tortured her and her sister Eudoxia, beating them with rods; and they parted her from her children and divorced her from her husband, and him they say, Prince Peter Urusov,[48] they married to another wife. But what was there to do? Let them torture those dear ones, they will go to their heavenly bridegroom. In every wise God will cause to pass this troublesome time and will call to himself the bridegroom to his heavenly palace, he the true Sun, our Light and our Hope. Let us turn again to the one first matter.

After this they took me again to the monastery of Pafnutiev, and there, having shut me up in the dark room, and put fetters on me, they kept me for well-nigh a year. There the cellarer Nikodemus was good to me at first, but he, poor fellow, smoked of tobacco more than that sixty poods the which they seized when they searched the house of the Metropolitan of Gaza,[49] and they seized a lute too and other hidden things of the monastery on the which they played and made merry withal. It is a

[45] Prince Ivan Vorotynsky: member of a wealthy aristocratic family who supported Avvakum and his movement.

[46] Prince Ivan Khovansky: a member of a conservative family that lent its support to Avvakum.

[47] Isaiah: the majordomo of the boyar, Peter Saltykov. He was burned for his faithfulness to the Old Belief.

[48] Prince Peter Urusov: the husband of Princess Eudoxia Urusova, and brother-in-law of Theodosia Morozova.

[49] Metropolitan Paisy of Gaza (Palestine): a Greek bishop who came to Russia in 1662 and became very influential at the court. He was the ideological leader of the opponents of Avvakum and the Old Believers, and was well known for his lack of scrupulousness and his participation in suspicious mercantile operations.

sin to speak of it, forgive me; it was not my business, let him
look to it, to his own Lord he must stand or fall. This is just by
the way. With them there were well-beloved teachers of Holy
Writ. I asked of this Nikodemus, the cellarer, on Easter Day, in
order that I might rest because of the holiday, that he would
bid them open the door that I might sit on the threshold, and
he abused me and refused me savagely as he willed. And after
that he came into my cell he fell suddenly ill, they anointed him
with oil and gave him the last sacraments and then and there
he died. That was on Easter Monday, and before, on the night
of Tuesday, there had come to him a man in the semblance of
myself with a censer, and in shining vestments, and having
censed him and taken him by the hand he moved himself and
was healed. And he came to me with the servitor by night into
the dungeon. And as he came he said, "Blessed is this dwelling
—what a dungeon doth it contain—how blessed is this dungeon
—what sufferings doth it hold! blessed are those bonds. . . ." And
he fell before me and clasped my chain and said, "Forgive me,
for God's sake! forgive, I have sinned before God and before
thee. I have insulted thee, and for this God hath punished me."
And I spake, "How hath he punished thee? Instruct me!" And
he, "Thou thyself," said he, "didst come to me and didst cense
me; thou didst have pity on me and didst raise me up. Why dost
thou deny it?" And the servitor standing there said, "Yes, my
Lord and Father, he took thee by the hand and led thee from
the cell, and bowed down before thee, and thou didst go hence."
And I charged him that he should say nothing to any man concerning this secret thing. And he questioned me how henceforth
he might live for Christ. "Ah," said he, "dost thou charge me to
go forth into the desert?" But I forbade him and would not
suffer him to give up his stewardship, if only in secret he would
preserve the ancient tradition of his fathers. And he bowed low
and went away to his own place and on the morrow at meat he
told it to all the brotherhood. And the people ceaselessly and
with boldness pressed in to see me, asking for a blessing and for
my prayers, and I taught them from Holy Writ and I healed
them by the Word of God. At that time I had some enemies,
but these were reconciled to me. Alas, when shall I quit this
life of vanity? It is written: "Woe to him when all men speak
well of him." In very truth I know now how I may endure to
the end; of good deeds there are none now; but I glorified God.
That he knows and with him it rests.

Thither there came to me in secret Theodore with his children; he that was strangled, God rest his soul! and he ques-

tioned me thus: "How wouldst thou have me walk? Shall I go
in my shift in the old fashion or shall I put clothes upon me?
The heretics," said he, "are seeking me, they would fain bring
me to ruin. I," said he, "was at Riazan under guard at the archbishop's palace at the court, and he, Hilarion,[50] did grievously
torment me: there was scarce a day when he did not beat me
with cords and he kept me bound in iron fetters, compelling me
to partake of the new communion of Antichrist. And I said, 'I
could not,' and I prayed in the night and wept and spake, 'O
Lord, if thou dost not save me, they will cause me to commit
abomination and I shall perish. What can I do?'" And weeping
much he said suddenly, said he, "My father, all my chains fell
rattling from me, and the door was opened of its own motion.
And I," said he, "bowed down to God, and I went forth. I came
to the outer gates and the gates were opened. I went straight
forth along the road to Moscow. It was scarce daylight," said
he, "when they gave chase on horseback; three men passed
quickly by me and they did not see me, and I," said he, "trusting in Christ, went on my way onwards. But," said he, "very
soon they came upon me and they were snarling at me; said
they, 'The son of a whore has escaped, where may one take
him?' And again," said he, "they passed by me and did not see
me. And I," said he, "again betook me to thee and asked
whether I should go again to be tortured or whether I should
don clothes and live in Moscow." And I, a sinner, bade him don
clothes and not to hide himself from the hands of the heretics.
They strangled him in Mezen, hanging him upon the gallows-
tree. Eternal be his memory together with Luke Lavrentievich.
My well-beloved children! They suffered for Christ. Glory to
God for them. And Theodore accomplished an exceeding mighty
deed above measure; by day he played the Fool of Christ, and
all night long he wept and prayed. I know many good men, but
I had never yet beheld such an ascetic. He lived with me in
Moscow about half a year, but I was still ill—two of us lived in
the same chamber with him and at the most he would lie an
hour or two and then he would get up, and then he would go
through a thousand genuflexions and would seat himself on the
ground, or else, standing up, he would weep for some three
hours; meantime I would continue lying and sometimes sleep,
but sometimes I was restless, and when he had his fill of violent
weeping then he would come up to me and say, "How long

---

[50] Hilarion, Bishop of Riazan: a former friend of Avvakum's who
became a staunch supporter of Nikon and the modernists.

wilt thou continue lying? Come to thyself. Thou art a priest.
How are thou not ashamed?" And I could not rise though he
lifted me up saying, "Stand up, my sweet father!" And he
pulled at me somehow or other. And he bade me say prayers
as I sat, and he kept bowing down instead of me. He *was*
my friend in very truth! He was sore vexed by his sufferings.
At one time his intestine issued forth from him three yards in
length, and at another five yards, and his guts were measure-
less—and it was both pitiful and laughable. At Ustiug for five
years he froze barefoot in the frost with only his shift. I saw
him myself. Then he became my spiritual son, and when I came
from Siberia he ran up to my stall in the church in order to
pray: he spoke thus: "When," said he, "one first began to thaw
after the frost and get warm, my father, it was very hard to
bear"; said he, "one stamps with one's feet on the brick floor as
though they were wooden legs, and on the morrow they did not
hurt."

He had with him there in his cell a psalter of those newly
printed. He knew but little as yet of those newfangled things.
But I told him all, word by word, concerning the new books—
and he snatched at the book and hurled it into the stove. And
he cursed all these newfangled ways. And he was exceeding
zealous for the faith of Christ. But why speak many words? As
he began, so he ended. And his great virtue lay not in idle
words, as is with me, miserable man, for whom he died pleading
to God.

A good man, too, was my dear old Afanasy, my spiritual son
—his name in religion was Avraany—whom the apostates baked
to death in Moscow on the fire, and like unto bread of sweet
savor he was offered to the Holy Trinity. Until he took the cowl,
he went about barefoot with only his shift, both winter and
summer, only he was milder than Theodore and fell short of his
asceticism. He dearly loved weeping, and weeping he would go
about and with whomsoever he spoke his words were soft and
sweet as though he wept. Theodore was very zealous and suffered much concerning the work of God. In every way he would
weary himself to bring sin to light and to destroy it. But enough
of them! As they lived, so they died, with Christ Jesus our Lord.

XIV. The Church Council of 1667 and the Final Schism

I will tell you yet more of my wanderings when they brought
me out of the Pafnutiev Monastery in Moscow and placed me
in the guesthouse, and after many wanderings they set me down
in the Miracle Monastery, before the patriarchs of all Christen-

dom, and the Russian Nikonites sat there like so many foxes. I
spoke of many things in Holy Writ with the patriarchs. God did
open my sinful mouth and Christ put them to shame. The last
word they spoke to me was this: "Why," said they, "art thou
stubborn? The folk of Palestine, Serbia, Albania, the Wallachians,
they of Rome and Poland, all these do cross themselves with
three fingers, only thou standest out in thine obstinacy and dost
cross thyself with two fingers; it is not seemly." And I answered
them for Christ thus: "O you teachers of Christendom, Rome
fell away long ago and lies prostrate,[51] and the Poles fell in the
like ruin with her, being to the end the enemies of the Christian.
And among you orthodoxy is of mongrel breed; and no wonder
—if by the violence of the Turkish Mohmut you have become
impotent, and henceforth it is you who should come to us to
learn. By the gift of God among us there is autocracy; till the
time of Nikon, the apostate, in our Russia under our pious
princes and tsars the Orthodox faith was pure and undefiled,
and in the church was no sedition. Nikon, the wolf, together
with the devil, ordained that men should cross themselves with
three fingers, but our first shepherds made the sign of the cross
and blessed men as of old with two fingers, according to the
tradition of our holy fathers, Meletina of Antioch, Theodoret,
the blessed Bishop of Cyrene, Peter of Damascus and Maxim
the Greek;[52] and so too did our own synod of Moscow, at the
time of the Tsar Ivan, bid them, putting their fingers together
in that wise, make the sign of the cross and give the blessing,
as of old the holy fathers Melety and others taught. Then in the
time of Ivan, the tsar,[53] there were the standard-bearers, Gury
and Varsanophy, wonder-workers of Kazan, and Phillip the
Abbot of Solovki among the Russian saints."[54] And the patriarchs
fell to thinking, and our people began to howl like wolf cubs
and to belch out words against their fathers saying, "Our Russian holy men were ignorant, and they understood nothing, they
are unlearned folk," said they. "How can one trust them? they
have no letters." O Holy God! How hast thou suffered so great
reviling of thy holy ones? I, miserable one, was bitter in my

[51] Here Avvakum quotes The *Tale of the White Cowl* (see Selection 31), which became one of the ideological foundation stones of
the Old Believer movement.

[52] Maxim the Greek was a Greek scholar whose writings were often
quoted by the Old Believers.

[53] This refers to Tsar Ivan IV.

[54] Sts. Gury and Varsanophy were Orthodox missionaries among
the Tatars after the taking of Kazan. St. Phillip, Abbot of Solovki,
later Metropolitan of Moscow.

heart, but I could do nothing. I abused them as hard as I could, and I spake as follows: "I am pure, and the dust that cleaves to my feet do I shake off before you, as it is written—'better one if he do the will of God than a thousand of the godless.'" Then louder than before they began to cry out against me: "Away with him, away with him; he hath outraged us all"; and they began to thrust at me and to beat me. And the patriarchs themselves threw themselves on me; about forty of them I think there must have been. Great was the army of Antichrist that gathered itself together. Ivan Uvarov seized me and dragged at me, and I cried aloud, "Stop, do not beat me!" Then they all sprang back and I began to speak to the interpreter, the archimandrite, thus: "Say to the patriarch, the Apostle Paul writes: 'For such an high priest became us, who is holy, harmless, and so forth,' but ye, having sorely mishandled a man, how then can ye straightway perform your office?" Then they sat down. I went away to the door and lay down on my side. "Ye sit down," I said to them, "but I lie down." At that they laughed. "The archpriest," said they, "is a silly fellow, and does not show honor to the patriarchs." And I said, "We are fools for Christ's sake. Ye are great and we without honor; ye are strong and we are weak." After that, again, the authorities came to me and began to talk with me on the question of the Alleluias: Christ put it in my heart and I put them to shame for their Romish heresy, through Dionysios the Areopagite, of whom mention has been made before. And Euphemy, the cellarer of the Miracle Monastery, spake: "Right art thou," said he, "there is no more to be said." And they took me along to chain me.

Then the tsar sent an officer with musketeers and they took me to the Vorobiev hills.[55]

There was the priest Lazar and the monk Epiphany, an elder.[56] They had been shorn and were ill treated as though they were village peasants, my dear ones. A wise man when he did but see them must needs fall aweeping when he looked at them. Well, let them suffer! Why grieve for them! Christ was better than them, and against him, our sweet Lord, evil was wrought by the forebears of the Nikonites, Annas and Caiaphas. No wonder, for they followed after an exemplar—we must grieve for

[55] Vorobiev, or Sparrow Hills—hills in the vicinity of Moscow where Moscow University is now located.

[56] Father Lazar and Monk Epiphany were condemned, together with Avvakum, by the Council of 1667. Both of them, as well as Avvakum and Deacon Fedor (Theodore), were deported to Pustozersk, and burned in 1682.

them, poor things! Woe to the hapless followers of Nikon! They have perished of their own wickedness and their stubbornness of soul!

Then they brought us from the Vorobiev hills to the guest-house of the Andreevsky Monastery to the Savin suburb, and as though we were robbers, followed after us and left us not, nay, even when we relieved nature. It was both pitable and laughable, as though the devil had blinded them.

Then again we were taken to the St. Nickolas Monastery at Ugresha. And there the tsar sent to me the officer Yury Lutokhin, that I might bless him, and we had much converse concerning this and that.

Then again they brought me to Moscow, to the guesthouse of the Nikolsky Monastery, and they demanded of us yet again a statement of the true faith. After that there were sent more than once to me gentlemen of the bedchamber, diverse persons, Artemon and Dementy.[57] And they spake to me in the name of the tsar: "Archpriest!" they said, "I see thy life that it is pure and undefiled and pleasing unto God, I and the tsarina and our children, be entreated of us." The envoy wept as he spake, and for him I weep always. I was exceeding sorry for him. And again he spake: "I beg of thee, hearken to me. Be thou reconciled with the patriarchs." And I said, "Even if God will that I should die, I will not be joined together with apostates. Thou art my tsar, but they, what have they to do with thee? They have lost their tsar and they have come here to gobble you up. I—say I—will not cease to uplift my hands to heaven until God give thee over to me."

The last word I got from the tsar was, "Wherever," said he, "thou shalt be, do not forget us in thy prayers." And I, sinful one, now, as far as I may, pray to God for him.

XV. BANISHMENT TO PUSTOZERSK

After scourging my friends, but not me, they banished me to Pustozersk. And I sent from Pustozersk to the tsar two letters, the first not long but the other longer, what I had said to him, that I wrote also in the letters, and also certain signs of God, which had appeared to me in my prison. Who reads will understand. Also a letter written by the deacon was sent to Moscow by me and the brotherhood as a gift to the True Believers. The

[57] This refers to Artemon Mateev and Dementy Bashmakov, who were important bureaucrats and close councilors of Tsar Alexis. The latter was the head of *Tainy Prikaz* (Department for Secret Affairs) under Alexis.

book was an answer of the Orthodox and was a conviction of the
heresy of the apostates—in it was written the truth concerning
the dogmas of the Church. Further, two letters had been sent by
the priest Lazar to the tsar and the patriarch, and of all this we
got a present. In Mezen of my household they hanged two men,
my spiritual children, the aforenamed Theodore, Christ's Fool,
and Luke Lavrentievich, servants of Christ. Luke was a dweller
in Moscow, the only son of his mother, who was a widow; he
was of the guild of banners, a youth in years about fifteen. He
came to Mezen, to his death, with my children. And when there
was a general slaughter in my house, Pilate asked him, "And
how do you, my man, cross yourself?" And he made answer with
all temperance: "I do believe and do cross myself so, placing my
fingers as doth my spiritual father, the archpriest Avvakum."
And Pilate ordered them to put him in the dungeon, and there
to put a noose round his neck, and he hanged him on a railing.
And so he passed from earth to heaven. Greater than that what
could they do for him? And if he were but a youth, he acted
like an old man. He went his way to the Lord. Well were it even
for an old man did he win through like that.

At this time the order was given to hang my two sons after
the flesh, Ivan and Prokopy, but they, miserable ones, were
weaklings and never thought them to lay hold on the crowns of
victory. Being soon afraid of death they made submission, and
so they buried them alive in the earth with their mother for
third. There was a death without death for you. Repent as ye
sit there, while the devil concocts something else! That death
be terrible is not wonderful! Time was when even Peter, dear
friend of Christ, made denial and went out and wept bitterly,
and for his tears he was forgiven, and for my children it is not
wonderful that, because of my sins, weakness was permitted
them. Well and good! So be it! Christ is mighty to save us all
and to have mercy upon us.

At this time the deputy, Ivan Elagin, was with us in Pustozersk,
having come from Mezen, and he received from us a statement,
and this was it: "Year and month," and again: "We keep the
tradition of the holy Fathers unaltered, and we proclaim as
accursed Paisy the Patriarch of Palestine with his fellows as an
assembly of heretics," and besides there were said there a few
words about Nikon, the fabricator of this heresy. For this they
brought us to the scaffold, and when they had read the sentence
they took me away without scourging me to the dungeon. They
read me the edict: "Let Avvakum be put into an underground

prison within the palisade and let there be given to him bread and water." But I spat on this and I desired to die, refraining from food, and I ate nothing for about eight days or more. But then my brethren bade me eat.

At the same time they took the priest Lazar, and cut out his whole tongue from his throat, but little blood flowed and soon stopped. And he spoke again without his tongue. Moreover, having placed his right hand upon the scaffold, they cut it off at the wrist, and the hand that had been cut off, lying upon the ground, of its own motion placed its fingers after the ancient use, and lying thus long time before the people, the poor thing made confession, and even unto death did not betray the sign of salvation. Even I am amazed at that; the lifeless thing convicts the living. And on the third day I felt in his mouth with my hand; it was all smooth, and there was no tongue, but it did not hurt. God had granted that with good hap it had healed up. In Moscow they had cut out his tongue and then there was some of it left, but now it was all cut away. But he spoke clearly for the space of two years as though he had a tongue. And when he had completed two years there was another wonder—in the space of three days his tongue grew again to its full size, but that it was a little stumpy, and again he spake, instantly praising God and railing at the apostates.

At this time they seized a hermit priest, an anchorite of strict rule, Epiphany, an elder, and cut out the whole of his tongue. And they cut off four fingers of his hand. And at first he spoke thickly, and at this time he prayed to the Virgin, the Mother of God, and there appeared to him in the air two tongues, that of Moscow and the present one. Now he, taking up one, put it in his mouth, and from that moment began to speak purely and clearly, and the whole tongue fitted itself into his mouth. Great are the works and unspeakable are the judgments of the Lord! He sendeth forth his judgments and again he healeth and hath mercy. But what availeth many words? God is an old hand at miracles. Out of nothing he brings life, and shall he not at the Last Day raise up all flesh in the twinkling of an eye; and who may discern concerning this thing? God is after this wise: he createth what is new and he reneweth that which is old. In all things glory be to him!

At this time they seized the deacon Theodore. They cut out the whole of his tongue, but left a little bit in his mouth, having cut it slantways across his throat. It healed just as it was at the time, but later on it grew again as it was before. It stuck out a little way from the lips, but stump-like. And they cut off his hand across the palm. By the gift of God it all healed, and he spake clearly and cleanly as before.

Then they covered us up with earth. There was a framework in the earth, and above the earth a second framework, and then again round the whole of it was a fence with four locks, and they set a watch to guard all the doors. Now we, both here and everywhere in dungeons, sing songs before the Lord Christ, the Son of God, such as Solomon sang when he beheld his mother Bathsheba: *"Thou art good, my fair one, thou art good, my beloved. Thine eyes burn like a flame of fire, thy teeth are as white as milk; the shining of thy face is brighter than the sun's rays, and altogether thou shinest like unto the day in its strength."*

Then Pilate journeyed from us, and having settled his business at Mezen he returned to Moscow. And others of us were burned and baked. They burned Isaiah to death and afterwards burned Avraamy and other defenders of the Church—the most of them did he undo. God will count the number of them. A wonder is it that they would not come to their right mind. They think to establish the faith by fire or the knout and gallows-tree! Which of the Apostles taught them that? I know not. My Christ did not teach his Apostles that fire and knout and gallows-tree should lead to the faith. But it was said to the Apostle by the Lord thus: *"Go ye into all the world and preach the Gospel to every creature; he that believeth and is baptized, the same shall be saved."* See now, my reader, Christ calls us to come if we will, but he does not bid the Apostles to burn with fire and to hang on the gallows-tree them that are disobedient. The Tatar god Mahmud[58] in his books wrote thus: "We bid ye lay low with the sword the heads of them that obey not our law and tradition." But Christ never gave such like command to his disciples, and these teachers, it is plain, are themselves Antichrists; they, who, leading men to the faith, destroy them and give them over to death—they bring forth works like unto their faith. It is written in the gospels: *"A good tree cannot bring forth evil fruit, neither a bad tree good fruit. Every tree is known by its fruit."* But why speak many words? "No Cross, no Crown." He that will be crowned, for *that* he had not need to go to Persia. We have our Babylon at home. Come, True Believer! Name thou the name of Christ, standing in the midst of Moscow, cross thyself with the sign of the Saviour our Christ, with two fingers as we have received from the holy Fathers. Lo! here at home

[58] This refers to Muhammad, the Prophet of Islam.

for thee is thy Kingdom of Heaven. Glory to God! Suffer tortures for the placing of thy fingers, reason not much, but I with thee am ready to die for this and for Christ. If I am a foolish man and one without learning, yet this I know, that all the traditions of the Church, handed down to us by the holy Fathers, are holy and incorrupt. I keep them even unto death, as I received them. I will not falsify the eternal boundaries—that which was laid down before our days, let it so remain to all eternity, but, O thou heretic, do not tamper with things, touch not the sacrifice of Christ, lay not thine hand on the cross, nay, stir not even the corporals! And they have planned with the devil to misprint books and falsify everything, and to alter the sign of the cross in the church, and on the wafers. Within the altar they have banished the priestly prayers, they have altered the "Lord have mercy upon us," and in baptism they bid to invoke the Evil One. I would fain spit in his eyes and in theirs! And round about the font the Evil One leads them against the course of the sun, and in like fashion they consecrate the church, and when they solemnize marriage they lead the married counterclockwise; plainly they do this in hostility. And in baptism they do not abjure the Evil One. How should they? They are his children and they do not desire to abjure their father. But why multiply words? Woe is me for the True Believer! Every spirit that is exalted is brought low. As Nikon, the hound of hell, spake, so did he do. Print the books, Arsen,[59] anyhow, only not after the ancient fashion. And so he did! More than that, one cannot alter things. It behooves every man to endure for this, even unto death. May these damnable ones be accursed, with all their devilish imaginations: and to them whom they made to suffer in their souls, may theirs be threefold eternal remembrance.

For this I ask forgiveness of every True Believer. Some things that I have said were perhaps best unsaid—but I may read through the Acts of the Apostle and the epistles of Paul. The Apostles proclaimed concerning themselves that God was working through them. *"Not unto us but to our God be the praise."* And I am of no account. So spake I again and again. I am a

[59] Arsen, a learned Greek, came to Moscow in 1649, and was invited to become a professor there. However, it was soon discovered that he had managed to become a Catholic three times, once a Moslem, and then, finally, Orthodox. For these successful conversions he was deported to Solovki Monastery. In 1652 Nikon invited him to revise the Russian missal, and this participation by Arsen in the re-editing of the holy books was largely responsible for the disrepute into which Nikon's reforms fell.

man that is a sinner. Wanton am I and a ravisher, a thief and a
robber, the friend of publicans and sinners, and to every man
am I a hypocrite accursed; forgive me and pray for me; to you
who read me and who hearken am I bound more than to any.
I know not how to live and what I am doing that I tell to men.
What matter that they talk vanity of me, in the days of judgment they shall all know of my deeds, whether they be good or
evil. But if I be unlearned in speech, yet am I not in thought;
I am untaught in rhetoric and in dialectic and in philosophy, but
the mind of Christ is our guide within us, as the Apostle saith,
though I be rude in speech yet not in knowledge.

XVI. Concluding Remarks to the Monk Epiphany

And now, my Elder, thou hast heard full much of my bab-
bling, and I bid thee, in the name of the Lord, write thou also
for thy servant in Christ, how the Mother of God kneaded this
devil in her hands and gave him over to thee, and how the ants
ate thee in thy secret parts, and how something devilish set fire
to the Word and how the cell was burnt to ashes, but all within
it were safe and sound. And how thou didst cry aloud to heaven:
and other things thou dost remember to the glory of Christ and
the Mother of God. Hearken to what I say; if thou dost not
write to me I shall be sorely angered! Thou lovest to hear of
me; of what thou art ashamed, tell me if even a little. The
Apostles, Paul and Barnabas, were wont to set forth, in the assembly at Jerusalem, before all, what sights and wonders God
had wrought by them among the Gentiles (see Acts 34 and
42), and the name of the Lord Jesus was magnified. And many
who believed came to them, making confession and telling their
deeds. And much of this is written by the Apostles and in the
Acts. Fear not to tell me, only keep thy conscience straitly; seek
not thine own glory, but speak thou for Christ and the Mother
of God. Let thy servant in Christ read and rejoice. When we
die, then shall this be read and we be remembered before God,
and we will pray to God for them who read and who hearken.
They shall be our people. They shall be there with Christ, and
we shall be theirs for ever and ever. Amen.

SECULAR TALES

40. Shemiaka's Judgment

Shemiaka's Judgment is one of the oldest Russian satirical stories with a purely fictitious plot. Indeed, the name "Shemiaka" can be traced back to the middle of the fifteenth century when Dmitry Shemiaka, prince of the northern city of Galych (not to be confused with Galich, capital of the southwestern province of Galicia), waged his endless feud against his cousin, Vasily III, Great Prince of Muscovy. The proper name "Shemiaka," however, subsequently became quite popular in Muscovite Russia, and there is no definite indication that the hero of the tale can be actually identified with Prince Dmitry Shemiaka or any other real historical figure.

The language and structure of the tale, its elements of popular satire and folk riddles, bring *Shemiaka's Judgment* somewhat closer to the oral folk tales (*skazki*) than to any literary narrative. Many Russian, Bielorussian, and Ukrainian tales and fairy tales about an unjust judge commonly employ the same motifs of crimes and court decisions that can be found in this tale. *Shemiaka's Judgment* satirizes Russian court mores of the sixteenth and seventeenth centuries, when judges often thought that their decisions should be a source of personal income. In those centuries this tale became extremely popular, and there have been preserved innumerable prose and verse versions of it.

The present translation follows the text of a seventeenth-century manuscript published by M. Skripil in *Russkaia povest XVII veka*, Moscow, 1954, pages 140–142.

◆ ◆ ◆

In a village of Russia there lived two peasant brothers. One was rich and the other poor. The rich one for many years lent money to his poor brother, but could not end his destitution.

Once the poor brother came to the rich one and asked him to lend him his horse because he hadn't one for bringing in wood. The rich brother did not want to give him the horse, and said, "On many occasions I have lent you money, but I cannot improve your condition." But he did lend him the horse, and then the poor brother asked to borrow the harness. The rich brother

371

felt offended, and began to abuse his brother, saying: "You! You don't even have your own harness," and he didn't give him the harness. The poor man left the house of the rich brother, took his own sledge, and attached it to the horse's tail. He then went to the forest and later returned to his house, but he forgot to take out the gate spike. The sledge got caught on the spike and could not move. He flayed the horse with the knout, and the horse pulled with all its might, finally tearing away its own tail. When the poor brother brought back the horse and the rich brother saw that it no longer had a tail, he began to abuse his poor brother for having ruined his horse. And he refused to take the horse back, but went to the city to lodge a complaint with the judge, Shemiaka.

And the poor brother, seeing that his brother went to court, followed him, because he knew that if he did not come of his own volition, he would be obliged to pay an additional fee to the court messenger.

And both of them stopped for the night in some township not far from the city. The rich brother went to pass the night with the parson of the township because the parson was an acquaintance of his. The poor man also came to the parson's, and, arriving there, went to sleep in an upper bunk. The rich brother began to tell the parson about the misfortune concerning his horse, and explained why he was going to the city. And then the parson began to sup with the rich brother. The poor one, however, was not invited. As the poor hungry brother looked from the upper bunk to see what the parson and his brother were eating, he fell from the upper bunk, accidentally crashing onto the cradle of the parson's infant son, killing him.

And then the parson went with the rich brother to the city to sue the poor brother for the death of his infant son. As they came to the city wherein lived the judge, the poor one was following them. They were walking over a bridge to the city. At that time one of the inhabitants of the city was transporting his father in a cart to a steambath under the bridge in order to wash him. The poor brother, who knew that he must expect the worst from his rich brother and from the parson, decided to commit suicide. He jumped from the bridge into the moat in order to kill himself; but the moat was dry, and in jumping he accidentally fell on the old man and killed him. He was seized and brought before the judge.

The poor man began to think how to avoid the misfortune of a penalty and how to bribe the judge. But since he couldn't find anything in his pocket, he took a stone and wrapped it in a kerchief and put it in his hat and presented himself to the judge. And now the rich brother lodged his complaint against him, requiring a compensation for his horse, and began to explain the case to the judge. Shemiaka listened to the complaints, and told the poor man, "Answer." The poor brother didn't know what to say. He took out of his hat the wrapped stone and showing it to the judge, bowed deeply. The judge, thinking the poor man promised him a bribe, told his rich brother: "Since he tore away the tail of your horse, don't accept the horse from your brother as long as the tail will not grow back. But as soon as the tail grows back, at that time take from him your horse."

And then began the second trial. The parson began to sue the poor brother for the death of his infant son, because the poor man had crushed his son. The poor brother once more took from the hat the same bundle and showed it to the judge. The judge saw it, and thought that in the second trial the poor man promised another bundle of gold. And he told the parson: "Since he crushed your son, give him your wife until a child is born from him. And at that time take back from him your wife and the child."

And then began the third trial, for the crushing of the son's old father by jumping from the bridge. The poor one, taking the wrapped stone from his hat, showed it for the third time to the judge. The judge, hoping that the poor man was promising him a third bundle of gold for this, the third trial, told the son of the old man: "Go onto the bridge, while the man who killed your father remains under the bridge. And you must jump down from the bridge and kill him in the same way in which he killed your father."

When, after the trial, the plaintiffs left the court with the defendant, the rich brother began to claim his horse from the poor brother. But the latter told him: "According to the judge's decision, as he told you, I will return the horse to you when its tail grows back." So the rich one gave him five rubles in order to get back the horse, even though it had no tail. The poor brother accepted the five rubles, and returned the horse to him.

Then the poor one, according to the decision of the judge, claimed from the parson his wife in order to have a child with her, and having had the child, to return the wife with the child to the parson. But the parson began to beg him not to take his wife. For this concession the poor man took ten rubles from the parson.

Then the poor one told the third plaintiff: "According to the judge's decision, I will stand under the bridge while you go on the bridge and jump on me in the same manner in which I jumped on your father."

And the plaintiff thought, if I jump on him, probably I will not crush him but myself," and he began to plead with the poor man, and gave him some money in order not to be obliged to jump on him. In this way the poor man got money from all three of them.

The judge sent a servant to the defendant, ordering him to get from the latter the three bundles that had been shown him. The servant told him: "Give me that which you showed to the judge from your hat. He has ordered me to take it from you."

And the latter, taking the wrapped stone from under his hat, showed it to the servant. "Well, but that is a stone," said the servant.

The defendant said: "Yes, it is for the judge. I would have killed him if he hadn't tried me to my advantage."

The servant came back and told everything to the judge. And the judge, after listening to the servant, said: "I thank and praise God that I tried him to his advantage. If I had not done so, he would have killed me."

And the poor man returned home, being overjoyed and praising God.

41. *The Tale of Savva Grudtsyn*

THE *Tale of Savva Grudtsyn* is a work characteristic of a transitional period when the new currents that were appearing in Russian literature modified previously well-established patterns. The story of Savva's life, which describes his adventures, his illicit affair with the wife of his father's close friend, and his military deeds during his service in regiments commanded by foreign soldiers according to Western tactics, reflects the new way of life and the new mentality of Muscovite Russia. Still, some elements of the earlier Russian hagiographic tradition persist, especially at the conclusion of the tale.

The basic theme of this work is the struggle between good and evil, illustrated by the fall of a man and his eventual redemption through repentance. Thus the *Tale of Savva Grudtsyn* has several thematic parallels with the poetic tale of *Misery-Luckless-Plight*. The style of *Savva Grudtsyn* is equally transitional, combining the solemn, archaic language and syntax with new, colloquial expressions and idioms.

It is worth noting that this tale begins in the Time of Troubles, when the Poles' intervention in Russia during the period 1605 to 1613 undermined the foundations of the old order in Russia. As in other Russian tales of the seventeenth century, most of the characters belong to well-known aristocratic and merchant families. The Grudtsyn-Usovs and the Vtorys were important merchants in northern Russia; the boyars Streshnev and Shein are well known from Russian history; and, finally, the tsar himself shows interest in Savva and actually influences the hero's destiny. The plot is certainly fictional and complex, but it does give vivid and realistic details of the life of a patriarchal Russian family of that time, of the life of the military, and of the mores of Muscovite society. The author was decidedly not a member of the literati of that period, for, despite the use of both archaic and colloquial expressions, his art is rather limited, and he often repeats word for word certain descriptions, speeches, and conceptions.

The translation follows an early eighteenth-century manuscript published, with some corrections, by M. Skripil in *Russkaia povest XVII veka*, Moscow, 1954, pages 82–102.

◆ ◆ ◆

This is a most truthful and true tale which has come to pass in these days and which reveals how God, who loves man, revealed his love to the Christian people. I wish to tell you, brethren, this most wonderful tale which is filled with awe and horror, which deserves inexplicable astonishment, and which explains the patience of our man-loving God who, awaiting our conversion, brings us to salvation through the most inexplicable of deeds.

On a day in 1606 (7114) God allowed, because of the multiplication of our sins, the God-offending apostate, heretic, and unfrocked monk Grishka Otrepiev[1] to attack the Muscovite state and to win the throne of the Russian land in a most robberlike, untsarlike manner. Also, at that time Russia was invaded by the

[1] Grishka, or Gregory, Otrepiev was a pretender to the Russian throne who claimed to be Prince Dmitry, the son of Ivan IV. See introduction to Selection 35. At that time Poland and Lithuania were united into one dominion, which explains the author's calling the foreign troops Polish in one case, Lithuanian in another.

increasing bands of faithless Lithuanians and Poles who performed all kinds of base deeds and who caused great misfortune
to the Russian people in Moscow and in other cities. Because
of these Lithuanian and Polish attacks, many people abandoned
their homes and fled from city to city.

In the year 1606 (7114), in the city of Great Ustiug,[2] there
lived a citizen named Foma, by surname, Grudtsyn-Usov, whose
descendants still reside in that city. Seeing much anarchy and
base deeds of the lawless Poles in Russia, this Foma decided to
forsake the city of Great Ustiug, to live no longer in his home,
but to migrate with his wife to the city of Kazan on the lower
Volga, for in this city on the lower Volga there were no base
Lithuanians or Poles.

And Foma and his wife lived in the city of Kazan until the
beginning of the reign of the God-fearing sovereign, Grand
Duke, and Tsar of All Russia, Michael Fedorovich. Foma had
an only son, Savva, who was twelve years old. It was Foma's
custom to make frequent business trips, traveling up and down
the Volga, sometimes going to Solikamsk,[3] sometimes to the city
of Astrakhan, and sometimes beyond the Caspian Sea to the
land of Persia. He also taught his son, Savva, so that he might
learn to attend to his business promptly and diligently, since
after Foma's death his only son would inherit his estate.

After some time, Foma decided to sail to Persia and began
the loading of his goods into the usual ships. He also loaded
other boats with customary goods and ordered his son to sail to
Solikamsk, there to learn the merchant's trade with all diligence.
Having bidden farewell to his wife and son, Foma set out on
his journey. Some days later, his son, Savva, sailed to Solikamsk
in the ships his father had ordered loaded. Having reached the
city of Orel, which is in the Usolsk region, he docked and, following his father's orders, went to live at the inn of a certain
respectable man. The innkeeper and his wife, remembering the
loving kindness of Savva's father, for he had done them many
favors, cared with diligence for the son, rendering him many
services and even treating him as their son.

In this city of Orel there lived a citizen, Bazhen Vtory by

[2] The city of Great Ustiug is located in northern Russia, between
Moscow and the White Sea, and in the seventeenth century was an
important merchant city.
[3] Solikamsk and Orel are located in the same region as Great
Ustiug. The city of Atraskhan is located at the delta of the Volga,
and was the main trading center for commerce with Persia and other
countries of the Near East.

name, who was both famous and well known. He was already old in years and was known in many cities for his virtuous way of life and for his wealth. He had befriended and was well acquainted with Savva's father. Having learned that the son of Foma Grudtsyn had come to this city from Kazan, he thought to himself: Since his father and I share much love and friendship, why should I neglect the son by not inviting him into my home, to live with me and to eat at my table?

Having come to this conclusion, when Bazhen saw Savva walking in the street he invited him to his house, saying: "My dear friend, Savva, do you know that your father and I share much love and friendship? Why did you neglect me by not coming to abide in my home? This time, do not disobey me, but come and live in my house and break bread with me. And, for the love of your father, I shall receive you even as if you were my own son."

Hearing these words from Bazhen, Savva was very happy to be received into the house of such a famous man, and he bowed low before him, and made haste to move from the inn to Bazhen's house. And there he lived, enjoying all the comforts, and rejoicing.

This old man, Bazhen, had a young wife who had never been married before, but who was Bazhen's third wife. The Devil, that enemy who hates all things not vile in the human kind, having seen this man's virtuous way of life, decided to bring strife into his house by inducing Bazhen's wife to have sinful relations with the young man. Thus the wife began to seduce him into sin with tempting words. Human nature knows how to lead the mind of a young man into iniquity. And thus Savva, influenced by the flattery of this woman, or, better to say, by the Devil's envy, was led to the sin of adultery. They sinned endlessly, but still they were unable to satiate their desires. And Savva remained for a long time in such a sinful relation with her. They sinned even on Sundays and on holy days and, having forgotten all fear of God, they wallowed continuously, like swine, in the filth that is sin. And for a long time they remained in such insatiable lust, like beasts.

When the holy day honoring the Ascension of our Lord Jesus Christ neared, Bazhen Vtory took the young man and went to vespers in the holy church, this being on the eve of that holy day. Then they went home again and, after the usual supping, went each to his own bed, giving thanks to God. As soon as the God-loving man, Bazhen Vtory, had fallen soundly asleep, his wife, incited by the devil, got up secretly from her couch, went to the young man's bed, woke him, and compelled him to wicked adultery. Though young, Savva was seized by the fear of God, as if pierced by an arrow. And, fearing God's judgment, he began to ponder, asking himself, How could I do such a wicked deed and on such a great holy day?

And having thought thusly, he wished to be rid of her and, taking an oath, said to her, "I do not want to lose my soul forever by profaning my body on such a great holiday."

But she, in the grip of an insatiable carnal desire, tried to force him by her caresses and threats to submit to her. But try as she would, she could not force him to yield to her desire. And some kind of divine power helped him. When this evil woman saw that she could not bring the youth to do her bidding, she at once became seized by a wicked rage. Hissing like a fierce serpent, she went away from his bed. Then she began to ponder how she might destroy him through a magic potion. And she decided to fulfill her evil intention of destroying him without delay.

And she did as she had decided. When the bells announced matins, God-loving Bazhen quickly got up from his bed, woke the young man, Savva, and went with him to the morning service to glorify God. They listened to the liturgy with attention and with the fear of God, and then they returned home. When the hour of the sacred liturgy arrived, they returned to the holy church with joy so that they might hear the glorification of God. In the meantime, this accursed woman carefully prepared a magic philter for the youth, for she, like a serpent, wanted to spit poison at him.

When the holy liturgy was ended, Bazhen and Savva left the church, intending to go home. However, the voevoda of the city invited Bazhen to take dinner with him. And he asked, concerning the youth, "Whose son is this and where is he from?"

Bazhen answered that he was Foma Grudtsyn's son from Kazan. Thereafter, the voevoda invited the young man to his home, for he had known Savva's father well. So they went to the voevoda's house and, as was the custom, ate together with the others, and afterward returned home.

Arriving home, Bazhen ordered that wine be brought out so that they might drink in his home to honor the holy day. He was not in the least aware of his wife's evil scheme. When the wine had been brought in, she poured it into a cup and offered it to her husband. He drank it and gave thanks to the Lord. Then she poured more and drank it herself. Then she poured out the poisoned philter she had prepared, and offered it to Savva. He drank this base potion without any apprehension or hesitation, for he expected no evil deed from her, thinking that she harbored no ill will toward him. But as soon as he had drunk it, a fire began to burn in his heart. And he thought to himself: I have drunk many drinks in my father's house, but never such a wine as this one.

When he had finished the drink, he began to grieve in his heart and to long for a woman. The wife, like a fierce lioness, looked furiously at Savva and showed him not the least friendliness. But she began rather to slander the young man to her husband, saying base words and ordering her husband to drive the youth from their house. God-fearing Bazhen, although he took pity on the young man, was finally ensnared by his wife's cajolery and ordered the youth out of his home, accusing him of various failings. And the youth went away from the house with great sorrow and grief in his heart, lamenting and grieving the evil deeds of that woman.

He went back to the house of the innkeeper where he had previously lived, and the innkeeper asked him by what fault he had left Bazhen's house. And Savva answered, "I did not wish to live longer with those people, for I did not have enough to eat."

But he continued to grieve for and long after this woman. And, because of his grief, his handsome face began to wane and his flesh to waste away. Seeing the youth so grieving and lamenting, the innkeeper could not ascertain what had happened.

Now in the same city there was a magician who, through sorcery and charms, could tell why and to whom sorrow had come. He was also able to divine who would live and who would die. The innkeeper and his wife, who were sensible and cared greatly for the young man, summoned this sorcerer secretly, for they wished to learn why the youth grieved so. The sorcerer came and, consulting his book of magic, told them the truth: "The youth has no sorrow for himself, but longs only for the wife of Bazhen Vtory, since he has fallen into sinful adultery with her. But he became ashamed of her, and since that time he has grieved, longing for her."

The innkeeper and his wife, hearing this from the sorcerer, did not believe him, because they knew Bazhen Vtory to be a pious and God-fearing man who could not be involved in such an affair. Savva, however, continued to lament incessantly and to long for that accursed woman. And from day to day he wasted away, as if he were afflicted by some overwhelming bereavement.

Once, Savva left the city and went into the fields, wishing to take a walk to alleviate his longings and grief. He went walking alone, seeing no one before him nor no one behind him, and thinking of nothing in particular, but only grieving and lamenting his separation from that woman. Then there came into his mind an evil thought, and he said to himself: "If someone, man or devil, would do something so that I might take sexual pleasure with this woman, then would I serve even the Devil."

And coming to such an idea, as if he had lost his mind, he continued walking through the field, but a short distance behind him he heard a voice that called him by name. He turned around and saw a youth who was dressed in fine garments and was running swiftly toward him, entreating him with his hand to wait. And the youth came up to Savva. It must be said that this was not a youth, but the Enemy and the Devil who searches for ways to destroy human souls.

The youth came up to Savva and, after they had bowed to each other, said: "Brother Savva. Why did you run from me? I have awaited you a long time, hoping that you would come to me and would have brotherly love for me. I have known you for a long time, and I know that you are of the Grudtsyn-Usov family of the city of Kazan. And if you wish to know me, I may say that I am also from the city of Great Ustiug. And since, by birth, I can be considered your brother, you should become my brother and friend from this time on. And never leave me, so that I can be of help to you in all things."

Savva, hearing such words from his false brother, that is to say, from the Devil, became very happy to find a relative in such a distant and unknown land. And they kissed each other with love and went together through the wilderness. And the Devil said to Savva: "Brother Savva, wherefore do you grieve? Why do you destroy your youthful beauty?"

Savva avoided the questions, however, telling him that he was afflicted by a malady.

The Devil cunningly smiled and said: "Why do you conceal the truth from me? I know your ailment, but what would you give me if I were to cure you of it?"

And Savva answered: "If you actually know the affliction I bear in my heart, then I shall believe that you can help me."

The Devil replied: "In your heart you long for the wife of Bazhen Vtory, since you are deprived of her love. What would you give me if I once more united you with her and she once more loved you?"

Savva answered: "In such a case, I shall give you all the merchandise and wealth of my father and all my profits! Only cause me to be once more with this women."

The Devil laughed and retorted: "Why do you tempt me? I know that your father actually is very rich. But you are not aware that my father is seven times richer than yours. What are your goods to me? Only give me a short note, and I shall fulfill your desire."

The youth was very happy, thinking to himself: The wealth of my father will remain intact, and I shall give him the letter and write whatever he wants.

The youth did not know what misfortune he was bringing upon himself. Actually, he did not read or write well. Oh, the madness of youth! Thus he was ensnared by a woman's treachery and, for her sake, he was going to the Devil.

Hardly had the Devil spoken these words about the letter, when the youth happily promised to give him the letter. The false brother, that is to say, the Devil, quickly took paper and ink from his pocket, gave them to the youth, and ordered him to write the letter. Savva still did not fully know what he was writing, but began to write senselessly. And by this letter Savva renounced Christ, the True God, and gave himself in the service of the Devil. Having written the letter in which he rejected God, he gave it to the Devil, his false brother.

Thus, they both arrived in Orel. Then Savva asked the Devil, "Tell me, my brother, where you live, so that I may know your house."

The Devil laughed, and said: "I have no particular house anywhere, but wherever it is convenient, there do I spend the night. However, if you wish to see me often, look always for me in the Horse Market, since I sometimes live there when buying horses. Now, go to the shop of Bazhen, and I know that you will be gladly invited to live in this house."

Savva, following the words of his brother, the Devil, happily ran to Bazhen's shop. Bazhen, upon seeing Savva, eagerly invited him into his house, say to him: "Master Savva! What a wrong I have done you? Why did you leave my house? I pray you, come back now and live in my house. I am truly happy, for the love of your father, to have you here as if you were my own son."

Hearing such words from Bazhen, Savva was overcome with joy, and quickly entered Bazhen's house. And when the youth had entered, the wife, being incited by the Devil, met him with

joy and greeted him, giving him a welcoming kiss. The youth
was ensnared in the woman's flattery, that is to say, by the
Devil, and was once more drawn into the sinful net with that
accursed woman. From that time on, he remembered neither
the holy days nor Sundays. He lost his fear of God, and wallowed with her constantly in the sin of lechery, as if he were a
swine.

After quite a time had passed, there came a rumor to Savva's
mother in the city of Kazan to the effect that her son was living
an unrighteous and sinful life and that the father's wealth that
was with him had all been squandered in lechery and drunkenness. Hearing such things about her son, the mother began to
grieve profoundly, and wrote him a letter in which she urged
him to return to his father's house in the city of Kazan. When
the letter arrived, he read it, and laughed, paying it no heed.
The mother sent him a second and a third letter in which she
besought and entreated him to return home immediately from
Orel to the city of Kazan. Savva, however, did not obey his
mother's commands and entreaties, but, paying no heed to anything, continued only to persevere in his sinful passions.

Some time later, the Devil took Savva and went with him
beyond the city of Orel into the fields of the countryside. As
soon as they had left the city, the Devil said to Savva: "Do you
know who I am? You were fully convinced that I am of the
Grudtsyn family, but it isn't so. Now, out of love, I shall reveal
the truth to you. Don't be afraid, and be not ashamed to call me
your brother, for verily I do love you as a brother. But if you
wish to know who I am, I am the son of a king. Let us go
farther, and I shall show you my glory and the wealth of my
father!"

Having said these words, he lead Savva to a certain hill and
showed him a fine city a short distance away. Its walls and roofs
were of pure gold, and gleamed.

And the Devil said to Savva: "This city is the work of my
father. Let us go and bow down before my father. And now,
take the letter you gave to me and present it to my father, and
you will be given a great honor by him."

And having said these words, the Devil returned the letter in
which Savva had renounced God.

Oh, the madness of youth! Didn't he know that there was no
kingdom near the Muscovite state that was not under the sway
of the tsar? If only he had made the sign of the cross, then all
these devilish temptations would have vanished like a shadow.

When they approached this chimerical city and came up to

the city gates, they were met there by youths with dark faces and in vestments and belts decorated with gold. These youths bowed to them, rendering honor to the king's son, who was actually the Devil, and also greeting Savva. When they entered the courtyard of the Kings' palace, they were met there by more youths, who wore still more brilliant raiment than the first ones they had met. And these youths also bowed to them. Then they entered the King's palace and were met by still more youths, who surpassed each other in their proud dignities and their magnificent vestments. And they also rendered honors to the King's son and to Savva.

Entering the palace, the Devil said: "Brother Savva, wait here for me awhile. I shall go and announce you to my father, and I shall later take you to him. When you appear before him, think of nothing and have no fears; only give him the letter." Having said this, he passed into the inner chambers, leaving Savva alone. In a short while he returned, came to Savva, took him by the hand, and let him before the Prince of Darkness. The Prince of Darkness was sitting on a high throne embellished with gold and jewels. He was distinguished by his proud glory and his magnificent raiment. Round his throne, Savva noticed a large number of winged youth, the faces of some being blue, while the faces of others were red, and still others had faces as black as pitch. Savva appeared before the King, fell to the floor, and genuflected before him.

The King asked him: "From whence do you come? What is your plight?"

The senseless youth presented him with his God-rejecting letter, and said, "I have come, great King, to serve you."

That ancient serpent, Satan, accepted the letter, read it, turned toward his dark-faced warriors, and said, "Although I accept this youth, I know not whether he will remain faithful to me." Then he summoned his son, Savva's false brother, saying to him, "Go to another room, and have dinner with your brother."

Both bowed to the King, went to another room, and began to dine. They were served unimaginably aromatic dishes, and the same kind of drink. Savva marveled, and said that he had never partaken of similar dishes or of similar drinks in his own father's house.

After the meal, the Devil took Savva, and together they left first the King's courtyard and then the city. And Savva asked his brother, the Devil, "Tell me, brother, who were those winged youths who surrounded your father's throne?"

The Devil smiled and answered: "Aren't you aware that many nations serve my father—the Indians, the Persians, and many, many others. Don't wonder about this and don't hesitate to call me your brother. From now on I will be your younger brother. However, when I tell you to do something, you must obey me. And I shall render you all kinds of good deeds."

Savva promised to be obedient, and the Devil became so confident that, when they had arrived back in the city of Orel, he left Savva alone and went away. Savva still went to the house of Bazhen Vtory and continued to indulge in his sinful lechery.

In the meantime, Savva's father, Foma Grudtsyn, returned to Kazan from Persia, having been very successful in his business. As usual and as is due, he gave a kiss to his wife and then inquired about their son, asking whether he were still alive. And she answered him, saying: "I have heard from many people about him. After you left for Persia, he went to Solikamsk, and from there to the city of Orel. And since then, he sins and, as people say, has squandered all our wealth and has dissipated his health in drunkenness and in lechery. And on many occassions I have written him asking that he return home from there. But not once has he answered my letters, and so I don't know whether he is alive or not."

Hearing this from his wife, Foma was in a quandry. Then he sat down and penned a letter to Savva, beseeching him to return without delay to the city of Kazan. "I would like, my child," he wrote, "once again to see your handsome face, for I haven't seen you in a long time."

Savva, having received and read the letter, paid it no heed and did not even think of returning to his father. He wished only to indulge in his insatiable lust. Foma, seeing that his letter had accomplished nothing, ordered boats and goods prepared for sailing, and began his travels to Solikamsk, telling his wife, "I shall myself look for our son, and bring him back to our home."

As soon as the Devil learned that Savva's father was traveling to Solikamsk, he decided to take Savva to Kazan. So he told Savva: "Brother Savva, how long are we going to remain in this small town? Let us visit other cities and have a good time there. Then we can return here."

Savva did not contradict him, but said: "You are right, brother. Let us go. But we should wait for a short while, since I want to obtain some money for my merchandise."

But the Devil prevented him from doing so, and said: "Haven't you looked upon my father's glory? Aren't you aware that he has estates everywhere? Wherever we go, we shall have as much money as we need."

Thus they left the city of Orel, and their departure was known to no one, neither to Bazhen Vtory nor to Bazhen's wife. In one night Savva and the Devil covered the distance of two thousand miles, from the city of Solikamsk to the city of Kozmodemiansk[4] on the river Volga. And the Devil said to Savva: "In case you should meet someone you know, and this person should ask from whence you have come, you should answer that you came from Solikamsk and have spent three weeks traveling to this place." And Savva did as he was told, following the Devil's order.

They passed several days in the city of Kozmodemiansk, and then the Devil and Savva covered the distance from the city of Kozmodemiansk to the village of Paul's Ferry (Pavel's Perevoz) on the river Oka in one night. They arrived there on Thursday, which was the market day. Walking through the market, Savva noticed a very old beggar who stood dressed in repulsive rags. This man observed Savva carefully, and then began to weep. Savva left the Devil's side for a short time and went up to the old man, wishing to learn what caused him to cry. Approaching the old man, Savva asked him: "Wherefore do you grieve? Why do you weep so incessantly?"

And the beggar, who was a holy elder, answered: "My child, I cry because you have lost your soul. You don't realize that you have lost it, but you have voluntarily turned to the Devil. Do you know, my child, with whom you walk and whom you call your brother? It is not a man, but the Devil who walks with you and who hopes to bring you to the very pit of hell."

As soon as the old man had spoken these words, Savva turned toward his false brother, or, better to say, to the Devil. The Devil was standing a short way from him and was threatening Savva and gnashing his teeth. The youth left the holy elder and went up to the Devil. The Devil began abusing him, and said: "Why do you talk with such an evil destroyer of souls? Aren't you aware that this base elder has brought many people to their downfall? He noticed your Sunday clothes and wanted to win you by flattery, to take you away from the crowd, and then to strangle you with a cord and steal your clothes. You will be lost without me, if I abandon you."

After saying these words, the Devil took Savva from that

---

[4] The city of Kozmodemiansk is located on the Upper Volga, north of Moscow.

village. He went with him to a city called Shuya,[5] and they remained there together for a time.

In the meantime, Foma Grudtsyn came to the city of Orel and began inquiring about his son's whereabouts, but no one was able to give him any information. Everyone had seen his son in the city before Foma had arrived, but then he suddenly disappeared without telling anyone of his departure. Some said that the son was frightened by the father's arrival, because he had squandered his father's wealth, and had therefore disappeared. Especially astounded by Savva's departure were Bazhen Vtory and his wife. And Bazhen told Foma: "He spent the night at our place and the next morning he went away. We waited for him to come to dinner, but since that morning he has not reappeared in this city. And neither myself nor my wife knows where he has disappeared to."

Foma shed many tears, and lived for a time in Orel waiting for his son, but since his expectations went unrequited, he returned home. And he told of the unhappy case to his wife. Together they grieved and lamented the disappearance of their only son. Foma Grudtsyn grieved for a long time, and then he entered into his Father's House. And his wife remained a widow.

While the Devil and Savva were living in the town of Shuya, the pious and great sovereign, Tsar, and Grand Duke, Michael Fedorovich, the Autocrat of All the Russias, sent his army against the city of Smolensk[6] to fight the King of Poland. According to the tsar's decree, soldiers were to be recruited throughout all Russia. For the recruiting of such soldiers, Stolnik Timothy Vorontsev was sent from the city of Moscow to Shuya. And he recruited soldiers and drilled them everyday according to military regulations. Savva and the Devil used to go and watch the drills. Once the Devil told Savva: "Brother Savva, would you like to serve the tsar? Let us volunteer for the army."

Savva answered: "Well, brother, you are right. Let us serve." And so they joined the ranks of the army and began to go together for drilling. The Devil gave Savva such a talent for

[5] The city of Shuya is located between Moscow and Nizhny-Novgorod (which is now called Gorky).

[6] The city of Smolensk, some 250 miles west of Moscow, was an important fortress on the Russian-Polish frontier in the seventeenth century. It was lost to Poland during the Time of Troubles. In the years 1632 to 1634, Russia was at war to win back this important city. The Russian armies were under the command of Boyar B. M. Shein. The author erroneously called him Feodor Ivanovich Shein. Tsar Michael Fedorovich, the first Romanov to be tsar, reigned from 1613 to 1645.

The siege of Smolensk by the Poles, 1604–1610. An early seventeenth-century engraving.

military studies that he very soon surpassed the old soldiers and even the commanders. The Devil himself served as Savva's orderly, and cared for Savva and carried his weapons.

When these recently recruited soldiers were transferred from Shuya to Moscow, a German colonel continued their training.[7] When this colonel came to inspect the newly recruited soldiers during drill, he noticed a very young man who behaved most properly, who acted by the regulations, and who was faultless in his military deportment, and who surpassed many old soldiers and commanders in his studies. He was astounded by Savva's acumen, called him aside, and inquired about his background. Savva told him the whole truth. The colonel took a liking to Savva, called him his own son, and gave him his hat, decorated with precious stones, from off his head. And he entrusted to Savva three companies of recruits. And so Savva began to drill and to instruct them in place of the colonel.

The Devil secretly approached Savva and hold him: "Brother Savva, in case you don't have sufficient money to pay your soldiers, tell me and I shall bring you as much as you need, so as to prevent complaints and dissatisfaction among your troops."

And all Savva's soldiers were always quiet and peaceful, while in other companies there were complaints and disorder because the soldiers were dying of starvation and from the lack of clothing and provisions. Among Savva's troops the soldiers were peaceful and well organized, and everyone marveled at Savva's acumen.

Once, the tsar himself learned of Savva. At that time in Moscow was the very powerful boyar and brother-in-law of the tsar, Simeon Streshnev.[8] When this boyar learned of Savva, he ordered that he be brought to him.

When Savva came, Boyar Streshnev asked him, "My youth, do you want to be received in my house and to receive considerable honors from me?"

Savva bowed and replied: "I have a brother, my lord; I will

---

[7] Since the sixteenth century, the Russians had begun hiring foreign instructors to drill and equip their armies according to the requirements of contemporary military science. They preferred to hire German and English instructors because they were Protestants and not Roman Catholics. They preferred Protestants because Russia was constantly at strife with Poland, which for centuries had been an outpost of Catholic expansion.

[8] Boyar Simeon Streshnev was a well-known Russian statesman of the second half of the seventeenth century. The author of this tale erroneously ascribed to him an active part in the first half of the seventeenth century.

ask him. If he orders me to do so, I will serve you with pleasure." The boyar had no objections, and permitted Savva to go and ask his brother.

When Savva came and told everything to his false brother, the Devil, the Devil answered him angrily, saying: "Why do you wish to disregard the tsar's service and become a servant of the tsar's servant? You are now in an important position and you have become favorably known to the tsar. No, you mustn't do this, but let us rather serve the tsar. When the tsar learns of your faithful service, you will be promoted by him to the higher ranks."

By the order of the tsar, all recruits were distributed among the regiments of streltsy[9] in order to swell their ranks. Savva was quartered in the city at the house of Jacob Shilov, a streltsy captain of the Zimin regiment. His house was located in the Istretenka neighborhood of the Earthen City. This captain and his wife, who were pious and decent people, highly respected Savva for his acumen.

The regiments were readied in Moscow for the campaign, when one day the Devil came to Savva and told him: "Brother Savva, let us go ahead of the regiment to Smolensk to see what the Poles are doing there, how they have fortified the city, and what kind of weapons they have." In one night they went from Moscow to Smolensk. Coming there, they remained in the city for three days and three nights, being invisible. There they saw and inspected all things and saw how the Poles were fortifying the city and how they were placing grenades in the places of possible storming. On the fourth day in Smolensk, the Devil revealed himself and Savva to the Poles. Upon seeing them, the Poles became alarmed and began to chase after them, trying to catch them. The Devil and Savva escaped from the city, fled to the river Dnieper, and the river parted before them and they crossed the river as if it were dry. The Poles opened fire on them, but did not succeed in injuring them. And they marveled, saying, "They, who have sojourned in our city, are demons in men."

However, Savva and the Devil returned to Moscow and once again were quartered with this same Captain Shilov. When, at the tsar's command, the regiments marched from Moscow against Smolensk, this Savva and his brother went with the soldiers. The commander over all regiments was Boyar Feodor Shein.

[9] Streltsy (sing., strelets) were professional infantrymen who were armed with muskets, halberds, and sabers. This standing infantry was first organized by John IV.

On the way to Smolensk, the Devil told Savva: "Brother Savva, when we arrive in Smolensk a giant Polish knight will ride out from the city, and will challenge one of our soldiers to a joust. Don't fear him, but go against him. I know and I assure you that you will defeat him. The next day there will come another giant from the Polish ranks who will seek to joust. Once again you must go against him, and I know that you will defeat him also. When the third day comes, the third Polish knight will ride forth from Smolensk. Don't fear him, but go against him, and you will defeat him. You will be wounded by him, but I shall cure you of your wounds." So Savva was advised. And the regiments came to the city of Smolensk and set up camp in a good place.

As the Devil had said, there rode forth from the city of Smolensk a most terrifying warrior who rode on his horse and looked through the Muscovite ranks for an adversary. But no one dared to oppose him. But then Savva announced that he would do so, saying: "If I had a good, spirited steed, I would go to fight against this enemy of the tsar." And when his friends heard of this, they told his intentions to the boyar. The boyar ordered that Savva be brought before him and that he be given a good steed and a weapon, but the boyar thought that the youth would perish at the hands of such a terrifying giant. Then Savva, as he was ordered by his brother, the Devil, galloped against this Polish knight, quickly defeated him, and brought him and his horse to the Muscovite regiments. And Savva was praised by all.

The next day there rode forth from Smolensk another glorious warrior who was in search of an adversary among the Muscovite armies. And once more Savva rode out, and defeated the knight. And everyone was stunned by his daring. However, Boyar Shein became wroth with Savva, but he concealed his rage in his heart.

On the third day, there once more came a warrior from the city of Smolensk, and this knight was more glorious than the previous two, and was looking for an adversary. Although Savva was afraid to ride against such a terrifying warrior, he followed the Devil's order and immediately rode against him. And then this Pole furiously charged Savva and wounded him in his left thigh with his lance. Savva recovered, however, charged this Pole, killed him, and brought his body and horse into the Russian camp. He terrified the Poles in Smolensk, while the entire army was stunned. Then the Polish sortie commenced, army clashed against army, and the battle began. And the flank of the Russian army, in which Savva fought with his brother, was winning, and the Poles turned their backs, and fled. The Devil and Savva killed an endless number of Poles, but they themselves were not injured by anyone.

When Boyar Shein learned of the courage of this youth, he could no longer conceal the wrath in his heart, but summoned Savva to his tent, and asked him, "Tell me, my youth, from which family are you and whose son are you?" And when Savva told him that he was the son of Foma Grudtsyn of Kazan, the boyar began to abuse him with all kind of crude words, and told him: "Why did you need to take part in such mortal combat? I know your father and your relatives. They are immensely wealthy. What is the reason for your forsaking your parent's home to come here? Was it persecution or poverty? I tell you, don't delay any longer, but return to the house of your parents and remain there, living in abundance with your parents. If you don't obey, and I hear about you once more and learn that you have remained here, then you will perish without mercy. I will order that you be beheaded!" Saying this to the youth, the raging boyar left him. And the youth left the tent in great sadness.

When he had left the tent, the Devil asked him: "Why are you troubled about this? If people do not want our services here, we shall return to Moscow and live there." And soon after, they left Smolensk for Moscow, and there they continued to live in the house of Captain Jacob Shilov. The Devil spent the day with Savva, while in the evening he would go to his abode in hell where he dwelt according to the ancient evil customs.

After a considerable length of time, Savva fell ill, and his illness was so severe, he was at death's door. The wife of the captain was a wise, God-fearing woman. She cared for Savva and told him on many occasions that he should summon a priest so that he might take Holy Communion and confess his sins. "You should do this," she said, "for you may die suddenly without having had the last rites."

Savva rejected her advice because, as he said, "My illness is certainly grave, but not fatal." His condition worsened from day to day, and the captain's wife incessantly urged him to take the last rites, because, as she said, "You may die without having taken them."

Finally Savva was forced by this God-loving woman to summon a priest. The captain's wife sent for a priest from the Church of St. Nicholas which is located in the Rooks' neighbor-

hood. The priest came to the ill man without delay. He was of
a mature age, with great experience, and was very devout.
When he came to the bedside of the ill man, he began to pronounce prayers before confession, as is the custom. When the
other people had left the room, the priest began to confess the
sick man.

Suddenly Savva noticed that the room had become filled with
a multitude of demons. His false brother, who was actually the
Devil, came with these demons, but this time he was not in the
image of man, but in his true bestial form. The Devil, who remained behind the crowd of demons, was in a frenzy of rage,
gnashing his teeth, and showing Savva the God-rejecting letter
Savva had given him in the vicinity of Solikamsk. And the Devil
told the ill man: "Look at this, you perjurer, do you realize what
it is? Did you write this or do you believe that by repenting
you can escape us? Oh, no, don't think that, for I will move
against you with all my forces." And the Devil told him this and
other evil threats. The sick man evidently heard them and was
as first frightened, but later he relied upon the power of God
and confessed everything in great detail to the priest. The priest,
although he was a man of the holy life, also became frightened,
since no one but he and Savva were in the room. And he was
deafened by the great uproar that came from the multitude of
demons, and only with great difficulty did the priest finish con-
fessing the sick man. Then he left for home without saying anything to anyone.

After the confession, the evil spirit assaulted Savva and began
to torture him mercilessly. One minute the Devil was beating
him against the wall; another minute he was throwing him
from the couch to the floor; then he throttled him until Savva
began to gasp and foam came from his mouth; then he tortured
him with many different kinds of torture. The aforementioned
captain, who was also a pious man, saw with his wife that the
youth was assaulted and tormented by the Devil. And they
grieved and bemoaned the fate of the youth, but were unable
to help him in any way. From day to day the assaults and
torments of the Devil became fiercer, and those who witnessed
them were terrified.

The master of the house, who saw the unusual fate of this
youth and who realized that, because of his courage, the youth
was known to the tsar himself, decided with his wife to inform
the tsar. They hoped that there might be some relative of the
youth in the tsar's palace. As soon as the man had decided this,

Portrait of a Russian boyar.
A seventeenth-century painting.

he sent his wife to her relative, telling her to inform the relative about everything and asking that she inform the tsar immediately. And he added, "In case the young man dies in such miserable plight, there may be litigation for not having informed the tsar."

His wife, without delay, hastened to her relative and told her exactly what she was ordered to say by her husband. Hearing these words, her relative was profoundly moved, grieved over the fate of the youth, and became sad at the situation of her relatives, fearing that this matter might bring them trouble. Therefore, without any delay, she went from her house to the tsar's palace and told the members of the tsar's court of these happenings. When the tsar heard about this youth, he showed mercy on him. He told the courtiers who were before him to send two sentries to the house of the captain where the sick man lay, whenever the daily changing of the sentries took place.

The tsar said, "They should watch over this youth with care so as to prevent him from killing himself by throwing himself into the fire or into the water, when he loses his senses because of the demons' torments."

And the pious tsar ordered that meals be sent daily to the sick man, and asked that the sick man appear before him in his palace as soon as he was cured. And so it was done. However, the sick man remained for a long time under the Devil's sway.

The first of July arrived, and on those days the youth was particularly tormented by the Devil. Finally he fell asleep, and while he was sleeping he began to talk as if he were awake and he shed tears from his exhausted eyes. And he said: "O Most Merciful Lady, Queen and Holy Virgin, have mercy upon me, our Lady, the Queen of Queens. I do not lie, I do not lie, but I shall do as I pledge."

The members of the captain's household and the sentries who watched him were astounded when they heard these words spoken by sick Savva, and they said, "He has a vision."

When the sick man woke from the sleep, the captain came to him, and said, "Tell me, Lord Savva, what kind of words did you speak while shedding tears in your sleep?"

And tears flowed steadily from Savva's eyes, and he said: "I saw that my couch was approached by a Lady from whom emanated light, and who shone with indescribable grace, and who was wearing a purple vestment. With her were two men distinguished by their venerable white hair. One of them was in an archbishop's vestment, while the other was wearing the robes of an Apostle. And I believe that they were none other than the Holy Virgin, the Friend of the Lord, John the Theologian, and Metropolitan Peter, the ever vigilant guardian of our city, Moscow, and the most glorious archbishop of bishops. I know well their images from the icons. And the Lady from whom emanated light said: 'What has happened to you, Savva? Why are you so full of sorrow?'

"And I said to her: 'I am full of sorrow, my Lady, because the Son of our God is wroth with me, and because you, the Intercessor for the Christians, are wroth with me.' And, smiling on me, she said: 'What do you think? How can you escape such a plight? How can you get your God-rejecting letter from hell?' And I told her: 'It cannot be done, my Lady, except with the succor of your Son and through your infinite mercy.' And she told me: 'I shall implore my Son and God in your behalf; only, you must follow to the word what I shall tell you. I shall deliver you from this misfortune, if you will decide to take monastic vows.'

"And so I vowed to her tearfully in my dream, and these were the words that you heard. And then she told me: 'Listen, Savva! On the holy day of my icon in my cathedral of the icon of Kazan, come to my church that is on the main square in the vicinity of the Rag Market. And then I shall perform a miracle for you in the presence of all.' And after this, she became invisible."

The captain and the sentries who kept watch over Savva marveled greatly upon hearing his words about his vision. And the captain and his wife began to ponder how they should inform the tsar of this vision, and decided to send their relative to inform the courtiers in the tsar's palace and let them tell of the vision to the tsar. When the aforementioned relative came to the captain's house, they told her of Savva's vision. When she learned of this, she went immediately to the tsar's palace in order to inform the courtiers in the tsar's palace and to let them inform the tsar of Savva's vision. When the tsar learned of it, he marveled greatly.

When, on July 8th, the holy day of the Icon of the Blessed Virgin of Kazan arrived, there was a church procession with holy icons and sacred crosses from the Cathedral of the Assumption of the Holy Virgin to the Holy Virgin of Kazan. In this procession participated the great sovereign, tsar, and grand duke, Michael, the holy patriarch, with the bishops, and a great many courtiers. And the tsar ordered that sick Savva be brought to this church. Then, by the tsar's order, the ill man was rapidly brought on a carpet to the Church of the Holy Virgin of Kazan and was laid before the entrance to the church.

When the holy Mass begun, ill Savva was assaulted by the evil spirit, and the Devil began to torment him ferociously, and Savva called in a loud voice, "Help me, my Lady and Holy Virgin! Help me, my Queen of Queens, the Mother of God!" And when the choir began to sing the Song of the Cherubim, people heard a sound like thunder, and there came a voice announcing: "Savva! Get up and come into my church!"

Then he got up from the carpet on which he had been brought, as if he had never been ill. He quickly came into the church, fell on his knees before the Icon of the Most Holy Virgin of Kazan, and prayed, shedding tears. At the same moment there fell from the cupola of the church the God-rejecting letter of Savva that he had given to the Devil at Solikamsk. And all writing was erased from the letter, as if nothing had ever been written there. And then the same voice repeated: "Savva! Here is the letter you wrote, and now fulfill my commandment, and don't commit the sin of disobedience." And he arose, picked up the letter, and, shedding tears, spoke in a loud voice before the icon: "Oh, Most Blessed Mother of God, Intercessor for all Christians, who prays for us to her Son and to our God, absolve me of my sins and save me from the very pit of hell. And I will fulfill what I have pledged."

When the tsar, the patriarch, and all who were there heard this and witnessed this most marvelous miracle, they thanked God and His Most Holy Mother, and greatly marveled about such divine mercy that had delivered him from the very pit of hell. And, after the divine liturgy, they began to glorify God, and the entire clergy gave a service of thanksgiving for the miracles that were performed before all.

Thereafter, the church procession with the holy icons and sacred crosses left the church and went to the cathedral. And the tsar returned to his palace rejoicing over this miracle, and thanking God. And Savva returned in good health to the house of the aforementioned Captain Shilov, and never again did he suffer from his disease. The captain and his wife saw this, marveled greatly, and thanked God for his great mercy for all men.

Savva remained living for a short time in the house of the captain. Then he distributed all his wealth to the poor and to the churches, and left for the Monastery of the Miracle of Archangel Michael, which is called the Miracle Monastery and which is located in the vicinity of the Cathedral of the Venerable and Glorious Assumption of the Most Holy Virgin. There he took his monastic vows, and remained laboring, fasting, and praying incessantly and thus pleasing God. There he lived for many years, and passed to the Lord in peace. And he was buried in this monastery.

42. *Frol Skobeev, the Rogue*

HARDLY any work of Russian seventeenth-century literature reflects so strikingly the drastic changes in both the way of life and the mentality of the Muscovite Russian as does the tale of *Frol Skobeev, the Rogue*. This story reveals the thorough secularization of Muscovite writings and the break with the traditions of the Age of Faith. The religious and moralistic tone in literature have vanished altogether. The solemn, ornate style, with an abundance of archaic Old Church Slavonic words, has given place to colloquial Russian and simple, short sentences. The subject itself of a rogue portrayed against the background of everyday Russian life was completely novel in Russian literature at that time, and the description of Frol Skobeev's life lacks the traditional clichés that dominated earlier biographical and hagiographic works. Amorous and erotic motifs now make their appearance. This work is a bitter satire on the new man who is shown as a rogue and cunning operator, and whose final success announced a new age for both Russian society and literature.

In some versions of this tale, the action takes places around 1680, the time when the customary barriers between the old, aristocratic boyars and the new gentry were crumbling, and the anonymous author gave the names of actual historical personages to his characters. The Skobeevs were small provincial squires of that time. Lovchikov actually did belong to the court and was a *stolnik* in the 1670's and 1680's. Only the name of Ordyn-Nashchekin, a famous statesman and diplomat during the reign of Tsar Alexis Mikhailovich, was slightly modified to Nadrin-Nashchekin. Still, it appears that the plot does not depict actual happenings, but reflects rather the new atmosphere and social trends in Muscovite Russia.

The present translation follows the oldest extant version of this tale, a manuscript written in the late seventeenth century

and published by N. Skripil in *Russkaia Povest XVII veka,*
Moscow, 1953, pages 155–166.

Some interesting passages indicating the further development
of satirical and erotic themes in later versions of this tale have
been interpolated from a manuscript published by N. K. Gudzy
in *Khrestomatiia po drevnei russkoi literature,* Moscow, 1956,
pages 415–425. These interpolated passages have been placed
in brackets.

◆ ◆ ◆

In the district of Novgorod there lived the nobleman Frol
Skobeev. In the same district were the estates of Stolnik[1]
Nadrin-Nashchekin; and the stolnik's daughter, Annushka, was
living at these Novgorodian estates.

Frol Skobeev, learning about the stolnik's daughter, came to
the decision that he should have a love affair with her. But since
he could not get to meet her, he decided to become acquainted
with the steward of estates of Nadrin-Nashchekin. And so he
began to visit him at his home. Some time later, Frol Skobeev
happened to be at the steward's home when Annushka's nurse
came to this steward. Frol Skobeev learned that the nurse lived
with Annushka. When the nurse left to return to her mistress'
home, Frol followed her and gave her a present of two rubles.
And the nurse said to him, "My lord Skobeev, the favor you
show me is beyond my service, for I haven't yet rendered you
any service." And returning home to her mistress, the nurse said
nothing to her of this matter. Frol spent a time at the steward's
house, and then went home.

When the time of the Christmas holidays arrived, during
which there is much merrymaking and the girls often have pre-
texts to pass the time gaily, the daughter of Stolnik Nadrin-
Nashchekin, Annushka, told her nurse to go to all noblemen who
had young daughters and whose estates were in the vicinity and
ask them to come to Annushka's party and have some fun. The
nurse went and asked all the daughters of noblemen, and they
all promised to come to Annushka's party. Since the nurse knew
that Frol Skobeev had a young sister who was unmarried, she
went to Frol's house and asked his sister to come to Stolnik
Nadrin-Nashchekin's house, to Annushka's party. The sister told

[1] Stolnik: an important rank at the Russian court in Moscow. At
official banquets and receptions the stolniks served the tsar at the
table. They usually were members of the aristocracy, and were often
high officials in various governmental agencies or commanders in the
army.

the nurse: "Wait a moment and I will go and ask my brother. Then I will tell you what he has decided."

The sister went to Frol and told him: "The nurse of Stolnik Nadrin-Nashchekin's daughter has arrived, and asks that I come to Annushka's party."

Frol Skobeev told his sister: "Go and tell this nurse that you will go, but with another girl, a nobleman's daughter."

The sister pondered on what her brother had told her to tell the nurse. However, she did not dare to disobey her brother, and told the nurse that she would go that very evening with the daughter of another nobleman. Then the nurse returned to her mistress, Annushka.

In the meantime Frol Skobeev began to speak with his sister, saying, "Well, sister, it is time for you to get dressed to go to the party." When his sister began to don feminine attire, Frol ordered her: "Sister, bring me also a girl's attire. I shall don it, and we shall go together to Annushka, the stolnik's daughter."

The sister was very much afraid that people might recognize him, and then certainly there would be much trouble for her brother, for the stolnik was much liked by the tsar. Still, she did not dare to disobey her brother, and she brought him the attire of a girl. Frol, having dressed himself as a girl, went with his sister to Annushka, the stolnik's daughter.

There had already gathered many daughters of noblemen, but no one was able to recognize Frol in his feminine attire. Then the girls began to play parlor games, and enjoyed themselves. Frol also played the games, and was not recognized by anyone. Finally Frol left the room for his needs, and was accompanied through the corridor by the nurse, who carried a taper. On leaving, he told her, "Oh, my dear nurse, there are many girls here, and many of them ask services of you, but none of them would give you any gift for such services." Still the nurse did not recognize him. Then Frol gave her five rubles, which she accepted gratefully.

Seeing that the nurse still did not recognize him, Frol fell on his knees and explained to her that he was a nobleman, Frol Skobeev, and that he had come in feminine attire so that he might marry Annushka. When the nurse realized that he really was Frol Skobeev, she became frightened and did not know what to do. Still, remembering both of his generous gifts, she said to him, "Well, my lord Skobeev, I am ready to do everything you may ask, in view of your gracious generosity."

Returning to the place where the girls were enjoing themselves, she spoke not a word about Frol Skobeev, but soon after she told her mistress: "Well, girls, you have had enough of these games. I suggest you play another game, one that was played when I was young."

Annushka did not wish to disobey her nurse, and said only: "Well, my dear nurse, we shall play the games according to your desires."

And the nurse told them of her game, saying: "Please, dear Annushka, play the role of the bride." Pointing to Frol Skobeev, she said: "And this girl will be the bridegroom." And then she led the two into a nice chamber, to the bed, as a bride and bridegroom are usually led after the wedding. The girls accompanied them to the bedroom and then, leaving the two alone, went to the rooms in which they had been playing their parlor games. And the nurse ordered the girls to sing loudly so that they might not hear any cries coming from the bedchamber. And Frol Skobeev's sister was very much afraid, fearing that her brother might get into trouble.

Lying with Annushka on the bed, Frol told her that he was a nobleman, Frol Skobeev, from the district of Novgorod, and not a girl. Annushka was seized by great fright. But Frol, despite the fact that he was himself afraid, became daring and forced her to submit to his will. Thereafter, Annushka begged Frol not to bring shame upon her by telling of this to others. Later on, when the nurse and the girls returned to the chamber where Frol and Annushka were, they realized from Annushka's expression that something had happened. [Annushka had undergone a tribulation she had never before experienced.] However, the girls still did not recognize Frol Skobeev, for he was again in feminine attire. But Annushka took her nurse by the hand, led her away from the girls, and said to her: "What have you done to me! The one who was with me was not a girl. He is a man, Frol Skobeev."

However, the nurse answered: "I tell you the truth, my gracious lady, when I say that I was not able to recognize him. I thought that he was a girl like the others. If he has committed such a shameful deed, we can kill him and hide his body in some secret place, for we have plenty of servants."

But Annushka took pity on Frol Skobeev [because she had begun to care for him, having lain with him in the bedchamber]. And she told the nurse, "Well, nurse, let it be this way, for never again shall I regain my chastity."

Thereafter, all the girls, as well as Frol Skobeev, went to the reception room, and all enjoyed themselves until late into the night. Afterward, all the girls went to bed. And Annushka went to bed with Frol Skobeev [telling herself, "I wouldn't be able to find a better girl with whom to sleep." And they enjoyed themselves throughout the night with carnal pleasures. And since that time a profound pity for Frol Skobeev dwelt in Annushka's heart. And only with great sorrow did she part from Frol Skobeev.]

In the morning, when everyone had got up, the girls returned to their homes. Frol Skobeev also wanted to leave with his sister, but Annushka, who permitted all the others to go, kept Frol Skobeev in her house. Frol Skobeev remained at Annushka's house for three days, always in feminine attire, so that he might not be recognized by the house servants. And he and Annushka enjoyed themselves, and only after three days did Frol go home with his sister. Before leaving, Annushka gave Frol three hundred rubles. Frol [returned home, overjoyed, and from that time the destitute Skobeev became richer, and began to live like a wealthy man and] began to have banquets with his fellow noblemen.

Sometime thereafter, Stolnik Nadrin-Nashchekin wrote from Moscow that Annushka should come to Moscow because there were many noble young men, sons of stolniks, who were seeking her hand in marriage. [Although Annushka was most unwilling to do so,] she did did not want to disobey her father. And so she soon left for Moscow. And when Frol Skobeev learned that she had gone to Moscow, he became confused, knowing not what he should do. Although he was a nobleman, he was quite poor, and made his living working in Moscow soliciting litigations at the court.[2] He decided [to mortgage his estate, which was just a wasteland, and] to go to Moscow in order to take Annushka as wife. He began to make preparations for his trip to Moscow, although his sister was greatly grieved, not wanting him to go.

Frol Skobeev [took leave of his sister and] said: "Dear sister, don't grieve over anything. Maybe I will lose my life, but I will not give up Annushka. I will be either a colonel or a corpse. If things happen according to my plans, I will not leave you in

---

[2] These solicitors were not formally trained, for there were no formally educated lawyers in Muscovite Russia. The functions of lawyers were performed by professional legal solicitors who represented their clients at the court and in governmental agencies. Many of these solicitors, however, gained positions of great influence in government administration.

need. However, in case misfortune occurs, please don't forget me in your prayers." And having made all the preparations, Frol went to Moscow.

Arriving in Moscow, he took quarters in the vicinity of Stolnik Nardin-Nashchekin's mansion. The next day Frol Skobeev went to Mass, and in the church he met Annushka's nurse. After the liturgy was over, Frol Skobeev left the church and awaited the nurse. When the nurse came out from the church, Frol Skobeev approached her, bowed deeply, and asked her to announce his arrival in Moscow to Annushka. [The nurse promised to support him.] Coming home, she told Annushka about Frol's arrival. Annushka became very happy, and told her nurse to take him twenty rubles when he went to Mass the next day. And the nurse did as she was told.

Stolnik Nadrin-Nashchekin had a sister who had taken vows in the Maiden's Convent.[3] Once the stolnik went to visit his sister in the convent. When he came there, the sister met him with all due honors. And the stolnik passed a long time with his sister. They had many conversations, and once the sister asked the brother to permit her niece to visit her, since she had not seen her niece in many years. Stolnik Nadrin-Nashchekin promised to permit his daughter to visit her at the convent. The sister added: "I would only ask you to give the necessary order in your home so that your daughter may come whenever I send my carriage, even if you yourself are not at home."

Some time later, Stolnik Nadrin-Nashchekin and his wife had to go to visit some friends, and he ordered his daughter: "In case my sister, your aunt, should send her carriage from the convent, please go to her." And he then went with his wife to visit the friends.

Annushka asked her nurse to go immediately to Frol Skobeev and to tell him that he should procure a horse and carriage as soon as possible and come to her house, saying that he was sent from the Maiden's Convent by the stolnik's sister for Annushka. The nurse went to Frol Skobeev and repeated the commands of her mistress.

When Frol Skobeev heard this, he didn't know what to do and whom to deceive in order to obtain a carriage, for all noble aristocrats knew that he was a poor nobleman and a great cheat, able only to solicit litigations. But he thought of a certain stolnik named Lovchikov who had always been very kind to

[3] The Maiden's Convent: the proper name of a convent in the vicinity of Moscow.

him. Therefore he went to this Lovchikov and had a long talk with him. Finally Frol began to beg Lovchikov to lend him his carriage and horses [so that he might go and look for a fiancée. Giving in to his requests, Lovchikov lent him his carriage and a coachman.] Frol went to his quarters and gave the coachman drinks until he was completely stupefied. Then he dressed himself in the lackey's clothes, sat on the coachbox, and went in the carriage to the home of Stolnik Nadrin-Nashchekin to get Annushka. There he was recognized by Annushka's nurse, who told Annushka that her aunt had sent her carriage for her from the convent. Annushka readied herself, sat in carriage, and went to Frol's quarters.

In the meantime Lovchikov's coachman had awakened, and Frol, realizing that the coachman was not sufficiently drunk, gave him more to drink. He then put him in the carriage, sat on the coachbox, and returned to Lovchikov's mansion. Arriving there, Frol opened the gate, drove the carriage into the yard, and left it there. When Lovchikov's servants found the carriage in the yard and the coachman inside, stupefied from drink, they went to Lovchikov and told him that the carriage was in the yard and that the coachman was dead drunk. Yet no one could learn who had brought the carriage and horses into the yard. Stolnik Lovchikov ordered the putting up of the horses and carriage in the stables, and added: "It's all right. At least the horses were not sold. What can one expect from Frol Skobeev?" In the morning Lovchikov asked the coachman where he went with Frol Skobeev, and the man answered, "I remember that we went to his quarters, but I do not actually know where I drove and what I did."

Soon afterward Stolnik Nadrin-Nashchekin returned from his friends and asked to see his daughter. He was told by the nurse that Annushka, by his order, had gone to the convent to his sister, since the sister had sent her carriage for her. Nadrin-Nashchekin answered, "Well, that's all right."

Thinking that his daughter lived with his sister in the convent, Nadrin-Nashchekin did not go for a while to his sister. In the meantime Frol and Annushka married. When Nadrin-Nashchekin finally did go to see his sister at the convent, and passed some time there without seeing his daughter, he remarked to his sister, "Well, sister, I haven't seen Annushka here." The sister answered: "Brother, don't joke. What can I do if you don't honor my requests? I asked you to send her to me, but apparently you don't trust me. As for myself, I haven't had time to send my carriage for her."

Stolnik Nadrin-Nashchekin replied: "My dear lady and sister, of what are you speaking? I don't understand a thing you have said, because Annushka left for your convent a month ago when you sent the carriage and horses after her. At that time I was visiting friends with my wife. She was permitted to go, as I ordered it so."

But the sister explained: "Brother, I have not sent a carriage and horses for her, and neither has Annushka ever been in this place."

Nadrin-Nashchekin grieved profoundly for his daughter, and cried bitterly, for she had vanished without leaving the slightest trace. Returning home, he told his wife that Annushka had disappeared and was not at the convent with his sister. And then he began to question the nurse, asking who had come and with whom Annushka had left. The nurse answered: "A coachman came with a carriage and said that he had come from the Maiden's Convent for Annushka. And Annushka left with him, according to your order."

The stolnik and his wife were greatly grieved, and wept bitterly. The next morning the stolnik went to the tsar to tell him that his daughter had vanished into thin air. The tsar ordered that the disappearance of the stolnik's daughter be made public, and he made the following pronouncement: "In case someone is keeping her secretly and does not come forward and admit it, this man will be sentenced to death when she is found."

Hearing this, Frol Skobeev didn't know what to do. Finally he decided to go to Stolnik Lovchikov, for this stolnik had always been good and kind toward him. When Frol came to Lovchikov, they had a long conversation during which Lovchikov asked, "Have you taken a bride?" And when Frol answered that he had, the stolnik asked, "And did you marry a wealthy wife?"

Frol answered, "Up to now I haven't seen much wealth, but we shall see what the future holds."

And Stolnik Lovchikov told Frol: "Well, Mr. Skobeev, now you must start living in upright ways. Stop soliciting. It would be much healthier if you were to live in your own domain." Thereafter, Frol began begging Stolnik Lovchikov to intervene for him.

Lovchikov answered: "Well, if it is a decent cause I shall intervene for you, but if it is something dishonest, don't be angry with me."

Frol then revealed to Lovchikov that he had married Stolnik

Nadrin-Nashchekin's daughter and that she was staying at this place.

Lovchikov answered, "You did this on your own, so accept the responsibility for it on your own."

But Frol threatened: "If you don't intervene for me, you also may be made responsible! I can testify against you, since you lent me the carriage and the horses to take her away. If you hadn't lent them to me, I wouldn't have been able to do it."

Lovchikov became very confused, and answered: "You are a real rogue! What are you trying to do to me? How can I intervene for you?" And then he suggested that Frol should go on the next day to the Cathedral of the Assumption of the Holy Virgin, for Nadrin-Nashchekin would be there for the Mass.[4] "After the Mass," he continued, "all of us will be standing together at St. John's Square. In this moment come and fall before the feet of Nadrin and tell him about his daughter. And I shall try to intervene on your behalf."

Frol Skobeev went the next morning to the Cathedral of the Assumption of the Holy Virgin and saw that Stolnik Nadrin-Nashchekin and several other stolniks were praying there. All of them, as was their wont, gather after Mass before the Bell Tower of John the Great[5] in John's Square. Nadrin-Nashchekin talked of his bereavement caused by the disappearance of his daughter. Lovchikov discussed the matter with him and was trying to convince him that he should be merciful no matter what happened. While they were talking, Frol Skobeev approached them and bowed to the stolniks, as was his custom, since they all knew him. Paying no heed to the others, Frol Skobeev fell to the feet of Nadrin-Nashchekin and began begging for forgiveness, saying: "My merciful lord and the first of the stolniks! Forgive me my guilt as if I were your humble slave who had daringly made an altercation with you!"

Nadrin-Nashchekin was already of advanced age and therefore had poor eyesight, and so could not recognize the man before him. He then drew Frol up with the handle of his cane, and asked: "Who are you? Tell me about yourself. What do you want from us?"

---

[4] In the seventeenth century the Cathedral of the Assumption of the Holy Virgin, which is located in the Kremlin, was in the center of the area of Muscovite governmental agencies.

[5] The Bell Tower of John the Great is the highest of the campaniles in the Kremlin. It was built by John IV, and, like the Cathedral of the Assumption of the Holy Virgin, was in the center of the area of governmental agencies.

But Frol repeated only, "Absolve me of my guilt."

Lovchikov came nearer, and said, "Before you stands Frol Skobeev, a nobleman who asks you to absolve him of his guilt."

Then Nadrin-Nashchekin exclaimed: "Get up, you rogue! For a long time have I known you, you rogue and knave! Tell me what has happened, you scoundrel! So you have once more got yourself into a predicament. If it is not too bad, I will help you. But if it is really base, then do as you want. For a long time I have told you, rogue, to live decently. Now get up and tell what is your evil-doing."

Frol got up from before the stolnik's feet and informed him that his daughter was at his place and that he had married her. Having heard that his daughter was Frol's wife, the stolnik began to sob, and lost consciousness. When he had slightly recovered himself, he began to rage: "What have you done, rogue? Do you know who you are? Who are you? Your evil-doing cannot be forgiven. How could you, such a rogue, dare to wed my daughter? I will go to the sovereign and ask that he punish you for this offense which is such a great affliction for me, you rogue!"

Lovchikov, for the second time, came near Nadrin-Nashchekin and tried to convince him not to go to the tsar, saying: "You had better go home and explain this to your spouse and then do your best as you both shall decide. You cannot undo what is already done. And he, Frol Skobeev, can find no shelter from your wrath."

Stolnik Nadrin-Nashchekin followed the advice of Lovchikov, and took his carriage and went home. In the meantime Frol Skobeev went to his house and told Annushka: "Well, Annushka, I don't know what will become of us. I have told your father of our marriage."

Stolnik Nadrin-Nashchekin came home, went to his wife's chambers, and, bitterly weeping and sobbing, told her: "My wife, my wife! Do you know what? I have found Annushka!"

And the wife asked him: "And where is she, Father?"

And Nadrin-Nashchekin told his wife: "That thief, rogue, and knave, Frol Skobeev, has married her."

When his wife heard these words, she knew not what to do, but only grieved deeply for her daughter. And both of them began to weep bitterly and to reprove their daughter. And knowing not what they should do, they cursed their daughter. When they had become calm, they began to ponder, and they deeply regretted the fate of their daughter. Finally they decided: "We must send a servant to learn where this rogue lives and if Annushka is still alive or not." And so they summoned a servant and ordered him to find the house of Frol Skobeev and to learn about Annushka and whether she was still alive and eating well.

When the servant came to the house of Frol Skobeev and Frol noticed that a man from his father-in-law's house had come into the yard, Frol told his wife to go to bed and to behave as if she were very ill. Annushka did as her husband willed. When the man, who was sent by her parents, entered the house and bowed deeply, as was the custom, Frol asked him, "What man are you and what is your business?" The man told Frol that he was sent by Stolnik Nadrin-Nashchekin to find out whether Annushka was in good health or not.

And Frol Skobeev told him: "Do you see, my friend, what kind of health she enjoys? This is the result of her parents' wrath, for, as you know, they reprimand her and curse her. They should at least give her their blessing."

The man bowed, left Skobeev, and returned to his master, Stolnik Nadrin-Nashchekin. And the stolnik asked him: "Did you find their quarters? Did you find Annushka? Is she alive or not?" The man answered that Annushka was very ill and would hardly remain alive much longer. And he asked them to send their blessings to their daughter. The stolnik and his wife grieved deeply and pondered what they should do with this rogue and knave.

Finally, the mother spoke: "Well, my friend, there is little we can do. Apparently God himself has willed that such a rogue be our daughter's husband. We, my friend, must send them the icon with our blessings. When our hearts become more merciful, then we shall see them." And they took down from the wall an icon decorated with gold and precious stones that were worth five hundred rubles. And they sent it with a servant, directing him to tell Annushka to pray to it and to tell Frol Skobeev not to sell the icon and then squander the money.

The servant took the icon and went to Frol Skobeev's house. Frol Skobeev saw the man coming, and told his wife: "Get up Annushka!" She got up and sat down with Frol. The servant entered the room and gave the icon to Frol. The latter accepted it, put it in a new place, and told the servant: "Such is the power of parental blessings. As soon as they had sent their blessings, God helped Annushka, and she recovered. And now, thanks be to God, she is in good health."

The servant returned to his master, told him that he had given the icon to Annushka, that her health had much improved, and that Annushka thanked her parents. The man then went to his lodgings.

Stolnik Nadrin-Nashchekin began to deliberate with his wife concerning their daughter. And they became sorry for her. The mother asked: "What should we do, my friend? Certainly this rogue will starve Annushka. How can this dog provide for her, when he himself is hungry? We must send her some provisions in a six-horse carriage." And so they sent provisions and a list of such to Frol Skobeev. Frol ordered that the provisions be put in an appropriate place without looking at the list. And he ordered the stolnik's servant to thank the parents for such gifts.

And from that time, Frol Skobeev lived like a wealthy man, and often visited important personages. And everyone wondered about Frol Skobeev and how he could have dared to carry through this affair.

Only a month later did the hearts of the parents become merciful to Frol and his wife. And they sent a man to them asking that they come to their house for dinner. And the man came and asked that they come that very day for dinner. And Frol answered the man, saying, "Report to the father that we are ready to come today to his grace." Frol and his wife dressed and went to the house of Frol's father-in-law, Stolnik Nadrin-Nashchekin. And when they came to the father-in-law's house, Annushka went to her father and fell before the feet of her parents. When Nadrin-Nashchekin and his wife saw their daughter, they began reprimanding her and visited their parental wrath upon her. But looking upon her, they began to weep bitterly because she had married against the will of her parents. Finally, their wrath subsided and they forgave her and ordered that she sit with them. But to Frol Skobeev they said: "And you, rogue, why are you standing? Sit down here. How can you, such a rogue, be married to our daughter?"

But Frol answered only: "Well, my lord and father, it was the will of God." And all sat down at the table, but Stolnik Nadrin-Nashchekin ordered the servants not to admit any visitors to the house, saying: "In the event that someone does come and asks if the stolnik is home, tell them that he is not, since I do not want to have other people see that we are eating with our son-in-law, that knave and rogue, Frol Skobeev."

After the meal, the stolnik asked, "Well, rogue, how will you make your living?"

And Frol answered: "Well, you know that better than I. I know only how to make my living by soliciting litigations."

And the stolnik told Frol: "Well, rogue, stop your soliciting.

In the district of Simbirsk I have an estate on which there are
three hundred peasant families. You, rogue, can have it for your
own, and live there permanently." Then Frol Skobeev and his
wife bowed deeply and thanked the parents for this gift. But
the stolnik said: "Don't bow, rogue. Better that you prepare the
deeds to this domain."

Frol and Annushka remained only a short while longer at
the parents' home, and then left. But on their way, Stolnik
Nadrin-Nashchekin ordered that they return, and asked: "Well,
rogue, how will you get supplies? Do you have any money?"

Frol answered: "Well, my father, you yourself know what
kind of money I have, but perhaps I should sell the peasants on
this estate."

Stolnik Nadrin-Nashchekin replied, saying: "No rogue, don't
sell them. I shall give you some money. Take it." And he ordered
that three hundred rubles be given to him. Frol Skobeev took
the money and returned to his quarters.

Sometime later he received the deeds to this estate. Stolnik
Nadrin-Nashchekin eventually was to make Frol Skobeev the
heir of all his capital and domains. After the death of his father,
Frol Skobeev married off his sister to the son of another stolnik,
while Annushka's nurse remained living with Annushka and her
husband in great honor to the end of her days.

43. *Misery-Luckless-Plight*

THE origin of *Misery-Luckless-Plight* has not been exactly
determined, and it is of mixed genre. Found in a single copy
that apparently was prepared in the eighteenth century, this
tale-poem, in its content, philosophy, and language, belongs to
the middle of the seventeenth century, when the problem of
religious regeneration became so acute during the period of the
movement of the Seekers After God (see Selection 39) and the
Great Schism. Its theme is the salvation of a sinner. The story
is in blank verse, and seems to have been written by a man well
acquainted with both the ancient Russian tradition and oral
folk poetry. The use of recurrent descriptions, its imagery, and
repetition of traditional nature symbols and metaphors (for
example, "The youth flew as a falcon," or "Misery after him as
a gray hawk") relate the work to both the written and folklore
traditions. The meter of four stresses is close to that of the

historical *bylina,* while the psychological depiction of the prodigal young man seems to indicate that the author was familiar with religious literature. The writer's originality lies in the fact that his portrayal of the youth is distinctly different from the stereotyped characterizations of hagiographic writers.

For the present edition Leo Wiener's translation of the poem has been used. For readability, however, it has been divided into songs and stanzas, and the original Russian verse form has been retained. The translation has been partially revised.

❖ ❖ ❖

I. The Nature of Man

By the will of the Lord, our God, and our Savior,
Jesus Christ, Almighty
from the beginning of the age of man.
In the beginning of this passing age
God created heaven and earth,
God created Adam and Eve.
He ordered them to live in holy paradise,
and gave them this divine command:
He told them not to eat the fruit of the grapevine,
from the great tree of Eden.

But the human heart is unthinking and unruly,
and Adam and Eve were tempted.
They forgot God's command,
ate of the fruit of the grapevine,
from the great and wonderful tree,
and for that great transgression of theirs,
God's wrath rose against Adam and Eve.
And God drove Adam and Eve from the holy paradise of
      Eden.
He settled them upon the lowly earth,
blessed them that they might grow and multiply,
and told them to appease their hunger through their own
      labor
from the fruits upon earth.

God gave them this commandment:
there should be weddings and marriages
for the propagation of the race of men,
and for having beloved children.

But the human heart was senseless and disobedient;
from the very start it was not submissive,
looked with disdain at the father's instruction,
did not obey the mother,
was untrue to the advice of friends.

Then there came a weak and wretched race
that turned to reckless deeds
and began to live in turmoil and wrong,
and discarded humility of spirit.
And God grew wroth with them,
and imposed great calamities upon them,
and permitted that great misery be accorded to them,
and immeasurable shame,
evil plight,
fiendish visitations.
and evil, immeasurable nakedness,
and endless poverty and extreme want.
And he did it to humble us, to punish us,
to lead us on the path of salvation.
Such is the nature of man from his very birth from father
        and mother.

II. Parents' Admonition

The youth had reached the age of discretion and absence of
        wantonness.
His father and mother loved him much,
and they began to teach and instruct him,
to prepare him for good deeds:

"Dear child of ours,
    listen to your parents' instruction,
    listen to their saws,
    good and cunning and wise,
    and you will not be in want,
    you will not be in great poverty.
    Go not, child, to feasts and carousings;
    do not seat yourself on a high place;
    drink not two beakers at once;
    be not tempted by good, beautiful women, fathers'
            daughters.

Lie not down in the back yards.
Fear not the wise man;

fear the fool
lest the fools lay hands on you
and take off your costly garments,
and cause you great shame and dishonor,
and expose you to the scorn and empty prattle of men.
Go not, my child, to the dice-players and innkeepers,
and keep no company with tavern-goers.
Make no friends with the foolish and simple.
Steal not, rob not,
nor deceive, nor tell a lie, nor do wrong.
Be not tempted by gold and silver;
collect not unrighteous wealth.

Be not a witness to false swearing,
and think no evil of father and mother
or any other man—
that God may protect you from all evil.
Dishonor not, child, the rich and the poor,
but regard them all alike.
Keep company with the wise and sensible,
and make friends with friends you may rely upon,
who will not deliver you to evil."

III. The Emancipation

The youth was then young and foolish,
not in his full senses, and imperfect in mind;
he was ashamed to submit to his father
and bow before his mother,
but wanted to live as he listed.
If the youth earned fifty rubles,
he found easily fifty friends,
and his honor flowed like a river;
the youth gained many friends for himself,
and they accounted themselves of his race.

And the youth had a trusted friend:
he named himself his plighted brother,
and he tempted him with tempting words;
he called him to the tavern yard,
led him into the hall of the inn,
brought him a cup of good wine,
handed him a beaker of heady beer,
and spoke to him the following words:

"Drink, my bosom friend, brother of mine,
to your joy and happiness and health.
Empty the cup of good wine
and follow it by a glass of sweet mead.
And if you drink, brother, until you be drunk,
lie down to sleep where you have drunk—
depend upon me, your plighted brother.
I shall sit down and keep watch over you:
at your head, dear friend,
I shall place a beaker of sweet mead,
by your side I shall place good wine,
and near you I shall place heady beer,
I shall watch well over you, dear friend,
and shall take you back to your father and mother."

At that time the youth depended
on his plighted brother; he did not wish to disobey him.
He settled himself near the heady drinks,
and emptied a cup of green wine,
followed it by a glass of sweet mead,
and he drank also the heady beer.
He drank until he lost his senses,
and where he had drunk, there he fell asleep;
he depended upon his plighted brother.

The day was inclining toward night
and the sun was in the west,
when the youth awoke from his sleep.
The youth looked all around him;
all the costly garments had been taken from him,
his shoes and stockings were all gone,
his shirt even was taken from him,
and all his property was stolen.
A brick was lying under his unruly head;
he was covered with a tavern sackcloth,
and at his feet lay ragged shoes;
at his head his dear friend was no more.

And the youth stood up on his bare feet
and began to clothe himself:
he put on the ragged shoes,
covered himself with the tavern sackcloth,
covered his white body
and washed his white face.

Sorrow entered the youth's heart,
and he spoke the following words:

> "Though God has granted me a good life,
> I have now nothing to eat or drink!
> Since my money is gone,
> even the last half-farthing,
> I have not a friend,
> not even half a friend.
> They no longer account themselves of my race,
> all my friends have disappeared!"

IV. THE EXPATRIATION

The youth felt ashamed to show himself
before father and mother,
and his race and family,
and to his former friends.
He went into a strange, distant, unknown land.
He found a court, a town in size,
and a house in that court, a palace in height.
In that house was given a splendid feast;
the guests drank, ate and made merry.

The youth came to the splendid feast,
made the sign of the cross over his white face,
bowed before the miraculous icons,
made his obeisance to the good people
on all four sides.

And when the good people saw the youth,
how well he made the sign of the cross,
how he acted according to the written rule,
they took him by the hands,
seated him at the oaken table,
not in the best place, nor in the worst,
they seated him in a middle place,
where the younger guests were seated.

And the feast was a merry one,
and all the guests at the feast were drunk and merry and
        boastful;
but the youth sat, not merry at all,
gloomy, sorrowful, joyless,

and neither ate, nor drank, nor made merry,
nor boasted of anything at the feast.
Said the good people to the youth:

"Wherefore, O good youth,
  do you sit, not merry at the feast,
  gloomy, sorrowful, joyless;
  you neither drink, nor make merry,
  nor boast of anything at the feast.
  Or has the cup of good wine not reached you,
  or is not your seat according to your father's worth?
  Or have small children insulted you?
  Or are our children not kind to you?
  Or foolish and unwise people made light of you, youth?"

But the good youth remained sitting, and said:

"My lords and good people!
  I will tell you of my great misfortune,
  of my disobedience to my parents,
  of my drinking at the inn, about the cup of mead,
  the tempting drinking of heady wine.

When I took to drinking the heady wine,
  I disobeyed both father and mother;
  their blessing departed from me;
  the Lord grew wroth with me
  and to my poverty were added
  many great and incurable sorrows
  and sadness without comfort,
  want, and misery, and extreme wretchedness.

Want has tamed my flowery speech;
  sadness has dried up my white body.
  For this my heart is not merry,
  and my white face is sad, and my eyes dim.
  I have lost my paternal honor,
  any my youthful valor has left me.
  My lords and good people!
  Tell me and teach me how to live in a strange land,
  among strange people,
  and how to find dear friends!"

Said the good people to the youth:

"You are a sensible youth!
  Be not haughty in a strange land;
  submit to friend and foe,
  bow to old and young,
  tell not of the affairs of others,
  neither what you hear nor see.
  Flatter not friends nor enemies;
  have no tortuous fits,
  nor bend as a cunning snake;
  be humble before all
  but withal keep to truth and right—
  and you will have a great honor and glory.
  When people will find you out
  they will respect and honor you
  for your great truth,
  your humility and wisdom—
  and you will have dear friends
  who will call themselves your plighted brothers."

V. Temptations of Misery-Luckless-Plight

And the youth went hence into a strange land
and began to live wisely,
and through his great wisdom acquired greater wealth than
        before.
He looked out for a bride according to custom,
for he wished to marry.
The youth prepared a splendid feast,
according to his father's worth
and as best he knew,
and invited the honored guests and friends.
But through his own sin,
by God's will and the devil's temptation,
he boasted before his honored guests
and friends and plighted brothers.
A boastful word is always rotten,
and self-praise brings the destruction of man.
"I, a youth, have gained more possessions than ever!"

Misery-Luckless-Plight heard the young man's boasting
and spoke the following words:

  "Young man, boast not of your fortune,
    praise not your wealth!
  I, Misery, have known people

who were wiser and richer than you,
but I, Misery, have outwitted them.
When a great misfortune befell them,
They struggled with me unto their death;
they were worsted by their luckless plight—
could not get away from me, Misery,
until they took their abode in the grave,
and I covered them forever with the earth.
Only then they were rid of nakedness,
and I, Misery, left them,
though luckless plight remained upon their grave."

And again it cawed ominously:

"I, Misery, attached myself to others,
for I, Misery-Luckless-Plight,
cannot live empty-handed; I, Misery,
wish to live among people
from whom I cannot be driven away with a whim;
but my chief seat and paternal home
is among the carousers!"

Spoke gray Misery the miserable:

"How am I to get at the youth?"

and evil Misery devised cunningly
to appear to the youth in his dream:

"Young man, renounce your beloved bride,
for you will be poisoned by your bride;
you will be strangled by that woman;
you will be killed for your gold and silver!
Go, young man, to the tsar's tavern,
save nothing, but spend all your wealth in drink;
doff your costly dress, put on the tavern sackcloth.
In the tavern Misery will remain,
and evil Luckless-Plight will stay—
for Misery will not gallop after a naked one,
nor will anyone annoy a naked man,
nor has assault any terrors for a barefooted man."

The young man did not believe his dream,
but evil Misery again devised a plan,

appeared as the archangel Gabriel,
and stuck once more to the youth for a new plight:

> "Are you not, youth,
>   acquainted with immeasurable nakedness,
>   and its great lightness and advantages?
>   What you buy for yourself is money spent,
>   but you are a brave fellow
>   and can live without expense!
>   They do not beat, nor torture naked people,
>   nor drive them out of paradise,
>   nor drag them down from the other world;
>   nor will anyone annoy a naked man,
>   nor has assault any terrors for a naked man!"

VI. THE LAST TRIAL

The young man believed that dream:
he went and spent all his wealth in drink;
he doffed his costly dress,
put on the tavern sackcloth,
covered his white body.
The youth felt ashamed to show himself to his dear friends.
He went into a strange, distant, unknown land.
On his way he came to a swift river.
On the other side were the ferrymen
and they asked for money to ferry him across;
but the youth had none to give,
and without money they would not take him across.
The youth sat a whole day,
until evening, and all that day until compline
the youth had nothing to eat,
not even half a piece of bread.
The young man arose on his swift feet,
and standing, he fell to grieving,
and he spoke the following words:

> "Woe to me, miserable Luckless-Plight!
>   It has overtaken me, young man,
>   has starved me, young man, with a hungry death.
>   Three unlucky days have I passed,
>   for I, young man, have not eaten half a piece of bread!
>   I, young man, will jump into the swift river:
>   swallow my body, swift river!
>   And eat, O fish, my white body!

And that will be better than my shameful life;
will I ever be able to escape the hands
of Misery-Luckless-Plight?"

At that hour Misery leaped from behind a rock
near the swift river;
Misery was barefooted and naked
and there was not a thread upon it,
and it was girded with a bast thong,
and it called out with a mighty voice:

"Wait, young man, you will not escape from me, Misery!
Jump not into the swift river,
nor be in your misery doleful!
Though you live in misery, you need not be doleful,
but let your dolefulness die in misery!
Remember, young man, your former life;
how your father spoke to you, and your mother
    instructed you!
Why did you not then obey them?
You would not submit to them,
and were ashamed to bow to them,
but wanted to live as you listed!
But he who will not listen to the good teaching of
    his parents
will be taught by me, Misery-Luckless-Plight!

Luckless-Plight spoke the following speech:

"Submit to me, impure Misery;
bow before me, Misery, to the damp earth,
for there is no one wiser in the whole world than I,
    Misery;
and you will be ferried across the swift river,
and the good people will give you to eat and drink."

The young man saw his inevitable calamity,
and he submitted to impure Misery,
bowed before Misery to the damp earth!

The good fellow went ahead with a light step over the steep,
    fair bank,
over the yellow sand.
He went happy, not at all doleful,

for he had appeased Misery-Luckless-Plight.
And as he went, he thought a thought.
    "Since I have nothing,
      I need not worry about anything!"
And as the youth was not sorrowful,
he started a fair song,
a mighty, sensible song it was:

    "Sorrowless mother has borne me:
      with a comb she combed my little locks,
      dressed me in costly garments,
      and stepping aside shaded her eyes
      and looked at me:
      'Does my child look well in costly garments?
      In costly garments my child is a priceless child!'
      Thus my mother always spoke of me!
      And then I learned and know it well,
      that a costly gown cannot be made without a master,
      nor a child be comforted without a mother,
      nor a drunkard ever become rich,
      nor a dice-player be in good renown,
      and I was taught by my parents to be a well-dressed boy
      who was born devoid of everything."

The ferrymen heard the good fellow's song,
took the young man across the swift river,
and took nothing from him for the ferrying.
The good people gave him to drink and to eat,
took off his tavern sackcloth,
gave him peasant's clothes.
And these good people spoke to him:

    "You are a good fellow,
      so go to your home,
      to your beloved, respected parents,
      to your father and mother dear,
      greet your parents, father and mother,
      and receive from them the parental blessing!"

From there the youth went to his home.
When he was in the open field,
evil Misery had gone before him;
it met the youth in the open field,
and began to caw above the youth,

like an ill-omened crow above a falcon.
Misery spoke the following words:

"Wait! you have not gone away from me, good fellow!
Not merely for a time have I, Misery-Luckless-Plight,
attached myself to you;
I shall labor with you to your very death!
And not I, Misery, alone, but all my relatives,
and there is a godly race of them:
we are all gentle and insinuating,
And he who joins our family will end his days among us!
Such is the fate that awaits you with us.
Even if you were to be a bird of the air,
or if you went into the blue sea as a fish,
I would follow you at your right hand."

The youth flew as a clear falcon,
and Misery after him as a white gyrfalcon;
the youth flew as a steel-blue dove,
and Misery after him as a gray hawk;
the youth went into the field as a gray wolf,
and Misery after him with greyhounds;
the youth became the feathergrass in the field,
and Misery came with a sharp scythe,
and Luckless-Plight railed at him:

"You, little grass, will be cut down;
you, little grass, will lie on the ground,
and the boisterous winds will scatter you!"

The youth went as a fish into the sea,
and Misery after him with close-meshed nets,
and Misery-Luckless-Plight railed at him:

"You, little fish, will be caught at the shore,
and you will be eaten up and die a useless death!"

The youth went on foot along the road
and Misery at his right hand.
It taught the youth to live as a rich man by killing and
robbing,
so that they might hang the young man for it,
or might put him with a stone in the water.

The youth bethought himself of the road to salvation
and at once the youth went to a monastery to be shorn a monk,
and Misery stopped at the holy gates—
no longer clung to the youth.

And this is the end of the story:
Lord, preserve us from eternal torment,
and give us, O Lord, the light of paradise!
Forever and ever, amen!

44. *Poems From the Collection of Baccalaureus Richard James*

IN 1619 a young British scholar, baccalaureus Richard James, visited Russia and brought back to England six short poems, or songs, which he had transcribed phonetically in Russian, using Latin letters. F. Buslaev, the first scholar to study and publish them, believed that they were specimens of Russian folklore, but contemporary scholars believe that all of the poems were written by an unknown Russian poet of the early seventeenth century. The use of rhymed verses, completely uncharacteristic of Russian folklore of the time, their vocabulary—which betrays an author well-versed in the Russian literary language—as well as their subjects strongly confirm the latter opinion. The poems reflect political events of the time, and one of them, "Ode on the Return to Moscow of Patriarch Filaret," even deals with an event that occurred in the same year as the transcription of these poems.

The first is about the second raid against Moscow by the Khan of Crimea, Devlet Girey. In 1571 the Tatars of Crimea, under Khan Devlet, cleverly circled Russian armies guarding the access to Moscow and attacked and burned the Russian capital. Over a million Russians perished during this raid, while hundreds of thousands of prisoners were captured by the Tatars, later to be sold on the Middle Eastern and Mediterranean slave markets. In 1572 Devlet repeated his raid, but was defeated by Russian troops under Prince M. Vorotynsky. Out of a hundred and twenty thousand Tatar warriors, only twenty thousand returned home. The poem depicts the Tatars' hope of inflicting a final blow on Moscow and of conquering the other Russian cities. The "seventy Apostles" mentioned in the poem are the Muscovite churches, dedicated to seventy pupils of Christ, while the expression "Holy Fathers" refers to the churches dedicated to the three theologians of the early Christian Church: St. Basil the Great, St. Gregory the Theologian, and St. John Chrysostom (Golden Mouth).

The second poem voices the feelings and lament over her fate of Princess (Tsarevna) Xenia, the daughter of Tsar Boris

Godunov. After the death of Tsar Boris, when the impostor,
Pseudo-Dmitry, seized Moscow and became tsar, he abused the
daughter of his enemy and then sent her to a convent in
Ustiuzhna-Zheleznaia, in northern Russia, where she was forced
to take monastic vows.

The last of the poems offered here from the James Collection
is an ode glorifying the return from a Polish prison of Metropolitan Filaret (who soon became Patriarch), father of Michael
Romanov, the first tsar of the dynasty which was to rule Russia
until the revolution of 1917. Fedor (Filaret was his monastic
name) Nikitich Romanov had been captured along with other
Russian aristocrats by the Poles during the Time of Troubles,
and only after the Russian-Polish armistice of 1618 was he permitted to leave the Polish-Lithuanian Condominium and return
to Moscow.

The text of the *Raid of the Crimean Tatars* and *Ode to the
Return of Filaret Romanov* follow the translations of Leo
Wiener, while the text of *Song of Princess Xenia* is taken from
W. R. Morfill's *Story of Russia*, New York and London, 1890.
All three texts have been revised by the present editor.

◆ ◆ ◆

RAID OF THE CRIMEAN TATARS

Not a mighty cloud has covered the sky,
Nor mighty thunders have thundered:
Whither travels the dog, Crimea's khan?—
To the mighty Tsardom of Muscovy.
 "Today we will go against stone-built Moscow,
  But coming back, we will take Riazan."
And when they were at the river Oka,
They began their white tents to pitch.
 "Now think a thought with all your minds:
  Who is to sit in stone-built Moscow,
  And who is to sit in the city of Vladimir,
  And who is to sit in the city of Suzdal,
  And who will hold the old city of Riazan,
  And who will sit in the city of Zvenigorod,
  And who will sit in the city of Novgorod?"
There stepped forward Divi Murza, son of Ulan:
 "Listen, our lord, Crimea's khan!
  You, our lord, shall sit in stone-built Moscow,
  And your son in Vladimir,

And your nephew in Suzdal,
And your relative in Zvenigorod,
And let the equerry hold old Riazan,
But to me, O lord, grant Novgorod:
There, in Novgorod, lies my luck."
The voice of the Lord called out from heaven:
"Listen, you dog, Crimea's khan!
Know you not the Tsardom of Muscovy?
There are in Moscow seventy Apostles,
Besides the three Holy Fathers.
And there is in Moscow still an Orthodox tsar."
And you fled, you dog, Crimea's khan,
Not over the highways, nor the main road,
Nor following the black banner.

SONG OF PRINCESS XENIA, DAUGHTER OF TSAR BORIS GODUNOV

There weepeth a little bird,
A little white quail:
"Alas, that I so young must grieve!
They wish to burn the green oak,
To destroy my little nest,
To kill my little ones,
To catch me, quail."
In Moscow the Princess weepeth:
"Alas that I so young must grieve!
For there comes to Moscow the impostor
Grishka Otrepiev, the defrocked monk,
Who wants to take me captive,
And having captured make me a nun,
To send me into the convent.
But I do not wish to become a nun,
To go into a monastery:
I shall keep my dark cell open,
To look at the fine fellows.
O our beautiful corridors!
Who will walk over you
After our life as the tsar's family
And after Boris Godunov?
O our beautiful palace halls!
Who will be sitting in you
After our life as the tsar's family
And after Boris Godunov?"

And in Moscow the Princess weepeth,
The daughter of Boris Godunov:
   "O God, our merciful Savior!
    Wherefore is our Tsardom perished—
    Is it for father's sinning,
    Or for mother's not praying?
    And you beloved palace halls!
    Who will rule in you,
    After our life as the tsar's family?
    Fine stuffs of drawn lace!—
    Shall we wind you around the birches?
    Fine gold-worked towels!
    Shall we throw you into the woods?
    Fine earrings of hyacinth
    Shall we hang you on branches,
    After our life as the tsar's family,
    After the reign of our father,
    Glorious Boris Godunov?
    Wherefore comes to Moscow the defrocked monk,
    And wants to break down the palaces,
    And to take me, princess, captive,
    And to send me to Ustyuzhna Zheleznaia,
    To make me, princess, a nun,
    To place me behind a walled garden?
    Why must I grieve,
    As they take me to the dark cell,
    And the abbess gives me her blessing?"

ODE TO THE RETURN OF FILARET ROMANOV, FATHER OF TSAR MIKHAIL, TO MOSCOW

The Tsardom of Muscovy was happy
And all the holy Russian land.
Happy was the sovereign, the Orthodox tsar,
The Grand Duke Mikhail Fedorovich,
For he was told that his father had arrived,
His father Filaret Nikitich,
From the land of the infidel, from Lithuania.
He had brought back with him many princes and boyars,
He had also brought the boyar of the tsar,
Prince Mikhail Borisovich Sheyn.
There had come together many princes, boyars, and
       dignitaries,

In the mighty Tsardom of Muscovy:
They wished to meet Filaret Nikitich
Outside the famous white stone-built Moscow.
'Tis not the beautiful sun in its orbit—
'Tis the Orthodox tsar that has gone out,
To meet his father dear,
Lord Filaret Nikitich.
With the tsar went his uncle,
Ivan Nikitich the boyar—
    "The Lord grant my father be well,
     My father, lord Filaret Nikitich."
They went not into the palace of the tsar,
They went into the cathedral of the most Holy Virgin,
To sing a holy Mass.
And he blessed his beloved child:
    "God grant the orthodox tsar be well,
     Grand Duke Mikhail Fedorovich!
     And for him to rule the Tsardom of Muscovy
     And the holy Russian land."

45. *Prince Ivan Khvorostinin: Autobiographical Verses*

PRINCE Ivan Khvorostinin (1585? to 1625) was one of the most controversial Russian writers of the first quarter of the seventeenth century. Scion of an ancient noble family and the son of the valiant defender of Pskov against King Stephen Bathory, Ivan Khvorostinin appeared at the Muscovite court quite early. He later became one of the intimate friends of Pseudo-Dmitry, who became tsar in 1605. After the fall of this impostor, Khvorostinin was banned from Moscow, but some years later he reappeared as commander of one of the armies that fought against the Poles in southwestern Russia. It seemed at the time that this talented aristocrat had a brilliant career before him, but his debauchery, dissoluteness, and unorthodox behavior caused him difficulty once more. He was apparently very unhappy in Moscow society, for he often criticized his surroundings, and complained that there weren't any clever people there, nor anyone worth being acquainted with. In one of his satirical verses, he claimed:

> "These Muscovite people
> cultivate much rye,
> but live only by the lie."

Such verses aroused the indignation of the court, and a new investigation of his case showed that he wanted to flee to the West, to Italy, and that he denied such basic dogmas of the Orthodox Church as resurrection after death, and the Trinity. He apparently followed the teachings of the Unitarians. This early Russian Westernizer was then sent to the Monastery of St. Cyril where, in 1623, he decided to recant, and was then permitted to return to Moscow. Soon after his return he wrote his monumental *Exposition Against the Blaspheming Heretics*, in which he ambitiously attacked both the Roman Catholic and Protestant churches. This exposition, which is about 1,333 verses long, is written in rhymed couplets. His verses have no meter, and the line varies from six to fourteen syllables. This first Russian poem of considerable length deserves attention not only because of its size, but also because of the great variations in rhyme and the autobiographical elements of its final part. In this last section Prince Khvorostinin bitterly complained of the unfaithfulness of his servants and friends, who apparently informed the government of his unorthodox behavior and thinking. Besides this religious poem, he was the author of a number of other historical and polemical works in which he displayed a skillful command of contemporary literary devices and in which he often introduced rhymed passages.

The following translation of the final part of the *Exposition Against the Blaspheming Heretics* is based on the text published in *Letopis zaniatii arkheograficheskoi komissii*, Volume XVIII, St. Petersburg, 1907, pages 77–80.

✦ ✦ ✦

> Look, reader, upon the Roman mores
> and be faithful to God's glories.
> Do not look for truth in any foreign creeds.
> Do not betray the holy fathers' deeds.
> Take care, for the Western Church's revelations
> can certainly destroy our foundations.[1]
> The Western Church is dark both day and night,
> and bitter fruits grow like a blight.

[1] Under the expression "Western Church" Prince Khvorostinin means both the Catholic and the Protestant churches.

Their Eighth Council[2] did many wrong deeds,
betraying many of the holy fathers' creeds.
They want to condemn us to evil torments,
and they give their warriors heretical armaments.
The wave of their wrath is great,
but ever shall I their teachings berate.
I have wanted to bequeath something to my nation,
which is built upon a holy and Christian foundation.
But there were many evil doers,
who have confused our blessed rulers.
I have wanted to lend my hand to the work of salvation,
and for the destruction of their heretical creation.
But in place of ink, I had to use tears
and in irons I found the end of my career.
In prison I passed many days,
for a long time I did not see the sun's rays.
I have wanted to escape their evil gold,
and for such, never have I my soul sold.
I was forced to hide from treacherous detestation,
and thus could not continue my affirmation.
As an army commander I was always brave,
not wanting to bring my friends to the grave.
On Him who knows my heart have I always relied,
and He has always been my friend, true and tried.
His commandments I have never rejected,
but to His protection have I myself directed.
And before the time of my misfortune,
I had always rejected a heretical fortune.
I did so by the Holy Scriptures,
and following the holy fathers' strictures.
I have remained the faithful son of my faith
and firmly stood for the Eastern Church's Grace.
It was not my wont to debate with the ignorant,
nor did I care for their argument.
By much misfortune have I been accosted,
but by the absence of friends I was sore exhausted.
And no one would fain take a stand for me,
but only the Lord His help granted me.
I have written many words against the enemy
of the faith,

[2] Eighth Council was the first council of the Western Christian
Church, which is considered by the Catholics an Ecumenical Council;
but it is not recognized by the Eastern Orthodox, who did not take
part in its works.

and still I was thrown into such a bitter place.
Many a friend denounced my writing
and launched against me bitter fighting.
They took me from my holy task,
and not a word of thanks could I ask.
As a heretic was I condemned,
and thus my task came to a bitter end.
Look upon their evil doings,
and contrite hearts be not eschewing.
Even my servants became my enemies,
thus depriving me of any serenity.
They took away from me their comfort and support,
and prepared against me the trial in court.
Their lawless hatred was evil,
and they prepared me for burial.
They did so, for they belong to a kind most base,
worse than if they were of a devilish race.
They spewed their poisons at me,
and in their betrayal they agreed.
Their weapons were denunciations,
spreading against me all kind of calumniation.
O Lord, our God, show your might
and judge whether they or I be right.
You alone know of all my devotions
and you will divine the truth in their motions.
They were fed on my bread,
yet they turned my good deed to one of dread.
Yet sweeter than the sweetest flower,
is being in the Lord's power.
Let the work of my slaves be cursed,
let us hope their design will be dispersed.
Don't throw pearls before swine,
for they will be defiled, whether they be yours
          or mine.
And I underwent many hardships because of my
          slaves,
and they nearly brought me to the brink of the
          grave.
They forgot the words of Christ's admonitions
and I could not escape their evil intentions.
Their words were as ensnaring as a spider's web,
and their hatred was like an evil web.
Over them I was placed by my Creator,

by God was I placed over these evil traitors.
I stood alone against this evil horde,
but I was raised above them by my dear Lord.
But they became my bitter enemies,
and they profaned their own souls with their
     calumnies.
To win their own freedom,
they wanted to escape their serfdom.
They hurled their words like arrows against their
     lord,
and I wonder about those who approve of such
     a horde.

46. *The Orderly of Colonel Theodore Zay*
A Love Letter from the Year 1698

THE accidental arrest of a certain Savva Kartsev, who was suspected of participating in political conspiracy, preserved in the archives of the Russian police a love letter written by the orderly of Colonel Theodore Zay. The letter was written for the colonel's son, who had recently married without parental consent, and was to be delivered by Savva Kartsev to the wife of this young man. The intervention of the police prevented its delivery, but preserved the letter for posterity. The rhymed couplets of this letter demonstrate a new poetic vogue, while the metre, epithets, and vocabulary resemble the love songs of Russian folklore.

This poem is translated from the text published by L. Maikov in *Ocherki po istorii russkoi literatury XVII i XVIII stoletii*, St. Petersburg, 1889, page 230.

✦ ✦ ✦

To the most glorious light which has ever appeared
     before my eyes,
to the nicest person whom I advise.
May my beloved live for many years,
and not forget the pledge given to me here.
Do not forget our pledge taken before the Lord,
when we exchanged rings of our future concord.

At that time we had our wedding crowns on our
        heads,
crowns of gold for the commemoration of the
        happy, holy event.
Do not forget me in your prayers,
for I shall forget you never.
And I am so sad without you,
that I could fly from here as if I were a bird,
and I would come to you, my beloved.
We could lock ourselves in our chambers,
and confide in each other's secrets.
O my dear, blue flower, the beloved of my life!
What did I do when I came to my lord-father
and when I saw my lady-mother?
When I looked into their eyes,
I saw that our joy was beshadowed.
I awaited kind words from their graces,
but their words betrayed my faith.
"You can marry
someone with considerable wealth,
but you should marry her that we would care for,
and whom you should love.
You should marry a girl from the house of a
        Muscovite nobleman."
But I, my dear nightingale, only thanked them
        for their advice,
and now I send you this love letter with my best
        regards.

47. *Peter Kvashnin*

AROUND 1680 Peter Kvashnin, a member of an ancient and
noble family, wrote about fifty lyric poems, some of which are
more than a hundred lines in length. This poetry was first published in 1932 by M. N. Speransky, who thought it was the
product of Russian folklore. But the form, vocabulary, and unusual epithets, as well as partially rhymed lines, seem to prove
that the poems are instead the personal creations of Kvashnin
or of one of his friends. Only in a few aspects do they follow the
folklore tradition. The fact, also, that many of them are unfin-

ished would indicate that they are the product of Kvashnin's own poetic creativeness. All the poems have a common topic, that of painful and unrequited love, and are filled with pathos.

The translations of the two poems given here are based on M. N. Speransky's texts published in *Izvestiia Akademii Nauk USSR*, Volume 7, 1932, pages 721–724.

The subject of the first poem is the tender love of a sister for her brother.

◆　◆　◆

DEAR BROTHER

It was not a she-turtledove that cooed with a
    turtledove.
It was a sister that spoke with her brother.
And speaking with her brother, the sister
began to praise the darling little brother:
"Oh, my dearest little brother, my fond heart,
my dearest of friends, my beloved.
I cannot cease my enjoyment of looking upon you.
You are my precious darling, beautiful as an apple.
You are handsome, my fair brother, like a poppy
    blossom.
You appear, my young, dear brother, as a cherry.
When I don't see you, my brother,
I could die from sorrow.
And I remember my brother,
but I can only sigh after him.
And I dream steadily of him,
my friendship for him is firm."
The sister speaks with her brother,
and the sister begins to lament:
"Bitter is my life, my brother,
for I hear nonsense and senseless rumors.
Why do those people hate me?
O God, judge those who envy us,
who want to abuse me, a young girl,
and who want to separate me from my brother.
I should rather lose my reputation
than be separated from my brother.
Even if they spread calumnies about me,
I shall never forsake my brother. . . ."

                              [This poem is unfinished.]

I THOUGHT

I thought, I pondered,
I followed the reasoning of another,
and I said no to my love, straight to his face.
[A hiatus of several lines]
And he decided to take a young wife, a maiden
fair.
Oh, come to me, my beloved, on the eve of your
wedding!
I shall give you, my beloved, a beautiful linen
shirt,
A shirt adorned with muslin.
I waited for my dear friend the whole day until
evening.
And my beloved came to me
early in the morning, when a beautiful sun had
risen.
And you, my nurses and servants, bring me my
trunk with iron bars.
And open this trunk with the iron bars,
and take from it two steel knives
for me and for my friend.
Since I could not keep him with me,
you had better open his white breast.
And then he, my beloved, will belong
neither to me, nor to my sister,
nor to that strumpet who separated us.
But you, my beloved, will belong to our mother,
the damp earth.
And only an oaken board will preserve my secret.

A Short Glossary of Some Russian Terms Used in This Anthology

I. Currency and Measures

Grivna   An old Russian unit of money equivalent to the old English pound. It was in the form of a silver ingot.

Kuna   From the Russian word for marten. A monetary unit, there being twenty-five *kunas* in a *grivna*.

Nogata   A unit of money, there being twenty *nogatas* in a *grivna*. It was a vair.

Rezana   A vair. There were fifty *rezanas* in a *grivna*.

Ruble   A Russian monetary unit since the fifteenth century. Equal to about one English pound at that time.

Versta or *poprishche*   Units of measure equal to about ⅗ of a mile.

II. Ranks and Titles

Metropolitan   The head of the national Orthodox Church, in particular head of the Russian Church until the end of the sixteenth century. Since the end of the sixteenth century the term has come to denote an archbishop in charge of a large diocese.

Posadnik   An elected high official in the cities of early Kievan Russia and in both the Novgorodian and Pskovian republics until the fifteenth century. Similar to rank of commissioner.

Sotnik   An officer who commanded a *sotnia*, a company of one hundred men. A centurion.

Stolnik   A high official at the tsar's court or of the civil administration.

Strelets   (pl. *streltsy*) Professional infantrymen. The corps of *streltsy* was created in the sixteenth century.

Tysiatsky   An elected commander of the army in the earlier Kievan period and in the Novgorodian and Pskovian republics.

Voevoda   A high-ranking officer either in the civil administration or in the army. A rank equivalent to that of general or governor.

Chronology of Russian History and Culture

Seventh Century B.C.   Occupation of the southern prairies of Russia by the Scythians, and the founding of Greek cities on the northern shore of the Black Sea.

Third Century A.D.   Goths occupy the southern prairie of Russia.

Fourth Century   The Huns penetrate into Europe from Asia, thus causing the Great Migration. The Antes (Slavs?) founded a state in what is present-day southern Russia.

Ninth Century   Appearance of the Viking (Varangian) tradesmen in Russia.

862   The legendary founding of the Russian state by Rurik.

907   Oleg's first campaign against Constantinople.

955   Olga travels to Constantinople, and takes baptism there.

988 or 989   The Christianization of Russia by Prince Vladimir.

Early Eleventh Century   The Kumans drive out the Pechenegs from the southern prairies of Russia.

Circa 1030   The oldest known Russian literary work, the *Sermon* of Luke Zhidiata.

1019–1054   The reign of Yaroslav the Wise.

Circa 1050   The writing of the *Primary Chronicle* begins.

1113   Monk Nestor ends the writing of the *Primary Chronicle*.

1113–1125   The reign of Vladimir Monomakh, the last great prince of the Kievan Period to be recognized as ruler of all Russia.

1185   Igor's unfortunate campaign against the Kumans.

1186 (?)   The writing of the *Lay of Igor's Campaign*.

1223   Russians are defeated by the Mongols at the river Kalka.

1237–1240   The Mongol conquest of Russia.

1283–1304   Daniel, Prince of Moscow, founds the Muscovite state.

1261   The beginning of the Muscovite branch of the Rurik dynasty.

1326   Metropolitan Peter, the head of the Russian Church, moves his office to Moscow.

1328   Ivan Kalita receives the title "Great Prince of All Russia."

1314–1392   St. Sergius of Radoniezh, the founder of monasticism in northern Russia.

1380   Russia defeats the Tatars at the Battle of Kulikovo.

1386 (?)   The writing of *Zadonshchina*.

1420   The death of Epiphanius the Wise, author of the lives of St. Sergius and St. Stephen of Perm.

1427 or 1430   Death of the greatest Russian painter of the medieval era, Andrew Rublev.

1462–1505   The reign of Ivan III, the unifier of northern Russia.

1533–1584   The reign of Ivan IV.

1550–1570   The compilation of *Chetii Minei (The Book of the Lives of Saints)*, of the *Book of Grades*, and Nikon's *Illustrated Codex*.

1598   The death of Tsar Fedor, and the consequent end of the Rurik dynasty.

1598–1605   The reign of Tsar Boris Godunov.

1605–1613   The Time of Troubles.

1613–1645   The reign of the first Romanov, Tsar Michael.

1620–1630   Avraamy Palitsyn, M. Katyrev-Rostovsky, and I. Khvorostinin write their works on the Time of Troubles. Probable time of the writing of the *Life of Yuliania Lazarevskaia*.

1645–1676   The reign of Tsar Alexis.

1653   The first reforms of Patriarch Nikon.

1663   Simeon Polotsky comes to Moscow. Beginning of Russian syllabic verse.

1667   The Church Council of Moscow and the consequent schism within the Russian Church.

1672   *Esther*, the first Russian play, is staged in the tsar's theatre.

1673   Avvakum writes his *Life*.

1682–1725   The reign of Peter the First, and the consequent westernization of Russia.